Cases and Materials on Land Law

Authors

Emily Allen
Matthew Carn
Julie Harris
Hugh McFaul
Jan Maltby

Consultant Editor

Christopher Howard

First edition July 2010

Fourth edition July 2015

Published ISBN: 9781 4727 3389 4

Previous ISBN: 9781 4727 2116 7

British Library Cataloguing-in-Publication Data
A catalogue record for this book is available
from the British Library

Published by
BPP Learning Media Ltd
BPP House, Aldine Place
London W12 8AA
www.bpp.com/learningmedia

Printed in the United Kingdom by
Charlesworth Press

Flanshaw Way
Flanshaw Lane
Wakefield
WF2 9LP

Your learning materials, published by BPP
Learning Media Ltd, are printed on paper
sourced from sustainable, managed forests.

Contents

Index of Cases   vii

Part I – The Foundation Concepts

1   The Meaning of 'Land'   3
2   Estates in Land   25
3   Interests in Land   49
4   Enforcement of Third Party Interests   61
5   Proprietary Estoppel   91

Part II – Three Key Proprietary Rights

6   Covenants in Freehold Land   121
7   Mortgages   149
8   Easements   177

Part III – The Landlord and Tenant Relationship

9   Essential Characteristics of the Leasehold Relationship   207
10   Covenants between a Landlord and Tenant   235
11   Termination of Leases and Extending Business Tenancies   263

Part IV – Co-ownership of Land Under a Trust

12   Legal Principles Governing Trusts of Land   289

Index of Cases

A

Abbey National Building Society v Cann [1991] 1 AC 56 71
Ackroyd v Smith (10 CB 164) 184
AG Securities v Vaughan and Others; Antoniades v Villiers and Another [1990] AC 417 .. 217
Akici v LR Butlin Limited [2005] EWCA Civ 1296, [2006] 1 WLR 201 274
Alford v Hannaford [2011] EWCA Civ 1099 203
Allan v Liverpool Overseers (1874) L.R. 9 Q.B. 180, 191-192 210
Alton Corporation [1985] B.C.L.C. 27, 33 60
Arlesford Trading Co Ltd v Servansingh [1971] 3 All ER 113 252
Armory v Delamirie (1722) 1 Str. 505 11
Aslan v Murphy [1990] 1 WLR 766 214

B

Barclays Bank plc v O'Brien and Another [1994] 1 AC 180 165
Batchelor v Marlow [2003] 1 WLR 764 187
Berkley v Poulett [1977] 1 EGLR 86 14
Berkley v Poulett and Others [1977] 261 EG 911 at 913 19
Bernstein v Skyviews General Ltd [1978] QB 479 6
BHP Petroleum Great Britain Ltd v Chesterfield Properties Ltd and another [2002] Ch 194 .. 260
Biggs v Hoddinott [1898] 2 Ch 307 151
Billson and others v Residential Apartments Limited [1992] 1 AC 494 278
Bircham & Co Nominees (No.2) Ltd v Worrell Holdings Ltd [2001] EWCA Civ 775,
    [2001] All ER (D) 269 (May) 57
Borman v Griffith [1930] 1 Ch 493 198
Boyer v Worbey [1953] 1 QB 234 255
Brew Bros Ltd v Snax (Ross) Ltd [1970] 1 QB 612 243
Bruton v London & Quadrant Housing Trust [2000] 1 AC 406 213
Burgess v Rawnsley [1975] Ch 429 300

C

Campbell v Griffin [2001] EWCA Civ 990 108
Chhokar v Chhokar [1984] FLR 313 73
City of London Building Society v Flegg [1988] AC 54 67
Cityland and Property (Holdings) Ltd v Dabrah [1968] Ch 166 161
Coatsworth v Johnson [1886-90] All ER Rep 547 46
Cobbe v Yeoman's Row Management Limited [2008] UKHL 55 102
Congleton Corporation v Pattison (1808) 10 East 130, 138 256
Copeland v Greenhalf [1952] Ch 488 186
Cordell v Second Clanfield Properties Limited [1969] 2 Ch 9 194
Crest Nicholson Residential (South) Limited v McAllister [2004] EWCA Civ 410,
    [2004] 1 WLR 2409 140

D

Davis and another v Smith [2011] EWCA Civ 1603 306
D'Eyncourt v Gregory [Law Rep. 3 Eq. 382 13
Diligent Finance Co Ltd v Alleyne (1972) 23 P & CR 346 81
Dresden Estates Limited v Collinson (1988) 55 P&CR 47 230

E

Elitestone Ltd v Morris and another [1997] 1 WLR 687 16
Esso Petroleum Co Ltd v Fumegrange Ltd and others [1994] 2 EGLR 90 232
Estates Gazette Ltd v Benjamin Restaurants Ltd and another [1995] 1 All ER 129 258
Expert Clothing Service & Sales Limited v Hillgate House Limited and another
    [1986] Ch 340 270

F

Facchini v Bryson [1952] 1 TLR 1386 226
Federated Homes Limited v Mill Lodge Properties Limited [1980] 1 WLR 594 137

G

G. and C. Kreglinger v New Patagonia Meat and Cold Storage Company [1914] AC 25 . 154
Gill and another v Lewis and another [1956] 2 QB 1 265
Gillett v Holt [2001] Ch 210 98
Glasgow Corporation v Johnstone [1965] AC 609 228
Gomm's case, 20 Ch.D. 562 , 582 54
Goodman v Gallant [1986] Fam 106 291
Gore and Snell v Carpenter [1990] 60 P&CR 456 305
Graham Charles Botham & Ors v TSB Bank plc [1997] 73 P & CR D1 19
Graysim Holdings Limited v P & O Property Holdings Limited [1996] AC 329 280
Griffith v Pelton [1958] Ch. 205 52
Grigsby v Melville [1972] 1 WLR 1355 191

H

Harris v Goddard [1983] 1 WLR 1203 293
Helby v Matthews [1895] AC 471, 482 52
Hill v Tupper (1863) 2 H&C 121 184
Holland and another v Hodgson and another (1872) LR 7 CP 328 13
Holland v Hodgson (1872) LR 7 CP 328 19
Hopwood v Cannock Chase District Council [1975] 1 All ER 796 239
Horsey Estate Ltd v Steiger [1899] 2 QB 79, 89 256
Hua Chiao Commercial Bank Ltd v Chiaphua Industries Ltd [1987] AC 99 256
Hunter v Babbage (1995) 69 P&CR 548 303

I

In re 88 Berkeley Road [1971] Ch 648..294

In re Buchanan-Wollaston's Conveyance [1939] Ch 738 308

In re Citro (Domenico) (A Bankrupt); In re Citro (Carmine) (A Bankrupt) [1991] Ch 142 312

In re Draper's Conveyance [1969] 1 Ch 486 292

In Re Ellenborough Park [1956] Ch 131 179

In re Evers' Trust [1980] 1WLR 1327 310

In re Mulholland's Will Trusts [1949] 1 All E.R. 460 54

In Reid v Smith (1905) 3 CLR 656 at 659...18

International Drilling Fluids Ltd v Louisville Investments (Uxbridge) Ltd [1986] Ch 513.........246

Irvine v Moran [1991] 1 EGLR 261 237

J

Javad v Aqil [1991] 1 WLR 1007 43

Jennings v Rice [2002] EWCA Civ 159..110

Jones v Challenger [1961] 1 QB 176 309

Jones v Morgan [2001] EWCA Civ 995, [2001] 82 P&CR D36 157

K

Keay v Morris Homes (West Midlands) Ltd..32

Kelsen v Imperial Tobacco Company (of Great Britain and Ireland) Ltd [1957] 2 QB 334 6

Kettel & Ors v Bloomfold Ltd [2012] EWHC 1422 193

Kinch v Bullard [1999] 1 WLR 423...296

Kingsnorth Finance v Tizard [1986] 1 WLR 783..85

Kling v Keston (1985) 49 P & CR 212...57

Knightsbridge Estates Trust, Limited v Byrne and Others [1939] Ch 441 156

L

Lace v Chantler [1944] KB 368...39

Ladies' Hosiery and Underwear Ltd v Parker [1930] 1 Ch 304.....................................40

Link Lending Ltd v Bustard (by her litigation friend Walker) [2010] EWCA Civ 424 74

Lister v Lane & Nesham [1893] 2 Q.B. 212..244

Lloyds Bank plc v Rosset [1989] Ch 350 77

London and Blenheim Estates Ltd v Ladbroke Retail Parks Ltd [1992] 1 WLR 1278, 1288...187

London and South Western Railway Co. v. Gomm (1882) 20 Ch.D. 562, 581 53

London County Council v Allen and others [1914] 3 KB 642 132

Lurcott v Wakely & Wheeler [1911] 1 KB 905...243

M

Marchant v Charters [1977] 1 WLR 1181 216
McCausland and another v Duncan Lawrie Ltd and another [1997] 1 WLR 38 36
Mercer v Liverpool, St Helen's and South Lancs Railway Co [1903] 1 KB 652 81
Midland Bank Trust Co Ltd v Green [1981] AC 513 82
Mikeover Limited v Brady [1989] 3 All ER 618 223
Moncrieff v Jamieson [2007] 1 WLR 2620 188
Moody v Steggles (1879) LR 12 ChD 261 185
Moule v Garrett and others (1872) LR 7 Exch 101 259
Multiservice Bookbinding Ltd and Others v Marden [1979] Ch 84 162

N

Nadia Laiqat v Abdul Majid, Arshad Majid, Tariq Majid [2005] EWHC 1305 (QB),
   [2005] All ER (D) 231 (Jun) 5
Newton Abbot Cooperative Society Limited v Williamson & Treadgold Limited
   [1952] Ch 286 135
Nielsen-Jones v Fedden and Others [1975] Ch 222 298
Noakes & Co v Rice [1902] AC 24 153
Norris v Checksfield [1991] 1 WLR 1241 227
North Eastern Properties Ltd v Coleman and another 32
Nunn v Dalrymple [1990] 59 P&CR 231 226

O

Oun v Ahmad [2008] EWHC 545 (Ch), [2008] 13 EG 149 33

P

P & A Swift Investments (a firm) v Combined English Stores Group plc [1989] AC 632 128
P&S Platt Limited v Crouch [2004] 1 P&CR 18 202
Parker v British Airways Board [1982] QB 1004 .... 7, 11
Pritchard v Briggs and Others [1980] Ch 338 55
Prudential Assurance v London Residuary Body [1992] 2 AC 386 41
Purchase v Lichfield Brewery Company [1915] 1 KB 184 254
Pwllbach Colliery Co Ltd v Woodman, 12 195

R

Re King, Robinson v Gray [1963] Ch 459 249
Re Wallis & Simmonds (Builders) Ltd. [1974] 1 WLR. 391 60
Record v Bell [1991] 1 WLR 853 28
Renals v Cowlishaw [9 Ch. D. 130] 134
Rhone and another v Stephens [1994] 2 AC 310 123
Rhone v Stephens 127
Rogers v Hosegood [1900] 2 Ch 388 .... 129, 133
Romano Barca v Malcolm John Mears Trustee of the estate of Romano Barca
    [2004] EWHC 2170 (Ch), [2005 2 FLR 1] 316
Ropaigealach v Barclays Bank plc [2000] QB 263 171
Royal Bank of Scotland v Etridge (No 2) and Other Appeals [2001] UKHL 44,
    [2002] 2 AC 773 167
Royal Philanthropic Society v County [1986] 18 HLR 83 229
Rugby School (Governors) v Tannahill [1935] 1 KB 87 267

S

Savva and Savva v Hussein (1997) 73 P & CR 150 273
Scala House & District Property Co. Limited v Forbes and others [1974] QB 575 268
Silven Properties Ltd and another v Royal Bank of Scotland plc and others [2004] 4
    All ER 484 172
Sledmore v Dalby (1996) 72 P&CR 196 114
Smith and Snipes Hall Farm Limited v River Douglas Catchment Board [1949] 2 KB 500.... 129
South Staffordshire Water Co. v. Sharman [1896] 2 QB 44 11
Sovmots Investments Limited v Secretary of State for the Environment [1979] AC 144......... 201
Spencer's Case (1582) 5 Coke Reports 16a 253
Spiro v Glencrown Properties Ltd. and Another [1991] Ch 537 51
Stockholm Finance v Garden Holdings Inc and Others [1995] NPC 162 76
Strand Securities v Caswell [1965] Ch 958 70
Street v Mountford [1985] AC 809 209
Stuart and Others v Joy and Another [1904] 1 KB 362 248

T

Taylor v Hamer [2002] EWCA Civ 1130, [2002] All ER (D) 512 (Jul) 21
Taylor's Fashions Limited and others v Liverpool Victoria Trustees Co Ltd [1982] QB 133 93
Thamesmead Town Limited v Allotey (1998) 3 EGLR 97 126
The Mortgage Corporation v Shaire and Others [2001] Ch 743 313
Thorner v Major [2009] UKHL 18 106
Tootal Clothing Ltd v Guinea Properties Management Ltd (1992) 64 P & CR 452 30
Tulk v Moxhay (1848) 2 Ph 774 131

U

United Bank of Kuwait Plc v Sahib and Others [1997] Ch 107..........................59

W

Walsh v Lonsdale (1882) LR 21 Ch D 9 45
Warren v Keen [1954] 1QB 15 242
Waverley Borough Council v Fletcher [1996] QB 334 10
Westminster City Council v Clarke [1992] AC 288... 211
Wheeldon v Burrows (1879) LR 12 ChD 31 196
Williams & Glyn's Bank Ltd v Boland [1981] AC 487 .... 64, 69, 72, 77
Williams v Hensman (1861) 1 J&H 546 298
Wilson v Wilson [1963] 1 WLR 601 292
Wong v Beaumont Properties Limited [1965] 1 QB 173.................................... 195
Wright v Macadam [1949] 2 KB 744.. 199
Wright v Mortimer [1996] 28 HLR 719 283
Wright v Robert Leonard (Developments) [1994] EG 69 (C.S.) 32
Wrotham Park Estate Co. Limited v Parkside Homes Limited and others
    [1974] 1 WLR 798 144

Y

Yaxley v Gotts and another [2000] Ch 162.. 37

Part I

The Foundation Concepts

1

The Meaning of 'Land'

Topic List

1   Does the Definition of Land include the Airspace above Land?

2   Ownership of Land – Things Found on the Land

3   The Distinction Between Fixtures and Chattels

Introduction

The concept of land encompasses in a legal sense much more than just the ground or the buildings on land. It is therefore vital to establish how land might be defined and what the concept includes.

It is particularly important to know what land comprises when land is sold: the buyer needs to know what is included with the land, and the seller needs to establish before contracts are exchanged whether he is retaining any part of the land for himself.

'Land' is defined in the Law of Property Act 1925 (LPA 1925) s 205(1)(ix), but even this statutory provision needs further clarification from the common law. There are three major issues which have been addressed by case law: (1) does land include the airspace above land?; (2) to whom do objects found on land belong?; and (3) the distinction between fixtures (objects forming part of the land) and chattels (objects not forming part of the land).

1.1 Does the Definition of Land include the Airspace above Land?

Nadia Laiqat v Abdul Majid, Arshad Majid, Tariq Majid [2005] EWHC 1305 (QB), [2005] All ER (D) 231 (Jun)

Panel: Silber J

Facts: The claimant was the freehold owner of a property in Bradford. The defendants occupied the adjacent property which comprised a house and a take-away shop. The defendants installed an extractor fan on their property which protruded by 750 millimetres into the claimant's back garden at a height of 4.5 metres. The claimant contended that the extractor fan trespassed into her back garden and sought an injunction to move or remove the fan. The judge at first instance dismissed the claim and the claimant appealed to the High Court.

MR JUSTICE SILBER

10. ...[T]he first issue is whether the position of the fan above the claimant's land constituted a trespass to her property.

11. The second issue only arises if it is decided that the defendants' fan extractor trespassed on the claimant's land, and that issue is then what the claimant's remedy should be. The claimant contends that an injunction should be granted requiring the defendants to remove or reposition the extractor fan so that it does not trespass on the claimant's land. ...

15. The question whether an invasion of air space amounts to a trespass has been the subject of judicial consideration on various occasions in recent years. ...

16. In *Kelsen v Imperial Tobacco Company (of Great Britain and Ireland) Ltd* [1957] 2 QB 334, an advertising sign erected by the defendants projected a few inches into the air space above the one-story [sic] shop of a neighbouring occupier, who commenced proceedings against the defendants.

17. McNair J held that the positioning of the advertising sign constituted a trespass as it invaded the claimant's air space. ...

18. ...McNair J also attached importance to the fact that Parliament had found it necessary expressly to negative the action of trespass arising from the mere fact that [sic] of an aeroplane passing through the air above land in ... section 40(1) of Civil Aviation Act 1949. Thus, the learned judge concluded that a trespass was created by the invasion of Kelsen's airspace by this sign. ...

20. In *Bernstein v Skyviews General Ltd* [1978] QB 479, Griffiths J (as he then was) held that when the defendants used an overflying aeroplane in order to obtain aerial photographs of the claimant's country residence, this invasion of airspace by the overflying aircraft did not constitute a trespass.

21. In explaining his decision Griffiths J said ... that:

    "it may be a sound and practical rule to regard any incursion into the air space at a height which may interfere with the ordinary user of the land as a trespass rather than a nuisance. Adjoining owners then know where they stand: they have no right to erect structures overhanging or passing over their neighbour's land and there is no room for argument whether they are thereby causing damage or annoyance to their neighbours about which there may be much room for argument and uncertainty"

22. I interject to add that that the learned judge's statement that adjoining owners "have no right to erect structures overhanging or passing over their neighbour's land" is supportive of the claimant's case... .

23. Griffiths J then proceeded to explain that different considerations arose in the case with which he was concerned as he was considering the passage of aircraft "at a height in which no way affects the user of the land" (page 486H – 487A) before he concluded that "I can find no support and authority for the view that a land owner's rights in the airspace above his property extend to an unlimited height" (page 487G).

24. ...Griffiths J continued by saying ... that:

    " ...The problem is to balance the rights of an owner to enjoy the use of his land against the rights of the general public to take advantage of all that science now offers in the use of airspace. This balance is in my judgment best struck in our present society by restricting the rights of an owner in the airspace above his land to such height as is necessary for the ordinary use and enjoyment of his land and the structures upon it, and declaring that above that height he has no greater rights in the airspace than any other member of the public". ...

 Alert

34. In my opinion, all the authorities establish that if a defendant interferes with a claimant's airspace, this amounts to trespass except that this conduct would not constitute trespass if the interference were at such great height - such as by high flying aircraft - that it does not interfere with the claimant's airspace. ...

The protrusion of the extractor fan was a trespass into the claimant's land. Mr Justice Silber cites a long line of prior authorities which support his finding that the protrusion of an object into the lower airspace above land constitutes a trespass and the object may therefore be removed. Interference with the airspace directly above someone else's land is sufficient to constitute a trespass. The citations from *Bernstein v Skyviews General Ltd* are particularly useful in demonstrating the distinction between the lower airspace and the upper airspace.

1.2 Ownership of Land – Things Found on the Land

Parker v British Airways Board [1982] QB 1004

Panel: Eveleigh and Donaldson LJJ and Sir David Cairns

Facts: The defendant was the tenant of an executive lounge at Heathrow Airport. The claimant found a gold bracelet on the floor of the lounge when he was awaiting his flight. He gave it to an employee of British Airways Board (BAB), together with his name and address, and asked for it to be returned to him if the true owner did not come forward to claim it. The employees of BAB had instructions as to the actions they should take when lost items were handed in but these were not published to the users of the lounge, and no searches were carried out in the lounge by BAB for lost articles. The true owner did not claim the bracelet. BAB sold the bracelet for £850 and kept the proceeds. Mr Parker sued and was awarded damages in the County Court. The defendant appealed.

LORD JUSTICE DONALDSON

On November 15, 1978, the plaintiff, Alan George Parker, had a date with fate - and perhaps with legal immortality. He found himself in the international executive lounge at terminal one, Heathrow Airport. And that was not all that he found. He also found a gold bracelet lying on the floor. ...

Neither the plaintiff nor the defendants lay any claim to the bracelet either as owner of it or as one who derives title from that owner. The plaintiff's claim is founded upon the ancient common law rule that the act of finding a chattel which has been lost and taking control of it gives the finder rights with respect to that chattel. The defendants' claim has a different basis. They cannot and do not claim to have found the bracelet when it was handed to them by the plaintiff. At that stage it was no longer lost and they received and accepted the bracelet from the plaintiff on terms that it would be returned to him if the owner could not be found. They must and do claim on the basis that they had rights in relation to the bracelet immediately before the plaintiff found it and that these rights are superior to the plaintiff's. The defendants' claim is based upon the proposition that at common law an occupier of land has such rights over all lost chattels which are on that land, whether or not the occupier knows of their existence. ...

Some qualification has also to be made in the case of the trespassing finder. The person vis à vis whom he is a trespasser has a better title. The fundamental basis of this is clearly public policy. Wrongdoers should not benefit from their wrongdoing. This requirement would be met if the trespassing finder acquired no rights. That would, however, produce the free-for-all situation to which I have already referred, in that anyone could take the article from the trespassing finder. Accordingly, the common law has been obliged to give rights to someone else, the owner ex hypothesi being unknown. The obvious candidate is the occupier of the property upon which the finder was trespassing.

Curiously enough, it is difficult to find any case in which the rule is stated in this simple form, but I have no doubt that this is the law. ...

In the interests of clearing the ground and identifying the problem, let me now turn to another situation in respect of which the law is reasonably clear. This is that of chattels which are attached to realty (land or buildings) when they are found. If the finder is not a wrongdoer, he may have some rights, but the occupier of the land or building will have a better title. The rationale of this rule is probably either that the chattel is to be treated as an integral part of the realty as against all but the true owner and so incapable of being lost or that the "finder" has to do something to the realty in order to get at or detach the chattel and, if he is not thereby to become a trespasser, will have to justify his actions by reference to some form of licence from the occupier. In all likely circumstances that licence will give the occupier a superior right to that of the finder. ...

Link

Waverley Borough Council v Fletcher

In a dispute of this nature there are two quite separate problems. The first is to determine the general principles or rules of law which are applicable. The second, which is often the more troublesome, is to apply those principles or rules to the factual situation. I propose to confront those two problems separately.

Rights and obligations of the finder

1. The finder of a chattel acquires no rights over it unless (a) it has been abandoned or lost and (b) he takes it into his care and control.

2. The finder of a chattel acquires very limited rights over it if he takes it into his care and control with dishonest intent or in the course of trespassing.

3. Subject to the foregoing and to point 4 below, a finder of a chattel, whilst not acquiring any absolute property or ownership in the chattel, acquires a right to keep it against all but the true owner or those in a position to claim through the true owner or one who can assert a prior right to keep the chattel which was subsisting at the time when the finder took the chattel into his care and control.

4.   Unless otherwise agreed, any servant or agent who finds a chattel in the course of his employment or agency and not wholly incidentally or collaterally thereto and who takes it into his care and control does so on behalf of his employer or principal who acquires a finder's rights to the exclusion of those of the actual finder.

5.   A person having a finder's rights has an obligation to take such measures as in all the circumstances are reasonable to acquaint the true owner of the finding and present whereabouts of the chattel and to care for it meanwhile.

Rights and liabilities of an occupier

1.   An occupier of land has rights superior to those of a finder over chattels in or attached to that land and an occupier of a building has similar rights in respect of chattels attached to that building, whether in either case the occupier is aware of the presence of the chattel.

2.   An occupier of a building has rights superior to those of a finder over chattels upon or in, but not attached to, that building if, but only if, before the chattel is found, he has manifested an intention to exercise control over the building and the things which may be upon it or in it.

 Alert

3.   An occupier who manifests an intention to exercise control over a building and the things which may be upon or in it so as to acquire rights superior to those [of] a finder is under an obligation to take such measures as in all the circumstances are reasonable to ensure that lost chattels are found and, upon their being found, whether by him or by a third party, to acquaint the true owner of the finding and to care for the chattels meanwhile. The manifestation of intention may be express or implied from the circumstances including, in particular, the circumstance that the occupier manifestly accepts or is obliged by law to accept liability for chattels lost upon his "premises," e.g. an innkeeper or carrier's liability.

4.   An "occupier" of a chattel, e.g. a ship, motor car, caravan or aircraft, is to be treated as if he were the occupier of a building for the purposes of the foregoing rules.

Application to the instant case

The plaintiff was not a trespasser in the executive lounge and, in taking the bracelet into his care and control, he was acting with obvious honesty. Prima facie, therefore, he had a full finder's rights and obligations. He in fact discharged those obligations by handing the bracelet to an official of the defendants' [sic] although he could equally have done so by handing the bracelet to the police or in other ways such as informing the police of the find and himself caring for the bracelet. ...

The defendants, for their part, cannot assert any title to the bracelet based upon the rights of an occupier over chattels attached to a building. The bracelet was lying loose on the floor. Their claim must, on my view of the law, be based upon a manifest intention to exercise control over the lounge and all things which might be in it. The evidence is that they claimed the right to decide who should and who should not be permitted to enter and use the lounge, but their control was in general exercised upon the basis of classes or categories of user and the availability of the lounge in the light of the need to clean and maintain it. I do not doubt that they also claimed the right to exclude individual undesirables, such as drunks, and specific types of chattels such as guns and bombs. But this control has no real relevance to a manifest intention to assert custody and control over lost articles. There was no evidence that they searched for such articles regularly or at all. Evidence was given of staff instructions which govern the action to be taken by employees of the defendants if they found lost articles or lost chattels were handed to them. But these instructions were not published to users of the lounge and in any event I think that they were intended to do no more than instruct the staff on how they were to act in the course of their employment.

It was suggested in argument that in some circumstances the intention of the occupier to assert control over articles lost on his premises speaks for itself. I think that this is right. If a bank manager saw fit to show me round a vault containing safe deposits and I found a gold bracelet on the floor, I should have no doubt that the bank had a better title than I, and the reason is the manifest intention to exercise a very high degree of control. At the other extreme is the park to which the public has unrestricted access during daylight hours. During those hours there is no manifest intention to exercise any such control. In between these extremes are the forecourts of petrol filling stations, unfenced front gardens of private houses, the public parts of shops and supermarkets as part of an almost infinite variety of land, premises and circumstances.

 Alert

This lounge is in the middle band and in my judgment, on the evidence available, there was no sufficient manifestation of any intention to exercise control over lost property before it was found such as would give the defendants a right superior to that of the plaintiff or indeed any right over the bracelet. As the true owner has never come forward, it is a case of "finders keepers."

I would therefore dismiss the appeal.

The appeal was dismissed and the claimant was entitled to the damages awarded at first instance.

The Court of Appeal has set out a clear test to establish whether objects found on land belong to the finder or to the owner/occupier of the land in the absence of the true owner. Lord Justice Donaldson sets out tests which are flexible and wide enough to be applied to cases decided in the future, including the following case.

Waverley Borough Council v Fletcher [1996] QB 334

Panel: Sir Thomas Bingham MR, Auld and Ward LJJ

Facts: Waverley Borough Council owned the freehold title to a public park. Mr Fletcher was using his metal detector in the park and found a medieval gold brooch buried in the ground. He dug down into the ground, to a depth of about nine inches, to retrieve the brooch. He reported his find to the coroner; the coroner held that the brooch was not treasure and it was awarded to Mr Fletcher. However, the council claimed ownership of the brooch. The judge at first instance found in favour of the defendant as finder of the brooch, approving his argument that he was allowed to use the property and that the council was not in actual occupation of the park at the time. The council appealed.

LORD JUSTICE AULD

This appeal concerns the collision of two familiar notions of English law: "finders keepers" and that an owner or lawful possessor of land owns all that is in or attached to it. ...

The starting point in considering those rival contentions is the firm principle established as long ago as 1722 in *Armory v. Delamirie* (1722) 1 Str. 505, that the finder of an object is entitled to possess it against all but the rightful owner. ...

The same principle applies as between the owner or lawful possessor of land and the finder in relation to unattached objects on land unless the former has made plain his intention to control the land and anything that might be found on it. ...A more recent example is Parker's case [1982] Q.B. 1004 where the finder of a gold bracelet dropped by an unknown traveller in an airline company's lounge at an airport was held to be entitled to it as against the airline company. In that case Donaldson L.J., giving the leading judgment, held, at p. 1014, that for the landowner's claim to prevail in such a case, he had to have both a right and a manifest intention to exercise control over anything which might be on his land.

As to articles found in or attached to land ... *South Staffordshire Water Co. v. Sharman* [1896] 2 QB 44 ... a case which, on its facts, was just on the "in" side of the borderline between objects found in and on land ... concerned a landowner which had instructed its employee to clean the bottom of a pool on land owned by it. In the course of doing so the employee found two gold rings in mud at the bottom of the pool. The landowner and the employee each claimed the rings. Lord Russell of Killowen C.J. ... expressly based his judgment, at pp. 46-47, on the following passage in Pollock and Wright, Possession in the Common Law, at p. 41, dealing with objects attached to or in land:

"The possession of land carries with it in general, by our law, possession of everything which is attached to or under that land, and, in the absence of a better title elsewhere, the right to possess it also. And it makes no difference that the possessor is not aware of the thing's existence. ...

...[I]t is clear from Pollock and Wright's statement ... that they regarded its application to objects in land to be free from the uncertainties inherent in disputes about entitlement to unattached objects found on land. Their proposition was that in practice possession of land should generally be taken as carrying with it an intent to possession of objects in or attached to it. ...

Donaldson L.J. in his review of the authorities and statement of the principles that he derived from them in *Parker v. British Airways Board* [1982] Q.B. 1004, appears to have been of the same view. ...

In my view, the authorities reveal a number of sound and practical reasons for the distinction.

First, as Donaldson L.J. said in *Parker v British Airways Board* [1982] Q.B. 1004, 1010, an object in land "is to be treated as an integral part of the realty as against all but the true owner" or that the finder in detaching the object would, in the absence of licence to do so, become a trespasser. ...

Second, removal of an object in or attached to land would normally involve interference with the land and may damage it... .

Third, putting aside the borderline case of a recently lost article which has worked its way just under the surface, in the case of an object in the ground its original owner is unlikely in most cases to be there to claim it. The law, therefore, looks for a substitute owner, the owner or possessor of the land in which it is lodged. Whereas in the case of an unattached object on the surface, it is likely in most cases to have been recently lost, and the true owner may well claim it. In the meantime, there is no compelling reason why it should pass into the possession of the landowner as against a finder unless he, the landowner, has manifested an intention to possess it. As to borderline cases ... potential absurdities can always be found at the margins in the application of any sound principle. It is for the trial judge to determine as a matter of fact and degree on which side of the line, on or in the land, an object is found. ...

In my view, the two main principles established by the authorities, and for good practical reasons, are as stated by Donaldson L.J. in *Parker v. British Airways Board* [1982] Q.B. 1004. I venture to restate them with particular reference to objects found on or in land, for he was concerned primarily with an object found in a building. (1) Where an article is found in or attached to land, as between the owner or lawful possessor of the land and the finder of the article, the owner or lawful possessor of the land has the better title. (2) Where an article is found unattached on land, as between the two, the owner or lawful possessor of the land has a better title only if he exercised such manifest control over the land as to indicate an intention to control the land and anything that might be found on it.

 Alert

...I can see no basis for not applying the general rule that an owner or lawful possessor of land has a better title to an object found in or attached to his land than the finder, or for modifying it in some way to produce a different result in the circumstances of this case. Mr. Fletcher did not derive a superior right to the brooch simply because he was entitled as a member of public to engage in recreational pursuits in the park. Metal detecting was not a recreation of the sort permitted under the terms under which the council held the land on behalf of the general public. In any event, digging and removal of property in the land were not such a permitted use, and were acts of trespass... .

As to the ... absence of a manifest intention to control, it is, for the reasons I have given in the earlier part of this judgment, not the test for objects found in or attached to land; and, for the reasons I have just given, there is no reason for its application to the circumstances of this case. ...

For those reasons I would allow the appeal.

The difference in this case is that the object was found in or attached to the land. In reliance on previous authorities, Auld LJ and his fellow Court of Appeal judges had little difficulty in allowing the council's appeal and awarding it possession of the brooch.

1.3 The Distinction Between Fixtures and Chattels

The cases relating to the distinction between fixtures and chattels show the range of approaches that may be taken by a court in assessing whether an object is a fixture or a chattel.

Holland and another v Hodgson and another (1872) LR 7 CP 328

Panel: Blackburn J

Facts: In April 1869, the owner of a mill mortgaged the mill and all its fixtures to the claimant. In July 1869, the mill owner transferred his property (still subject to the mortgage) to his trustees in bankruptcy, the defendants. The defendants sold some of the objects in the mill as part of the resolution of the mill owner's bankruptcy problems, but the claimant claimed possession of 436 looms in the mill as forming part of the security due to their status as fixtures. The looms could not work properly if they rested on their own weight so had to be nailed into the floor. The defendants contended that the looms were only slightly annexed to the floor so that they could be more conveniently used and they were therefore chattels.

MR JUSTICE BLACKBURN

There is no doubt that the general maxim of the law is, that what is annexed to the land becomes part of the land; but it is very difficult, if not impossible, to say with precision what constitutes an annexation sufficient for this purpose. It is a question which must depend on the circumstances of each case, and mainly on two circumstances, as indicating the intention, viz., the degree of annexation and the object of the annexation. When the article in question is no further attached to the land, then [sic] by its own weight it is generally to be considered a mere chattel... . But even in such a case, if the intention is apparent to make the articles part of the land, they do become part of the land: see *D'Eyncourt v Gregory* [Law Rep. 3 Eq. 382]. Thus blocks of stone placed one on the top of another without any mortar or cement for the purpose of forming a dry stone wall would become part of the land, though the same stones, if deposited in a builder's yard and for convenience sake stacked on the top of each other in the form of a wall, would remain chattels. On the other hand, an article may be very firmly fixed to the land, and yet the circumstances may be such as to shew [sic] that it was never intended to be part of the land, and then it does not become part of the land. ...Perhaps the true rule is, that articles not otherwise attached to the land than by their own weight are not to be considered as part of the land, unless the circumstances are such as to shew [sic] that they were intended to be part of the land, the onus of shewing [sic] that they were so intended lying on those who assert that they have ceased to be chattels, and that, on the contrary, an article which is affixed to the land even slightly is to be considered as part of the land, unless the circumstances are such as to shew [sic] that it was intended all along to continue a chattel, the onus lying on those who contend that it is a chattel. ...

Alert

Link

Elitestone v Morris

The Court held that the looms were fixtures and formed part of the security.

Mr Justice Blackburn sets out what have become the classic tests for distinguishing between a fixture and a chattel, which are now commonly described as the degree of annexation and purpose of annexation tests. This case focuses on the degree of annexation test, but over time this test has been superseded by the purpose of annexation test. The following case demonstrates the different approaches taken by judges in applying these two tests.

Berkley v Poulett [1977] 1 EGLR 86

Panel: Stamp, Scarman and Goff LJJ

Facts: The claimant bought part of an estate belonging to the defendant. The claimant claimed that certain contents of the property were fixtures which should have passed to him on purchase. The contents included six pictures in one room and two in another room of the house, which were fixed into the wooden panelling of the rooms where they were displayed, a marble statue weighing half a tonne standing on a plinth and a sundial resting on a stone pedestal. These had been removed by the defendant prior to the purchase. The judge at first instance dismissed the claim and Mr Berkley appealed.

LORD JUSTICE SCARMAN

The first question, therefore, is whether the objects … were fixtures. …I find myself in agreement with the [judge]. None of the objects … was, in my judgment, a fixture. …In my judgment, since the contract was silent as to the items in dispute, it is necessary to determine whether under the general law they are to be considered as fixtures, which pass with the realty, or as chattels, in which event they remain the property of the vendor.

As so often, the difficulty is not the formulation but the application of the law. I think there is now no need to enter into research into the case law prior to *Leigh v Taylor* [1902] AC 157. The answer today to the question whether objects which were originally chattels have become fixtures, that is to say part of the freehold, depends upon the application of two tests: (1) the method and degree of annexation; (2) the object and purpose of the annexation. The early law attached great importance to the first test. It proved harsh and unjust… .

Since *Leigh v Taylor* the question is really one of fact. The two tests were explained in that case by the Lord Chancellor … who commented that not the law but our mode of life has changed over the years; that what has changed is "the degree in which certain things have seemed susceptible of being put up as mere ornaments whereas at our earlier period the mere construction rendered it impossible sometimes to sever the thing which was put up from the realty." In other words, a degree of annexation which in earlier times the law would have treated as conclusive may now prove nothing. If the purpose of the annexation be for the better enjoyment of the object itself, it may remain a chattel, notwithstanding a high degree of physical annexation. Clearly, however, it remains significant to discover the extent of physical disturbance of the building or the land involved in the removal of the object. If an object cannot be removed without

 Alert

serious damage to, or destruction of, some part of the realty, the case for its having become a fixture is a strong one. The relationship of the two tests to each other requires consideration. If there is no physical annexation there is no fixture. ...Nevertheless an object, resting on the ground by its own weight alone, can be a fixture, if it be so heavy that there is no need to tie it into a foundation, and if it were put in place to improve the realty. Prima facie, however, an object resting on the ground by its own weight alone is not a fixture: see Megarry and Wade, p 716. Conversely, an object affixed to realty but capable of being removed without much difficulty may yet be a fixture, if, for example, the purpose of its affixing be that "of creating a beautiful room as a whole" (Neville J in *In Re Whaley* [1908] 1 Ch 615 at p 619). ...Today so great are the technical skills of affixing and removing objects to land or buildings that the second test is more likely than the first to be decisive. Perhaps the enduring significance of the first test is a reminder that there must be some degree of physical annexation before a chattel can be treated as part of the realty.

When one seeks to apply the law to the facts of this case, it is necessary to discriminate between what is relevant but not decisive and what is decisive. ...It is enough to say that the pictures were firmly fixed and that their removal needed skill and experience if it were to be done without damage to the wall and panelling. Certainly they were firmly enough fixed to become fixtures if that was the object and purpose of their affixing. But, if ordinary skill was used, as it was, in their removal, they could be taken down, and in the event were taken down, without much trouble and without damage to the structure of the rooms. The decisive question is therefore as to the object and purpose of their affixing. ...I find, applying the second test, that the pictures were not fixtures. They were put in place on the wall to be enjoyed as pictures. The panelling presented a technical problem in putting them up. The way the carpenter, or whoever it was, solved the problem is not decisive in determining their legal character. But the purpose in putting them there is.

The statue and the sundial give rise in my judgment to no difficulty. Neither was at the time of the sale physically attached to the realty. The sundial was a small object and, once the Earl had detached it (as he did many years earlier) from its pedestal, it ceased to be part of the realty. The [statue] was heavy. ...There is an issue as to whether it was cemented into the plinth or rested on its own weight. The question is not decisive, for, even if it was attached by a cement bond, it was (as events proved) easily removable. However, upon the balance of probability, I agree with the [judge] in thinking it was not attached. The best argument for the statue being a fixture was its careful siting in the West Lawn so as to form an integral part of the architectural design of the west elevation of the house. The design point is a good one so far as it goes: it explains the siting of the plinth, which undoubtedly was a fixture. But what was put upon the plinth was very much a matter for the taste of the occupier of the house for the time being. We know that at one time the object on the plinth had been a sundial. At the time of the sale it was this statue of a Greek athlete. The plinth's position was architecturally important: it ensured that whatever stood on it would be correctly positioned. But the object it carried could be whatever appealed to the occupier for the time being. Sundial or statue - it did not matter to the design, so long as it was in the right place - a result ensured by the plinth which was firmly fixed into the ground.

> Being, as I think, unattached, the statue was, prima facie, not a fixture, but, even if it were attached, the application of the second test would lead to the same conclusion.
>
> Accordingly, I agree with the [judge]. ...I would dismiss the appeal.

The pictures, statue and sundial were held to be chattels and did not pass to the purchaser.

The three judgments in this case are interesting for their different approaches to the application of the law. Lord Justice Scarman focuses on the second test, the purpose of annexation and concluded that all the objects in question remained chattels. Lord Justice Stamp agreed with him, but his approach is very different. He looked at the first test, the degree of annexation, and set out in minute detail in several paragraphs how the pictures were affixed to the wall (they were attached to the wall and fitted into the surrounding wooden panelling) and how difficult it was for the carpenters to remove them (he looked at the evidence and thought that the pictures had not been particularly difficult to remove). He asserted that they were chattels before they were hung on the walls and remained chattels even after they were hung. He also agreed with Scarman LJ's view of the statue and the sundial.

Interestingly, Goff LJ dissented from the majority judgment. He agreed with the principle for deciding whether an object is a fixture or a chattel but he disagreed with how the other judges had applied the test. He focused on the statue and the sundial in his judgment (and conceded that the sundial was in fact a chattel) and thought that the statue formed part of an architectural design. He also considered the pictures and the wooden panelling fixed to the walls into which the pictures were fitted: "I think the panelling and pictures were made one integral whole", going against the view of Stamp LJ.

In later cases, such as the following two examples, the judges tend to follow Scarman LJ's approach and focus on the purpose of annexation test. This is now the more important test in establishing whether an object is a fixture or a chattel.

Elitestone Ltd v Morris and another [1997] 1 WLR 687

Panel: Lord Browne-Wilkinson, Lord Lloyd of Berwick, Lord Nolan, Lord Nicholls of Birkenhead and Lord Clyde

Facts: The claimant was the freehold owner of a parcel of land, divided into 27 plots, upon one of which was a bungalow occupied by the defendants. The bungalow rested on concrete foundation blocks in the ground. The claimant wished to redevelop the land and to remove the bungalow and its occupants for that purpose, so the claimant served notice on the occupiers of all the plots, claiming possession from them. The defendants asserted that the bungalow formed part of the land and that they were tenants of that land, protected by statute. The claimant claimed that the bungalow was a chattel, not a fixture, and that the defendants were only licensees whose licence could be terminated at any time. The judge (the assistant recorder at first instance) held that the bungalow was a fixture as it had become part of the land. The Court of Appeal allowed the appeal by the claimant and held that the bungalow was a chattel as it rested on the concrete pillars and was not attached to them. The defendants appealed to the House of Lords.

LORD LLOYD OF BERWICK

The assistant recorder held, correctly, at the end of what was necessarily a very lengthy judgment that the question in Mr Morris's case turned on whether or not the bungalow formed part of the realty. …

Having visited the site, the assistant recorder had this to say:

'While the house rested on the concrete pillars which were themselves attached to the ground, it seems to me clear that at least by 1985 and probably before, it would have been clear to anybody that this was a structure that was not meant to be enjoyed as a chattel to be picked up and moved in due course but that it should be a long-term feature of the realty albeit that, because of its construction, it would plainly need more regular maintenance.'

The Court of Appeal disagreed. Aldous LJ, who gave the leading judgment, was much influenced by the fact that the bungalow was resting by its own weight on concrete pillars, without any attachment. …

[T]he Court of Appeal did not have the advantage of having seen the bungalow. Nor were they shown any of the photographs, some of which were put before your Lordships. These photographs were taken only very recently. Like all photographs they can be deceptive. But if the Court of Appeal had seen the photographs, it is at least possible that they would have taken a different view. For the photographs show very clearly what the bungalow is, and especially what it is not. It is not like a Portakabin, or mobile home. The nature of the structure is such that it could not be taken down and re-erected elsewhere. It could only be removed by a process of demolition. This, as will appear later, is a factor of great importance in the present case. If a structure can only be enjoyed in situ, and is such that it cannot be removed in whole or in sections to another site, there is at least a strong inference that the purpose of placing the structure on the original site was that it should form part of the realty at that site, and therefore cease to be a chattel. …

It will be noticed that in framing the issue for decision I have avoided the use of the word 'fixture'. There are two reasons for this. The first is that 'fixture,' though a hallowed term in this branch of the law, does not always bear the same meaning in law as it does in everyday life. In ordinary language one thinks of a fixture as being something fixed to a building. One would not ordinarily think of the building itself as a fixture. …

For my part, I find it better in the present case to avoid the traditional twofold distinction between chattels and fixtures, and to adopt the threefold classification set out in Woodfall Landlord and Tenant release 36 (1994) vol 1, p 13/83, para 13.131:

 Alert

'An object which is brought onto land may be classified under one of three broad heads. It may be (a) a chattel; (b) a fixture; or (c) part and parcel of the land itself. Objects in categories (b) and (c) are treated as being part of the land.'

 Alert

So the question in the present appeal is whether, when the bungalow was built, it became part and parcel of the land itself. The materials out of which the bungalow was constructed, that is to say the timber frame walls, the feather boarding, the suspended timber floors, the chipboard ceilings and so on, were all, of course, chattels when they were brought onto the site. Did they cease to be chattels when they were built into the composite structure? The answer to the question, as Blackburn J pointed out in *Holland v Hodgson* (1872) LR 7 CP 328 at 334, [1861-73] All ER Rep 237 at 242, depends on the circumstances of each case, but mainly on two factors, the degree of annexation to the land and the object of the annexation.

Degree of annexation

The importance of the degree of annexation will vary from object to object. In the case of a large object, such as a house, the question does not often arise. Annexation goes without saying. ...[T]here is a more recent decision of the High Court of Australia which is of greater assistance. In *Reid v Smith* (1905) 3 CLR 656 at 659 Griffith CJ stated the question as follows:

 Alert

'The short point raised in this case is whether an ordinary dwelling-house, erected upon an ordinary town allotment in a large town, but not fastened to the soil, remains a chattel or becomes part of the freehold.'

The Supreme Court of Queensland had held that the house remained a chattel. But the High Court reversed this decision, treating the answer as being almost a matter of common sense. The house in that case was made of wood, and rested by its own weight on brick piers. The house was not attached to the brick piers in any way. It was separated by iron plates placed on top of the piers, in order to prevent an invasion of white ants. There was an extensive citation of English and American authorities. It was held that the absence of any attachment did not prevent the house forming part of the realty. ...

Purpose of annexation

Many different tests have been suggested, such as whether the object which has been fixed to the property has been so fixed for the better enjoyment of the object as a chattel, or whether it has been fixed with a view to effecting a permanent improvement of the freehold. This and similar tests are useful when one is considering an object such as a tapestry, which may or may not be fixed to a house so as to become part of the freehold (see *Leigh v Taylor* [1902] AC 157, [1900-3] All ER Rep 520). These tests are less useful when one is considering the house itself. In the case of the house, the answer is as much a matter of common sense as precise analysis. A house which is constructed in such a way so as to be removable, whether as a unit or in sections, may well remain a chattel, even though it is connected temporarily to mains services such as water and electricity. But a house which is constructed in such a way that it cannot be removed at all, save by destruction, cannot have been intended to remain as a chattel. It must have been intended to form part of the realty. I know of no better analogy than the example given by Blackburn J in *Holland v Hodgson* (1872) LR 7 CP 328 at 335, [1861-73] All ER Rep 237 at 242:

 Alert

'Thus blocks of stone placed one on the top of another without any mortar or cement for the purpose of forming a dry stone wall would become part of the land, though the same stones, if deposited in a builder's yard and for convenience sake stacked on the top of each other in the form of a wall, would remain chattels.'

Applying that analogy to the present case, I do not doubt that when Mr Morris's bungalow was built, and as each of the timber frame walls were placed in position, they all became part of the structure, which was itself part and parcel of the land. ...

...[T]he Court of Appeal may have been misled by Blackburn J's use of the word 'intention' in *Holland v Hodgson* (1872) LR 7 CP 328, [1861-73] All ER Rep 237. ...[T]he intention of the parties is only relevant to the extent that it can be derived from the degree and object of the annexation. The subjective intention of the parties cannot affect the question whether the chattel has, in law, become part of the freehold... .

For the above reasons, I would allow this appeal and restore the order of the assistant recorder.

The House of Lords held unanimously that the bungalow was a fixture forming part of the land.

Lord Lloyd of Berwick picked up on the confusion surrounding the word 'intention', as used by Blackburn J in *Holland v Hodgson* and emphasised that it is the objective intention which is vital in deciding whether an object is a fixture or a chattel. The purpose of the annexation should be inferred from all the circumstances.

Graham Charles Botham & Ors v TSB Bank plc [1996] 73 P & CR D1

Panel: Sir Richard Scott, Roch and Henry LJJ

Facts: The appellant was the owner of a flat which was mortgaged in favour of the respondent bank. When the mortgage payments went into arrears, the bank obtained possession of the flat and sold it. An issue arose as to which of the contents of the flat were fixtures and could be sold by the bank and which were chattels and so still belonged to the appellant. The judge at first instance held that all the objects except for one wall-mounted electric razor were fixtures. Mr Botham appealed to the Court of Appeal.

LORD JUSTICE ROCH

The most helpful statement of the legal principles in this area of the law, in my opinion, is to be found in the judgment of the Court of Exchequer Chamber delivered by Blackburn J in the case of *Holland -v- Hodgson* [1872] LR 7CP 328... .

...These principles have to be applied with the observations of Scarman LJ, as he then was, in *Berkley v Poulett and Others* [1977] 261 EG 911 at 913, in mind. At page 912 Scarman LJ identified the two tests as being:

"(1) the method and degree of annexation;

(2) the object and purpose of the annexation." ...

The tests, in the case of an item which has been attached to the building in some way other than simply by its own weight, seem to be the purpose of the item and the purpose of the link between the item and the building. If the item viewed objectively, is, intended to be permanent and to afford a lasting improvement to the building, the thing will have become a fixture. If the attachment is temporary and is no more than is necessary for the item to be used and enjoyed, then it will remain a chattel. Some indicators can be identified. For example, if the item is ornamental and the attachment is simply to enable the item to be displayed and enjoyed as an adornment that will often indicate that this item is a chattel. ...The ability to remove an item or its attachment from the building without damaging the fabric of the building is another indicator. ...It must be remembered that in many cases the item being considered may be one that has been bought by the mortgagor on hire purchase, where the ownership of the item remains in the supplier until the instalments have been paid. ...The type of person who instals or attaches the item to the land can be a further indicator. Thus items installed by a builder, eg the wall tiles will probably be fixtures, whereas items installed by eg a carpet contractor or curtain supplier or by the occupier of the building himself or herself may well not be.

 Alert

The judge's directions to himself [at first instance] on the law were these: that the primary test whether an item is or is not a fixture is the degree of annexation of the item to the building. ...

The judge then went on to direct himself that the second matter relevant to the issue was the purpose of the annexation of the item to the land or building. That consideration could in some cases render an item a chattel in law although it was attached to the land. The judge continued that the conventional test was whether or not the purpose of annexation was or was not to effect a permanent improvement in the land or was merely to enable the owner of the chattel to enjoy it as a chattel. ...Finally the judge directed himself that the purpose test was objective and could not depend on the particular intention of the person who had attached the item to the building. ...

In my judgment, no criticism can be made of the judge's statement of the tests and principles which had to be applied in this case ...Nevertheless, it remains to be considered whether the judge correctly applied those principles and tests to the 8 classes of items which remained in dispute. ...

Applying the principles which I have sought to identify and taking account of what can be seen in [the] photographs certain classes of items can, in my judgment, safely be found to be fixtures.

I have no hesitation in agreeing with the judge that ... the bathroom fittings namely the taps, plugs and showerhead together with the towel rails, soap dishes and lavatory roll holders ... are fixtures.

Those items are attached to the building in such a way as to demonstrate a significant connection with the building, and are of a type consistent with the bathroom fittings such as the basins, baths, bidets and lavatories, as to demonstrate an intention to effect a permanent improvement to the flat. They are items necessary for a room which is used as a bathroom. They are not there ... to be enjoyed for themselves, but they are there as accessories which enable the room to be used and enjoyed as a bathroom. Viewed objectively, they were intended to be permanent and to afford a lasting improvement to the property. ...

This leaves ... the fitted carpets, ... the light fittings, ... the four gas fires, ... the curtains and blinds ... and the white goods in the kitchen ... .

I would allow the appeal with regard to the fitted carpets and the curtains and blinds ... . These items, although made or cut to fit the particular floor or window concerned, are attached to the building in an insubstantial manner. Carpets can easily be lifted off gripper rods and removed and can be used again elsewhere. In my judgment neither the degree of annexation nor the surrounding circumstances indicate an intention to effect a permanent improvement in the building. ...The removal of carpets and curtains has no effect damaging or otherwise on the fabric of the building. In my opinion, the method of keeping fitted carpets in place and keeping curtains hung are no more than is required for enjoyment of those items as curtains and carpets. Such items are not considered to be or to have become part of the building. They are not installed, in the case of new buildings, by the builders when the building is constructed, but by the occupier himself or herself or by specialist contractors who supply and install such items. ...There may be cases where carpeting or carpet squares are stuck to a concrete screed in such a way as to make them part of the floor and thus fixtures. In this case, there was no evidence, in my opinion, to justify the judge's finding that the carpets in this flat were fixtures. ...

This leaves the final group ... the white goods in the kitchen. ...No one, I venture to suggest would look on these as fixtures. Here the judge should have reminded himself that the degree of annexation was slight: no more than that which was need[ed] for these items to be used for their normal purposes. In fact these items remain in position by their own weight and not by virtue of the links between them and the building. All these items can be bought separately, and are often acquired on an instalment payment basis, when ownership does not pass to the householder immediately. ...The degree of annexation is therefore slight. Disconnection can be done without damage to the fabric of the building and normally without difficulty. ...

Consequently I would allow the appeal in respect of these group of items.

Apart from the items found in the bathroom, all the other items were held to be chattels, which remained in the ownership of the mortgagor.

This case is an informative one in relation to the status of household objects and shows that each object must be viewed on its own merits. The Court of Appeal did not dispute the law as stated by the judge at first instance, but did not agree with his application of it in a blanket fashion, grouping the objects into broad classes. The tests must be applied to each object individually, which is how Roch LJ proceeded in his judgment.

Taylor v Hamer [2002] EWCA Civ 1130, [2002] All ER (D) 512 (Jul)

Panel: Sedley and Arden LJJ and Wall J

Facts: Mr Taylor inspected a property belonging to Mrs Hamer, prior to entering into a contract to purchase it. Part of the property comprised a number of gardens, one of which (known as the 'dog garden') was partially covered in old flagstones. The sales particulars for the property stated that the property included landscaped gardens but it did not contain a picture or description of the dog garden. The sales particulars stated that the items mentioned in the particulars were included in the sale but that all other fixtures were excluded. Prior to exchange of contracts and after inspection by Mr Taylor, many of the flagstones were removed from the dog garden by Mr Hamer and stacked up on neighbouring land, and grass was laid in their place. Mr Taylor's solicitor, who inspected the property prior to exchange of contracts but after the flagstones had been moved, raised an enquiry about the stacked-up flagstones, asking whether they had been removed from the property. Mr Hamer lied and said that they had not been removed from the property and that they did not form part of the sale. After the purchase, the claimant sued the defendant, claiming that the flagstones were fixtures and should have passed with the property. The judge at first instance held that the flagstones were not fixtures and so were not included in the sale. Although he did confirm that the husband had been fraudulent when answering the solicitor's enquiry, the judge relied on a term of the contract which stated that the buyer was deemed to have inspected the property just prior to exchange of contracts and therefore was deemed to know that the flagstones had been removed from the garden. Mr Taylor appealed to the Court of Appeal for damages to replace and re-lay the flagstones.

LORD JUSTICE SEDLEY

82. A house and grounds are put on the market. A prospective buyer looks them over and decides to buy. Before contracts are exchanged the vendor removes valuable fixtures without telling the purchaser. The purchaser exchanges and completes in the reasonable belief that the property he is buying is the property he was shown. Common sense and common decency both suggest that, if there is no good reason to do otherwise, the law ought to give the purchaser what he was led to think he was getting.

...

84. ...The "Property" ... includes things fixed to and forming part of the land, so that to speak of the property is to speak of everything it is composed of. On conveyance all of it will pass unless excluded. ...

85. None of the terms of the agreement has, in my judgment, the effect of excluding these flagstones from the sale. ...

92. ...[A]ny reasonable person, in my judgment, would have understood the property which was being bid for and contracted for to include the flagstones in the dog garden. The case falls outside the caveat emptor paradigm ... because the vendor, by his conduct in inviting an offer for the property as shown to the purchaser and without any explicit subtraction from it, represented that it was to include the flagged garden.

93. In everyday house purchases people are entitled to be confident that, unless some different agreement is reached and recorded, the property which is to pass includes its fixtures. If before the sale takes place the seller has given the buyer no reason to think that the fixtures (at least those the buyer knows of) are not part of the premises for which an offer is being invited, simple morality says that he cannot remove them without telling the buyer that they are no longer for sale. To fail to do so is to invite a bid for something which is no longer what the bidder still reasonably believes it to be: not to put too fine a point on it, it is cheating. Surreptitiously removing fixtures does not mean that the seller is stealing them, for they are his. It means that if the sale goes through he will be failing to convey what the eventual buyer has become entitled to have conveyed. ...

94. For my part, accordingly, I would allow this appeal and order the respondent to restore the flagstones to their former location in the dog garden or to indemnify the appellant for the cost of doing so. ...

The flagstones were fixtures and ought to have passed with the property on purchase.

Although the case appears to be complicated, the fundamental question that the Court of Appeal had to answer was whether the flagstones formed part of the property and had therefore passed to the purchaser. Both Wall J and Sedley LJ concluded that the flagstones were fixtures and no clause of the contract excluded them from the sale under the LPA 1925 s 62(4). The lie by Mr Hamer only served to muddy the waters in the opinion of the majority; if Mr Hamer had not removed them, the flagstones would have passed to the purchaser because they formed part of the property.

Lady Justice Arden did not agree with the majority judgment. She thought that the flagstones were chattels, not fixtures, at the date of the contract, because they were not mentioned or shown in the sales particulars. The sales particulars contained a warning to purchasers that they should not make assumptions about parts of the property which were not pictured in the sales particulars. She thought that a buyer should not rely on his inspection as to what was included in the purchase; this depends on the terms of the contract. However, both Wall J and Sedley LJ thought that the contract did not affect the status of the flagstones and they should have passed on purchase by Mr Taylor.

Further Reading

Cheshire and Burn *Modern Law of Real Property,* (17th Edition), pp 156-161, 173-176

Gray & Gray *Elements of Land Law,* (5th Edition), pp 14-15, 23-48

MacKenzie & Phillips *Textbook on Land Law,* (15th Edition), Oxford University Press, Chapter 28

Megarry & Wade *The Law of Real Property,* (8th Edition), pp 52-63, 1103-1113

2

Estates in Land

Topic List

1   The Freehold Estate (Fee Simple Absolute in Possession)

2   The Leasehold Estate (Term of Years Absolute)

Introduction

Only two estates in land can exist in England and Wales: the freehold (or fee simple absolute in possession) and leasehold (or term of years absolute) as contained in the Law of Property Act 1925 (LPA 1925) s 1(1). Essentially, the freehold estate is land ownership for an unlimited duration of time while the leasehold estate is for a fixed and certain period of time. Once the leasehold, or term of years absolute, expires then the leasehold land will revert back to the freehold owner, who retains the freehold reversion.

We will see in this chapter the manner in which the freehold and leasehold estates are subject to their respective formalities. For the transfer of the freehold estate a contract or contracts of sale complying with the Law of Property (Miscellaneous Provisions) Act 1989 (LP(MP)A 1989) s 2 may be exchanged prior to completion. Should the contract(s) not comply with s 2 due to a term being omitted then the courts may, depending on the circumstances, apply the remedy of rectification or find the existence of a separate contract, which would not invalidate the statutory requirements.

With the leasehold estate, one must first establish the essential characteristics of the leasehold before a lease may be found by the courts. Case law has examined the need for certainty of term and, should one not be expressly mentioned by the parties, then alternatively there is the possibility of implying a period to satisfy this requirement. We will also examine the length of this period and the reasoning behind the implied periodic tenancy as mentioned above, together with the additional requirement of an intention to create legal relations, ie to grant a lease.

The freehold estate will be examined first.

2.1 The Freehold Estate (Fee Simple Absolute in Possession)

The transfer of the freehold from one party to another must be effected by deed as prescribed by the LPA 1925 s 52(1) and can take place in a number of ways including by will, gift and sale. To be a legal transfer, the transferee must also be registered as the new owner of the property under the Land Registration Act (LRA) 2002 s 4(1) for unregistered land or s 27(1) for registered land.

2.1.1 Exchange of contracts

Prior to transfer, however, binding contracts for sale will usually be exchanged between the vendor and purchaser outlining the agreed terms of the sale and the intentions of the parties. As these are contracts for the sale of an interest in land, they must comply with the LP(MP)A 1989 s 2 if they were created on or after 27 September 1989. Contracts created before this time are governed by the LPA 1925 s 40.

Under the LP(MP)A 1989 s 2 all of the agreed terms must be included in the contract otherwise it is void and unenforceable and, therefore, cannot be the basis for claims by either party. There have been occasions, however, where one or more of the agreed terms were excluded from the final contract, which was then relied upon by an aggrieved party. The courts are faced with the question of whether or not they can uphold the incomplete contract or must declare it void for non-compliance with the LP(MP)A 1989 s 2.

Record v Bell [1991] 1 WLR 853

Panel: Judge Paul Baker QC sitting as a Judge of the High Court

Statute: Law of Property (Miscellaneous Provisions) Act 1989 s 2

Facts: The claimant sought specific performance of two contracts: one for the purchase of a house by the defendant and the other for purchase of chattels within the house. A further agreement was made under which the defendant would not purchase the house until the claimant produced evidence that he was the registered proprietor of the land in question. This agreement was not included in the final written sale contract between the parties and so the defendant claimed that it was void for non-compliance with the LP(MP)A 1989 s 2.

JUDGE PAUL BAKER QC sitting as a judge of the High Court

The other ground for giving leave to defend is that the contract does comply with the terms of s 2 of the Law of Property (Miscellaneous Provisions) Act 1989. It is a point of some general importance arising under a new statute which has made very substantial changes in the law relating to contracts for the sale of land. The particular area I am concerned with is where a contract in two parts has been duly signed by the respective parties and is awaiting exchange. Then some term is orally agreed immediately prior to exchange and confirmed by the exchange of letters. Is the statute satisfied? That, as I see it, is a very common situation, especially where there is some pressure to get contracts exchanged, as there frequently is, and one often finds that at exchange not all the loose ends are tidied up and it is necessary to have some last minute adjustment of the contract which takes the form of side letters.

Turning to the part of the contract signed by the defendant one sees that it has this letter from Offenbach & Co dated 1 June fixed to it:

'Dear Mr Berns, (solicitor of the claimant)

RE: 6 SMITH SQUARE LONDON SW1
This letter is written to be attached to the Contract of Sale and is part of the contract between the parties. It is agreed that: (1) Office Copies to be delivered to the Purchaser will show the registered proprietor as Anthony Record and there will be no other entries different from the copy Charge Certificate supplied to the Purchaser's solicitors other than in respect of financial charges. (2) The blue colouring referred to on the Office Copy filed plan is the same as the yellow copy on the Office Copy Transfer supplied to us.'

That is the version of this arrangement that Mr Offenbach put forward and I should say that in due course up-to-date office copies become available and they showed exactly as was anticipated in the letter, namely that Mr Record was the registered proprietor, there were no other charges other than financial ones and the colouring on the plan was as stated.

Those, I think, are all the facts that I need refer to in relation to this point. Now I must return to the Law of Property (Miscellaneous Provisions) Act 1989, s 2. Subsections (1) to (3) are the relevant parts for the purposes of this matter.

1.   A contract for the sale or other disposition of an interest in land can only be made in writing and only by incorporating all the terms which the parties have expressly agreed in one document or, where the contracts are exchanged, in each.

2.   The terms may be incorporated in a document either by being set out in it or by reference to some other document.

3.   The document incorporating the terms or, where contracts are exchanged, one of the documents incorporating them (but not necessarily the same one) must be signed by or on behalf of each party to the contract.'

… In his submissions to me on this Mr Halpern for the defendant said, first, that the section does not cater for side letters of the sort involved in this case unless they are incorporated into the main agreement. Secondly, he says, that the letters in this case were not incorporated as required by the section, and thirdly in any event they had to be in identical terms when there are two parts to the contract, and these letters were not in identical terms. He also says, indeed, these letters in this case were not more than memoranda of a pre-existing oral contract between the solicitors and that was a situation which it was the purpose of the Act to outlaw.

In reply to that Mr Ritchie submitted first of all that side letters may amount to a collateral contract outside the 1989 Act. As regards that point Mr Halpern concedes that there is a possibility of side letters being a collateral contract and unless they are themselves a contract for the sale of land the 1989 Act would not bite.

   …Turning to Mr Berns's letter, I observed it to be stated that the contracts were exchanged conditionally upon the following basis: that the office copies would reveal Anthony Record and that there were no other entries on the register other than financial charges. I do not find in the terms of these letters any difference between what Mr Offenbach has put forward and what Mr Berns has put forward as to what the vendor is purporting to guarantee. Mr Berns's letter, as one might expect, explains the reasons why it is necessary to put that forward, that he had failed to obtain up-to-date copies of the Land Registry entries up to the point of exchange. He describes it that contracts 'were exchanged conditional upon the following basis', but myself I would not regard that as fatal to this being a warranty of the sort described in *De Lassalle v Guildford*, and indeed my conclusion on this is unhesitating. This was, in my judgment, an offer of a warranty by Mr Berns to Mr Offenbach as to the state of the title, and it was done to induce him to exchange. That offer was accepted by exchanging contracts. It would be

 Decipher
The term 'collateral' has a specific meaning within contract law and cannot be used to describe a contract, term, or warranty that does not serve as an inducement to enter into the main contract from one party to another.

unfortunate if common transactions of this nature should nevertheless cause the contracts to be avoided. It may, of course, lead to a greater use of the concept of collateral warranties than has hitherto been necessary.

It may be seen, therefore, that a collateral contract designed to induce a party into the main contract does not need to comply with the LP(MP)A 1989 s 2 unless it is itself a contract of land. As such, the collateral contract in this case was valid, as was the main contract. The term 'collateral contract' should not be used loosely but rather only with reference to a situation similar to that in *Record v Bell*.

Should the contract in question not be designed to induce entry into the contract for sale or disposition of land then another approach is required where agreed terms have been omitted from a land contract.

Tootal Clothing Ltd v Guinea Properties Management Ltd (1992) 64 P & CR 452

Panel: Parker and Scott LJJ and Boreham J

Statute: Law of Property (Miscellaneous Provisions) Act 1989 s 2

Facts: Tootal Clothing (the claimant at first instance; the appellant in the Court of Appeal) were granted a lease by the respondents for 25 years. The appellant was to carry out shop-fitting works to the leased property and, upon satisfactory completion of these works, the respondent was to pay them £30,000. The respondent failed to pay these monies to the appellant and claimed in their defence that the contract relied on by the appellants was void as it did not comply with the LP(MP)A 1989 s 2.

LORD JUSTICE SCOTT

Formal agreements were prepared embodying the terms that had been agreed between the parties. The formal agreements were signed by each of the parties. They were dated August 10 1990 and exchanged on that date. There were two agreements that were signed, dated and exchanged. One was an agreement for a lease whereby it was agreed: (i) that Guinea Properties would grant and Tootal would accept the grant of a 25-year lease in the form of the draft lease annexed thereto; (ii) that the grant of the lease would be completed on August 17 1990; (iii) that Tootal would within 12 weeks from the date of the agreement (or a later date in the event of certain delays occurring) carry out the shop-fitting works at its own expense; (iv) that rent under the lease would commence to be payable three months from the date of the grant thereof; and (v) that "this Agreement sets out the entire agreement of the parties...".

This agreement, which I will hereafter call "the lease agreement", contained no reference to the other agreement, also dated August 10 1990 and exchanged on that date.

The other agreement (which I will call the "supplemental agreement") contained a recital that "the parties have agreed that this Agreement is supplemental to the [Lease] Agreement and have agreed terms whereby the Landlord will contribute towards the cost of the Tenant's works referred to in Clause 3 of the [Lease] Agreement". There was also a recital of the lease agreement. This supplemental agreement, after the two recitals to which I have referred, then set out the terms on which the £30,000 would be payable by Guinea Properties to Tootal. I have said before, and I repeat, that both agreements were signed by each of the parties thereto.

The lease agreement was duly completed on August 31 1990. A lease bearing that date in the form of the draft lease annexed to the lease agreement was granted by Guinea Properties to Tootal. Tootal thereupon set about carrying out the necessary shop-fitting works. Having completed the shop-fitting works, I assume satisfactorily because the contrary has not been suggested, Tootal applied to Guinea Properties for payment of the £30,000. Guinea Properties declined to pay, contending that section 2 of the Law of Property (Miscellaneous Provisions) Act 1989 barred recovery by Tootal of the £30,000. Tootal, not surprisingly, commenced proceedings. The only defence pleaded by Guinea Properties to the claim by Tootal for the £30,000 was the section 2 point. It was pleaded in Guinea Properties' defence that:

7.   The terms embodied in the Document [ie the supplemental agreement] were not incorporated into the Agreement [ie the lease agreement] or the Lease and are void and/or unenforceable by virtue of section 2 of the Law of Property (Miscellaneous Provisions) Act 1989.

In my opinion, the reliance in Guinea Properties' defence on section 2 of the 1989 Act misses the point about the purpose and effect of section 2.

...[S]ection 2 is of relevance only to executory contracts. It has no relevance to contracts which have been completed. If parties choose to complete an oral land contract or a land contract that does not in some respect or other comply with section 2, they are at liberty to do so. Once they have done so, it becomes irrelevant that the contract they have completed may not have been in accordance with section 2.

In the present case, the parties having agreed all the terms under which the new 25-year lease would be granted, including those relating to the shop-fitting works and the contribution by Guinea Properties of £30,000 towards the cost incurred by Tootal in carrying out the shop-fitting works, chose to incorporate the terms in two documents instead of one, namely the lease agreement and the supplemental agreement. They then completed the lease agreement. The lease agreement thereupon ceased to be an executory contract. The question whether section 2 of the 1989 Act would, because not all the terms of the contractual bargain had been incorporated into the lease agreement, have rendered the lease agreement unenforceable became irrelevant. All that was left was the supplemental agreement. The supplemental agreement was not and is not by itself a land contract or, at least, if it is, by incorporation therein of the terms of the lease agreement, a land contract, then there is no issue in the case that need detain the court. But on the footing that the supplemental agreement by itself is not a land contract, which is the contention of Mr Ritchie for Guinea Properties, there was no longer, after the completion of the lease agreement, any executory land contract in existence to which section 2 of the 1989 Act could apply. There was simply a contract recorded in writing, signed by each party, for the payment of £30,000 in a certain event by one party to the other.

I am of the opinion, speaking for myself, that even before completion of the lease agreement on August 31 1990, section 2 would not have prevented the enforcement of the lease agreement. If parties choose to hive off part of the terms of their composite bargain into a separate contract distinct from the written land contract that incorporates the rest of the terms, I can see nothing in section 2 that provides an answer to an action for enforcement of the land contract, on the one hand, or of the separate contract on the other hand. Each has become, by the contractual choice of the parties, a separate contract.

But it is not necessary for us on the present appeal to decide that point. It suffices, in my judgment, to say that, once the lease agreement had been executed by completion, section 2 had no relevance to the contractual enforceability of the supplemental agreement, whether or not that supplemental agreement was negotiated as part of one bargain that included the terms of the lease agreement.

I would, therefore, allow this appeal. Guinea Properties has, in my opinion, no defence to the action.

Lord Justice Scott's decision was based on two reasons. The first was that the contract for the lease had already been completed, thereby rendering s 2 LP(MP)A 1989 irrelevant with respect to the contract for the lease. This part of the decision has now been doubted by the Court of Appeal in the case of **Keay v Morris Homes (West Midlands) Ltd** [2012] EWCA Civ 900. The second reason for Lord Justice Scott's decision was that the contract for the shop-fitting was clearly distinct from the contract for the granting of the lease as indicated by the actions of the parties and, as it was not a contract for land, s 2 did not need to apply. It seems, therefore, that when a term or number of terms are 'hived off' (in the words of Scott LJ) by the parties then this can form a separate contract and need not comply with s 2 if it is not a contract for land. As in *Record v Bell* this means that the main contract is still valid too, notwithstanding that it does not contain the other term.

Note that the later case of **North Eastern Properties Ltd v Coleman and another** [2010] 2 EGLR 161 has restricted this principle by stating that if the main land contract is conditional on the terms in the separate contract, then those terms cannot be hived off in this manner.

Should a collateral or separate contract not be found to exist, as seen in the respective cases of *Record v Bell* and *Tootal Clothing v Guinea* above, then yet another situation may arise with respect to a missing term. This may occur when the term in question cannot be seen to be of a distinctly different nature to the contract of land (as in *Tootal Clothing v Guinea*) or collateral to the contract of land (as in *Record v Bell*).

Wright v Robert Leonard (Developments) [1994] EG 69 (C.S.)

Panel: Dillon, Leggatt, and Henry LJJ

Statute: Law of Property (Miscellaneous Provisions) Act 1989 s 2

Facts: The defendant, Robert Leonard (Developments), had agreed to sell the leasehold of a show-flat to the claimant, Wright. The original agreement had included an oral understanding that the furnishings and fixtures were to be included with the sale on the basis that completion would occur within 21 days. A schedule of the fixtures and fittings was attached to the claimant's contract. The completion date was not met but the purchase price was eventually paid by the claimant at a later date; the defendant then removed the fixtures and fittings. At first instance it was found that a separate contract for the sale of the fixtures and fittings existed that did not have to comply with the LP(MP)A 1989 s 2 as it was not for the sale of land. The defendant appealed.

While judgment at first instance was given in favour of the claimant, upon appeal the rationale for the decision was clarified by Dillon LJ. He disagreed with the judge at first instance in that he could not justify the existence of two separate contracts as in *Record v Bell* and *Tootal Clothing v Guinea*, which were considered. Instead, the contract for the sale of the flat had two separate *elements*, one being for the sale of the land and the other for the inclusion of the fixtures and fittings. As they were part of a single transaction for the sale of land they were inseparable and, therefore, the whole arrangement needed to comply with the LP(MP)A 1989 s 2.

The term regarding the inclusion of the fixtures and fittings was oral, however, and was not included in the contract for sale of the land as prescribed by s 2. The court decided that the remedy of rectification was available where it would be unjust not to grant it; in the present situation the written contract did not include the term regarding fixtures and fittings even though it had previously been agreed by the parties. Therefore, under s 2(4), fixtures and fittings were included in the rectified contract.

In this case it is established that the remedy of rectification may be available when a term, previously agreed by the parties and intended to be included in the contract, is omitted and it would be unjust not to amend the contract. This principle from *Wright v Robert Leonard (Developments)* was to be applied to a number of similar situations, though not always with the same outcome.

Oun v Ahmad [2008] EWHC 545 (Ch), [2008] 13 EG 149

Panel: Morgan J

Statutes: Law of Property (Miscellaneous Provisions) Act 1989 s 2; Land Registration Act 2002 s 111

Facts: The defendant owned the long lease of a property consisting of an off-licence on the lower floor and a residence on the upper floor. The claimant and defendant then came to an arrangement whereby the claimant would purchase the lease from the defendant. Two documents were drawn up to reflect this arrangement, the first entitled 'Contract to Sell' and the second containing provisions as to how the purchase monies were to be apportioned. A disagreement as to the sale of the property arose and the claimant sued for breach of the first contract. It was held by an adjudicator that the first contract did not comply with the LP(MP)A 1989 s 2 and was, therefore, void and unenforceable. Furthermore, rectification was not available to the claimant.

MR JUSTICE MORGAN

28. Section 2(1) requires the written document to incorporate all the terms which the parties have expressly agreed.

29. The first matter to be explored is a question of fact: what were all the terms which the parties had expressly agreed?

30. Once one has found all the terms which the parties have expressly agreed, then one can examine the written document to see if it incorporates all those terms or whether it omits any.

31. If, on examination of the written document, it is found that it does not incorporate all the terms which the parties have expressly agreed, then prima facie there is no binding contract at all. There cannot be a binding contract for all the terms expressly agreed because not all the terms expressly agreed have been incorporated into the written document. There cannot be a binding contract for only those terms which have been incorporated because they are not the complete set of terms which were expressly agreed.

32. The prima facie position may be displaced in two cases, in particular.

33. The first particular case is where there are two separate contracts and not one composite contract. If it is possible to hold that the terms which have been incorporated into the written document include all of the express terms of a separate and independent contract for the sale or other disposition of an interest in land and other terms agreed between the parties are terms of a second independent contract, then the written document complies with section 2 in relation to the first contract.

34. The second particular case is where the written document, which does not incorporate all of the terms expressly agreed, can be rectified to include in the written document all of the terms expressly agreed. Following such rectification, the written document by definition does include all of the terms expressly agreed and therefore complies with section 2.

35. Section 2(4) of the 1989 Act expressly contemplates that a court can order rectification in some cases where the written document does not incorporate all of the terms expressly agreed. However, there is an important issue in the present appeal as to the cases in which rectification is available. Is it every case where the written document does not incorporate all of the terms expressly agreed (whatever the reason for that might be) or is it only those cases where, applying conventional principles, the equity of rectification is available?

At this stage it was considered, therefore, whether the remedy of rectification in land law was treated differently to rectification in contract law, which was long established and subject to a number of principles and conditions.

36. The process of rectification which is referred to appears to differ somewhat from the normal process of rectification. In this context, before the order for rectification the written document does not have contractual effect (because it does not contain all the terms expressly agreed) but after the order for rectification the rectified written document does have contractual effect. This feature of rectification in this context is acknowledged in section 2(4) of the 1989 Act which refers to the contract "com[ing] into being" as a result of the order for rectification. Further, section 2(4) contemplates that the court has power to specify the date when the contract comes into being and this is different from the usual retrospective effect of rectification.

42. In the first type of case, the written document does not incorporate all the terms expressly agreed, by reason of a mistake in the recording of the agreement. In such a case, the court can rectify the written document so as to incorporate all the terms expressly agreed and then the document as rectified complies with section 2.

43. The second (rather more unusual) type of case is as follows. Say the parties expressly agree upon five terms of their agreement. They agree to record four of them in a written document and they do so. They agree that the fifth term shall remain unrecorded in writing. The result is that the written document does not comply with section 2 and is of no effect. Can one party seek an order for rectification to the effect that the fifth term should be incorporated into the written document so that the written document will then comply with section 2?

55. In my judgment, this express agreement to omit the term means that there is no defect or mistake in the recording of, or the expression of, the arrangement and it is beyond the ambit of rectification to write into the written agreement a term which the parties expressly agreed should not be so recorded. I reach this conclusion applying what I understand to be conventional principles as to the availability of rectification and not some special set of rules as to rectification for the purposes of section 2(4) of the 1989 Act. In my judgment, this approach serves the legislative objective of section 2 of the 1989 Act.

...

Here we can also see the role of statutory interpretation by the courts as Morgan J looks to the legislative objective behind s 2 rather than merely its wording.

69. On my findings of fact, the parties expressly agreed not to record the terms as to apportionment in the first document. On my understanding of the law, it is beyond the ambit of the court's power to rectify to write in terms which the parties agreed should not be recorded in the first document.

70. The result is that Mr Oun did not have the benefit of a binding contract to buy the property.

71. The appeal must be dismissed.

Oun v Ahmad gives us a number of useful points regarding the remedy of rectification in land, together with the need to comply with LP(MP)A 1989 s 2. A clear distinction is drawn between the situation in *Wright v Robert Leonard,* where an agreed term was excluded by mistake, and the present situation where an agreed term was expressly excluded despite the consequence that the initial contract, thought by both parties to be binding, was void and unenforceable. Rectification is only available therefore in a small number of situations and cannot be applied by the courts to remedy a defect in law.

Upon the exchange of a s 2 compliant contract there exists a binding relationship between the purchaser and vendor that cannot be broken unilaterally without incurring liability. However, it is quite common that the situation arises whereby the parties wish to vary an existing term of their contract. When this occurs and one party seeks to rely upon the variation, the courts are faced once more with the application of the LP(MP)A 1989 s 2 to the new term.

McCausland and another v Duncan Lawrie Ltd and another [1997] 1 WLR 38

Panel: Neill and Morritt LJ and Tucker J

Statute: Law of Property (Miscellaneous Provisions) Act 1989 s 2

Facts: The claimants had contracted with the defendants to purchase a house and paid a small holding deposit with the remainder payable upon completion. A price was agreed along with a completion date, after which the full 10% deposit on the property would become due. The defendants' solicitors subsequently discovered that the agreed completion date was a Sunday and telephoned the solicitors of the claimants requesting that it be moved to the preceding Friday, 24 March 1995, instead. This was orally agreed by the claimants. However, completion failed to take place on 24 March and the defendants issued a completion notice for the full amount of the deposit. This was paid but without prejudice to the claimants' right to sue for specific performance of the contract for sale, the final price of which would reflect the full deposit paid. The first instance judge found in favour of the defendants, stating that the LP(MP)A 1989 s 2 did not apply to the variation of the contract and, therefore, the completion date had been 24 March 1995. The claimants appealed.

LORD JUSTICE MORRITT

The question here is whether the contract for the sale of the land was varied so as to justify the notice to complete served by the vendor. Thus the vendor has to establish that the contract with the purchaser provided that the sale of the property was to be completed on Friday, 24 March. For that purpose he has to demonstrate that there is a document or two documents which were exchanged containing all the terms of that contract and signed by both parties. Obviously he cannot do that for the completion date he relies on is different from that specified in the contract and there is no other document which is signed by both parties.

The choice lies between permitting a variation, however fundamental, to be made without any formality at all and requiring it to satisfy s 2. In my view it is evident that Parliament intended the latter. There would be little point in requiring that the original contract comply with s 2 if it might be varied wholly informally. Further, the respect in which the Act differs from the Bill proposed by the Law Commission indicates that Parliament intended more, rather than less, formality than that recommended by the Law Commission.

Thus, whilst understanding the reasons which the judge considered justified his conclusion and having had more time than he did to consider the point, I do not agree with him. In my judgment, the variation of a term material to a contract for the sale or other disposition of an interest in land must comply with the formalities prescribed by s 2 of the 1989 Act if either party is to be able to enforce such contract as varied. Accordingly, I think that the judge was wrong to have struck out the statement of claim on the footing that s 2 did not apply in this case.

Whenever a material term in a contract for the sale or disposition of land is varied, therefore, that variation must comply with the LP(MP)A 1989 s 2 also. To deem it otherwise would defeat the purpose of needing s 2 as any number of terms could be varied at a later date. Neither Morritt LJ nor any other on the panel specifically defined what is meant by a 'material' term, however, and so there is little guidance as to whether specific variations will need to comply with s 2 in the future. It seems, however, that where a term, such as the completion date, as in this case, is essential to the nature of the contract, then it will be considered 'material' and any variation must comply with the LP(MP)A 1989 s 2.

2.1.2 Exceptions to s 2 LP(MP)A 1989

As we have seen the LP(MP)A 1989 s 2 is rigorously applied to contracts for the sale or other disposition of land. However, as with many areas of law, there are exceptions upon which one can rely should the necessary formalities not be complied with.

Yaxley v Gotts and another [2000] Ch 162

Panel: Beldam, Robert Walker and Clarke LJJ

Statute: Law of Property (Miscellaneous Provisions) Act 1989 s 2

Facts: The claimant was a builder who requested a loan from the father of the defendant so that he could purchase freehold land to develop as flats. The father of the defendant purchased the land instead but with the provision that the claimant could acquire the ground floor flats if he completed building work on the upper floor flats and operated as the managing agent for the entire building. The defendant then took over the freehold from his father and excluded the claimant despite a large amount of work already having been completed on the building. It was held at first instance that the defendant took over the freehold with knowledge of the claimant's interest and held the leasehold of the ground floor flats for a period of 99 years on constructive trust for the claimant. Alternatively, the doctrine of proprietary estoppel could have been relied upon, but the effect would have been virtually identical to that of the constructive trust. The defendant appealed.

LORD JUSTICE ROBERT WALKER

Section 2 of the 1989 Act has repealed and replaced s 40 of the Law of Property Act 1925, which itself replaced part of s 4 of the Statute of Frauds 1677. It is not in dispute that s 2 is an entirely new provision which marks a radical change in the law: *Firstpost Homes Ltd v Johnson* [1995] 4 All ER 355 at 358, [1995] 1 WLR 1567 at 1571 per Peter Gibson LJ and *McCausland v Duncan Lawrie Ltd* [1996] 4 All ER 995 at 1001, [1997] 1 WLR 38 at 44 per Neill LJ.

Parliament's requirement that any contract for the disposition of an interest in land must be made in a particular documentary form, and will otherwise be void, does not have such an obviously social aim as statutory provisions relating to contracts by or with moneylenders, infants, or protected tenants. Nevertheless it can be seen as embodying Parliament's conclusion, in the general public interest, that the need for certainty as to the formation of contracts of this type must in general outweigh the disappointment of those who make informal bargains in ignorance of the statutory requirement. If an estoppel would have the effect of enforcing a void contract and subverting Parliament's purpose, it may have to yield to the statutory law which confronts it, except so far as the statute's saving for a constructive trust provides a means of reconciliation of the apparent conflict.

To give it what I take to be its [s 2(5) LP(MP)A 1989] natural meaning, comparable to that of s 53(2) of the Law of Property Act 1925 in relation to s 53(1), would not create a huge and unexpected gap in s 2. It would allow a limited exception, expressly contemplated by Parliament, for those cases in which a supposed bargain has been so fully performed by one side, and the general circumstances of the matter are such, that it would be inequitable to disregard the claimant's expectations, and insufficient to grant him no more than a restitutionary remedy.

To give the saving a narrow construction would not to my mind be a natural reading of its language. Moreover, it would often require the court to embark on minute inquiries into informal negotiations, between parties acting without legal advice, in order to decide whether or not the parties' 'agreement, arrangement or understanding' would have amounted to a complete and legally binding contract but for the single fatal defect of non-compliance with s 2. The course which this case has taken vividly illustrates the problems involved.

For those reasons I would dismiss this appeal.

LORD JUSTICE BELDAM

For my part I cannot see that there is any reason to qualify the plain words of s 2(5). They were included to preserve the equitable remedies to which the Commission had referred. I do not think it inherent in a social policy of simplifying conveyancing by requiring the certainty of a written document that unconscionable conduct or equitable fraud should be allowed to prevail.

In my view the provision that nothing in s 2 of the 1989 Act is to affect the creation or operation of resulting, implied or constructive trusts effectively excludes from the operation of the section cases in which an interest in land might equally well be claimed by relying on constructive trust or proprietary estoppel.

That, to my mind, is the case here. There was on the judge's findings, as I interpret them, a clear promise made by Brownie Gotts to the plaintiff that he would have a beneficial interest in the ground floor of the premises. That promise was known to Alan Gotts when he acquired the property and he permitted the plaintiff to carry out the whole of the work needed to the property and to convert the ground floor in the belief that he had such an interest. It would be unconscionable to allow either Alan or Brownie Gotts to resile from the representations made by Brownie Gotts and adopted by Alan Gotts. For my part I would hold that the plaintiff established facts on which a court of equity would find that Alan Gotts held the property subject to a constructive trust in favour of the plaintiff for an interest in the ground floor and that that interest should be satisfied by the grant of a 99-year lease. I consider the judge was entitled to reach the same conclusion by finding a proprietary estoppel in favour of the plaintiff. I, too, would dismiss the appeal.

Yaxley v Gotts is, therefore, a case that serves to both clarify and establish the position of constructive trusts and the equitable doctrine of estoppel following the implementation of the LP(MP)A 1989 s 2. The facts of the case and the interpretation of s 2(5) used here allow us to see how a constructive trust may arise and the possible use of proprietary estoppel following the repeal of the LPA 1925 s 40. These are, therefore, possible exceptions to the general operation of the LP(MP)A 1989 s 2 should the circumstances justify them.

We shall now look at the second type of legal estate.

2.2 The Leasehold Estate (Term of Years Absolute)

Unlike the freehold estate, the leasehold estate is granted for a fixed and definite period of time by one party to another. The most basic example is that of a freehold owner granting a lease to another for a certain number of years subject to specific conditions. The grant of a lease is also a more intricate matter than the sale of a freehold with specific definitional requirements needing to be satisfied (details of these can be found in the Study Notes).

2.2.1 Certainty of Term

An essential characteristic of the leasehold is that of a certain term and, if one is not specified or able to be implied, then the lease will ultimately fail.

Lace v Chantler [1944] KB 368

Panel: Lord Greene MR, MacKinnon and Luxmoore LJJ

Facts: A lease was granted by the defendant to the claimant for a period defined as 'the duration of the war', referring to World War II. The defendant argued that a weekly tenancy had been created and, following the giving of the required notice, sought to repossess the property inhabited by the claimant. It was argued by the claimant that this lease was not of a weekly duration but of a certain longer duration, the period of which could be defined at a later date.

LORD GREENE MR

Apart from one circumstance, there could be no question that this was an ordinary weekly tenancy, duly determinable at a week's notice. But the parties in the rent-book agreed to a term which appears there expressed by the words "furnished for duration"—which must mean the duration of the war. The question immediately arises whether a tenancy for the duration of the war creates a good leasehold interest. In my opinion, it does not. A term created by a leasehold tenancy agreement must be a term which is either expressed with certainty and specifically, or is expressed by reference to something which can, at the time when the lease takes effect, be looked to as a certain ascertainment of what the term is meant to be. In the present case, when this tenancy agreement took effect, the term was completely uncertain. It was impossible to say how long the tenancy would endure. Counsel for the tenant in his argument has maintained that such a lease would be a good lease; and that, even if the term is uncertain at the beginning of the term, when the lease takes effect, the fact that at some future time it will be made certain is sufficient to make it a good lease. In my opinion, that argument is not to be sustained.

In this succinct *ratio decidendi* Lord Greene MR does not overly complicate the issues, and it is clear that a lease must be created for a certain term before the lease takes effect and, if not, then a period must be implied instead. The term purporting to be certain in this case was invalid and, therefore, a period of one week was found and inserted in its place.

Other authorities had specifically addressed the issue of such a tenancy where the term is uncertain before the lease takes effect; a necessary clarification was exactly how an implied period was to be determined.

Ladies' Hosiery and Underwear Ltd v Parker [1930] 1 Ch 304

Panel: Maugham J

Facts: The claimant company obtained the freehold of land upon which the defendant leased a shed for business purposes. At a later date the Midland Bank became the owner of the freehold and leased a part of their land back to the claimant company. The claimant company refused to lease the land which the defendant occupied to the defendant and instead sought possession of the land from them. The defendant counterclaimed for a declaration that they were yearly tenants of the land.

MR JUSTICE MAUGHAM

The question is whether the holding over under an agreement in the terms of that of 10 Oct 1914, with the continuance of the payment of the weekly rent of 2 pounds, would create the relationship of landlord and tenant on the terms of a yearly tenancy. The agreement was to let the premises for the term of three years commencing from 12 Oct 1914, at a weekly rent of 2 pounds to be paid every week, and with a right of re-entry on failure to pay the rent for seven days. It is well known, I think, that "tenancy from year to year" is a tenancy which originally used to be described as a tenancy at will, with a provision that not less than six months' notice had to be given to put an end to it, expiring at the time of the year at which the original tenancy expired. The authorities on that point are referred to in REDMAN'S LAW of LANDLORD AND TENANT (8th Edn) pp 4, 5. At the end of each year, if not determined by proper notice, another year is added to the term. The inference that that is the intention of the parties is an inference drawn from the fact that, in the ordinary case, the payment of rent is by reference to a yearly rent. It is true that the rent may be paid each year, or half-yearly or quarterly, or even weekly; but in those cases, at any rate so far as the authorities are concerned, the rent is always a payment by reference to a year's rent.

My conclusion, therefore, is that when the defendant Mr Parker, after the expiration of that agreement, paid the sum of 2 pounds a week to his landlord, Mr Jenkins, he was prima facie not paying it with reference to a year or an aliquot part of a year, but was paying it with reference to the week in respect of which he made the payment.

While the language of the judgment may seem to lack strength, the general principle laid down by Maugham J has remained intact and was not challenged in this case when it was sent to the Court of Appeal. A yearly tenancy was seen to be created when rent was calculated annually; conversely in this case, when rent was calculated weekly then a weekly tenancy was implied. This principle has been used by the courts ever since. The issue of a periodic tenancy was later examined in much greater detail, and the rationale behind it espoused in much more unambiguous language.

Prudential Assurance v London Residuary Body [1992] 2 AC 386

Panel: Lord Templeman, Lord Griffiths, Lord Goff of Chieveley, Lord Browne-Wilkinson and Lord Mustill

Facts: Land was leased by the London County Council (later the London Residuary Body – the defendant) to the claimant's predecessor until such time as the defendant needed to widen the road to which it was attached. Notice to quit was given to the claimant a number of years later; the claimant argued that the defendant could not give notice as they did not have the power to widen the road and, therefore, could not need the land for road widening. The defendant was granted judgment at first instance; upon appeal the decision was overturned. The defendant appealed.

LORD TEMPLEMAN

When the agreement in the present case was made, it failed to grant an estate in the land. The tenant however entered into possession and paid the yearly rent of £30 reserved by the agreement. The tenant entering under a void lease became by virtue of possession and the payment of a yearly rent, a yearly tenant holding on the terms of the agreement so far as those terms were consistent with the yearly tenancy. A yearly tenancy is determinable by the landlord or the tenant at the end of the first or any subsequent year of the tenancy by six months' notice unless the agreement between the parties provides otherwise.

...My Lords, I consider that the principle in *Lace v Chandler* (sic) [1944] 1 All ER 305, [1944] KB 368 reaffirming 500 years of judicial acceptance of the requirement that a term must be certain applies to all leases and tenancy agreements. A tenancy from year to year is saved from being uncertain because each party has power by notice to determine at the end of any year. The term continues until determined as if both parties made a new agreement at the end of each year for a new term for the ensuing year. A power for nobody to determine or for one party only to be able to determine is inconsistent with the concept of a term from year to year.

This part of the judgment provides justification for the existence of an implied periodic tenancy, therefore, and clearly sets out the reasoning behind it. The term is not uncertain even though, in theory, the tenancy could go on indefinitely as the tenant may continue to renew.

A lease can be made for five years subject to the tenant's right to determine if the war ends before the expiry of five years. A lease can be made from year to year subject to a fetter on the right of the landlord to determine the lease before the expiry of five years unless the war ends. Both leases are valid because they create a determinable certain term of five years. A lease might purport to be made for the duration of the war subject to the tenant's right to determine before the end of the war. A lease might be made from year to year subject to a fetter on the right of the landlord to determine the lease before the war ends. Both leases would be invalid because each purported to create an uncertain term. A term must either be certain or uncertain. It cannot be partly certain because the tenant can determine it at any time and partly uncertain because the landlord cannot determine it for an uncertain period. If the landlord does not grant and the tenant does not take a certain term the grant does not create a lease.

In the present case the Court of Appeal was bound by the decisions in *Charles Clay & Sons Ltd v British Railways Board* and the *Ashburn* case. In my opinion both those cases were wrongly decided. A grant for an uncertain term does not create a lease. A grant for an uncertain term which takes the form of a yearly tenancy which cannot be determined by the landlord does not create a lease. I would allow the appeal. The trial judge, Millett J, reached the conclusion that the six months' notice was a good notice. He was of course bound by the Court of Appeal decisions but managed to construe the memorandum of agreement so as to render cl 6 ineffective in fettering the right of the landlord to serve a notice to quit after the landlord had ceased to be a road widening authority. In the circumstances this question of construction need not be considered. For the reasons which I have given the order made by Millett J must be restored.

The case reaffirmed the need for certainty of term before a tenancy takes effect but also firmly established the doctrine of an implied periodic tenancy should the expressly stated term fail for uncertainty. Lord Templeman justified this conclusion by stating that each period would be certain as each party has the power to determine at the end of each period. Should determination not occur then the period renews as if it was a new agreement.

However, in the Supreme Court case of *Berrisford v Mexfield Housing Co-operative Limited* [2011] UKSC 52, the Supreme Court held that a lease for an uncertain term to an individual, Mrs Berrisford, did not take effect as an implied periodic tenancy, but took effect as a lease for her life, which statute converts into a lease for 90 years under the Law of Property Act 1925 s 149(6). The Supreme Court made clear its dissatisfaction with the law regarding certainty of term and hoped for a change in the law in this area, although it did not go so far as to overrule *Prudential Assurance v London Residuary Body* or to jettison the requirement for certainty of term.

The following case on periodic tenancies demonstrates a further requirement for the creation of a lease: intention to create legal relations. Should there be a lack of intention to create a tenancy by the payment of rent then this will overrule any potential implied periodic tenancy and will create a tenancy at will instead.

Javad v Aqil [1991] 1 WLR 1007

Panel: Mustill, Ralph Gibson and Nicholls LJJ

Facts: The claimant entered into negotiations to lease his property to the defendant, who was a manufacturer of leather goods. The defendant paid one quarter's rent in advance (£2,500) and, while negotiations continued, subsequently made payment of a further two quarters' rent. Negotiations eventually broke down, and the claimant sought possession of the property by way of two weeks' notice to quit. The defendant argued that he held a yearly tenancy as he was in possession and paying rent, which had been accepted by the claimant. Possession was ordered by the county court and the defendant appealed.

LORD JUSTICE NICHOLLS

This case turns on the distinction between a tenancy at will and a periodic tenancy. Shortly stated, a tenancy at will exists where the tenancy is on terms that either party may determine it at any time. A periodic tenancy, on the other hand, is one which continues from period to period indefinitely until determined by proper notice. For example, from year to year, quarter to quarter, month to month, or week to week. Failing agreement to the contrary, the notice of determination required is half a period in the case of a yearly tenancy but a full period in other cases.

Much of the argument before us was directed at the legal consequence which follows from proof of possession and payment of rent by reference to a quarterly period. For the defendant it was submitted that proof of those facts raises a presumption in favour of a periodic tenancy which can only be rebutted, and the occupant be held to be a tenant at will, by an express agreement to that effect. Alternatively, this presumption is not rebutted by the fact that the grant of a lease is under discussion, in a case where a substantial sum has been paid over as rent in advance.

I cannot accept the defendant's submissions. They are contrary both to principle and to authority. I shall consider first the position in principle. A tenancy, or lease, is an interest in land. With exceptions immaterial for present purposes, a tenancy springs from a consensual arrangement between two parties: one person grants to another the right to possession of land for a lesser term than he, the grantor, has in the land. The extent of the right thus granted and accepted depends primarily on the intention of the parties.

As with other consensually-based arrangements, parties frequently proceed with an arrangement whereby one person takes possession of another's land for payment without having agreed or directed their minds to one or more fundamental aspects of their transaction. In such cases the law, where appropriate, has to step in and fill the gaps in a way which is sensible and reasonable. The law will imply, from what was agreed and all the surrounding circumstances, the terms the parties are to be taken to have intended to apply. Thus if one party permits another to go into possession of his land on payment of a rent of so much per week or month, failing more the inference sensibly and reasonably to be drawn is that the parties intended that there should be a weekly or monthly tenancy. Likewise, if one party permits another to remain in possession after the expiration of his tenancy. But I emphasise the qualification: 'failing more'. Frequently there will be more. Indeed, nowadays there normally will be other material surrounding circumstances. The simple situation is unlikely to arise often, not least because of the extent to which statute has intervened in landlord-tenant relationships. Where there is more than the simple situation, the inference sensibly and reasonably to be drawn will depend on a fair consideration of all the circumstances, of which the payment of rent on a periodical basis is only one, albeit a very important one. This is so, however large or small may be the amount of the payment.

To this I add one observation, having in mind the facts of the present case. Where parties are negotiating the terms of a proposed lease, and the prospective tenant is let into possession or permitted to remain in possession in advance of, and in anticipation of, terms being agreed, the fact that the parties have not yet agreed terms will be a factor to be taken into account in ascertaining their intention. It will often be a weighty factor. Frequently in such cases a sum called 'rent' is paid at once in accordance with the terms of the proposed lease: for example, quarterly in advance. But, depending on all the circumstances, parties are not to be supposed thereby to have agreed that the prospective tenant shall be a quarterly tenant. They cannot sensibly be taken to have agreed that he shall have a periodic tenancy, with all the consequences flowing from that, at a time when they are still not agreed about the terms on which the prospective tenant shall have possession under the proposed lease, and when he has been permitted to go into possession or remain in possession merely as an interim measure in the expectation that all will be regulated and regularised in due course when terms are agreed and a formal lease granted.

Of course, when one party permits another to enter or remain on his land on payment of a sum of money, and that other has no statutory entitlement to be there, almost inevitably there will be some consensual relationship between them. It may be no more than a licence determinable at any time, or a tenancy at will. But when and so long as such parties are in the throes of negotiating larger terms, caution must be exercised before inferring or imputing to the parties an intention to give to the occupant more than a very limited interest, be it licence or tenancy. Otherwise the court would be in danger of inferring or imputing from conduct, such as payment of rent and the carrying out of repairs, whose explanation lies in the parties' expectation that they will be able to reach agreement on the larger terms, an intention to grant a lesser interest, such as a periodic tenancy, which the parties never had in contemplation at all.

[At first instance] Judge Stucley held that no periodic tenancy was created when the defendant moved his stock into 188 Brick Lane on 26 June 1985, because there were too many outstanding differences between the parties. He mentioned, as an example, the disagreement over sub-letting. For good measure, he reached the same conclusion regarding the defendant's status when the defendant returned to the property and, eventually, the workmen went away and the defendant was left in sole possession. He said that the matter was so nebulous that there was nothing sufficiently material to grasp on to find a periodic tenancy existing.

I can see no ground for disturbing the judge's conclusion. On a fair reading of the necessarily imperfect note of his judgment, it is clear that the judge approached the issue before him in the correct way. From the conclusions he expressed, it is apparent that the essential question to which he directed his attention was whether in all the circumstances it was right to infer the creation of a periodic tenancy.

Where there is no intention to create legal relations, therefore, a lease or tenancy will not be found despite the fact that one party has moved into possession and begun to pay consideration to the estate holder. Here, the occupation was granted on the basis that a lease would be agreed and concluded rather than as a tenancy in and of itself; when the negotiations broke down it was reasonable for the estate holder to serve notice upon the party in possession.

2.2.2 Equitable Leases

It is an established principle that where there is a valid agreement for a lease then equity will support the existence of a lease notwithstanding the fact that the lease has not been granted at law. There may be a situation, therefore, where both an equitable lease and a legal lease could exist where there is a valid agreement for a lease and the court would be willing to imply a legal lease with reference to a period (as described above).

Walsh v Lonsdale (1882) LR 21 Ch D 9

Panel: Sir George Jessel MR, Cotton and Lindley LJJ

Facts: The claimant and the defendant entered into a lease agreement for a mill, subsequent to which the claimant entered into possession and began paying rent. The defendant commenced an action for distress in contravention of the lease agreement. The claimant then counter-claimed for damages for illegal distress, specific performance, and an injunction. For various reasons the question before the court was whether the lease in equity prevailed over the lease at common law.

SIR GEORGE JESSEL MR

It is not necessary on the present occasion to decide finally what the rights of the parties are. If the Court sees that there is a fair question to be decided it will take security so that the party who ultimately succeeds may be in the right position. The question is one of some nicety. There is an agreement for a lease under which possession has been given. Now since the Judicature Act the possession is held under the agreement. There are not two estates as there were formerly, one estate at common law by reason of the payment of the rent from year to year, and an estate in equity under the agreement. There is only one Court, and the equity rules prevail in it. The tenant holds under an agreement for a lease. He holds, therefore, under the same terms in equity as if a lease had been granted, it being a case in which both parties admit that relief is capable of being given by specific performance. That being so, he cannot complain of the exercise by the landlord of the same rights as the landlord would have had if a lease had been granted. On the other hand, he is protected in the same way as if a lease had been granted; he cannot be turned out by six months' notice as a tenant from year to year. He has a right to say, "I have a lease in equity, and you can only re-enter if I have committed such a breach of covenant as would if a lease had been granted have entitled you to re-enter according to the terms of a proper proviso for re-entry." That being so, it appears to me that being a lessee in equity he cannot complain of the exercise of the right of distress merely because the actual parchment has not been signed and sealed.

Where there is a conflict between equity and the common law, therefore, it will be equity that prevails. A further point raised by *Walsh v Lonsdale* regards the enforcement of an agreement (in that case for a lease). Not only do appropriate formalities for the agreement need to be complied with but it must also be possible for specific performance to be granted. For this to be the case we must look at equitable maxims such as 'clean hands' and investigate whether any of the parties have acted in such a manner as to affect their ability to claim the equitable remedy of specific performance.

Coatsworth v Johnson [1886-90] All ER Rep 547

Panel: Lord Esher MR, Lindley and Lopes LJJ

Facts: The claimant and the defendant entered into a lease agreement for a farm for 21 years, which was not under seal and, therefore, did not satisfy the requisite formalities for a legal lease at that time. One of the covenants contained within the lease was that the claimant must keep the farm in a good and husband-like manner. The claimant never paid any rent and did not keep the farm in the manner prescribed in the agreement for the lease and the defendant demanded that the claimant quit the property. The claimant then sued the defendant for damages.

LORD ESHER MR

The law seems to me to be perfectly well established with regard to their relation. Until the payment of rent, that tenancy is a tenancy at will only. If a rent, on the terms of its being part of an annual rent, had been paid, then the landlord would have been estopped, on the failure of the payment of that rent, from saying that there was not a tenancy from year to year. But it is a payment of rent, as part of the annual rent, which raises estoppel where there is an agreement for a lease. Where there has been rent paid, which is part of an annual payment of rent, then there is a tenancy from year to year upon such of the terms of the agreement (which is not a lease) as are applicable to a tenancy from year to year. The agreement as a lease is void, although the circumstances will then have raised a tenancy. But until there has been a payment of rent it is only a tenancy at will.

If there is a tenancy at will, how is the landlord to put an end to it? By giving notice to quit, and that is all. He has not to assign any reasons for giving that notice. Supposing there had been no breach of any covenant, he could have given that notice to quit so far as it is a tenancy at will. If it is a tenancy at will, the question of whether there is a breach of covenant or not is immaterial. But it is argued that it was not a tenancy at will, because, under the circumstances, the court of equity would have decreed specific performance of the lease; and it is said that now both sides of the court would consider that as done which the court of equity would have decreed to be done. That proposition is not to be denied.

That raises this question! Would the court of equity in this case have decreed specific performance? If it would, then that is to be considered as done, and then there is a lease. But if it would not, then, there being no lease at common law, it being in the position that the court of equity would not decree specific performance for a lease, then it is no lease at common law. But the proposition is this: It is admitted that, before the Conveyancing Act, 1881, if there had been a breach of the contract as to cultivation, the court of equity would not have decreed specific performance. But it is said that, although the tenant has declined or neglected to cultivate in the way mentioned in the agreement, nevertheless the court of equity would decree specific performance, because it is said that the Conveyancing Act, 1881, by s 14, has altered the contract; and that now there is no breach of the contract to cultivate in a particular way, unless, besides the non-cultivation, there has been a demand by the landlord, or a notice by the landlord, not properly observed by the tenant In other words, that s 14 of the Conveyancing Act, 1881, has altered the contract, and that it is not confined merely to relief in the case of breach of the contract.

It is clear to my mind that s 14 of the Conveyancing Act, 1881, has not altered the contract at all. It has merely dealt with relief, or non-relief, on the assumption that that particular stipulation of the contract has been broken. If the contract is not altered, then by the non-cultivation there is a breach of the contract. Would the court of equity then decree specific performance, there being in existence at the time this state of facts? The moment the plaintiff went into equity, and asked for specific performance, and it was proved that he himself was guilty of the breach of contract, which the defendant says he is by not cultivating, the court of equity would refuse to grant specific performance, and would leave the parties to their other rights. Then, if the court of equity would not grant specific performance, we are not to consider specific performance as granted. Then the case is at an end. It is a lease at will.

Further Reading

Gray & Gray *Elements of Land Law,* (5th Edition), Oxford University Press, pp 1044-1051, 306-332

MacKenzie & Phillips *Textbook on Land Law,* (15th Edition), Oxford University Press, Chapter 5 and paras 7.6,10.1- 10.4.4 and 10.10

Megarry & Wade *The Law of Real Property,* (8th Edition), Sweet & Maxwell, pp 618-645, 743-797

3

Interests in Land

Topic List

1   Options to Purchase
2   Rights of Pre-Emption
3   Equitable Mortgages

Introduction

Interests in land cover the lesser proprietary rights which fall short of possession of land (estates). Interests in land generally allow a person to do something on another's land or restrict the landowner from doing something on his land, but do not allow a person to occupy the land.

In order for a right to be an interest in land, it must meet the necessary definitional requirements and must be created in accordance with the appropriate formalities. If these formalities are not complied with, the right will not be proprietary, but personal.

It is also necessary to consider whether an interest will take effect at law or in equity. The Law of Property Act 1925 (LPA 1925) s 1(2) provides a closed list of five interests that can take effect at law (easements, rent charges, legal charges, other charges and rights of entry). All other interests can only take effect in equity under s 1(3). This chapter will consider options to purchase, rights of pre-emption and equitable mortgages.

3.1 Options to Purchase

An option to purchase allows the holder of the option to compel a landowner to sell the land to him within an agreed period of time on agreed terms. It is an estate contract and must comply with the formalities contained in the Law of Property (Miscellaneous Provisions) Act 1989 (LP(MP)A 1989) s 2. *Spiro v Glencrown Properties Ltd and Another* [1991] Ch 537 considered whether the document *creating* the option, or the document *exercising* the option has to comply with these formalities.

Spiro v Glencrown Properties Ltd. and Another [1991] Ch 537

Panel: Hoffmann J

Statutes: The Law of Property (Miscellaneous Provisions) Act 1989 s 2

Facts: The vendor brought an action for damages for breach of contract by the purchaser. The vendor had granted the purchaser an option to purchase a property in a LP(MP)A 1989 s 2 compliant document (in writing, signed by both parties, containing all the terms); the option was exercisable until 5pm that day. The purchaser gave notice in signed writing before 5pm to exercise this option, but subsequently failed to complete. The vendor sued the purchaser for damages for breach of contract for the sale of land. The purchaser argued that as the document exercising the option was not a valid contract (it had only been signed by him), there was no binding contract to sell.

MR JUSTICE HOFFMANN

The only question for decision is whether the contract on which the vendor relies complied with the provisions of section 2 of the Law of Property (Miscellaneous Provisions) Act 1989, which came into force on 27 September 1989, some seven weeks before the grant and exercise of the option... The relevant provisions are as follows:

"(1) A contract for the sale or other disposition of an interest in land can only be made in writing and only by incorporating all the terms which the parties have expressly agreed in one document or, where contracts are exchanged, in each. (2) The terms may be incorporated in a document either by being set out in it or by reference to some other document. (3) The document incorporating the terms or, where contracts are exchanged, one of the documents incorporating them (but not necessarily the same one) must be signed by or on behalf of each party to the contract."

If the "contract for the sale . . . of an interest in land" was for the purposes of section 2(1) the agreement by which the option was *granted*, there is no difficulty. The agreement was executed in two exchanged parts, each of which incorporated all the terms which had been agreed and had been signed by or on behalf of the vendor and purchaser respectively. But the letter which *exercised* the option was of course signed only on behalf of the purchaser. If the contract was made by this document, it did not comply with section 2.

Apart from authority, it seems to me plain enough that section 2 was intended to apply to the agreement which created the option and not to the notice by which it was exercised. Section 2, which replaced section 40 of the Law of Property Act 1925 , was intended to prevent disputes over whether the parties had entered into a binding agreement or over what terms they had agreed. It prescribes the formalities for recording their mutual consent. But only the grant of the option depends upon consent. The exercise of the option is a unilateral act. It would destroy the very purpose of the option if the purchaser had to obtain the vendor's countersignature to the notice by which it was exercised. The only way in which the concept of an option to buy land could survive section 2 would be if the purchaser ensured that the vendor not only signed the agreement by which the option was granted but also at the same time provided him with a countersigned form to use if he decided to exercise it. There seems no conceivable reason why the legislature should have required this additional formality.

 Alert

The language of section 2 places no obstacle in the way of construing the grant of the option as the relevant contract. An option to buy land can properly be described as a contract for the sale of that land conditional on the exercise of the option. A number of eminent judges have so described it. In *Helby v Matthews* [1895] AC 471, 482, which concerned the sale of a piano on hire-purchase, Lord Macnaughten said:

"The contract, as it seems to me, on the part of the dealer was a contract of hiring coupled with a conditional contract or undertaking to sell. On the part of the customer it was a contract of hiring only until the time came for making the last payment."

In *Griffith v Pelton* [1958] Ch. 205, which raised the question of whether the benefit of an option was assignable, Jenkins L.J. said, at p. 225:

"An option in gross for the purchase of land is a conditional contract for such purchase by the grantee of the option from the grantor, which the grantee is entitled to convert into a concluded contract of purchase, and to have carried to completion by the grantor, upon giving the prescribed notice and otherwise complying with the conditions upon which the option is made exercisable in any particular case."

In the context of section 2, it makes obvious sense to characterise it in this way. So far, therefore, the case seems to me to be clear...

[F]rom the buyer's point of view... the essence of an option is that while the seller may be said to be conditionally bound, the buyer is free...

The granting of the option imposes no obligation on the purchaser and an obligation on the vendor which is contingent on the exercise of the option. When the option is exercised, vendor and purchaser come under obligations to perform as if they had concluded an ordinary contract of sale and the analogy of an irrevocable offer is, as I have said, a useful way of describing the position of the purchaser between the grant and exercise of the option...

But the irrevocable offer metaphor has much less explanatory power in relation to the position of the vendor. The effect of the "offer" which the vendor has made is, from his point of view, so different from that of an offer in its primary sense that the metaphor is of little assistance. Thus in the famous passage in *London and South Western Railway Co. v. Gomm* (1882) 20 Ch.D. 562, 581, Sir George Jessel M.R. had no use for it in explaining why the grant of an option to buy land confers an interest in the land upon the grantee:

"The right to call for a conveyance of the land is an equitable interest or an equitable estate. In the ordinary case of a contract for purchase there is no doubt about this, and an option for repurchase is not different in its nature. A person exercising the option has to do two things, he has to give notice of his intention to purchase, and to pay the purchase money; but as far as the man who is liable to convey is concerned, his estate or interest is taken away from him without his consent, and the right to take it away being vested in another, the covenant giving the option must give that other an interest in the land."...

Thus in explaining the vendor's position, the analogy to which the courts usually appeal is that of a conditional contract. This analogy might also be said to be imperfect, because one generally thinks of a conditional contract as one in which the contingency does not lie within the sole power of one of the parties to the contract. But this difference from the standard case of a conditional contract does not destroy the value of the analogy in explaining the *vendor's* position. So far as he is concerned, it makes no difference whether or not the contingency is within the sole power of the purchaser. The important point is that "his estate or interest is taken away from him without his consent."...

An option is not strictly speaking either an offer or a conditional contract. It does not have all the incidents of the standard form of either of these concepts. To that extent it is a relationship sui generis. But there are ways in which it resembles each of them. Each analogy is in the proper context a valid way of characterising the situation created by an option. The question in this case is not whether one analogy is true and the other false, but which is appropriate to be used in the construction of section 2 of the Law of Property (Miscellaneous Provisions) Act 1989 ...

 Alert

Perhaps the most helpful case for present purposes is *In re Mulholland's Will Trusts* [1949] 1 All E.R. 460. A testator had let premises to the Westminster Bank on a lease which included an option to purchase. He appointed the bank his executor and trustee and after his death the bank exercised the option. It was argued for his widow and children that the bank was precluded from exercising the option by the rule that a trustee cannot contract with himself. Wynn-Parry J. was pressed with the irrevocable offer metaphor, which, it was said, led inexorably to the conclusion that when the bank exercised the option, it was indeed entering into a contract with itself. But Wynn-Parry J. held that if one considered the purpose of the self-dealing rule, which was to prevent a trustee from being subjected to a conflict of interest and duty, the only relevant contract was the grant of the option. The rule could only sensibly be applied to a consensual transaction. While for some purposes it might be true to say that the exercise of the option brought the contract into existence, there could be no rational ground for applying the self-dealing rule to the unilateral exercise of a right granted before the trusteeship came into existence. Wynn-Parry J. quoted, at p. 464, from Sir George Jessel M.R. in *Gomm's case*, 20 Ch.D. 562 , 582, and said:

"As I understand that passage, it amounts to this, that, as regards this option, there was between the parties only one contract, namely, the contract constituted by the provisions in the lease which I have read creating the option. The notice exercising the option did not lead, in my opinion, to the creation of any fresh contractual relationship between the parties, making them for the first time vendors and purchasers, nor did it bring into existence any right in addition to the right conferred by the option."...

In my judgment there is nothing in the authorities which prevents me from giving section 2 of the Act of 1989 the meaning which I consider to have been the clear intention of the legislature. On the contrary, the purposive approach taken in cases like *Mulholland* [1949] 1 All E.R. 460 encourages me to adopt a similar approach to section 2 and the plain purpose of section 2 was, as I have said, to prescribe the formalities for recording the consent of the parties. It follows that in my view the grant of the option was the only "contract for the sale or other disposition of an interest in land" within the meaning of the section and the contract duly complied with the statutory requirements. There must be judgment for the plaintiff against both defendants with costs.

Thus, Hoffmann J indicated that an option to purchase could be characterised as an irrevocable offer from the purchaser's point of view, or a conditional contract from the vendor's point of view. In reality he concluded an option creates a 'relationship sui generis'. He concluded that only the document creating the option needs to comply with the requirements of a contract for land under the LP(MP)A 1989 s 2; by contrast, the exercise of an option is a unilateral act and therefore need not comply with these stringent formalities.

3.2 Rights of Pre-Emption

A right of pre-emption can be characterised as a right of first refusal; if the landowner decides to sell, he must offer it to the holder of the right of pre-emption before offering it to any other party. In registered land, a right of pre-emption is an interest in land from the moment of creation under the Land Registration Act 2002 (LRA 2002) s 115. In unregistered land, the position is less certain. The cases below provide guidance on rights of pre-emption in *unregistered* land.

Pritchard v Briggs and Others [1980] Ch 338

Panel: Stephenson, Goff and Templeman LJJ

Facts: Major and Mrs Lockwood granted Mr and Mrs Briggs' predecessor in title a right of pre-emption over a property. They agreed to offer to sell the property at a fixed price to the Briggs' predecessor before selling or agreeing to sell the property to any other party during the parties' lifetime. This right of pre-emption was subsequently transferred to the Briggs. Later, the Lockwoods granted an option to purchase the same property after their deaths to Mr Pritchard. Both the right of pre-emption and the option to purchase were properly registered. The matter for the court to decide was whether the Briggs' right of pre-emption could take precedence over Mr Pritchard's option.

LORD JUSTICE TEMPLEMAN

The question is whether a right of pre-emption exercisable during the lifetime of the grantor is subject to an option subsequently granted but only exercisable after the death of the grantor. In my opinion the answer to the question depends on whether the grant of the option made the right of pre-emption exercisable.

Rights of option and rights of pre-emption share one feature in common; each prescribes circumstances in which the relationship between the owner of the property which is the subject of the right and the holder of the right will become the relationship of vendor and purchaser. In the case of an option, the evolution of the relationship of vendor and purchaser may depend on the fulfilment of certain specified conditions and will depend on the volition of the option holder. If the option applies to land, the grant of the option creates a contingent equitable interest which, if registered as an estate contract, is binding on successors in title of the grantor and takes priority from the date of its registration. In the case of a right of pre-emption, the evolution of the relationship of vendor and purchaser depends on the grantor, of his own volition, choosing to fulfil certain specified conditions and thus converting the pre-emption into an option.

The grant of the right of pre-emption creates a mere spes which the grantor of the right may either frustrate by choosing not to fulfil the necessary conditions or may convert into an option and thus into equitable interest by fulfilling the conditions. An equitable interest thus created is protected by prior registration of the right of pre-emption as an estate contract but takes its priority from the date when the right of pre-emption becomes exercisable and the right is converted into an option and the equitable interest is then created. The holder of a right of pre-emption is in much the same position as a beneficiary under a will of a testator who is still alive, save that the holder of the right of pre-emption must hope for some future positive action by the grantor which will elevate his hope into an interest. It does not seem to me that the property legislation of 1925 was intended to create, or operated to create an equitable interest in land where none existed...

 Alert

After the grant of Mr Pritchard's option, Major Lockwood was not in a position to make an offer to Mr. and Mrs. Briggs or to grant an option to them pursuant to their right of pre-emption or at all save subject to Mr. Pritchard's option. After the registration of Mr. Pritchard's option, Mr. and Mrs. Briggs could not accept an offer or exercise an option granted by Major Lockwood pursuant to the right of pre-emption or at all save subject to Mr. Pritchard's option. In short Major Lockwood could only sell and the Briggs could only purchase subject to Mr. Pritchard's option.

LORD JUSTICE STEPHENSON

Major and Mrs. Lockwood made two promises... I can see no inconsistency in the two promises, only that the second promise confined the first to a promise not to sell the retained lands during the lifetime of... (Mr. and Mrs. Briggs' predecessor) and the Lockwoods... [The right of pre-emption] promise did not promise to offer the retained lands to... [Mr. And Mrs. Briggs' predecessor] either before or after the death of the last of the Lockwoods... Mr. and Mrs. Briggs got no promise of an offer after that death. Indeed, they got no promise of an offer at any time should the Lockwoods keep the retained lands until they were both dead...

Now unless that right of pre-emption, which may never become exercisable because the grantor has it in his power to permit or prevent its exercise, is as good as that more valuable right to buy first, which will become exercisable independently of the volition of the grantor, that weaker right cannot, in my opinion, prevail or defeat the stronger right.

The...conveyance [granting the right of pre-emption] refers to giving the option of purchasing but as a future act, not as a present right... what is granted as a right of pre-emption, on the true construction of the grant, is only properly called an option when the will of the grantor turns it into an option by deciding to sell and thereby binding the grantor to offer it for sale to the grantee. That it thereby becomes an interest in land is a change of the nature of the right to which, unlike Goff LJ, I see no insuperable objection in logic or principle.

Thus, under *Pritchard v Briggs*, a right of pre-emption in unregistered land only becomes an interest in land at the time when the grantor decides that he wishes to sell (at this time, the right of pre-emption becomes an option to purchase, as the purchaser is from this point entitled to demand the property be sold to him). Interests which are properly protected prior to the right of pre-emption becoming an interest in land will therefore take precedence. Following criticism, this decision has been disapplied in registered land by LRA 2002 s 115.

The decision in *Pritchard v Briggs* was considered in detail in *Kling v Keston* (1985) 49 P & CR 212.

Kling v Keston (1985) 49 P & CR 212

Panel: Vinelott J

Facts: The defendant's agent agreed to grant the claimant a right of pre-emption regarding a garage. The defendant subsequently granted a long lease to a third party, without having first made an offer to the claimant. The claimant sought specific performance of the right of pre-emption.

MR JUSTICE VINELOTT

The question whether a right of pre-emption or first refusal over land creates an equitable interest in the land capable of binding a purchaser was for many years a controversial one. It was settled so far as this court is concerned by the decision of the Court of Appeal in *Pritchard v. Briggs*...[the judge considered the case in some detail]

Applying these principles to the instant case, it is, I think, clear that the right of pre-emption became an option and created an equitable interest in the garage not later than the moment when the agreement for the grant of a lease was executed. A vendor can hardly evince a desire to sell land more clearly than by contracting to sell it. The defendant company must have intended actually to sell... or have wished to sell on a long lease... immediately before it entered into the agreement [with the third party] ... It follows that the plaintiff had a valid option to purchase the garage at the moment when the agreement... came into existence. Accordingly, the plaintiff then had and continued to have an equitable interest in the garage...

In *Kling v Keston* the claimant's right of pre-emption became an interest in land once the defendant showed an intention to sell the land (in this case, by contracting to grant a long lease). At this moment, the right of pre-emption became an option to purchase the property. The claimant therefore had an interest in the land and, as he was in actual occupation at the relevant time under LPA 1925 s 70(1)(g) (the forerunner to Schedule 3 Paragraph 2 LRA 2002), this was binding on the purchaser. *Kling v Keston* dealt with registered land, but, as it predated the LRA 2002, it was still subject to the principles set out in *Pritchard v Briggs*.

Bircham & Co Nominees (No. 2) Ltd v Worrell Holdings Ltd [2001] EWCA Civ 775, [2001] All ER (D) 269 (May) considered the nature of the obligation imposed by a right of pre-emption. It considered how long a grantor of a right of pre-emption was obliged to leave an offer to sell the property open to the grantee, before he could sell the property to a third party.

Bircham & Co Nominees (No.2) Ltd v Worrell Holdings Ltd [2001] EWCA Civ 775, [2001] All ER (D) 269 (May)

Panel: Schiemann and Chadwick LJJ and Sir Christopher Staughton

Facts: A third party made an offer to the vendor to buy a property over which the claimant held a right of pre-emption. The vendor made enquiries whether the claimant intended to exercise the right of pre-emption. Soon thereafter the vendor sold his interest in the property to the third party.

LORD JUSTICE CHADWICK

The covenant under consideration in *Pritchard v Briggs* [1980] Ch 338 required that the offer, when made to the person entitled to the right of pre-emption, "shall not be revoked or altered within 21 days". It may be that Lord Justice Goff did not have the terms of the particular covenant in mind when he said, at [1980] Ch 338, 389C, in a passage to which I have already referred:

"Moreover, even if the grantor decides to sell and makes an offer it seems to me that so long as he does not sell to anyone else he can withdraw that offer at any time before acceptance."

That was a course which was not open to the grantors in *Pritchard v Briggs* – at least, not until the period of twenty one days had expired. The importance of the point is this. Where an offer is made upon terms that it will remain open for acceptance for a specified time it has the characteristic which has led the courts, since at least the decision in *London & South Western Railway Co v Gomm* (1881) 20 ChD 562, to hold that the offeree obtains an immediate equitable interest in land. In the words of Mr Justice Street in *Mackay v Wilson* (1947) 47 SR (NSW) 315, 325 there is, in those circumstances:

". . . a positive obligation on the prospective vendor to keep the offer open during the agreed period so that it remains available for acceptance by the optionee at any moment within that period. It has more than a mere contractual operation and confers on the optionee an equitable interest in the land, the subject of the agreement; . . ."

An offer made on terms that it will remain open for acceptance for a specified time is indistinguishable from an option – indeed, to my mind, an offer made on such terms is properly described as an option. But, where the offer is made on terms that it can be withdrawn at any time before acceptance, it does not have the characteristic essential to an option. Such an offer is indistinguishable from any other contractual offer. The offeror remains free, at any time before acceptance, to decide that he will not part with the land – see *Tuck v Baker* [1990] 32 EG 46.

On the facts of the case, the vendor was entitled to sell his interest to a third party once he had made the offer to the purchaser and it had not been accepted. Chadwick LJ indicated that the appeal would have failed in any event, as the right of pre-emption did not comply with the LP(MP)A 1989 s 2, another important outcome of the case in confirming the need for such formality.

3.3 Equitable Mortgages

One way an equitable mortgage will arise is where the parties have contracted to enter into a legal mortgage, but there has been a failure to actually grant the legal mortgage. Such a contract must, as a contract for land, comply with the conditions of the LP(MP)A 1989 s 2. In *United Bank of Kuwait Plc v Sahib and Others* [1997] Ch 107 it was considered what formalities should be complied with where, in unregistered land, an equitable mortgage was entered into, secured by the deposit of the title deeds.

United Bank of Kuwait Plc. v Sahib and Others [1997] Ch 107

Panel: Leggatt, Peter Gibson and Phillips LJJ

Statute: Law of Property (Miscellaneous Provisions) Act 1989 s 2

Facts: One of the defendants claimed an equitable mortgage over the first defendant's property on the basis that the mortgage had been secured by the deposit of the title deeds. The court had to decide whether an equitable mortgage secured by the deposit of the title deeds must comply with the formalities set out in LP(MP)A 1989 s 2.

LORD JUSTICE PETER GIBSON

The section 2 point

Section 2 of the Act of 1989 was enacted to give effect to the substance of that part of the Law Commission's Report, Transfer of Land: Formalities for Contracts for Sale etc. of Land (Law Com. No. 164) (1987) which recommended the repeal of section 40 of the Law of Property Act 1925 and the abolition of the doctrine of part performance and proposed new requirements for the making of a contract for the sale or other disposition of an interest in land. The material parts of section 2 are:

"(1) A contract for the sale or other disposition of an interest in land can only be made in writing and only by incorporating all the terms which the parties have expressly agreed in one document or, where contracts are exchanged, in each. (2) The terms may be incorporated in a document either by being set out in it or by reference to some other document. (3) The document incorporating the terms or, where contracts are exchanged, one of the documents incorporating them (but not necessarily the same one) must be signed by or on behalf of each party to the contract. . . . (5) . . . nothing in this section affects the creation or operation of resulting, implied or constructive trusts. (6) In this section—'disposition' has the same meaning as in the Law of Property Act 1925; 'interest in land' means any estate, interest or charge in or over land or in or over the proceeds of sale of land. . . . (8) Section 40 of the Law of Property Act 1925 (which is superseded by this section) shall cease to have effect."

"Disposition" in section 205(1)(ii) of the Law of Property Act 1925 includes a conveyance, and "conveyance" includes a mortgage or charge. Section 40, which replaced section 4 of the Statute of Frauds, contained provisions less stringent than the Act of 1989 governing formalities relating to contracts for the sale or other disposition of land or any interest in land, and by subsection (2) had preserved the law relating to part performance.

The effect of section 2 of the Act of 1989 is, therefore, that a contract for a mortgage of or charge on any interest in land or in the proceeds of sale of land can only be made in writing and only if the written document incorporates all the terms which the parties have expressly agreed and is signed by or on behalf of each party. ...

I would emphasise the essential contractual foundation of the rule as demonstrated in the authorities. The deposit by way of security is treated both as prima facie evidence of a contract to mortgage and as part performance of that contract. It is sufficient to refer briefly to the more recent of the multitude of authorities. In *re Wallis & Simmonds (Builders) Ltd.* [1974] 1 WLR. 391 Templeman J. held that the equitable charge resulting from a deposit of title deeds was contractual in nature and specifically rejected an argument that the charge arose by operation of law. In *In re Alton Corporation* [1985] B.C.L.C. 27, 33 Sir Robert Megarry V.-C. said in relation to a loan accompanied by the deposit of title deeds:

". . . I have to remember that the basis of an equitable mortgage is the making of an agreement to create a mortgage, with the deposit of the land certificate and, since *Steadman v. Steadman* [1976] A.C. 536 . . . probably the paying of the money as well, ranking as sufficient acts of part performance to support even a purely oral transaction. But some contract there must be."

Thus, it is clear following the decision in *United Bank of Kuwait Plc. v Sahib and Others* that a mortgage secured by the deposit of title deeds must be created by a contract compliant with the LP(MP)A 1989 s 2 for it to take effect in equity, as it is considered to be a contract to enter into a mortgage. This is a change from the position prior to LPMPA 1989 s 2, when an equitable mortgage secured by the deposit of title deeds would be valid without any further formality. It also confirms the wider principle that whenever there is a failure to create a legal interest due to a lack of formalities, the grant can only take effect in equity where there exists a contract compliant with the LPMPA 1989 s 2.

It is clear from the cases above that an interest in land must be created in accordance with the correct formalities for it to be enforced by the courts. Where an interest has been properly created, it will be binding against the grantor, and potentially enforceable against third parties. The next chapter considers what requirements must be met for properly created interests to be enforceable against a third party in registered and unregistered land.

Further Reading

Peta Dollar, Laying Foundations, *Estate Gazette* 10 October 2009, EG 2009, 0940, 122, 124

4

Enforcement of
Third Party Interests

Topic List

1   Registered Land

2   Unregistered Land

Introduction

An important aspect of proprietary rights that exist in land is that they are capable of being enforced against successors in title to the party who originally created them.

A purchaser of an estate in land will wish to know whether any third party rights exist over that estate and, if they do, whether they will be enforceable against them. Likewise, the holder of such a right over the estate will wish to know whether or not that right will survive a sale of the estate to become enforceable against the new owner.

In deciding whether a right in land is enforceable against a purchaser of the estate the first step is to establish that the right in question is indeed held as an interest in the land, rather than as a merely personal right against the grantor. This issue was dealt with in Chapter 3. Once it has been established that the interest was created properly, it must be determined whether the interest is in fact enforceable against a purchaser.

The rules on enforceability differ depending upon whether the land to be sold has already been registered. If it has, then the issue of enforceability is governed by the Land Registration Act 2002 (LRA 2002). If the land has not yet been registered the issue of enforceability depends upon a combination of the pre-1926 rules on enforceability and the provisions of the Land Charges Act 1972 (LCA 1972). This chapter will deal with registered land first and then consider the rules as they relate to unregistered land.

4.1 Registered Land

Many interests are protected by entry on the register of the servient (ie burdened) estate by entering a **notice** on the charges register. However, 'overriding interests' bind the purchaser even though they do not appear on the register. These are listed in the LRA 2002 Sch 3. They include legal leases not exceeding seven years, implied legal easements and interests held by persons in actual occupation.

4.1.1 Interests of Persons in Actual Occupation under Schedule 3 para 2

The cases cited below often refer to the Land Registration Act 1925 (LRA 1925) s 70(1)(g): 'The rights of every person in actual occupation of the land or in receipt of the rents and profits, save where enquiry is made of such a person and the rights are not disclosed.' This was the predecessor of the LRA 2002 Sch 3 para 2 (which now supersedes s 70(1)(g)) and was different in two key ways:

(a)   The LRA 1925 s 70(1)(g) contained an alternative to actual occupation as being 'in receipt of rent or profits'; and

(b)   The LRA 1925 s 70(1)(g) did not require that the occupation be obvious on reasonable inspection or within the actual knowledge of the purchaser.

The cases below have been included on the basis that the principles still apply to the new LRA 2002 rules.

Williams & Glyn's Bank Ltd v Boland [1981] AC 487 is an example of an interest that can take effect as an overriding interest in actual occupation.

Williams & Glyn's Bank Ltd v Boland [1981] AC 487

Panel: Lord Wilberforce, Viscount Dilhorne, Lord Salmon, Lord Scarman and Lord Roskill

Statute: Land Registration Act 1925 s 70(1)(g)

Facts: Two cases were conjoined in this appeal to the House of Lords. In both cases wives had an equitable interest in their matrimonial homes. The legal owner in both cases was the husband. The wives' interests resulted from financial contributions to the purchase of the property and repayment of the mortgage. In both cases the husbands had remortgaged the home to the appellant bank. The bank did not make inquiry regarding the wives' interests. The husbands defaulted on the loan and the banks obtained orders for possession of the homes. These orders were reversed on appeal and the bank appealed to the House of Lords.

LORD WILBERFORCE

My Lords, these appeals ... raise for decision the same question: whether a husband or a wife, (in each actual case a wife) who has a beneficial interest in the matrimonial home, by virtue of having contributed to its purchase price, but whose spouse is the legal and registered owner, has an "overriding interest" binding on a mortgagee who claims possession of the matrimonial home under a mortgage granted by that spouse alone. ...

The essential facts behind this legal formulation are as follows. Each wife contributed a substantial sum of her own money toward the purchase of the matrimonial home or to paying off a mortgage on it. This, indisputably, made her an equitable tenant in common to the extent of her contribution. Each house, being registered land, was transferred into the sole name of the husband who became its registered proprietor. Later each husband mortgaged the house by legal mortgage to the appellant bank, which made no enquiries of either wife. Default being made, the bank started proceedings ... for possession, with a view to sale. In each case the judge made an order for possession but his decision was reversed by the Court of Appeal. So the question is whether the legal and registered mortgage takes effect against the matrimonial home, or whether the wives' beneficial interest has priority over it.

The legal framework within which the appeals are to be decided can be summarised as follows.

Under the Land Registration Act 1925, legal estates in land are the only interests in respect of which a proprietor can be registered. Other interests take effect in equity as "minor interests," which are overridden by a registered transfer. But the Act recognises also an intermediate, or hybrid, class of what are called "overriding interests": though these are not registered, legal dispositions take effect subject to them. The list of overriding interests is contained in section 70 and it includes ... the relevant paragraph being section 70 (1) (g):

"The rights of every person in actual occupation of the land or in receipt of the rents and profits thereof, save where enquiry is made of such person and the rights are not disclosed;..."

The first question is whether the wife is a "person in actual occupation" and if so, whether her right as a tenant in common in equity is a right protected by this provision.

...

I now deal with the first question. Were the wives here in "actual occupation"? These words are ordinary words of plain English, and should, in my opinion, be interpreted as such. ...

 Alert

They were taken up in the judgment of the Privy Council in *Barnhart v. Greenshields* (1853) 9 Moo.P.C.C. 18 The purpose for which they were used, in that case, was evidently to distinguish the case of a person who was in some kind of legal possession, as by receipt of the rents and profits, from that of a person actually in occupation as tenant. Given occupation, i.e., presence on the land, I do not think that the word "actual" was intended to introduce any additional qualification, certainly not to suggest that possession must be "adverse": it merely emphasises that what is required is physical presence, not some entitlement in law. So even if it were necessary to look behind these plain words into history, I would find no reason for denying them their plain meaning.

Then, were the wives in actual occupation? I ask: why not? There was physical presence, with all the rights that occupiers have, including the right to exclude all others except those having similar rights. The house was a matrimonial home, intended to be occupied, and in fact occupied by both spouses, both of whom have an interest in it: it would require some special doctrine of law to avoid the result that each is in occupation. Three arguments were used for a contrary conclusion. First, it was said that if the vendor (I use this word to include a mortgagor) is in occupation, that is enough to prevent the application of the paragraph. This seems to be a proposition of general application, not limited to the case of husbands, and no doubt, if correct, would be very convenient for purchasers and intending mortgagees. But the presence of the vendor, with occupation, does not exclude the possibility of occupation of others. There are observations which suggest the contrary in the unregistered land case of *Caunce v. Caunce* [1969] 1 W.L.R. 286, but I agree with the disapproval of these, and with the assertion of the proposition I have just stated by Russell L.J. in *Hodgson v. Marks* [1971] Ch. 892, 934. Then it was suggested that the wife's occupation was nothing but the shadow of the husband's – a version I suppose of the doctrine of unity of husband and wife. This expression and the argument flowing from it was used by Templeman J. in *Bird v. Syme-Thomson* [1979] 1 W.L.R. 440, 444, a decision preceding and which he followed in the present case. The argument was also inherent in the judgment in *Caunce v. Caunce* [1969] 1 W.L.R. 286 which influenced the decisions of Templeman J. It somewhat faded from the arguments in the present case and appears to me to be heavily obsolete. The appellant's main and final position became in the end this: that, to come within the paragraph, the occupation in question must be apparently inconsistent with the title of the vendor. This, it was suggested, would exclude the wife of a husband-vendor because her apparent occupation would be satisfactorily accounted for by his. But, apart from the rewriting of the paragraph which this would involve, the suggestion is unacceptable. Consistency, or inconsistency, involves the absence, or presence, of an independent right to occupy, though I must observe that "inconsistency" in this context is an inappropriate word. But how can either quality be predicated of a wife, simply qua wife? A wife may, and everyone knows this, have rights of her own, particularly, many wives have a share in a matrimonial home. How can it be said that the presence of a wife in the house, as occupier, is consistent or inconsistent with the husband's rights until one knows what rights she has? and if she has rights, why, just because she is a wife (or in the converse case, just because an occupier is the husband), should these rights be denied protection under the paragraph? If one looks beyond the case or [sic] husband and wife, the difficulty of all these arguments stands out if one considers the case of a man living with a mistress, or of a man and a woman – or for that matter two persons of the same sex – living in a house in separate or partially shared rooms. Are these cases of apparently consistent occupation, so that the rights of the other person (other than the vendor) can be disregarded? The only solution which is consistent with the Act (section 70 (1) (g)) and with common sense is to read the paragraph for what it says. Occupation, existing as a fact, may protect rights if the person in occupation has rights. On this part of the case I have no difficulty in concluding that a spouse, living in a house, has an actual occupation capable of conferring protection, as an overriding interest, upon rights of that spouse.

This brings me to the second question, which is whether such rights as a spouse has under a trust for sale are capable of recognition as overriding interests ... . In my opinion, the wives' equitable interests, subsisting in reference to the land, were by the fact of occupation, made into overriding interests, and so protected by section 70 (1) (g). ...

I would only add, in conclusion, on the appeal as it concerns the wives a brief observation on the conveyancing consequences of dismissing the appeal. These were alarming to Templeman J., and I can agree with him to the extent that whereas the object of a land registration system is to reduce the risks to purchasers from anything not on the register, to extend (if it be an extension) the area of risk so as to include possible interests of spouses, and indeed, in theory, of other members of the family or even outside it, may add to the burdens of purchasers, and involve them in enquiries which in some cases may be troublesome.

But conceded, as it must be, that the Act, following established practice, gives protection to occupation, the extension of the risk area follows necessarily from the extension, beyond the paterfamilias, of rights of ownership, itself following from the diffusion of property and earning capacity. What is involved is a departure from an easy-going practice of dispensing with enquiries as to occupation beyond that of the vendor and accepting the risks of doing so. To substitute for this a practice of more careful enquiry as to the fact of occupation, and if necessary, as to the rights of occupiers can not, in my view of the matter, be considered as unacceptable except at the price of overlooking the widespread development of shared interests of ownership. In the light of section 70 of the Act, I cannot believe that Parliament intended this, though it may be true that in 1925 it did not foresee the full extent of this development.

Appeals dismissed.

Compare the case of *City of London Building Society v Flegg* [1988] AC 54 where the interest was held not to be overriding, because it had been overreached.

City of London Building Society v Flegg [1988] AC 54

Panel: Lord Bridge of Harwich, Lord Templeman, Lord Mackay of Clashfern, Lord Oliver of Aylmerton and Lord Goff of Chieveley

Statutes: Law of Property Act 1925 s 14, s 27 and s 28; Land Registration Act 1925 s 70(1)(g)

Facts: The plaintiffs, City of London Building Society, were mortgagees of a residential property called Bleak House. Bleak House was purchased to accommodate a married couple (the Maxwell-Browns) and the wife's parents (Mr & Mrs Flegg). Mr & Mrs Flegg contributed £18,000 to the purchase and the couple raised their share of the purchase price via a mortgage. The couple were registered as the legal owners of the property. The couple borrowed more money by granting two further legal mortgages over the property, without Mr & Mrs Flegg's knowledge. City of London made no enquiries regarding Mr & Mrs Flegg's occupation of the property. The couple defaulted on the loan and City of London sought a declaration that the mortgage was binding on Mr & Mrs Flegg. Mr & Mrs Flegg argued that their beneficial interest, by virtue of their contribution to the purchase price, combined with their occupation of the property gave them an overriding interest binding on City of London as mortgagees. At first instance the court found that their interest had been overreached by the plaintiffs. The Court of Appeal found in favour of Mr & Mrs Flegg. The plaintiffs appealed to the House of Lords.

LORD TEMPLEMAN

By a legal charge by way of mortgage dated 8 January 1982 the Maxwell-Browns charged Bleak House to secure £37,500 advanced by the appellants to the Maxwell-Browns. The respondents knew nothing of the legal charge which was granted by the Maxwell-Browns for their own purposes and in breach of trust. The appellants knew nothing of the respondents.

By section 27 of the Law of Property Act 1925 (as amended by the Law of Property (Amendment) Act 1926, Schedule):

"(1) A purchaser of a legal estate from trustees for sale shall not be concerned with the trusts affecting the proceeds of sale of land subject to a trust for sale ... or affecting the rents and profits of the land until sale ... (2) Notwithstanding anything to the contrary in the instrument (if any) creating a trust for sale of land or in the settlement of the net proceeds, the proceeds of sale or other capital money shall not be paid to or applied by the direction of fewer than two persons as trustees for sale, except where the trustee is a trust corporation ..."

...

Thus the appellants advancing money in good faith to two trustees for sale on the security of a charge by way of legal mortgage of Bleak House were not concerned with the trusts affecting the proceeds of sale of Bleak House or with the propriety of the trustees entering into the legal charge. As a result of the legal charge the interests of the beneficiaries in Bleak House pending sale were transferred to the equity of redemption vested in the Maxwell-Browns and to the sum of £37,500 received by the Maxwell-Browns from the appellants in consideration for the grant of the legal charge. The Maxwell-Browns did not account to the respondents for any part of the sum of £37,500 and defaulted in the performance of their obligations to the appellants under the legal charge. The appellants seek possession of Bleak House with a view to enforcing its security.

The respondents resist the claim of the appellants to possession of Bleak House and rely on section 14 of the Law of Property Act 1925 . Sections 27 and 28 of that Act which overreach the interests of the respondents under the trust for sale of Bleak House are to be found in Part I of the Act. Section 14 provides:

"This Part of this Act shall not prejudicially affect the interest of any person in possession or in actual occupation of land to which he may be entitled in right of such possession or occupation."

The respondents were in actual occupation of Bleak House at the date of the legal charge. It is argued that their beneficial interests under the trust for sale were not overreached by the legal charge or that the respondents were entitled to remain in occupation after the legal charge and against the appellants despite the overreaching of their interests.

My Lords, the respondents were entitled to occupy Bleak House by virtue of their beneficial interests in Bleak House and its rents and profits pending the execution of the trust for sale. Their beneficial interests were overreached by the legal charge and were transferred to the equity of redemption held by the Maxwell-Browns and to the sum advanced by the appellants in consideration of the grant of the legal charge and received by the Maxwell-Browns. After the legal charge the respondents were only entitled to continue in occupation of Bleak House by virtue of their beneficial interests in the equity of redemption of Bleak House and that equity of redemption is subject to the right of the appellants as mortgagee to take possession. Sections 27 and 28 did not "prejudicially" affect the interests of the respondents who were indeed prejudiced but by the subsequent failure of the trustees for sale to account to their beneficiaries for capital money received by the trustees. A beneficiary who is entitled to share in the proceeds of sale of land held on trust for sale relies on the trustees. Section 26(3) of the Act (as amended) requires trustees for sale to consult their beneficiaries and to give effect to the wishes of the majority of the beneficiaries "but a purchaser shall not be concerned to see that the provisions of this subsection have been complied with." If the

Decipher
So overreaching has the effect of the purchaser taking the land free of the beneficial interest. The beneficial interests transfers from the land to the purchase monies.

argument for the respondents is correct, a purchaser from trustees for sale must ensure that a beneficiary in actual occupation is not only consulted but consents to the sale. Section 14 of the Law of Property Act 1925 is not apt to confer on a tenant in common of land held on trust for sale, who happens to be in occupation, rights which are different from and superior to the rights of tenants in common, who are not in occupation on the date when the interests of all tenants in common are overreached by a sale or mortgage by trustees for sale.

...

It follows that when the legal charge in the present case is registered, the appellants will take free from all the interests of the beneficiaries interested under the trust for sale in the proceeds of sale and rents and profits until sale of Bleak House but subject to any overriding interest.

Section 70(1) of the Land Registration Act 1925 defines overriding interests which include:

"(g) The rights of every person in actual occupation of the land or in receipt of the rents and profits thereof, save where inquiry is made of such person and the rights are not disclosed; ..."

In my view the object of section 70 was to reproduce for registered land the same limitations as section 14 of the Law of Property Act 1925 produced for land whether registered or unregistered. The respondents claim to be entitled to overriding interests because they were in actual occupation of Bleak House on the date of the legal charge. But the interests of the respondents cannot at one and the same time be overreached and overridden and at the same time be overriding interests. The appellants cannot at one and the same time take free from all the interests of the respondents yet at the same time be subject to some of those interests. The right of the respondents to be and remain in actual occupation of Bleak House ceased when the respondents' interests were overreached by the legal charge save in so far as their rights were transferred to the equity of redemption. As persons interested under the trust for sale the respondents had no right to possession as against the appellants and the fact that the respondents were in actual occupation at the date of the legal charge did not create a new right or transfer an old right so as to make the right enforceable against the appellants.

...

The Court of Appeal took a different view, largely in reliance on the decision of this House in *Williams & Glyn's Bank Ltd. v Boland* [1981] A.C. 487. In that case the sole proprietor of registered land held the land as sole trustee upon trust for sale and to stand possessed of the net proceeds of sale and rents and profits until sale upon trust for himself and his wife as tenants in common. This House held that the wife's beneficial interest coupled with actual possession by her constituted an overriding interest and that a mortgagee from the husband, despite the concluding words of section 20(1), took subject to the wife's overriding interest. But in that case the interest of the wife was not overreached or overridden because the mortgagee advanced capital moneys to a sole trustee. If the wife's interest had been overreached by the mortgagee advancing capital moneys to two trustees there would have been nothing to justify the wife in remaining in occupation as against the mortgagee. There must be a combination of an interest which justifies continuing occupation plus actual occupation to constitute an overriding interest. Actual occupation is not an interest in itself.

...

Appeal allowed.

We can see from *Williams & Glyn's Bank Ltd v Boland* [1981] AC 487 that 'occupation' should be given its ordinary meaning. In *Strand Securities v Caswell* [1965] Ch 958 the Court of Appeal had to consider whether someone could occupy on behalf of another.

Strand Securities v Caswell [1965] Ch 958

Panel: Lord Denning MR, Russell and Harman LJJ

Statute: Land Registration Act, 1925 s 70(1)(g)

Facts: The first defendant allowed his stepdaughter, the second defendant, to live in a London flat rent free. The first defendant did not live in the flat but used it as an occasional London base. The first defendant was the subleasee of the flat. The sublease was not protected by registration and the court had to consider whether the first defendant had an overriding interest binding on a purchaser under the LRA 1925 s 70(1)(g).

LORD JUSTICE RUSSELL

... On the facts, was the first defendant, at April 24, 1962, a person in actual occupation, though he was not in any ordinary sense residing there or treating it as his home, and the second defendant [his stepdaughter] and her family were allowed by him to reside there? As a matter of the ordinary use of language I would not consider the first defendant to be such. For him it was argued that the phrase "in actual occupation" derives from cases in which "actual occupation" and "actual possession" are used indifferently to describe a condition of enjoyment of the land itself, and that the phrase "actual occupation" here involves that form of the legal concept of possession as distinct from the other or notional forms of that concept consisting of the receipt of money payments derived from land, or of the right to possession though the land be vacant and it was argued that "actual possession" was avoided by the draftsman as a phrase because of the difficulty which would flow from the definition of "possession" in section 3 (xviii) of the Land Registration Act, 1925. Reference was made to a number of authorities, including cases in the fields of rating, poor law, and landlord and tenant, with a view to showing that possession, and therefore occupation, may be had through the medium of another. Suppose, it was said, that the first defendant employed a resident caretaker to look after the flat in question, would the first defendant not be a person in actual occupation? I think that is correct. Then, it was argued, that is because the caretaker would be his licensee, bound to go at his will, and that was the position of the second defendant. But I think that here is the distinction between occupation by the caretaker as a matter of duty on behalf of the first defendant and the occupation of the second defendant on her own behalf; both were licensees, but the former, by her occupation for which she was employed, was the representative of the first defendant and her occupation may therefore be regarded as his. The proposition that in each case the first defendant was in actual occupation because neither the caretaker nor the second defendant had a right to occupy independently of him seems to me too broadly stated and to ignore that distinction. I do not say that a contract of employment or agency with the person residing there is essential to actual occupation by the other person. I think that it might well be that if a house was used as a residence by a wife, separated from the tenant, her husband (whether or not in desertion), he could also be regarded as in actual occupation through her; the question whether the husband was also a person in actual occupation did not, of course, arise in *National Provincial Bank Ltd. v. Hastings Car Mart Ltd.* But this conception, even if valid, could not extend to the relationship in the present case.

Nor, it seems to me, can the presence on the premises of some of the first defendant's furniture, nor the previously mentioned use by him and others of the family of the flat, nor the fact, which I am prepared to assume though it was not proved, that he had a key, nor a combination of those matters, constitute actual occupation by him.

...

See also the case of *Abbey National Building Society v Cann* [1991] 1 AC 56 where Lord Oliver of Aylmerton in the House of Lords made *obiter* comments concerning whether occupation could exist without the personal presence of the party claiming an overriding interest.

Abbey National Building Society v Cann [1991] 1 AC 56

Panel: Lord Bridge of Harwich, Lord Griffiths, Lord Ackner, Lord Oliver of Aylmerton and Lord Jauncey of Tullichettle

Statute: Land Registration Act 1925 s 70(1)(g)

Facts: The first defendant intended to purchase a house for his mother and her fiancé (the second and third defendants). The first defendant arranged a loan from the plaintiff Building Society to be secured by a mortgage over the property. The completion of the mortgage and the purchase took place simultaneously at 12:30pm on 13 August 1984. The second defendant was away on holiday on this date but at 11:45am carpet layers laid carpets on her behalf and with the consent of the vendor. Her furniture was also taken into the house. The first defendant defaulted on the loan and the Building Society sought possession of the property. The second defendant claimed an overriding interest in actual occupation under the LRA 1925 s 70(1)(g) based on a contribution to the purchase and assurances made by the first defendant.

LORD OLIVER OF AYLMERTON

I have, up to this point, been content to assume that the facts of the instant case justify the proposition which found favour with Dillon L.J., that she was in actual occupation of the property at the material time. This is, of course, essentially a question of fact, but there is the serious question of what, in law, can amount to 'actual occupation' for the purposes of section 70(1)(g). In *Williams & Glyn's Bank Ltd. v Boland* [1981] A.C. 487, 504, Lord Wilberforce observed that these words should be interpreted for what they are, that is to say, ordinary words of plain English. But even plain English may contain a variety of shades of meaning. At the date of completion Mrs. Cann was not personally even in England, leave alone in personal occupation of the property, and the trial judge held that the acts done by Mr. Abraham Cann and Mr. George Cann amounted to

'no more than the taking of preparatory steps leading to the assumption of actual residential occupation on or after completion, whatever the moment of the day when completion took place . . . '

For my part, I am content to accept this as a finding of fact which was amply justified by the evidence before him, and I share the reservations expressed by Ralph Gibson and Woolf L.JJ. in the Court of Appeal. It is, perhaps, dangerous to suggest any test for what is essentially a question of fact, for 'occupation' is a concept which may have different connotations according to the nature and purpose of the property which is claimed to be occupied. It does not necessarily, I think, involve the personal presence of the person claiming to occupy. A caretaker or the representative of a company can occupy, I should have thought, on behalf of his employer. On the other hand, it does, in my judgment, involve some degree of permanence and continuity which would rule out mere fleeting presence. A prospective tenant or purchaser who is allowed, as a matter of indulgence, to go into property in order to plan decorations or measure for furnishings would not, in ordinary parlance, be said to be occupying it, even though he might be there for hours at a time. Of course, in the instant case, there was, no doubt, on the part of the persons involved in moving Mrs. Cann's belongings, an intention that they would remain there and would render the premises suitable for her ultimate use as a residential occupier. Like the trial judge, however, I am unable to accept that acts of this preparatory character carried out by courtesy of the vendor prior to completion can constitute 'actual occupation' for the purposes of section 70(1)(g). Accordingly, all other considerations apart, Mrs. Cann fails, in my judgment, to establish the necessary condition for the assertion of an overriding interest...

Appeal dismissed.

Thus, it can be concluded that occupation by proxy will only be successful if the party is an employee (or, possibly, a spouse – *Strand Securities v Caswell* [1965] Ch 958).

The issue of whether actual occupation could withstand either temporary or much longer absences was considered in the following two cases.

In the case of *Chhokar v Chhokar* [1984] FLR 313, the High Court held (affirmed by the Court of Appeal [1984] Fam Law 269) that the wife had been in actual occupation at the relevant time and therefore had an overriding interest binding upon the purchaser.

Chhokar v Chhokar [1984] FLR 313

Panel: Ewbank J

Facts: The defendant husband was the legal owner of the matrimonial home. The claimant wife had an interest in the house by virtue of a contribution to the purchase price. The husband sold the home to a purchaser without her knowledge. The sale was completed while the wife was in hospital giving birth. The wife claimed an overriding interest in actual occupation that would bind the purchaser.

MR JUSTICE EWBANK

The husband was willing and anxious to sell the house at whatever price he could get in order to evict the wife when she was in hospital having the baby. There was a mortgage of about £8,500 on the house. The equity accordingly was about £4,000 and at that time the wife's share would be about £2,000.

The contracts were exchanged in January. The wife's expected date of delivery was 12 February. The solicitors for the husband wrote to the solicitors for the purchaser saying that the contracts had to be exchanged within 10 days and that completion must take place during the beginning of the week starting 12 February 1979.

The husband says that he did not know that his solicitors were insisting on completion during that week. I do not accept the husband's evidence on that point at all. This was planned by him so that when the wife came out of hospital the house would have been sold and would have been in the hands of the new purchaser. In the event, the wife's confinement was on 16 February and not 12 February. She actually went into hospital on 15 February.

As might be expected with a scheme of this sort, the completion had to be put off accordingly, and so it was. Completion in fact was postponed to 19 February 1979. The husband did not remove all the furniture from the house and he asserts that the furniture was sold with the house but there are no documents to support this assertion.

Just before the date of the postponed completion the husband visited the wife in hospital. This was during the week-end of 17 and 18 February. The husband asserts that he told the wife of the sale of the house and that she was annoyed. She was like dynamite, he says, and threatened him with prison. If this evidence is true, it does not support in any way the husband's assertion that the wife had consented to him selling the house and knew all about it.

On 19 February, the date of completion, the husband made special arrangements to have the net proceeds of sale in cash in his hands. He paid his debts and then he set off for India. That was the last the wife saw of him for some 2 years. The wife and the baby were discharged from hospital on 22 February. They went home. They found the locks had been changed and so they went to spend the night with an aunt with whom the elder child had been staying while the wife was in hospital. On the following day, 23 February, the wife went home. Mr Parmar, who had bought the house, ejected her. On 1 March 1979 Mr Parmar registered the conveyance to him at the Land Registry. The wife on that date was not in the house because he had put her out, but some of her furniture was there. I have to consider whether she was in actual occupation on the day of the registration of the conveyance. I have no difficulty in deciding that she was in actual occupation. Her interest, accordingly, in the house is an overriding interest and Mr Parmar, in my judgment, took the conveyance of the house into his name subject to her overriding interest. He accordingly has held the house since then, subject to a half share belonging to the wife. ...

Appeal allowed with costs.

> **Link**
> See *Lloyds Bank v Rosset* which shows the relevant date is completion.

Link Lending Ltd v Bustard (by her litigation friend Walker) [2010] EWCA Civ 424

Panel: Mummery, Jacob and Sullivan LJJ

Facts: Ms Bustard was the registered owner of a freehold property. She was suffering from severe mental health problems, which affected her memory, judgement and understanding, and had been receiving hospital treatment. In 2004, Ms Bustard transferred the property to Mrs Hussain for the price of £100,000 and Mrs Hussain was later registered as the freehold owner. Ms Bustard did not receive any money for the property, but continued to live there. In 2007, she was sectioned under the Mental Health Act 1983 and moved firstly into a psychiatric hospital and then into a residential care home, leaving her property vacant, although her furniture and belongings were left there, and she made brief weekly visits to collect her post.

On 29 February 2008, Mrs Hussain decided to mortgage the property and granted Link Lending Ltd ('Link') a legal charge over the property. Ms Bustard was still in residential care at this time. Mrs Hussain failed to pay the loan to Link, which commenced possession proceedings. When Ms Bustard found out about the proceedings, she claimed that she was in actual occupation of the property at the time of the charge. Link disagreed. The judge at first instance dismissed Link's claim for possession, held that Ms Bustard had an equity in the property (the right to have the 2004 transfer set aside) and that she was in actual occupation of the property. Link appealed to the Court of Appeal.

LORD JUSTICE MUMMERY

20.   [Counsel for Link] contends that, although Ms Bustard could be in actual occupation of the Property without being personally present in it, her occupation ceased to have that quality of permanence and continuity required for actual occupation after a year of residence at [the residential care home]. After such an extended period of absence it could not be said that her connection with the Property was any longer one of actual occupation.

...

22.   [Counsel for Link] contends that in this case also Ms Bustard's absence from the Property had been so prolonged (a year, as in Stockholm [see below]) that "the notion of her continuing to be in actual occupation of it becomes insupportable".

...

25. The facts are not all one way. Some of the primary facts point against Ms Bustard's actual occupation of the Property at the relevant date: she was not personally present in the Property on 29 February 2008; she had been in a residential care home since January 2007; she was incapable of living safely in the Property; and her visits to the Property were brief and supervised.

26. Some of the primary facts point to Ms Bustard's continuing actual occupation of the Property: it was her furnished home and the only place to which she genuinely wanted to return; she continued to visit the Property because she still considered it her home; those who had taken responsibility for her finances regularly paid the bills ...; she was in the process of making an application to the Mental Health Review Tribunal in order to be allowed to return home; and no-one took a final and irrevocable decision that she would not eventually be permitted to return home.

27. ...The trend of the cases shows that the courts are reluctant to lay down, or even suggest, a single legal test for determining whether a person is in actual occupation. The decisions on statutory construction identify the factors that have to be weighed by the judge on this issue. The degree of permanence and continuity of presence of the person concerned, the intentions and wishes of that person, the length of absence from the property and the reason for it and the nature of the property and personal circumstances of the person are among the relevant factors.

...

29. In my judgment, this court should not disturb the decision that Ms Bustard was a person in actual occupation of the Property. The judge did not misconstrue the 2002 Act or the authorities. Nor did he misapply the law by making an insupportable evaluation of Ms Bustard's situation regarding the Property. The decisions of the courts on the different facts of other cases have been cited against his conclusion, but they do not demonstrate that he was wrong.

30. The assistance given in the authorities is in clarifying the legal principles, exploring the range of decisions available to the court and identifying the factors to which weight should be given. It is clear from the citations that Ms Bustard's is not a case of a "mere fleeting presence", or a case, like Cann, of acts preparatory to the assumption of actual occupation. It is also distinguishable from Stockholm, which involved the domestic living arrangements of a Saudi princess living with her mother in Saudi Arabia and owning a house in London, where there was furniture and clothing and caretaking arrangements in place, but where she had not lived for more than a year. In this case the new and special feature is in the psychiatric problems of the person claiming actual occupation. The judge was, in my view, justified in ruling, at the conclusion of a careful and detailed judgment, that Ms Bustard was a person in actual occupation of the Property. His conclusion was supported by evidence of a sufficient degree of continuity and permanence of occupation, of involuntary residence elsewhere, which was satisfactorily explained by objective reasons,

and of a persistent intention to return home when possible, as manifested by her regular visits to the Property.

Compare these two decisions to that in *Stockholm Finance v Garden Holdings Inc and Others* [1995] NPC 162.

Stockholm Finance v Garden Holdings Inc and Others [1995] NPC 162

Panel: Robert Walker J

Facts: The plaintiff finance company, Stockholm Finance, sought to enforce a mortgage granted on 20 February 1990 on registered property in Hampstead, London. A Saudi Princess, Princess Madawi, and her mother, Princess Hend, claimed to have a beneficial interest in the property that was binding on Stockholm Finance as an overriding interest in actual occupation. Neither Princess had lived in the property as their main residence but Princess Madawi left belongings in the property and used it when visiting London. Princess Madawi had not visited the property for a year prior to 20 February 1990. A family cleaner, Mrs Soledad Tabbada, visited the property once every seven to ten days and a driver, Mr Baghapour, was asked by Princess Madawi to keep an eye on the property. Mr Baghapour visited the property, on average, twice a week.

MR JUSTICE ROBERT WALKER

... Whether a person's intermittent presence at a house which is fully furnished, and ready for almost immediate use, should be seen as continuous occupation marked (but not interrupted) by occasional absences, or whether it should be seen as a pattern of alternating periods of presence or absence, is a matter of perception which defies deep analysis. Not only the length of any absence, but also the reason for it, may be material (a holiday or a business trip may be easier to reconcile with continuing and unbroken occupation than a move to a second home, even though the duration of absence may be the same in each case). But there must come a point where the person's absence from his own home is so prolonged that the notion of him continuing to be in actual occupation of it becomes unsupportable; and in my judgment that point must have been reached, in this case, long before Mr Dawkins [the surveyor] visited the house on 4 January 1990 (and still more so long before 20 February 1990). By then Princess Madawi had not set foot in the property for over a year: she had for over a year been living with her mother in the Islamic household at Riyadh.

Neither Mr Baghapour's visits in order to give the property a lived-in look (with occasional overnight stays, for his own convenience, in the accommodation over the garage) nor Mrs Tabbada's visits in order to clean, could in my judgment result in Princess Madawi being treated as in occupation through resident employees: both of them were employed by Mr Durani, and neither was in actual occupation of the property. I think ... that though Mr Baghapour's witness statement spoke of his exertions being so that visitors "would be alerted to the fact that there were people living in the house" it would have been more accurate to have spoken of their being persuaded of the fiction that there were people living in the house; because in truth no one was living in the house for more than a year.

For these reasons I conclude that there must be an order for possession of the property against Princess Madawi and Princess Hend.

Judgment accordingly.

In *Lloyds Bank plc v Rosset* [1989] Ch 350 the Court of Appeal considered what should be the relevant date of occupation and also the impact of the nature and state of the land occupied. (Later affirmed by House of Lords in *Lloyds Bank v Rosset* [1991] 1 AC 107.)

Lloyds Bank plc v Rosset [1989] Ch 350

Panel: Purchas, Mustill and Nicholls LJJ

Statute: Land Registration Act 1925 s 70(1)(g)

Facts: A husband was the legal owner of a semi-derelict property which the wife helped to renovate. The husband defaulted on a loan secured by a mortgage over the property. The wife claimed a beneficial interest in the property that took effect as an overriding interest binding on the lender.

LORD JUSTICE NICHOLLS

This is another case concerned with the operation of section 70(1)(g) of the Land Registration Act 1925 in the context of a claim by a wife that she has a beneficial interest in a house registered in the sole name of her husband and that her interest has priority over the rights of a bank under a legal charge executed without her knowledge. The case raises a point of importance in the law of registered conveyancing. Shortly stated, the point is whether, to have the protection afforded to overriding interests in respect of registered land, the wife needs to be in actual occupation of the house when the legal charge is executed as distinct from being in actual occupation by the later date on which the bank's charge is registered in the Land Registry.

The case also raises the question of what is meant by actual occupation within section 70(1)(g) in the case of a semi-derelict house which is in the course of being renovated ...

Lord Wilberforce observed in *Williams & Glyn's Bank Ltd. v Boland* [1981] A.C. 487, 504, that the words "actual occupation" are ordinary words of plain English and that they should be interpreted as such. The bank submitted that in ordinary, every day speech the wife would not have been regarded as being in occupation of Vincent Farmhouse on 17 December. Residential premises are occupied only by those who live in them.

I agree with this submission to the extent that I accept that in ordinary speech one normally does equate occupation in relation to a house with living there. If a person is intending to move into a house but has not yet done so, he would not normally be regarded as having gone into occupation. That is the normal position, with a house which is fit for living in. But that does not provide the answer in the present case, where the house was semi-derelict. In the first place, I do not think that in every day speech actual occupation of a house can never exist short of residence. Take Vincent Farmhouse. I do not think that it is as clear as the bank suggests that in every day speech the wife would not have been regarded as being in occupation on 17 December 1982 when the purchase was completed. Had the defendants been asked on the day "are you in occupation?" I am not sure that their answer would have been a simple "no." Their answer might well have been to the effect "We are not living there yet. The farmhouse was semi-derelict when we found it. No one could have lived there with the house as it was then. But we have the builders in. They have been there for over five weeks now. Diana spends almost every day there. Progress has been slower than we had hoped. We had intended to move in by Christmas but that will not be possible now." Secondly, if the words "actual occupation" are given the rigid, restricted meaning submitted by the bank in relation to residential premises, and that meaning is applied to a house in course of being built or renovated, the result in some cases will be to defeat the purpose intended to be achieved by paragraph (g) of section 70(1). If, day after day, workmen are actively building a house on a plot of land, or actively and substantially renovating a semi-derelict house, it would be contrary to the principle underlying paragraph (g) if a would be purchaser or mortgagee were entitled to treat that site as currently devoid of an occupant for the purpose of the paragraph. If, for example, the owner had granted a tenancy in return for a premium, so that the tenancy did not qualify as an overriding interest under section 70(1)(k), but the tenant himself and workmen employed by him were on site, building or renovating as I have described, why should he not be as much entitled to the protection afforded to occupants by section 70(1)(g) as he would be once the work had been finished and he was living in the house?

In my view, the test of residence propounded by the bank is too narrow. As the judge observed, what constitutes occupation will depend upon the nature and state of the property in question. I can see no reason, in principle or in practice, why a semi-derelict house such as Vincent Farmhouse should not be capable of actual occupation whilst the works proceed and before anyone has started to live in the building.

The bank further submitted that the presence of the builder and his men in the property could not constitute actual occupation by the defendants. I am unable to agree. I can detect nothing in the context in which the expression "actual occupation" is used in paragraph (g) to suggest that the physical presence of an employee or agent cannot be regarded as the presence of the employer or principal when determining whether the employer or principal is in actual occupation. Whether the presence of an employee or agent is to be so regarded will depend on the function which the employee or agent is discharging in the premises in the particular case. I am fortified in this approach by noting that it accords with the view, espoused in passing by Ormrod L.J. in *Williams & Glyn's Bank Ltd. v. Boland* [1979] Ch. 312 , 338, that a person may be in occupation through another, and with the views expressed in *Strand Securities Ltd. v. Caswell* [1965] Ch. 958, 981, 984. In the latter case both Lord Denning M.R. and Russell L.J. accepted that, if a tenant puts a resident caretaker into a residential flat to look after it, that would be actual occupation by the tenant. Russell L.J. observed that the caretaker, by her occupation for which she was employed, would be the representative of the tenant and her occupation might therefore be regarded as his. Likewise, in my view, the presence of a builder engaged by a householder to do work for him in a house is to be regarded as the presence of the owner when considering whether or not the owner is in actual occupation.

In the Boland case [1981] A.C. 487, Lord Wilberforce, at p. 505, explained the significance of the word "actual" in the phrase "actual occupation" as merely emphasising that what is required is physical presence, not some entitlement in law. He referred to the origin of the phrase "actual possession," and commented that in the judgment of the Privy Council in *Barnhart v. Greenshields* (1853) 9 Moo. P.C. 18, 34, the expression was used to distinguish the case of a person who was in some kind of legal possession, as by receipt of the rents and profits, from that of a person actually in occupation as tenant. I can see nothing in that exposition inconsistent with the views expressed in *Strand Securities Ltd. v. Caswell* [1965] Ch. 958 or with those I have sought to state.

I turn to the facts of the present case, which I have already summarised. The vendors had ceased to be in actual occupation long before 17 December. The house was empty and semi-derelict. They permitted the husband to go on to the property before completion. From 7 November until after Christmas the builder and his men were there every working day. One of them slept in the property on most nights. The wife spent almost every weekday at the property, from 10 a.m. to 4 p.m. Thus, there was physical presence on the property throughout the period leading up to completion on 17 December, and that physical presence was to the extent that one would expect of an occupier, having regard to the then state of the property.

Thus far I am in agreement with the judge. Where I feel obliged to part company from him is his conclusion that, although (as I read his judgment) the husband, through the presence of the builder and his men, was in actual occupation of the property on 17 December, the wife was not. As appears from the second extract from his judgment that I have quoted above, in reaching that conclusion the judge attached importance to the answer which Mr. Griffin, the builder, would have given to the question, "who occupies the building?" With all respect to the judge, I do not think that was the right question to pose. What mattered was not the builder's views on who occupied the building, but on whose behalf the builder was in the building. The judge himself had observed earlier that that was the vital question. As to that, the facts seem reasonably clear. Mr. Griffin regarded himself as being employed by both the husband and the wife. There was no clear evidence that in this he was mistaken. Mr. Griffin addressed his invoices to both Mr. and Mrs. Rosset. He looked to both of them for payment. In those circumstances, even though the husband alone was the contracting purchaser of the property, it seems to me that the presence of the builder and his men on the property was as much on behalf of the wife as it was on behalf of the husband. Mr. Griffin was working there under a contract made with both of them, renovating the property for both of them. He was there on behalf of both of them. There was no sound basis for distinguishing between the two of them. If the builder's presence was sufficient to constitute occupation by the husband, it was equally sufficient to constitute occupation by the wife. This was so even after the incident mentioned by the judge. A stage was reached when the workmen complained that both the husband and the wife were giving them instructions. The husband then "laid it down" that the workmen should take their instructions from him alone.

So the position was that the builder and his men were in the building, carrying out a contract made with the husband and the wife. Additionally, the wife herself was there almost every weekday. In my view, those facts amounted to actual occupation of the property by the wife on 17 December 1982. There was, I repeat, physical presence on the property by the wife and her agent of the nature, and to the extent, that one would expect of an occupier having regard to the then state of the property: namely, the presence involved in actively carrying out the renovation necessary to make the house fit for residential use.

Decipher
This shows what counts as occupation can depend on the nature and state of the premises occupied.

In my view, therefore, the judge erred in the inference he drew from the primary facts which he found. The reality was that before completion the husband and the wife had already taken over this semi-derelict house, under a revocable licence granted to the husband by the vendors. By 17 December renovation was well under way. Completion took place on 17 December, but no physical change then took place in their use of the property, save that the wife slept there more frequently. Eventually in February 1983 the family began to live there.

This conclusion has the attraction that it gives effect to the purpose of paragraph (g). Had a representative of the bank inspected the property before 17 December to check if anyone was in actual occupation, he would have seen that, indeed, someone was there. Builders were working there, day after day, plainly on behalf of someone. Had he gone up to the door, he would probably have found the wife in the house. In such circumstances the bank really has only itself to blame if it lends money without looking into the position further. In particular, I find it surprising that the bank, knowing that this was to be the matrimonial home, did not seek the wife's written consent to the grant of the charge. This was in December 1982. The *Boland* case [1981] A.C. 487 was decided by the House of Lords over two years earlier, in June 1980. …

LORD JUSTICE PURCHAS

As Nicholls L.J. has pointed out in his judgment, although for many of the categories of interest listed the date of registration would be the obvious and logical date from which the overriding interest should be effective to defeat the interest to be registered, e.g. a local land charge under paragraph (i), this does not apply to paragraph (g). To allow an overriding interest to arise after the completion of a sale or the creation of a legal charge upon registered land which does not itself have to be registered and of which the purchaser has no notice would be a conveyancing absurdity.

One is, therefore, driven to the conclusion that for the various purposes disclosed in the paragraphs of section 70(1) the effective date upon which to consider the existence of the overriding interest may differ. The historical background of section 70(1)(g) was to prevent in the case of persons living in the property transferred or charged whose presence was obvious and should put an intending purchaser or chargee on notice from having their interests prejudiced by the registration of a subsequent charge or transfer. If the effective date at which the presence of the overriding interest for the purposes of section 70(1)(g) is taken as the date of registration then the underlying purpose of protecting the interest of an occupant in being at the time when the purchaser is making his decision to buy is frustrated. I agree, with respect, with Nicholls L.J. that, unless for the purposes solely of section 70(1)(g) the effective date is taken to be the date at which the interest to be registered is created, then the paragraph has little value or effect. ...The effective date at which the wife's interest, if any, is to be considered is, therefore, 17 December 1982. ...

Appeal allowed.

Thus the relevant date for determining occupation is the date of completion rather than registration and the intensity of occupation must be considered against the nature and state of the premises occupied.

4.2 Unregistered Land

4.2.1 Legal interests

Where a person has a legal interest over land, generally, they will be able to enforce that interest automatically against a purchaser of that land. This continues the pre 1926 position that 'legal rights bind the whole world', see *Mercer v Liverpool, St Helen's and South Lancs Railway Co* [1903] 1 KB 652.

4.2.2 Equitable interests

Equitable interests in unregistered Land are dealt with in three ways:

(i)   Equitable interests subject to registration under the LCA 1972;

(ii)   Equitable interests subject to overreaching; and

(iii)   Equitable interests which neither fall into (i) or (ii) above and thus are still subject to the doctrine of notice.

Equitable interests subject to registration under the LCA 1972 must be entered on the Land Charges Register.   The LPA 1925 s 198(1) shows that registration will constitute actual notice of the right.   Registration must be against the correct name(s) of the estate owner(s).

Diligent Finance Co Ltd v Alleyne (1972) 23 P & CR 346

Panel: Foster J

Statute: Land Charges Act 1925 s 1 7(3)

Facts: The first defendant Erskine Owen Alleyne granted a second mortgage over his unregistered property to the plaintiff. Subsequent to this his estranged wife (the second defendant) registered a Class F land charge against her husband under the name Erskine Alleyne. The defendant then arranged a larger loan from the plaintiff and a new charge was registered and the old one cancelled. The plaintiff had searched the register under Erskine Owen Alleyne and found only the first mortgage. The court had to consider whether the Class F charge had priority over the second mortgage.

MR JUSTICE FOSTER

In my judgment, in the absence of any other evidence—and there is none—it is right for the court, following Ungoed-Thomas J.'s statement in the court below and Russell L.J. in the Court of Appeal, to assume in the absence of evidence to the contrary that the proper name of a person is that in which the conveyancing documents have been taken. It is unfortunate, to say the least, that the Class F registration was not made against the proper name Erskine Owen Alleyne but only against Erskine Alleyne, but that is a mistake which I for my part cannot unfortunately rectify. It follows that the official certificate granted to the plaintiff on February 13, 1970, under section 17 (3) of the Land Charges Act 1925 is conclusive and that the Class F charge does not rank ahead of the legal charge of the plaintiff.

Failure to register a land charge will mean that the equitable interest will be void against a purchaser. This can be illustrated in relation to *Midland Bank Trust Co Ltd v Green* [1981] AC 513. The events of the case below took place before the Land Charges Act 1972 was in force. However the substance of the Land Charges Act 1925, in so far as an option to purchase had to be registered as a land charge and failure to do so would mean it would be void against a purchaser for money or money's worth of a legal estate, remained unchanged by the 1972 Act.

Midland Bank Trust Co Ltd v Green [1981] AC 513

Panel: Lord Wilberforce, Lord Edmund-Davies, Lord Fraser of Tullybelton, Lord Russell of Killowen and Lord Bridge of Harwich

Statute: Land Charges Act 1925 ss 13(2) and 20(8)

Facts: In 1961 a tenant farmer (Geoffrey Green) was granted an option by his father (Walter) to purchase an unregistered farm in Lincolnshire. The son did not register the option. Six years later the father, intending to deprive his son of the option, sold the land to his wife (Evelyne) for £500. The farm had a market value of £40,000. On discovering the sale to his mother the son attempted to exercise the option. Both the son and the mother had died before the case reached the House of Lords who had to consider whether the option was binding on the mother's estate. At first instance the court found in favour of the son and that decision was reversed on appeal to the Court of Appeal.

LORD WILBERFORCE

...The trial took place before Oliver J. in 1977. A number of issues arose which are no longer relevant. The learned judge, in an admirable judgment with which I wholly agree, decided (i) that the sale and conveyance to Evelyne was not a sham and was a genuine sale by the vendor to a "purchaser," as defined by the Land Charges Act 1925 for money or money's worth, and accordingly that the option was not specifically enforceable; (ii) that Walter's estate had no answer to a claim for damages, and that an inquiry as to damages must be made; (iii) that any claim for damages against the estate of Evelyne was statute-barred by virtue of the Law Reform (Miscellaneous Provisions) Act 1934.

An appeal was brought to the Court of Appeal which, by a majority, reversed the judge's decision on point (i), and declared the option specifically enforceable. The ground of this decision appears to have been that the sale in 1967 was not for "money or money's worth," within the meaning of section 13 of the Land Charges Act 1925. In addition Lord Denning M.R. was prepared to hold that the protection of the Act was not available in a case of fraud meaning thereby "any dishonest dealing done so as to deprive unwary innocents of their rightful dues." The respondents, however, did not seek to support this except to the extent that they relied upon lack of good faith on the part of Evelyne.

My Lords, section 13 (2) of the Land Charges Act 1925 reads as follows:

"A land charge of class B, class C or class D, created or arising after the commencement of this Act, shall (except as hereinafter provided) be void as against a purchaser of the land charged therewith ... unless the land charge is registered in the appropriate register before the completion of the purchase: Provided that, as respects a land charge of class D and an estate contract created or entered into after the commencement of this Act, this subsection only applies in favour of a purchaser of a legal estate for money or money's worth."

As regards the word "purchaser" section 20 (8) of the same Act reads: "'Purchaser' means any person... who, for valuable consideration, takes any interest in land..."

Thus the case appears to be a plain one. The "estate contract," which by definition (section 11) includes an option of purchase, was entered into after January 1, 1926; Evelyne took an interest (in fee simple) in the land "for valuable consideration" - so was a "purchaser": she was a purchaser for money - namely £500: the option was not registered before the completion of the purchase. It is therefore void as against her.

In my opinion this appearance is also the reality. The case is plain: the Act is clear and definite. Intended as it was to provide a simple and understandable system for the protection of title to land, it should not be read down or glossed: to do so would destroy the usefulness of the Act. Any temptation to remould the Act to meet the facts of the present case, on the supposition that it is a hard one and that justice requires it, is, for me at least, removed by the consideration that the Act itself provides a simple and effective protection for persons in Geoffrey's position - viz. - by registration.

 Alert

...

My Lords, I recognise that the inquiring mind may put the question: why should there be an omission of the requirement of good faith in this particular context? I do not think there should be much doubt about the answer. Addition of a requirement that the purchaser should be in good faith would bring with it the necessity of inquiring into the purchaser's motives and state of mind. The present case is a good example of the difficulties which would exist. If the position was simply that the purchaser had notice of the option, and decided nevertheless to buy the land, relying on the absence of notification, nobody could contend that she would be lacking in good faith. She would merely be taking advantage of a situation, which the law has provided, and the addition of a profit motive could not create an absence of good faith. But suppose, and this is the respondents' argument, the purchaser's motive is to defeat the option, does this make any difference? Any advantage to oneself seems necessarily to involve a disadvantage for another: to make the validity of the purchase depend upon which aspect of the transaction was prevalent in the purchaser's mind seems to create distinctions equally difficult to analyse in law as to establish in fact: avarice and malice may be distinct sins, but in human conduct they are liable to be intertwined. The problem becomes even more acute if one supposes a mixture of motives. Suppose - and this may not be far from the truth - that the purchaser's motives were in part to take the farm from Geoffrey, and in part to distribute it between Geoffrey and his brothers and sisters, but not at all to obtain any benefit for herself, is this acting in "good faith" or not? Should family feeling be denied a protection afforded to simple greed? To eliminate the necessity for inquiries of this kind may well have been part of the legislative intention. Certainly there is here no argument for departing - violently - from the wording of the Act.

...

My Lords, I can deal more shortly with the respondents' second argument. It relates to the consideration for the purchase. The argument is that the protection of section 13 (2) of the Land Charges Act 1925 does not extend to a purchaser who has provided only a nominal consideration and that £500 is nominal. A variation of this was the argument accepted by the Court of Appeal that the consideration must be "adequate" - an expression of transparent difficulty. The answer to both contentions lies in the language of the subsection. The word "purchaser," by definition (section 20 (8)), means one who provides valuable consideration - a term of art which precludes any inquiry as to adequacy. This definition is, of course, subject to the context. Section 13 (2), proviso, requires money or money's worth to be provided: the purpose of this being to exclude the consideration of marriage. There is nothing here which suggests, or admits of, the introduction of a further requirement that the money must not be nominal.

...

This conclusion makes it unnecessary to determine whether £500 is a nominal sum of money or not. But I must say that for my part I should have great difficulty in so holding. "Nominal consideration" and a "nominal sum" in the law appear to me, as terms of art, to refer to a sum or consideration which can be mentioned as consideration but is not necessarily paid. To equate "nominal" with "inadequate" or even "grossly inadequate" would embark the law upon inquiries which I cannot think were contemplated by Parliament.

I would allow the appeal.

 Decipher

It is clear that a purchaser does not have to pay the market value for the property. Consideration can be nominal for a purchaser to take free of an unregistered land charge.

So entry onto the register, or failure to do so, is conclusive as to notice, regardless of any knowledge the purchaser may have of any rights existing over the land. The facts of this case gave rise to varied and lengthy litigation including an action against the negligent solicitor and a claim of conspiracy. In the connected case *Midland Bank Trust Co. Ltd and Another v Green and Another* [1980] Ch 590 Lord Denning MR observed that '[t]his story might be called the Green Saga' and that '[i]t bids fair to rival in time and money the story of *Jarndyce v. Jarndyce.*'

Decipher
This is the ruinous fictional property law case featured in the novel *Bleak House* by Charles Dickens.

4.2.2.1 Doctrine of Notice

Some equitable interests, such as pre 1926 easements, pre 1926 freehold covenants and beneficial interests that have not been overreached, are enforceable against anyone except 'Equity's Darling' – a *bona fide* purchaser for value of a legal estate without notice' of the equitable interest. Often the critical issue is whether the purchaser has notice of the interest. Notice can be actual, constructive or implied.

Kingsnorth Finance v Tizard [1986] 1 WLR 783

Panel: Judge John Finlay QC

Statute: Law of Property Act 1925 ss 70(1)(g) and 199(1)(ii)(b)

Facts: Mr Tizard, the first defendant, held the legal title of the unregistered matrimonial home (Willowdown House) on trust for himself and his wife, the second defendant. The marriage broke down and Mrs Tizard moved out of the matrimonial home. She returned to the house in the mornings and evenings to look after her and Mr Tizard's twin children; getting them ready for school and cooking them meals. She kept her clothing in three of the four wardrobe compartments in the master bedroom and also kept toiletries and a dressing gown at the property. She would also stay in the house overnight when Mr Tizard was away on business. Mr Tizard negotiated a loan secured by a legal mortgage with the plaintiff finance company. On the application form for the loan Mr Tizard described himself as single. When the plaintiff finance company sent a surveyor to inspect the property, Mr Tizard apologised for state of the property and explained that he was married but that his wife had left him and was no longer living at the property. The surveyor made no further enquiries and, on the basis of his report, the loan was agreed. Mr Tizard emigrated to America with the boy twin and defaulted on the loan. The court had to consider if Mrs Tizard's equitable interest was binding on the plaintiff finance company.

JUDGE JOHN FINLAY QC

I find that Mrs. Tizard contributed substantially to the successive property ventures by putting up money for the first deposit, by contributing through the earnings of hers which went into the common pool out of which mortgage instalments and building costs were paid, and by her labour. No accounts were kept of the spouses' respective contributions whether in money or in labour either before or after they were married. I find that they contributed substantially equally. Mrs. Tizard is entitled to half of the equity. Furthermore, I find that Mrs. Tizard remained at all material times in occupation of Willowdown House. Mr. Tizard, the owner of the legal estate, was in occupation, until he departed for the Americas in about June 1983. That circumstance does not however prevent Mrs. Tizard also being in occupation.

Mrs. Tizard was, in my judgment, in occupation of Willowdown notwithstanding that Mr. Tizard was living there also; and notwithstanding the fact that on numerous occasions she slept elsewhere. The "physical presence" to which Lord Wilberforce refers does not connote continuous and uninterrupted presence; such a notion would be absurd. Nor, indeed, do I consider that the requisite "presence" is negatived by regular and repeated absence. I find that Mrs. Tizard was in Willowdown virtually every day for some part of the day; that her life and activities were based on her presence, interrupted though it was, in Willowdown; there she prepared herself for work; there she cared for her children; there she looked after the house and the concerns of herself and the children; she went in the morning and returned in the evening to discharge her duties as housewife and mother. It is clear that prior to the time, November 1982, when she ceased always to sleep in the house when her husband was there, she had been in occupation; and, in my judgment, she did not cease to be in occupation simply because she made that change in her habits, significant though the change was.

Link
See *Williams & Glynn's Bank v Boland* above

Willowdown, however, is not registered land. If it were, my findings that Mrs. Tizard had equitable rights in the house and was at the material time in occupation would protect those rights against the mortgagee by reason of section 70(1)(g) of the Land Registration Act 1925. Do these two matters bring about the like result where the land is not registered?

Mr. Wigmore submits that although in the case of registered land the fact of occupation confers protection, in the case of unregistered land it is not enough that the claimant is in occupation; she must be found to be in occupation by the purchaser or mortgagee, or, at any rate, the circumstances must be such that she would have been found had proper inspections, inquiries and searches been made. ...

The [mortgage] brokers whose fee was to be £1240 were Bradshaws. They instructed a chartered surveyor, Mr. Marshall, to carry out an inspection. He did so on 13 March 1983, and made a report dated 15 March. Mr. Wigmore, for the plaintiffs, accepts that Mr. Marshall must be treated as the agent of the plaintiffs. If he were not, then the plaintiffs would not have inspected the property at all and could not rely, as the plaintiffs do, on what Mr. Marshall did not find. After receiving Mr. Marshall's report the plaintiffs wrote to him asking him to confirm that his report could be taken as addressed to the plaintiffs, and Mr. Marshall confirmed that it could.

...Mr. Tizard signed ... a printed form of application to the plaintiffs then Kingsnorth Trust Ltd. (that name heads the form) for an advance of £66000. The form is filled up so as to give various particulars about Mr. Tizard and about the property. Inter alia it states that he is "single," the word "married" being deleted. Although the marriage has now been dissolved it had not been at the time of the mortgage. This form of application is signed by Mr. Tizard and the date inserted in it is 16 March 1983.

...

When Mr. Marshall inspected on Sunday, 13 March there was no one at the property except Mr. Tizard. Mr. Tizard showed him round and then he inspected the property inside and outside on his own. He found evidences of occupation by two teenagers, a boy and a girl, from clothes, posters, etc. that he found in their respective rooms; he saw males clothes in the main bedroom; he had an impression that the fourth bedroom seemed to be used for storage, there were suitcases in it, but he could not in evidence recollect whether it contained a bed, dressing table, and so on; and he found no evidence at all of occupation by a female, other than the teenage daughter. Mr. Tizard, in apologising for the state of the house, said to Mr. Marshall that his wife had gone many months ago, that they were separated and that she was living with someone nearby.

Mr. Marshall's valuation report dated 15 March was made on a printed form headed with the logo and the name of "Ian Bradshaw Financial Consultants." Bradshaws had provided Mr. Marshall with a supply of these forms. He took one with him to do the valuation and made rough notes on it. Afterwards he produced the dated report which is completed in typescript. It gives the address of the property; and Mr. Tizard's name is typed in the space for the name of the applicant. The section titled "occupants" contains three questions: Who occupies the property? Are there any tenancies known to You or apparent on inspection? If yes, please give full details, including rental. The second question was answered "no" so there is no answer to the third. In answer to the first question there is typed, rather surprisingly in upper case (save for names and addresses, the remainder of the typescript uses upper and lower case in a normal way), the words "APPLICANT, SON AND DAUGHTER."

...

In my judgment, the fact that Mr. Tizard was married was a fact material to the transaction. ... In his evidence Mr. Marshall made it clear that he was suspicious; he was on the lookout for signs of female occupation; not the occupation of a wife, but that of a girl friend. He found no such signs, but his evidence made it clear that he regarded it as his duty to look for them. He drew the line however at opening cupboards and drawers. Mr. Marshall's understanding of his duty to look for signs of occupation by anyone else accords with mine. That being the scope of his duty, I consider that he should have enlarged on his answer to the question, "Who occupies the property?" The answer that he gave was, "Applicant, son and daughter." That was founded in part on his own observation; in part on what Mr. Tizard told him. He should, in my view, have added, either in the "Occupation" or in the "General observations" section, "Applicant states that he is separated from wife who lives nearby," or something to that effect.

My reason for that view is this. It is common ground that Mr. Marshall was acting as agent of the plaintiffs. He was not instructed by the plaintiffs. He was instructed by Bradshaws. Before Mr. Marshall inspected the property, Bradshaws had the document dated 12 March 1983 which Mr. Tizard signed. What Mr. Tizard told Bradshaws about his marital status at that stage can be inferred from what he told them later when he signed the plaintiffs' form, namely, that he was namely, "married," "single" must signify either bachelor or spinster as the case may be, or a widow or widower, or a person whose marriage has been dissolved. It cannot mean "married but separated." As Bradshaws were instructing Mr. Marshall to make an inspection on behalf of the plaintiffs, they were acting as the plaintiffs' agents for that purpose. The fact that Mr. Marshall was looking for evidence of the occupation of a female cohabitee coupled with what I infer from the two documents signed by Mr. Tizard was Bradshaw's understanding of Mr. Tizard's marital status, implies that Mr. Marshall approached his inspection on the footing that Mr. Tizard was not married; when it appeared that he was, I consider that he had a duty to communicate this new information to his principals. It follows in my judgment that the knowledge of the agent, Mr. Marshall, that Mr. Tizard had a wife is to be taken to be the knowledge of the principal, the plaintiffs.

...Primarily, the plaintiffs are to be taken to have been aware that Mr. Tizard was married and had described himself as single; and in these circumstances their further inquiries should have led them to Mrs. Tizard.

...

Although a spouse's statutory rights of occupation under section 1 of the Matrimonial Homes Act 1983, and the statutory provisions replaced by that Act are capable of protection by registration as a Class F. land charge, by virtue of the Land Charges Act 1972, the equitable interest of such a spouse in the matrimonial home is not capable of being so protected. The plaintiffs were prejudicially affected by the knowledge of their agent, Mr. Marshall, that Mr. Tizard, contrary to what he had said in his application, was married: see section 199(1)(ii)(b). That put them on notice that further inquiries were necessary; the inquiries which in these circumstances ought reasonably to have been made by the plaintiffs would, in my judgment, have been such as to have apprised them of the fact that Mrs. Tizard claimed a beneficial interest in the property; and accordingly, they would have had notice of such equitable rights as she had and the mortgage in these circumstances takes effect subject to these rights: see section 199(1)(ii)(a) . ...

It follows that the plaintiffs' claim for possession fails. ...

Action dismissed.

 Alert

Note that if the plaintiff finance company had paid the loan to two trustees , instead of only Mr Tizard (who was the sole legal owner; Mrs Tizard was only a beneficial owner), then they would have overreached Mrs Tizard's equitable interest in the property by virtue of the LPA 1925 ss 2 and 27. If Mrs Tizard's interest had been overreached then her interest would have transferred from the land to the loan monies, allowing the finance company to take the land free of her interest on default of the loan.

Further Reading

Gray & Gray: *Elements of Land Law*, (5th Edition), pp. 1083-1156

MacKenzie & Phillips: *Textbook on Land Law*, (15th Edition), Chapters 6 & 7

Megarry & Wade: *The Law of Real Property*, (8th Edition), Chapters 7 & 8

5

Proprietary Estoppel

Topic List

1 Assurance

2 Detriment

3 Proportionality

Introduction

Proprietary Estoppel is an equitable doctrine which enables someone who has relied to his detriment on an assurance or expectation made or encouraged by a landowner to claim a remedy in court. The court application may result in the award of an estate or interest in the land. The criteria which had to be met to enable a claim to be made used to be extremely strict. However, there has been a flurry of cases on proprietary estoppel in the last few decades resulting in a much broader formulation of the requirements of estoppel and a more flexible approach than was set out in the early cases. The 'modern' approach, founded on the concept of unconscionability, was set out by Oliver J in the following case.

Taylor's Fashions Limited and others v Liverpool Victoria Trustees Co Ltd [1982] QB 133

Panel: Oliver J

Facts: Old & Campbell Ltd (Old) owned the freehold of unregistered commercial premises ('21' and '22').

This following sequence of events occurred:

(i)   In 1948 Old granted a 28 year lease of 22, including an option to renew the lease for a further 14 years if the tenants installed a lift at the premises. The option to renew was not protected by entry of a Class C(iv) Land Charge.

(ii)   Later in 1948 Old sold the freehold of the premises to Liverpool Victoria Trustees Co Ltd ('Liverpool') who already owned the freehold of number 20.

(iii)   After the sale of the freehold Old was granted a 42 year lease of 21 which would terminate after 28 years if the tenants of 22 did not exercise the option to renew.

(iv)   In 1958 the lease of 22 was assigned to Taylor's Fashions Ltd (Taylor's). They installed a lift with the knowledge and acquiescence of Liverpool.

(v)   In 1962, Old was granted a 14 year lease of number 20, with an option to renew if the tenants of 22 exercised their option to renew. Old, now the tenant of 20 and 21, carried out extensive work on both premises.

In 1976, when the lease of 22 was about to run out (along with the leases of 20 and 21) Taylor's purported to exercise the option. Liverpool argued that as the option had not been protected by a Land Charge, it was void against them. This effectively meant that as Taylor's lease of 22 terminated in 1976 so did Old's leases of 20 and 21 (see points iii and v above). Liverpool served notice to quit on Taylor's and Old.

Oliver J confirmed that the option was void as against Liverpool as it had not been properly protected by a Class C(iv) Land Charge (s13 Land Charges Act 1925 (now replaced by s4(6) Land Charges Act 1972)). The question therefore was whether

Liverpool was estopped from relying on the strict legal rule to assert its rights, having regard to the expenditure incurred by both plaintiffs with Liverpool's concurrence.

He first of all reviewed the arguments of both sides.

MR JUSTICE OLIVER

The starting point of both Mr. Scott's and Mr. Essayan's arguments [for the Plaintiff] on estoppel is the same and was expressed by Mr. Essayan in the following proposition: if under an expectation created or encouraged by B that A shall have a certain interest in land, thereafter, on the faith of such expectation and with the knowledge of B and without objection by him, acts to his detriment in connection with such land, a Court of Equity will compel B to give effect to such expectation. This is a formulation which Mr. Millett [for the respondent] accepts but subject to one important qualification, namely that at the time when he created and encouraged the expectation and (I think that he would also say) at the time when he permitted the detriment to be incurred (if those two points of time are different) B not only knows of A's expectation but must be aware of his true rights and that he was under no existing obligation to grant the interest.

This is the principal point upon which the parties divide. Mr. Scott and Mr. Essayan contend that what the court has to look at in relation to the party alleged to be estopped is only his conduct and its result, and not - or, at any rate, not necessarily - his state of mind. It then has to ask whether what that party is now seeking to do is unconscionable. Mr. Millett contends that it is an essential feature of this particular equitable doctrine that the party alleged to be estopped must, before the assertion of his strict rights can be considered unconscionable, be aware both of what his strict rights were and of the fact that the other party is acting in the belief that they will not be enforced against him.

The point of contention therefore was whether the five probanda had to be strictly complied with. Counsel for Liverpool contended that they were not all met as Liverpool did not know what its legal rights were, and did not know that it was under no obligation to give effect to the option. He said that estoppel had no place in circumstances where both parties were acting under a mistake of law as to their rights. In order to see whether the test was strict, Oliver J reviewed *Ramsden v Dyson* (1866) LR 1 HL 129 and *Willmot v Barber* (1880) 15 Ch D 96.

The point is a critical one in the instant case and it is one upon which the authorities appear at first sight to be divided. The starting point is Ramsden v. Dyson (1866) L.R. 1 H.L. 129 where a tenant under a tenancy at will had built upon the land in the belief that he would be entitled to demand a long lease. The majority in the House of Lords held that he would not, but Lord Kingsdown dissented on the facts. There was no - or certainly no overt - disagreement between their Lordships as to the applicable principle, but it was stated differently by Lord Cranworth L.C. and Lord Kingsdown and the real question is how far Lord Cranworth was purporting to make an exhaustive exposition of principle and how far what he stated as the appropriate conditions for its application are to be treated, as it were, as being subsumed sub silentio in the speech of Lord Kingsdown. Lord Cranworth expressed it thus, at pp. 140-141:

"If a stranger begins to build on my land supposing it to be his own, and I, perceiving his mistake, abstain from setting him right, and leave him to persevere in his error, a court of equity will not allow me afterwards to assert my title to the land on which he had expended money on the supposition that the land was his own. It considers that, when I saw the mistake into which he had fallen, it was my duty to be active and to state my adverse title; and that it would be dishonest in me to remain wilfully passive on such an occasion, in order afterwards to profit by the mistake which I might have prevented. But it will be observed that to raise such an equity two things are required, first, that the person expending the money supposes himself to be building on his own land; and, secondly, that the real owner at the time of the expenditure knows that the land belongs to him and not to the person expending the money in the belief that he is the owner. For if a stranger builds on my land knowing it to be mine, there is no principle of equity which would prevent my claiming the land with the benefit of all the expenditure made on it. There would be nothing in my conduct, active or passive, making it inequitable in me to assert my legal rights."

 Alert

So here, clearly stated, is the criterion upon which Mr. Millett relies. Lord Kingsdown stated the matter differently and rather more broadly although in the narrower context of landlord and tenant. He says, at p. 170:

"The rule of law applicable to the case appears to me to be this: If a man, under a verbal agreement with a landlord for a certain interest in land, or, what amounts to the same thing, under an expectation, created or encouraged by the landlord, that he shall have a certain interest, takes possession of such land, with the consent of the landlord, and upon the faith of such promise or expectation, with the knowledge of the landlord, and without objection by him, lays out money upon the land, a court of equity will compel the landlord to give effect to such promise or expectation. This was the principle of the decision in Gregory v. Mighell (1811) Ves.Jun. 328, and as I conceive, is open to no doubt."

 Alert

So here, there is no specific requirement, at any rate in terms, that the landlord should know or intend that the expectation which he has created or encouraged is one to which he is under no obligation to give effect.

Mr. Millett does not - nor could he in the light of the authorities - dispute the principle. What he contends is that even if (which he contests) this is a case where the defendants could be said to have encouraged the plaintiffs' expectations - and that it is not necessarily the same as having encouraged or acquiesced in the expenditure - the principle has no application to a case where, at the time when the expectation was encouraged, both parties were acting under a mistake of law as to their rights...

... So far as proprietary estoppel or estoppel by acquiescence is concerned, he supports his submission by reference to the frequently cited judgment of Fry J. in Willmott v. Barber (1880) 15 Ch.D. 96 which contains what are described as the five "probanda." The actual case was one where what was alleged was a waiver by acquiescence. A lease contained a covenant against assigning subletting or parting with possession without the lessor's consent and the lessee had let a sublessee into possession of part of the land under an agreement with him which entitled him to occupy that part for the whole term and conferred an option to purchase the remaining land for the balance of the term outstanding when the option was exercised. The sublessee built on the land and the head landlord was aware that he was in possession and was expending money. It was, however, proved that he did not then know that his consent was required to a sub-letting or assignment. The question arose between the sublessee and the head landlord when the sublessee tried to exercise his option over the remaining land and found himself met with the response that the head landlord refused consent to the assignment. The case was, on Fry J.'s finding of fact, one simply of acquiescence by standing by and what was being argued was that the landlord was estopped by his knowledge of the plaintiff's expenditure on the part of the land of which the plaintiff was in possession from withholding his consent to an assignment of that part of which he was not. It having been found as a fact that the landlord did not, at the time of the plaintiff's expenditure, know about the covenant against assignment and that there was nothing in what had passed between them to suggest either that the landlord was aware that the plaintiff was labouring under the belief that no consent was necessary or to encourage that belief, Fry J. dismissed the plaintiff's claim. It has to be borne in mind, however, in reading the judgment, that this was a pure acquiescence case where what was relied on was a waiver of the landlord's rights by standing by without protest. It was a case of mere silence where what had to be established by the plaintiff was some duty in the landlord to speak. The passage from the judgment in Willmott v. Barber, 15 Ch.D. 96 most frequently cited is where Fry J. says, at pp. 105-106:

Alert

"A man is not to be deprived of his legal rights unless he has acted in such a way as would make it fraudulent for him to set up those rights. What, then, are the elements or requisites necessary to constitute fraud of that description? In the first place the plaintiff must have made a mistake as to his legal rights. Secondly, the plaintiff must have expended some money or must have done some act (not necessarily upon the defendant's land) on the faith of his mistaken belief. Thirdly, the defendant the possessor of the legal right, must know of the existence of his own right which is inconsistent with the right claimed by the plaintiff. If he does not know of it he is in the same position as the plaintiff, and the doctrine of acquiescence is founded upon conduct with a knowledge of your legal rights. Fourthly, the defendant, the possessor of the legal right, must know of the plaintiff's mistaken belief of his rights. If he does not, there is nothing which calls upon him to assert his own rights. Lastly, the defendant, the possessor of the legal right, must have encouraged the plaintiff in his expenditure of money or in the other acts which he has done, either directly or by abstaining from asserting his legal right. Where all these elements exist, there is fraud of such a nature as will entitle the court to restrain the possessor of the legal right from exercising it, but, in my judgment, nothing short of this will do."

Mr. Millett's submission is that when one applies these five probanda to the facts of the instant case it will readily be seen that they are not all complied with. In particular, Mr. Millett submits, the fourth probandum involves two essential elements, viz., (i) knowledge by the possessor of the legal right of the other party's belief; and (ii) knowledge that that belief is mistaken. In the instant case the defendants were not aware of their inconsistent right to treat the option as void and equally they could not, thus, have been aware that the plaintiffs' belief in the validity of the option was a mistaken belief. The alternative approach via estoppel by representation is not, he submits, open to the plaintiffs in this case because so far as Taylors were concerned the defendants made no representation to them at all and so far as Olds were concerned the representation of the continuing validity of the option, if there was one at all. was a representation of law.

Now, convenient and attractive as I find Mr. Millett's submissions as a matter of argument, I am not at all sure that so orderly and tidy a theory is really deducible from the authorities - certainly from the more recent authorities, which seem to me to support a much wider equitable jurisdiction to interfere in cases where the assertion of strict legal rights is found by the court to be unconscionable. It may well be (although I think that this must now be considered open to doubt) that the strict Willmott v. Barber, 15 Ch.D. 96 probanda are applicable as necessary requirements in those cases where all that has happened is that the party alleged to be estopped has stood by without protest while his rights have been infringed.

The judge decided that the probanda were useful in what can be called 'acquiescence' cases but were too strict in others. He then reviewed the plaintiffs' arguments and more recent authorities

Mr. Scott submits, however, that it is historically wrong to treat these probanda as holy writ and to restrict equitable interference only to those cases which can be confined within the strait-jacket of some fixed rule governing the circumstances in which, and in which alone, the court will find that a party is behaving unconscionably. Whilst accepting that the five probanda may form an appropriate test in cases of silent acquiescence, he submits that the authorities do not support the absolute necessity for compliance with all five probanda, and, in particular, the requirement of knowledge on the part of the party estopped that the other party's belief is a mistaken belief, in cases where the conduct relied on has gone beyond mere silence and amounts to active encouragement. In Lord Kingsdown's example in Ramsden v. Dyson, L.R. 1 H.L. 129, for instance, there is no room for the literal application of the probanda, for the circumstances there postulated do not presuppose a "mistake" on anybody's part, but merely the fostering of an expectation in the minds of both parties at the time but from which, once it has been acted upon, it would be unconscionable to permit the landlord to depart. As Scarman L.J. pointed out in Crabb v. Arun District Council [1976] Ch. 179, the "fraud" in these cases is not to be found in the transaction itself but in the subsequent attempt to go back upon the basic assumptions which underlay it.

Certainly it is not clear from the early cases that the courts considered it in all cases an essential element of the estoppel that the party estopped, although he must have known of the other party's belief, necessarily knew that that belief was mistaken...

...Furthermore the more recent cases indicate, in my judgment, that the application of the Ramsden v. Dyson, L.R. 1 H.L. 129 principle - whether you call it proprietary estoppel, estoppel by acquiescence or estoppel by encouragement is really immaterial - requires a very much broader approach which is directed rather at ascertaining whether, in particular individual circumstances, it would be unconscionable for a party

 Alert

to be permitted to deny that which, knowingly, or unknowingly, he has allowed or encouraged another to assume to his detriment than to inquiring whether the circumstances can be fitted within the confines of some preconceived formula serving as a universal yardstick for every form of unconscionable behaviour.

So regarded, knowledge of the true position by the party alleged to be estopped, becomes merely one of the relevant factors - it may even be a determining factor in certain cases - in the overall inquiry.

… The inquiry which I have to make therefore, as it seems to me, is simply whether, in all the circumstances of this case, it was unconscionable for the defendants to seek to take advantage of the mistake which, at the material time, everybody shared…

 Alert

5.1 Assurance

The first requirement for proprietary estoppel is that there must be an assurance or representation by, or an expectation encouraged by the landowner. The nature of the assurance and the form it should take was examined in the following case.

Gillett v Holt [2001] Ch 210

Panel: Beldam, Waller and Robert Walker LJJ

Facts: Gillett worked for Holt for almost 40 years as farm manager and subsequently as his business partner. Over the course of time, Holt assured Gillett in private and in front of witnesses that Gillett would inherit the farm under Holt's will. In fact, Holt made several wills which reflected this. However, relations between the two became strained and Holt made a final will under which he left nothing to Gillett. Gillett claimed a substantial part of Holt's estate, including the farm, by estoppel. At first instance, the claim was rejected. Gillett appealed. Robert Walker LJ first of all looked at the nature of the assurance which was needed. In rejecting Gillett's claim, the judge at first instance relied on the decision in *Taylor v Dickens* [1998] 1FLR 806. In that case, the claim was dismissed because the claimant knew that the landowner's will was revocable.

LORD JUSTICE ROBERT WALKER

Taylor v Dickens has itself attracted a good deal of criticism: see, for instance, Professor M P Thompson, "Emasculating Estoppel" [1998] Conv 210, and William Swadling [1998] RLR 220; but compare the contrary view in M Dixon, "Estoppel: A panacea for all wills?" [1999] Conv 39, 46. Mr Swadling's comment is short and pithy:

"This decision is clearly wrong, for the judge seems to have forgotten that the whole point of estoppel claims is that they concern promises which, since they are unsupported by consideration, are initially revocable. What later makes them binding, and therefore irrevocable, is the promisee's detrimental reliance on them. Once that occurs, there is simply no question of the promisor changing his or her mind."

Mr McDonnell [for the appellant] has added his voice to the criticism. In his skeleton argument he has submitted that *Taylor v Dickens* is "simply wrong". Mr Martin [for the respondents], while reminding the court that it is not hearing an appeal in *Taylor v Dickens*, has not given the case whole-hearted support. He has been inclined to concede that Judge Weeks should have focused on the promise which was made and whether it was of an irrevocable character, instead of looking for a second promise not to revoke a testamentary disposition...

... In my judgment these criticisms of *Taylor v Dickens* are well founded. The actual result in the case may be justified on the other ground on which it was put (no unconscionability on the facts); or (as Mr Swadling suggests later in his note) the gardener's unremunerated services might have merited some modest restitutionary relief. But the inherent revocability of testamentary dispositions (even if well understood by the parties, as Mr Gillett candidly accepted that it was by him) is irrelevant to a promise or assurance that "all this will be yours" (the sort of language used on the occasion of The Beeches incident in 1975). Even when the promise or assurance is in terms linked to the making of a will (as at the 1974 Golf Hotel dinner) the circumstances may make clear that the assurance is more than a mere statement of present (revocable) intention, and is tantamount to a promise. *Attorney General of Hong Kong v Humphreys Estate (Queen's Gardens) Ltd* [1987] AC 114, on which Judge Weeks relied, is essentially an example of a purchaser taking the risk, with his eyes open, of going into possession and spending money while his purchase remains expressly subject to contract. Carnwath J observed that the advice to the claimant in *Taylor v Dickens* "not to count his chickens before they were hatched" is [1998] 3 All ER 917, 929:

"an apt statement of how, in normal circumstances, and in the absence of a specific promise, any reasonable person would regard--and should be expected by the law to regard--a representation by a living person as to his intentions for his will."

In the generality of cases that is no doubt correct, and it is notorious that some elderly persons of means derive enjoyment from the possession of testamentary power, and from dropping hints as to their intentions, without any question of an estoppel arising. But in this case Mr Holt's assurances were repeated over a long period, usually before the assembled company on special family occasions, and some of them (such as "it was all going to be ours anyway" on the occasion of The Beeches incident) were completely unambiguous. With all respect to the judge, I cannot accept the conclusion which he reached on this point (at p 932, a passage which I have already quoted). The judge attached weight to The Beeches incident in reaching his conclusion. To my mind it is highly significant, but its significance goes the other way. I find it wholly understandable that Mr and Mrs Gillett, then 10 years married and with two young sons, may have been worried about their home and their future depending on no more than oral assurances, however emphatic, from Mr Holt. The bitterly fought and ruinously expensive litigation which has ensued shows how right they would have been to be worried. But Mr Gillett, after discussing the matter with his wife and his parents, decided to rely on Mr Holt's assurances because "Ken was a man of his word." Plainly the assurances given on this occasion were intended to be relied on, and were in fact relied on.

Then he considered what 'detriment' meant in the context of an estoppel claim.

The overwhelming weight of authority shows that detriment is required. But the authorities also show that it is not a narrow or technical concept. The detriment need not consist of the expenditure of money or other quantifiable financial detriment, so long as it is something substantial. The requirement must be approached as part of a broad inquiry as to whether repudiation of an assurance is or is not unconscionable in all the circumstances.

 Alert

There are some helpful observations about the requirement for detriment in the judgment of Slade LJ in Jones v Watkins 26 November 1987. There must be sufficient causal link between the assurance relied on and the detriment asserted. The issue of detriment must be judged at the moment when the person who has given the assurance seeks to go back on it. Whether the detriment is sufficiently substantial is to be tested by whether it would be unjust or inequitable to allow the assurance to be disregarded– that is, again, the essential test of unconscionability. The detriment alleged must be pleaded and proved.

 Alert

As authority for the second of these observations Slade LJ referred to *Spencer Bower & Turner on Estoppel by Representation*, 3rd ed (1977), p 110, which in turn cites the judgment of Dixon J in *Grundt v Great Boulder Pty Gold Mines Ltd* (1938) 59 CLR 641, 674-675 (High Court of Australia):

"One condition appears always to be indispensable. That other must have so acted or abstained from acting upon the footing of the state of affairs assumed that he would suffer a detriment if the opposite party were afterwards allowed to set up rights against him inconsistent with the assumption. In stating this essential condition, particularly where the estoppel flows from representation it is often said simply that the party asserting the estoppel must have been induced to act to his detriment. Although substantially such a statement is correct and leads to no misunderstanding, it does not bring out clearly the basal purpose of the doctrine. That purpose is to avoid or prevent a detriment to the party asserting the estoppel by compelling the opposite party to adhere to the assumption upon which the former acted or abstained from acting. This means that the real detriment or harm from which the law seeks to give protection is that which would flow from the change of position if the assumption were deserted that led to it. So long as the assumption is adhered to, the party who altered his situation upon the faith of it cannot complain. His complaint is that when afterwards the other party makes a different state of affairs the basis of an assertion of right against him then, if it is allowed, his own original change of position will operate as a detriment. His action or inaction must be such that, if the assumption upon which he proceeded were shown to be wrong, and an inconsistent state of affairs were accepted as the foundation of the rights and duties of himself and the opposite party, the consequence would be to make his original act or failure to act a source of prejudice."

This passage was not directed specifically to proprietary estoppel, but Slade LJ was right, in my respectful view, to treat it as applicable to proprietary estoppel as well as to other forms of estoppel.

The point made in the passage may be thought obvious, but sometimes it is useful to spell out even basic points. If in a situation like that in *Inwards v Baker* [1965] 2 QB 29, a man is encouraged to build a bungalow on his father's land and does so, the question of detriment is, so long as no dispute arises, equivocal. Viewed from one angle (which ignores the assurance implicit in the encouragement) the son suffers the detriment of spending his own money in improving land which he does not own. But viewed from another angle (which takes account of the assurance) he is getting the benefit of a free building plot. If and when the father (or his personal representative) decides to go back on the assurance and assert an adverse claim then, as Dixon J put it in the passage just quoted from *Grundt v Great Boulder Pty Gold Mines Ltd*, "if [the assertion] is allowed, his own original change of position will operate as a detriment".

The matters which Mr Gillett pleaded as detriment, and on which he adduced evidence of detriment, included, apart from the level of his remuneration, (i) his continuing in Mr Holt's employment (through KAHL [Mr Holt's company]) and not seeking or accepting offers of employment elsewhere, or going into business on his own account; (ii) carrying out tasks and spending time beyond the normal scope of an employee's duty; (iii) taking no substantial steps to secure his future wealth, either by larger pension contributions or otherwise; and (iv) expenditure on improving The Beeches farmhouse which was, Mr Gillett said, barely habitable when it was first acquired by KAHL in 1971. That company paid for some structural work, with a local authority improvement grant, but Mr Gillett paid for new fittings and materials and carried out a good deal of the work himself. The details are set out in part 3 and appendix 1 of Mr Gillett's witness statement.

I have to say that I see some force in Mr McDonnell's criticism of the judge's approach to this part of the evidence (although the judge, having decided the main action on the issue of assurances, was not obliged to cover the issue of detriment in great detail). After listening to lengthy submissions about the judgment, and after reading much of Mr Gillett's evidence both in his witness statement and under cross-examination, I am left with the feeling that the judge, despite his very clear and careful judgment, did not stand back and look at the matter in the round. Had he done so I think he would have recognised that Mr Gillett's case on detriment (on the facts found by the judge, and on Mr Gillett's uncontradicted evidence) was an unusually compelling one.

Gillett v Holt was a 'family' type of case rather than a case where the parties were operating in a commercial environment at arm's length. In such a 'family' situation, the parties probably would not talk in terms of precise proprietary rights; they would be much more vague and informal. This case is authority for saying that in such a context, imprecise statements can 'count' as assurances to found an estoppel claim.

However, where the parties are commercially experienced or are acting in a business capacity, the bar as to what 'counts' as an assurance or expectation is set much higher. Indeed, in *Cobbe v Yeoman's Row Management Limited* [2008] UKHL 55, it appeared that the informal type of assurance in *Gillett v Holt* could no longer form the basis of an estoppel claim, even in a domestic or family type of situation.

Cobbe v Yeoman's Row Management Limited [2008] UKHL 55

Panel: Lord Hoffman, Lord Scott, Lord Walker, Lord Brown and Lord Mance

Facts: Cobbe was a property developer who reached a 'gentleman's agreement' with Yeoman's Row Management Limited ('Yeoman's Row') (a company represented by Mrs Lisle-Mainwaring) to develop a site in Knightsbridge. Yeoman's Row owned the building. The parties agreed that Cobbe would obtain planning permission to demolish a block of flats and to build houses. Once planning permission had been granted, Yeoman's Row would sell the land to Cobbe for £12 million. He would then develop the site and sell the houses. If the sale proceeds he received exceeded £24 million, the surplus would be split between the parties. Cobbe incurred considerable expense in applying for planning permission. When it was granted, Yeoman's Row demanded £20 million instead of £12 million as the purchase price of the land. Cobbe claimed an interest in the land based on his reliance on the gentleman's agreement. He succeeded in his estoppel claim at first instance and in the Court of Appeal, but when the matter came before the House of Lords, he failed in his claim.

LORD SCOTT

14. Both the learned judge and the Court of Appeal regarded the relief granted as justified on the basis of proprietary estoppel. I respectfully disagree. The remedy to which, on the facts as found by the judge, Mr Cobbe is entitled can, in my opinion, be described neither as based on an estoppel nor as proprietary in character. There are several important authorities to which I want to refer but I want first to consider as a matter of principle the nature of a proprietary estoppel. An "estoppel" bars the object of it from asserting some fact or facts, or, sometimes, something that is a mixture of fact and law, that stands in the way of some right claimed by the person entitled to the benefit of the estoppel. The estoppel becomes a "proprietary" estoppel - a sub-species of a "promissory" estoppel - if the right claimed is a proprietary right, usually a right to or over land but, in principle, equally available in relation to chattels or choses in action. So, what is the fact or facts, or the matter of mixed fact and law, that, in the present case, the Appellant is said to be barred from asserting? And what is the proprietary right claimed by Mr Cobbe that the facts and matters the Appellant is barred from asserting might otherwise defeat?

15. The pleadings do not answer these questions. The terms of the oral "agreement in principle", the second agreement, relied on by Mr Cobbe are pleaded but it is accepted that there remained still for negotiation other terms. The second agreement was, contractually, an incomplete agreement. The terms that had already been agreed were regarded by the parties as being "binding in

honour", but it follows that the parties knew they were not legally binding. So what is it that the Appellant is estopped from asserting or from denying? The Appellant cannot be said to be estopped from asserting that the second agreement was unenforceable for want of writing, for Mr Cobbe does not claim that it was enforceable; nor from denying that the second agreement covered all the terms that needed to be agreed between the parties, for Mr Cobbe does not claim that it did; nor from denying that, pre 18 March 2004, Mr Cobbe had acquired any proprietary interest in the property, for he has never alleged that he had. And what proprietary claim was Mr Cobbe making that an estoppel was necessary to protect? ...

... Etherton J concluded, in para 85 of his judgment, that the facts of the case "gave rise to a proprietary estoppel in favour of Mr Cobbe", but nowhere identified the content of the estoppel. Mummery LJ agreed (paras 60 and 61 of his judgment, concurred in by Dyson LJ (para 120) and Sir Martin Nourse (para 141)), but he, too, did not address the content of the estoppel. Both Etherton J and Mummery LJ regarded the proprietary estoppel conclusion as justified by the unconscionability of Mrs Lisle-Mainwaring's conduct. My Lords, unconscionability of conduct may well lead to a remedy but, in my opinion, proprietary estoppel cannot be the route to it unless the ingredients for a proprietary estoppel are present. These ingredients should include, in principle, a proprietary claim made by a Claimant and an answer to that claim based on some fact, or some point of mixed fact and law, that the person against whom the claim is made can be estopped from asserting. To treat a "proprietary estoppel equity" as requiring neither a proprietary claim by the Claimant nor an estoppel against the Defendant but simply unconscionable behaviour is, in my respectful opinion, a recipe for confusion.

Lord Scott readily found that Mrs Lisle-Mainwaring on behalf of the company had acted unconscionably, but he required something more than that. He wanted to see an expectation on the part of the claimant of a particular interest in land, which was not subject to any contingency.

20. Lord Kingsdown's requirement that there be an expectation of "a certain interest in land", repeated in the same words by Oliver J in the *Taylors Fashions* case, presents a problem for Mr Cobbe's proprietary estoppel claim. The problem is that when he made the planning application his expectation was, for proprietary estoppel purposes, the wrong sort of expectation. It was not an expectation that he would, if the planning application succeeded, become entitled to "a certain interest in land". His expectation was that he and Mrs Lisle-Mainwaring, or their respective legal advisers, would sit down and agree the outstanding contractual terms to be incorporated into the formal written agreement, which he justifiably believed would include the already agreed core financial terms, and that his purchase, and subsequently his development of the property, in accordance with that written agreement would follow. This is not, in my opinion, the sort of expectation of "a certain interest in land" that Oliver J in the *Taylors Fashions* case or Lord Kingsdown in *Ramsden v Dyson* had in mind...

25. ... The reason why, in a "subject to contract" case, a proprietary estoppel cannot ordinarily arise is that the would-be purchaser's expectation of acquiring an interest in the property in question is subject to a contingency that is entirely under the control of the other party to the negotiations...

27. ... But debate about subject-to-contract reservations has only a peripheral relevance in the present case, for such a reservation is pointless in the context of oral negotiations relating to the acquisition of an interest in land. It would be an unusually unsophisticated negotiator who was not well aware that oral agreements relating to such an acquisition are by statute unenforceable and that no express reservation to make them so is needed. Mr Cobbe was an experienced property developer and Mrs Lisle-Mainwaring gives every impression of knowing her way around the negotiating table. Mr Cobbe did not spend his money and time on the planning application in the mistaken belief that the agreement was legally enforceable. He spent his money and time well aware that it was not. Mrs Lisle-Mainwaring did not encourage in him a belief that the second agreement was enforceable. She encouraged in him a belief that she would abide by it although it was not. Mr Cobbe's belief, or expectation, was always speculative. He knew she was not legally bound. He regarded her as bound "in honour" but that is an acknowledgement that she was not legally bound...

28. ... The advantage taken was the benefit of his services, his time and his money, in obtaining planning permission for the property. The advantage was unconscionable because immediately following the grant of planning permission, she repudiated the financial terms on which Mr Cobbe had been expecting to be able to purchase the property. But to leap from there to a conclusion that a proprietary estoppel case was made out was not, in my opinion, justified... Proprietary estoppel requires, in my opinion, clarity as to what it is that the object of the estoppel is to be estopped from denying, or asserting, and clarity as to the interest in the property in question that that denial, or assertion, would otherwise defeat. If these requirements are not recognised, proprietary estoppel will lose contact with its roots and risk becoming unprincipled and therefore unpredictable, if it has not already become so. This is not, in my opinion, a case in which a remedy can be granted to Mr Cobbe on the basis of proprietary estoppel.

Lord Walker draws a distinction between family and commercial cases, attributing a far greater level of legal awareness in commercial cases than in domestic arrangements. Nevertheless, it is clear that although the parties in a domestic case need not be talking in terms of precise rights, the claimant must show that he believed that the assurance could not be revoked. This would be difficult to show in many family cases.

LORD WALKER

63.	The present appeal is not a case of imperfect gift, like *Dillwyn v Llewelyn*. Nor is it a case of unilateral mistake to which the *Willmott v Barber* probanda would be appropriate - that is, a case of the Defendant taking advantage of a mistake as to title of which he is well aware. This case is, in the terminology used by Gray and Gray, a case of "common expectation" if it is anything. The critical issue, to my mind, is whether there was, on the judge's findings, a common expectation of the type capable of raising an equitable estoppel. Although they are not based on common mistake (as in the "imperfect gift" cases) or unilateral mistake (as in the "standing by" cases) "common expectation" cases often have at least a flavour of mistake, or at any rate what restitution lawyers call misprediction (Mr Cobbe predicted, wrongly, that Mrs Lisle-Mainwaring would not withdraw from the non-binding arrangement). Was it also necessary for Mr Cobbe to believe, wrongly, that Mrs Lisle-Mainwaring had no legal right to withdraw from it?...

66.	The point that hopes by themselves are not enough is made most clearly in cases with a commercial context, of which *Attorney General of Hong Kong* is the most striking example. It does not appear so often in cases with more of a domestic or family flavour... They may not have had a clear idea of the quantum of what they expected to get (in *Grundy v Ottey*, unusually, the expected quantum was precisely defined). But in those cases in which an estoppel was established, the Claimant believed that the assurance on which he or she relied was binding and irrevocable.

68.	It is unprofitable to trawl through the authorities on domestic arrangements in order to compare the forms of words used by judges to describe the Claimants' expectations in cases where this issue (hope or something more?) was not squarely raised. But the fact that the issue is seldom raised is not, I think, coincidental. In the commercial context, the Claimant is typically a business person with access to legal advice and what he or she is expecting to get is a contract. In the domestic or family context, the typical Claimant is not a business person and is not receiving legal advice. What he or she wants and expects to get is an interest in immovable property, often for long-term occupation as a home. The focus is not on intangible legal rights but on the tangible property which he or she expects to get. The typical domestic Claimant does not stop to reflect (until disappointed expectations lead to litigation) whether some further legal transaction (such as a grant by deed, or the making of a will or codicil) is necessary to complete the promised title...

71.	So the judge found that Mr Cobbe believed that Mrs Lisle- Mainwaring was, and regarded herself as, bound in honour to enter into a formal written contract if planning permission was granted; and that Mr Cobbe regarded himself as similarly bound. It is implicit - in my view necessarily and deliberately implicit - in the judge's carefully chosen language that neither Mrs Lisle-Mainwaring nor Mr Cobbe regarded herself or himself as legally bound. They were both very experienced in property matters and they knew perfectly well that that was not the position.

Cobbe seemed to set a new test as to what counts as an assurance. The circumstances in which this new test was to apply were clarified in *Thorner v Major* [2009] UKHL 18.

Thorner v Major [2009] UKHL 18

Panel: Lord Hoffman, Lord Scott, Lord Rodger, Lord Walker and Lord Neuberger

Facts: David Thorner was the cousin of a landowner and farmer, Peter. Peter was unmarried and had no children. David helped Peter on the farm, mostly unpaid, for 30 years. There was never any express statement to the effect that David would inherit the farm, but David came to hope that he would do so, following oblique remarks and actions by Peter. In 1990, Peter handed to David an insurance policy bonus notice, telling him that the money was to pay Peter's death duties. Peter did in fact make a will in David's favour, but subsequently destroyed it as he intended to make a new one. The new will, which was never made, would have contained minor changes, but would still have left the bulk of Peter's estate to David. The question for the House of Lords was whether there had been an assurance intended to be relied upon.

LORD WALKER:

56. I would prefer to say (while conscious that it is a thoroughly question-begging formulation) that to establish a proprietary estoppel the relevant assurance must be clear enough. What amounts to sufficient clarity, in a case of this sort, is hugely dependent on context. I respectfully concur in the way Hoffmann LJ put it in *Walton v Walton* (in which the mother's "stock phrase" to her son, who had worked for low wages on her farm since he left school at 15, was "You can't have more money and a farm one day"). Hoffmann LJ stated at para 16:

"The promise must be unambiguous and must appear to have been intended to be taken seriously. Taken in its context, it must have been a promise which one might reasonably expect to be relied upon by the person to whom it was made."

...

59. In this case the context, or surrounding circumstances, must be regarded as quite unusual. The deputy judge heard a lot of evidence about two countrymen leading lives that it may be difficult for many city-dwellers to imagine - taciturn and undemonstrative men committed to a life of hard and unrelenting physical work, by day and sometimes by night, largely unrelieved by recreation or female company. The deputy judge seems to have listened carefully to this evidence and to have been sensitive to the unusual circumstances of the case.

60. I respectfully consider that the Court of Appeal did not give sufficient weight to the advantage that the trial judge had in seeing and hearing the witnesses. They concentrated too much, I think, on the 1990 incident of the bonus notice. That was certainly an important part of the narrative. For David it marked the transition from hope to expectation. But it did not stand alone. The evidence

showed a continuing pattern of conduct by Peter for the remaining 15 years of his life and it would not be helpful to try to break down that pattern into discrete elements (and then treat each as being, on its own, insignificant). To my mind the deputy judge did find, in paras 94 and 98 of his judgment, that Peter's assurances, objectively assessed, were intended to be taken seriously and to be relied on…

Thus Lord Walker said that everything depended on the context in which the words were said or actions made, saying that the assurance should be 'clear enough' in the circumstances. Lord Neuberger posed a slightly different test:

LORD NEUBERGER

84. It should be emphasised that I am not seeking to cast doubt on the proposition, heavily relied on by the Court of Appeal (eg [2008] EWCA Civ 732, paras 71 and 74), that there must be some sort of an assurance which is "clear and unequivocal" before it can be relied on to found an estoppel. However, that proposition must be read as subject to three qualifications. First, it does not detract from the normal principle, so well articulated in this case by Lord Walker, that the effect of words or actions must be assessed in their context. Just as a sentence can have one meaning in one context and a very different meaning in another context, so can a sentence, which would be ambiguous or unclear in one context, be a clear and unambiguous assurance in another context. Indeed, as Lord Walker says, the point is underlined by the fact that perhaps the classic example of proprietary estoppel is based on silence and inaction, rather than any statement or action - see per Lord Eldon LC ("knowingly, though but passively") in *Dann v Spurrier* (1802) 7 Ves 231, 235-6 and per Lord Kingsdown ("with the knowledge . . . and without objection") in *Ramsden v Dyson* LR 1 HL 129, 170.

85. Secondly, it would be quite wrong to be unrealistically rigorous when applying the "clear and unambiguous" test. The court should not search for ambiguity or uncertainty, but should assess the question of clarity and certainty practically and sensibly, as well as contextually. Again, this point is underlined by the authorities, namely those cases I have referred to … above, which support the proposition that, at least normally, it is sufficient for the person invoking the estoppel to establish that he reasonably understood the statement or action to be an assurance on which he could rely.

86. Thirdly, as pointed out in argument by my noble and learned friend Lord Rodger of Earlsferry, there may be cases where the statement relied on to found an estoppel could amount to an assurance which could reasonably be understood as having more than one possible meaning. In such a case, if the facts otherwise satisfy all the requirements of an estoppel, it seems to me that, at least normally, the ambiguity should not deprive a person who reasonably relied on the assurance of all relief: it may well be right, however, that he should be accorded relief on the basis of the interpretation least beneficial to him.

Thus Lord Neuberger poses a test of 'clear and unequivocal' but then goes on to state that everything depends on the circumstances, and the court should not be 'unrealistically rigorous'. He therefore applies a more stringent test in a flexible way to achieve the same result as Lord Walker.

5.2 Detriment

Not only must the claimant show a relevant assurance, he must also show that he has suffered detriment. The issue of detriment was explored the following case where it was held that the 'detriment' need not be quantifiable in purely financial terms.

Campbell v Griffin [2001] EWCA Civ 990

Panel: Dame Butler-Sloss, Thorpe and Robert Walker LJJ

Facts: The claimant lodged with Mr and Mrs Ascough from 1978 to 1997. Over the years, the Ascoughs became increasingly dependent on the claimant, and from 1987 onwards made repeated assurances that he would have a home for life. Mrs Ascough died after her husband but left no valid will. The claimant claimed the right to reside in the house for life, based on estoppel. At first instance the judge dismissed the claim on the basis that the detriment was not suffered in reliance on any assurance as to a proprietary right, but simply because he was a decent human being who wanted to look after his friends. The claimant's appeal was allowed.

LORD JUSTICE ROBERT WALKER

22. ...I feel bound to disagree with the judge on the issue of detriment. If necessary I would say that his conclusion was against the weight of the evidence. The judge (who seems to have given an ex tempore judgement after what must have been a long day in court) seems not to have been sufficiently clear as to the admittedly confused chronology of the case. It covered a long period (the Ascoughs were in their late seventies when they first met Mr Campbell, and Mrs Ascough was nearly 100 when she died) and the pattern of events changed markedly during that period as the elderly couple became increasingly frail, helpless and incontinent. In re-examination Mr Campbell made clear that the incontinence had begun before the Ascoughs went to The Beeches for respite care, and he said it was "quite a regular occurrence" after they came home from The Beeches.

23. Another possible explanation of the judge's conclusion that there was no detriment might be that he was looking at quantifiable financial detriment, rather than simply looking for something substantial "as part of a broad enquiry as to whether repudiation of an assurance is or is not unconscionable in all the circumstances" (*Gillett v Holt* [2001] 3 Ch 210, [2000] 3 WLR 815, at 836 of the latter, following guidance given by Slade LJ in *Jones v Watkins*, 26 November 1987). The judge's references to "cheap and good accommodation" and "almost minimal cost" may tend to support that view.

24. The judge did not explain the reasons for his conclusion and so it is not possible to be sure whether he overlooked parts of the evidence, or erred in law in setting too demanding a test for detriment. Both factors may have contributed to his conclusion. But in any case I respectfully differ from it. As Mr Timothy Sisley has said in his skeleton argument, a lodger does not normally cook his landlords' evening meals, or delay going to work or go short of sleep in order to look after them, or clean up after incontinence. That is true even if the lodger is paying a low rent, or no rent. The court can take judicial notice that a live-in carer looking after a couple as frail as Mr and Mrs Ascough would expect to be paid a very substantial wage in addition to free board and lodging, and would expect to be fully reimbursed for all out-of-pocket expenditure. From some time in the late 1980's, or from 1990 at the very latest (but any particular date is bound to be arbitrary) Mr Campbell must in my judgment have been suffering and accepting detriment in his devoted care of the Ascoughs.

25. On the issue of reliance the judge's finding was that Mr Campbell acted "out of friendship and a sense of responsibility". The judge did not refer to the judgment of Balcombe LJ in *Wayling v Jones* (1993) 69 P&CR 170, 173, in which Balcombe LJ (with whom Hoffmann LJ, and probably also Leggatt LJ, agreed) stated as a principle:

"Once it has been established that promises were made, and that there has been conduct by the plaintiff of such a nature that inducement may be inferred then the burden of proof shifts to the defendants to establish that he did not rely on the promises - *Greasley v Cooke* [1980] 1 WLR 1306; *Grant v Edwards* [1986] Ch 638, 657."

...

27. Cases of this sort ought not to be decided by meticulous analysis of every single answer made during cross-examination by an honest but diffident witness who was (to his credit) not trying to exaggerate his claim. It is more difficult to differ from the judge on the issue of reliance, since he did see and hear the witnesses and he was able to observe Mr Campbell's demeanour when he was giving the evidence which is set out above. But just as this court reversed the trial judge in *Wayling v Jones*, I have after anxious consideration concluded that the judge overlooked the presumption of reliance and failed to address his mind to the different phases of the long history of this relationship. From 1978 to 1982 it was a very friendly relationship of elderly landlords and lodger, with both sides very contented with the relationship. By 1990 at latest there was a much closer, family-type relationship, with assurances of a home for life being given from about 1987. By 1990 Mr Campbell was doing much more for the Ascoughs than could be ascribed to even the most friendly lodger. He had become part of the family, and there was a strong presumption that the assurances given to him (to treat him, in effect, as a member of the family with moral claims on the Ascoughs) were influencing his conduct.

28. The fact that Mr Campbell agreed, under skilful cross-examination, that he would not in any event have ignored his elderly landlord ". . . if he had been lying on the floor, and had not eaten for two days" is not sufficient to rebut that presumption. In my judgment the judge was wrong on the issue of reliance also. In cases of this sort it is inevitable that claimants should be asked hypothetical questions of the "what if" variety but the court is not bound to attach great importance to the answers to such hypothetical questions. As Lord Denning MR said in *Greasley v Cooke* [1980] 3 All ER 710, [1980] 1 WLR 1306, at 1311 of the former report,

"No one can say what she [the claimant] would have done if Kenneth and Hedley [the two brothers who owned the property] had not made those statements."

29. The court must of course pay close attention, and give due weight, to the oral evidence given by the witnesses who have lived through the events into which the court has to enquire. But it would do no credit to the law if an honest witness who admitted that he had mixed motives were to fail in a claim which might have succeeded if supported by less candid evidence. As Balcombe LJ said in *Wayling v Jones* (at p 173):

"The promises relied upon do not have to be the sole inducement for the conduct: it is sufficient if they are an inducement."

In my judgment the assurances given by the Ascoughs were an inducement to Mr Campbell's conduct, from 1990 at latest. With respect to the judge, I consider that he erred (either in his evaluation of the evidence, or in his application of the legal presumption) in his conclusion that there was no sufficient causal connection between the assurances given by the Ascoughs and the detriment suffered by Mr Campbell.

5.3 Proportionality

Once an estoppel is established, the courts have a discretion as to what remedy to award to satisfy the equity. There have been two basic approaches, based on what the claimant expected to receive, and on the detriment he suffered.

In *Jennings v Rice* [2002] EWCA Civ 159, the Court of Appeal examined the basis on which awards were made. Bearing in mind the broad principles that the award should not exceed the claimant's expectation, and that the award should be the minimum to do justice, it adopted the 'expectation' approach as its starting point, then looked at whether the award should be more limited, introducing the notion of proportionality.

Jennings v Rice [2002] EWCA Civ 159

Panel: Aldous, Mantell and Robert Walker LJJ

Facts: The claimant worked for Mrs Royle from 1970 until Mrs Royle's death in 1997. At first he worked as a part-time gardener, but over the years his duties increased as Mrs Royle became heavily dependent on him. The claimant worked unpaid, and if ever he mentioned this to Mrs Royle, she made statements such as, 'this will all be yours one day'. Eventually, the claimant stayed at Mrs Royle's house most nights, to provide security. Mrs Royle died intestate. The claimant made a claim to her entire estate, valued at £1,285,000, based on proprietary estoppel. Alternatively, he claimed a sum equal to the value of the house and furniture, valued at £435,000. At first instance the claimant was awarded £200,000. He appealed. There was no argument that an estoppel had arisen; it was clearly established that there had been an expectation or assurance, detrimental reliance and unconscionability. The appeal centred on the amount awarded. Aldous LJ first of all explained what the decision had been at first instance, and summarised the arguments on appeal.

LORD JUSTICE ALDOUS

15. The judge then had to decide what was the appropriate relief. He started by referring to *Crabb v Arun District Council* [1976] Ch 179, [1975] 3 All ER 865 at p 198 of the former report. He went on to refer to a number of authorities and concluded that he should be guided by the approach of Robert Walker LJ and the other members of the Court of Appeal in *Gillett v Holt* [2001] Ch 210, [2000] 2 All ER 289. He concluded that he had a discretion to be exercised judicially in the light of all the relevant circumstances. He took into account, first that Mr Jennings did not know the extent of Mrs Royle's wealth and second, that the value of her actual estate and even the part known to Mr Jennings was out of all proportion to what Mr Jennings might reasonably have charged for the services he provided free. He then considered whether it would be equitable for Mr Jennings to take the house and the furniture which were the minimum he expected, and also what the judge called the problem of proportionality. The judge reminded himself that the house was valued at £420,000 and was not a suitable house for Mr Jennings to reside in on his own and he took into account that Mrs Royle had no special obligations to her family. He said that to reward an employee on the scale of £420,000 was excessive. He also compared the cost of full-time nursing care, which he estimated at £200,000, with the value of the house. He reasoned that Mr Jennings would probably need £150,000 to buy a house. He concluded:

"I do not think that he could complain that he had been unfairly treated if he had been left £200,000 in Mrs Royle's will. Most people would say that she would, at least, then have performed her promise to see him all right. The quality of her assurance affects not only questions of belief, encouragement, reliance and detriment, but also unconscionability and the extent of the equity.

In my judgment the minimum necessary to satisfy the equity in the present case is the sum of £200,000."

The Appeal

16. Mr Warner, who appeared for Mr Jennings, submitted that in a case like the present, where the claimant had established his claim of proprietary estoppel, the basic rule was that the established equity should be satisfied by making

good the expectation. He accepted that there were exceptions, for example where there had been misconduct, but this case did not fall within any of them. Mr Warner went on to submit that Mr Jennings had expected to be left Mrs Royle's whole estate and that is what the judge should have ordered. If the expectation was only the house and furniture, then that was the minimum that the judge should have awarded.

17. The first submission, that the award should equal the whole estate, cannot succeed having regard to the findings of fact made by the judge. He held that Mrs Royle had said she would see him all right and "This will all be yours one day." By the word "this" the judge must have been referring to the house and furniture. He also held that Mr Jennings had no idea what Mrs Royle owned, apart from the house and furniture and therefore could not have expected to receive anything more. There was no finding that Mrs Royle had led Mr Jennings to believe that he would get more than the house and furniture. That being so, any award upon the basis that the equity should be satisfied by awarding a sum equal to the expectation of Mr Jennings could not exceed the value of the house and furniture (£435,000), perhaps reduced by the amount of inheritance tax that the property would bear.

18. Miss Rich, who appeared for the Respondents, supported the conclusion and reasoning of the judge. She submitted that to arrive at the correct award, the starting point was the claimant's expectation as that would indicate the maximum extent of the equity. However the court's task did not end there. The ultimate aim was to achieve justice. That was achieved by making the award proportionate to the expectation and the detriment suffered.

In deciding the appropriate remedy, Aldous LJ surveyed the authorities. He concluded that in *Crabb v Arun DC* the award of an easement without any payment exceeded the claimant's expectations, but was awarded because it was just to do so. In *Pascoe v Turner,* the perfection of the gift of the fee simple was ordered, not because that was what was expected, but because that was what was just in all the circumstances. He further acknowledged that in *Sledmore v Dalby,* proportionality was at the heart of the judgments. He continued:

36. ... There is a clear line of authority from at least Crabb to the present day which establishes that once the elements of proprietary estoppel are established an equity arises. The value of that equity will depend upon all the circumstances including the expectation and the detriment. The task of the court is to do justice. The most essential requirement is that there must be proportionality between the expectation and the detriment.

 Alert

37. Mr Warner warned against the conclusion I have reached. He submitted that it led to uncertainty and that the appropriate course was to satisfy the expectation. I accept that the flexible approach adopted in the past may mean that there is room for what has been referred to as a judicial discretion, but the rigidity of the approach advocated by Mr Warner can lead to injustice which could not form the basis of an equitable result. One only has to alter the facts of this case to

illustrate the unsatisfactory nature of Mr Warner's submissions. The expectation was that Mr Jennings would receive the house and furniture valued at £435,000. If he had been left £5 or £50,000 or £200,000 in Mrs Royle's will, or she had died one month, one year or twenty years after making the representation relied on, should the court award the same sum? Yes, said Mr Warner. The result could then have been that Mr Jennings would receive £635,000 made up of the expectation and the legacy of £200,000, or perhaps, £435,000 in total, even when the detriment was say £800.

38. The judge was right to conclude that the award must be proportionate. He took into account the relevant factors as placed before him, namely the expectation, the detriment, the position of Mr Jennings and the amount available. His conclusion was the result of a judgment to which he was entitled to come. I would not interfere with it and would dismiss the appeal.

LORD JUSTICE ROBERT WALKER

50. To recapitulate: there is a category of case in which the benefactor and the claimant have reached a mutual understanding which is in reasonably clear terms but does not amount to a contract. I have already referred to the typical case of a carer who has the expectation of coming into the benefactor's house, either outright or for life. In such a case the court's natural response is to fulfil the claimant's expectations. But if the claimant's expectations are uncertain, or extravagant, or out of all proportion to the detriment which the claimant has suffered, the court can and should recognise that the claimant's equity should be satisfied in another (and generally more limited) way.

 Alert

51. But that does not mean that the court should in such a case abandon expectations completely, and look to the detriment suffered by the claimant as defining the appropriate measure of relief. Indeed in many cases the detriment may be even more difficult to quantify, in financial terms, than the claimant's expectations. Detriment can be quantified with reasonable precision if it consists solely of expenditure on improvements to another person's house, and in some cases of that sort an equitable charge for the expenditure may be sufficient to satisfy the equity (see Snell's Equity 30th ed para 39-21 and the authorities mentioned in that paragraph). But the detriment of an ever-increasing burden of care for an elderly person, and of having to be subservient to his or her moods and wishes, is very difficult to quantify in money terms. Moreover the claimant may not be motivated solely by reliance on the benefactor's assurances, and may receive some countervailing benefits (such as free bed and board). In such circumstances the court has to exercise a wide judgmental discretion.

52. It would be unwise to attempt any comprehensive enumeration of the factors relevant to the exercise of the court's discretion, or to suggest any hierarchy of factors. In my view they include, but are not limited to, the factors mentioned in Dr Gardner's third hypothesis (misconduct of the claimant as in *J Willis & Sons v*

Willis 277 EG 1133, [1986] 1 EGLR 62 or particularly oppressive conduct on the part of the defendant, as in *Crabb v Arun District Council* or *Pascoe v Turner*). To these can safely be added the court's recognition that it cannot compel people who have fallen out to live peaceably together, so that there may be a need for a clean break; alterations in the benefactor's assets and circumstances, especially where the benefactor's assurances have been given, and the claimant's detriment has been suffered, over a long period of years; the likely effect of taxation; and (to a limited degree) the other claims (legal or moral) on the benefactor or his or her estate. No doubt there are many other factors which it may be right for the court to take into account in particular factual situations...

55. ...I have made some references to the general trend of Australian jurisprudence in this area. It is unnecessary to attempt any detailed study of the different views expressed by the High Court in the *Verwayen* case (which was concerned with estoppel in the very different context of litigation arising out of personal injuries suffered in a collision between two warships) or of Australian cases since then.

56. However I respectfully agree with the view expressed by Hobhouse LJ in *Sledmore v Dalby* (1996) 72 P&CR 196, that the principle of proportionality (between remedy and detriment), emphasised by Mason CJ in *Verwayen*, is relevant in England also. As Hobhouse LJ observed at p 209, to recognise the need for proportionality:

" . . . is to say little more than that the end result must be a just one having regard to the assumption made by the party asserting the estoppel and the detriment which he has experienced."

The essence of the doctrine of proprietary estoppel is to do what is necessary to avoid an unconscionable result, and a disproportionate remedy cannot be the right way of going about that.

Sledmore v Dalby (1996) 72 P&CR 196

Panel: Butler-Sloss, Roch and Hobhouse LJJ

Facts: This case involved a dispute between a mother-in-law and her son-in-law. Mr and Mrs Sledmore owned the freehold of a house. Mr and Mrs Dalby, who were the owners' daughter and son-in-law, moved into the property in the 1960s as tenants. However, the Dalbys stopped paying rent when they hit hard times. The tenancy came to an end in 1976 but the Dalbys continued to live there. The Sledmores told the Dalbys that they intended to give the property to them. Mr Dalby, with the encouragement of the Sledmores, carried out substantial improvement work to the property, including building a new bathroom and bedroom, installing central heating and renovating the kitchen. Mr Sledmore gave his share of the property to Mrs Sledmore. She made a will leaving it to her daughter, Mrs Dalby, to the exclusion of Mr Dalby. Mr Sledmore and Mrs Dalby both died in the early 1980s. Mr Dalby met a new partner. He spent only a few nights of the week at the property, which was by now occupied by one of his grown up daughters. Mrs Sledmore wanted possession of the property as her own house was too big for her and in a state of disrepair. At first instance the judge dismissed the claim for possession and awarded Mr Dalby a licence to occupy for as long as he wished. Mrs Sledmore appealed.

LORD JUSTICE ROCH

The respondent's expectation, in my opinion, would have been that he would remain in the house certainly as long as his wife was alive and he was living with her and, probably, whilst his daughters were still living with their parents or, following his wife's death with him, if only because the prime reason for the improvement in the house was that the elder daughter had by 1977 reached the age where she needed a bedroom of her own.

The task for a court in determining the extent of an equity created by proprietary estoppel is set out in the 29th Edition of Snell's Equity at page 576.

"The extent of the equity is to have made good, so far as may fairly be done between the parties, the expectations of A which O has encouraged. A's expectation or belief is the maximum extent of the equity, so that if, for example, A's expectation is that he could stay in a house for the rest of his life, this will not be given effect to in such a way as to confer on him the rights of a tenant for life under the Settled Land Act 1925, for that, with its concomitant right of sale, would give him a greater interest than he was entitled to expect. Accordingly A may have to be content with something less than his expectations, eg some form of lease at a rent. In other cases a full life interest operating under the Settled Land Act 1925 may be given. Further, the position of O has to be considered. Thus the courts are reluctant to compel two persons to live together when they have fallen out, and even after O has died, the due administration of his estate and the rights of those taking under it are factors to be considered."

I would respectfully adopt that passage as an accurate statement of the decided cases and the law. In the present case the respondent clearly has assumed that he will be allowed to stay in this house for the rest of his life rent free. In my judgment this is a case where the respondent has to be content with something less than his expectations. The Recorder should have considered the position of the appellant and her needs and balanced those against the present use of the premises made by the respondent and his present need for them.

 Alert

Although the Recorder acknowledged the existence of the principles stated in the passage from Snell which I have cited, ... nowhere does the Recorder make any assessment of the Respondent's present use of and need for the house on the one hand or of the appellant's situation and need for the house on the other. Nor does the Recorder at any point ask himself the question whether it was still inequitable to allow the respondent's expectation to be defeated by permitting the appellant to enforce her legal rights, as owner of the property.

The conclusion that I have reached is that it is no longer inequitable to allow the expectation created in the respondent's mind by Mr Sledmore's oral statements and by his encouragement of the respondent to carry out the improvements to the house which were carried out between 1976 and 1979 to be defeated. The respondent has lived

 Alert

rent free in this accommodation for over 18 years. During that time the insurance of the property has been paid for by the Sledmore family and the property has been reroofed at their expense. The use made by the respondent of the house at the time of the trial was minimal and it is clear that there was accommodation for him elsewhere. He is a man in employment and therefore capable of paying for his accommodation. Whilst the respondent has lived in this house his elder daughter has married and left home and his younger daughter has reached the age of 27 and is able to maintain herself.

On the other hand, the evidence indicates that the appellant is vulnerable in that she is liable to lose her present accommodation and that she has a pressing need for this house which is her property…

I would allow this appeal and make an order for possession in the appellant's favour on the basis that the minimum equity to do justice to the respondent on the facts of this case was an equity which has now expired.

The judge decided that any rights which Mr Dalby may have had, had been satisfied over the years. Hobhouse LJ went further in his criticism of the first instance decision.

HOBHOUSE L.J:

…The decision of the County Court Judge in the present case was said to be an application of the principles of equitable estoppel, yet his conclusion produces a clearinjustice. The doctrine of estoppel exists for the purpose of enabling courts to do justice, modifying what otherwise might be the strict legal rights of the parties. If the supposed application of such a doctrine produces injustice not justice, then something has gone wrong.

He reviewed the facts and the first instance decision and continued:

The disproportion of this result is obvious as, in my judgment, is its injustice. The Defendant by virtue of carrying out very limited improvements to number 15A between 1976 and 1978 and incurring an expenditure which was likewise limited, has been held to have acquired a right to occupy number 15A for the remainder of his natural life rent free to the exclusion of Mrs Sledmore, although his tenancy has been lawfully terminated and he has no right to an extension of that tenancy. Further, he has, since 1976, had the benefit of the occupation of number 15A, together with such members of the family as were living there from time to time, without paying any rent for such occupation. The primary case which he has been presenting to the courts, right up to the time that he abandoned it before this Court, was that his expenditure in 1976 to 1978 entitled him without more to have transferred to him the freehold title.

He then explained the difference in emphasis between a claim based on promissory estoppel and one based on proprietary estoppel:

…In estoppel by representation or promise, a representation or promise must be clear and unequivocal; provided that there is reliance, the detriment element may be limited. In proprietary estoppel the emphasis is the other way round: the detriment must be distinct and substantial; the conduct of the affected party may be no more than acquiescence. It is said that the effect of proprietary estoppel is permanent, whereas estoppel by representation is merely temporary.

He quoted from the judgment of Mason CJ in the Australian case of *Commonwealth of Australia v Verwayen* (1990) 95 ALR 321 and continued:

The other aspect clearly illustrated by the quotations which I have made from Mason CJ is the need for proportionality. This is to say little more than that the end result must be a just one having regard to the assumptions made by the party asserting the estoppel and the detriment which he has experienced. Here it is unreal to suggest that the conclusion of the County Court Judge is proportionate to what happened over 15 years earlier. Similarly, it is unreal to say that the Defendant has suffered any injustice. He expended money in 1976 to 1978 upon his then family home and he and his family fully enjoyed the benefits of such expenditure. He has also enjoyed within the same framework over a period of over 15 years the rent-free occupation of the property. By the same token it cannot be properly said that there was anything unconscionable in Mrs Sledmore seeking the possession of number 15A in 1990.

In my judgment there is no estoppel operating against the Plaintiff. Her claim in this action falsifies no legitimate assumption or expectation. The effect of any equity that may at any earlier time have existed has long since been exhausted and no injustice has been done to the Defendant. The Plaintiff is entitled to an order for possession...

Further Reading

MacKenzie & Phillips, *Textbook on Land Law*, (15th Edition), Chapter 21

Further Reading

Part II

Three Key Proprietary Rights

6

Covenants in Freehold Land

Topic List

1   Common Law
2   Equity

Introduction

Covenants are frequently made between freehold owners of land where an owner sells part of his land to a buyer and asks the buyer to enter into a covenant to protect the value of the seller's retained land. The covenant may be a positive one, obliging the 4covenantor to take some action to comply with it, or a negative one, preventing the covenantor from taking some action. The covenant is binding between the original parties under normal contract law rules.

When the two pieces of land are sold by the original parties, the issue to address is whether the successor in title to the dominant land (the land with the benefit of the covenant) is able to enforce the covenant against the successor in title to the servient land (the land with the burden of the covenant). There are different rules to apply in order to establish whether the benefit has run with the dominant land and the burden with the servient land. There are also different rules depending on whether the benefit and burden are being enforced at common law or in equity.

6.1 Common Law

Generally the burden of a covenant will not run with the servient land at common law. This was confirmed in 1885 in *Austerberry v Corporation* of Oldham (1885) 29 ChD 750 and was reconfirmed over one hundred years later in the following case.

Rhone and another v Stephens [1994] 2 AC 310

Panel: Lord Templeman, Lord Oliver of Aylmerton, Lord Woolf, Lord Lloyd of Berwick and Lord Nolan

Facts: The owner of a freehold house divided it into two separate properties, Walford House and Walford Cottage. Part of the roof of Walford House hung over part of Walford Cottage and each property enjoyed a right of support from the other. The owner sold Walford Cottage (and retained the house), and he covenanted in clause 3 of the conveyance to maintain in a wind and watertight condition the part of the roof of Walford House that covered Walford Cottage. After the claimants had purchased Walford Cottage, the condition of the roof covering the cottage started to deteriorate and water began to leak into the cottage. The claimants said that they had the benefit of the covenant as it had been expressly assigned to them when the cottage was conveyed to them. They sued the defendant, the successor in title to the original common owner and owner of Walford House, for breach of covenant. In the County Court, the judge held that the claimants were entitled to enforce the covenant. The defendant appealed to the Court of Appeal, who allowed the appeal, holding that positive covenants do not run with freehold land. The claimants then appealed to the House of Lords.

LORD TEMPLEMAN

My Lords, this appeal raises the question of the enforceability of positive covenants between owners of freehold estates and involves consideration of the rule in *Austerberry v. Oldham Corporation* (1885) 29 Ch.D. 750.

...As between persons interested in land other than as landlord and tenant, the benefit of a covenant may run with the land at law but not the burden: see the Austerberry case.

Thus clause 3 of the ... conveyance ... did not confer on the owner for the time being of Walford Cottage the right at common law to compel the owner for the time being of Walford House to repair the roof or to obtain damages for breach of the covenant to repair. ...

My Lords, equity supplements but does not contradict the common law. ... In *Tulk v. Moxhay* (1848) 2 Ph. 774, a purchaser of land covenanted that no buildings would be erected on Leicester Square. A subsequent purchaser of Leicester Square was restrained from building. The conveyance to the original purchaser deprived him and every subsequent purchaser taking with notice of the covenant of the right, otherwise part and parcel of the freehold, to develop the square by the construction of buildings. Equity does not contradict the common law by enforcing a restrictive covenant against a successor in title of the covenantor but prevents the successor from exercising a right which he never acquired. ...

Link

see Equity

Equity can thus prevent or punish the breach of a negative covenant which restricts the user of land or the exercise of other rights in connection with land. Restrictive covenants deprive an owner of a right which he could otherwise exercise. Equity cannot compel an owner to comply with a positive covenant entered into by his predecessors in title without flatly contradicting the common law rule that a person cannot be made liable upon a contract unless he was a party to it. Enforcement of a positive covenant lies in contract; a positive covenant compels an owner to exercise his rights. Enforcement of a negative covenant lies in property; a negative covenant deprives the owner of a right over property. ...

...[I]n *Haywood v. Brunswick Permanent Benefit Building Society* (1881) 8 Q.B.D. 403 ... land had been conveyed in consideration of a rent charge and a covenant to build and repair buildings; a mortgagee of the land was held not to be liable on the covenant either at law or in equity although the mortgagee had notice of the covenant. Brett L.J. said, at p. 408, that *Tulk v. Moxhay*:

"decided that an assignee taking land subject to a certain class of covenants is bound by such covenants if he has notice of them, and that the class of covenants comprehended within the rule is that covenants restricting the mode of using the land only will be enforced. ..."

...Cotton L.J. also said that *Tulk v. Moxhay*:

"lays down the real principle that an equity attaches to the owner of the land. ...The covenant to repair can only be enforced by making the owner put his hand into his pocket, and there is nothing which would justify us in going that length." ...

In the *Austerberry case*, 29 Ch.D. 750 the owners of a site of a road covenanted that they and their successors in title would make the road and keep it in repair. The road was sold to the defendants and it was held that the repair covenant could not be enforced against them. Cotton L.J. said, at pp. *773-774*:

"undoubtedly, where there is a restrictive covenant, the burden and benefit of which do not run at law, courts of equity restrain anyone who takes the property with notice of that covenant from using it in a way inconsistent with the covenant. But here the covenant which is attempted to be insisted upon on this appeal is a covenant to lay out money in doing certain work upon this land; and, that being so ... that is not a covenant which a court of equity will enforce: it will not enforce a covenant not running at law when it is sought to enforce that covenant in such a way as to require the successors in title of the covenantor to spend money, and in that way to undertake a burden upon themselves. ..."

...For over 100 years it has been clear and accepted law that equity will enforce negative covenants against freehold land but has no power to enforce positive covenants against successors in title of the land. To enforce a positive covenant would be to enforce a personal obligation against a person who has not covenanted. To enforce negative covenants is only to treat the land as subject to a restriction.

Alert

...[Y]our Lordships were invited to overrule the decision of the Court of Appeal in the *Austerberry case*. To do so would destroy the distinction between law and equity and to convert the rule of equity into a rule of notice. It is plain ... that judicial legislation to overrule the *Austerberry case* would create a number of difficulties, anomalies and uncertainties and affect the rights and liabilities of people who have for over 100 years bought and sold land in the knowledge, imparted at an elementary stage to every student of the law of real property, that positive covenants, affecting freehold land are not directly enforceable except against the original covenantor. ...

Conditions can be attached to the exercise of a power in express terms or by implication. *Halsall v. Brizell* [[1957] Ch. 169] was just such a case and I have no difficulty in wholeheartedly agreeing with the decision. It does not follow that any condition can be rendered enforceable by attaching it to a right nor does it follow that every burden imposed by a conveyance may be enforced by depriving the covenantor's successor in title of every benefit which he enjoyed thereunder. The condition must be relevant to the exercise of the right. In *Halsall v. Brizell* there were reciprocal benefits and burdens enjoyed by the users of the roads and sewers. In the present case ... the 1960 conveyance imposes reciprocal benefits and burdens of support but clause 3 which imposed an obligation to repair the roof is an independent provision. In *Halsall v. Brizell* the defendant could, at least in theory, choose between enjoying the right and paying his proportion of the cost or alternatively giving up the right and saving his money. In the present case the owners of Walford House could not in theory or in practice be deprived of the benefit of the mutual rights of support if they failed to repair the roof.

In the result I would dismiss the appeal… .

The House of Lords unanimously dismissed the appeal and refused to overturn *Austerberry v Corporation of Oldham*.

The general rule, therefore, is that the burden of positive covenants will not run with the land at common law (or in equity). However, there is an exception to this rule which was examined in the case of *Halsall v Brizell*, referred to in Lord Templeman's judgment above, and confirmed in the following case.

Thamesmead Town Limited v Allotey (1998) 3 EGLR 97

Panel: Butler-Sloss, Peter Gibson and Hobhouse LJJ

Facts: A housing estate known as the Thamesmead Estate (the Estate) was constructed and leased by London County Council to local tenants. The freehold title to the whole Estate was later transferred to the claimant. Mr and Mrs Boorman bought the freehold title to one of the houses on the Estate and the transfer of the property to them included rights to use the roads and paths on the Estate and to the passage of water, gas and electricity through the pipes, drains and wires running under the Estate. Mr and Mrs Boorman covenanted that they would contribute a proportion of the repair and maintenance costs of the roads, paths, pipes, drains and wires and the communal garden areas on the Estate (although the Boormans had not been granted any rights to use the communal garden areas). Mr and Mrs Boorman later sold the house to the defendant. Mr Allotey refused to pay the contributions and the claimant sued him for the outstanding payments. The judge at first instance held that the defendant was only liable to pay the costs relating to the rights that he had chosen to exercise, which totalled £41.65. The claimant appealed to the Court of Appeal.

LORD JUSTICE PETER GIBSON

At law it has long been the rule that the benefit of a covenant, whether positive or negative, made with a covenantee having an interest in the land to which it relates runs with the land but that the burden of a covenant does not… . Although equity relaxed the rigours of the common law by the doctrine of *Tulk v. Moxhay* (1848) 2 Ph. 774, it did so only in relation to restrictive covenants. It was held by this court in *Austerberry v. Oldham Corporation* (1885) 29 Ch D 750 that the *Tulk v. Moxhay* doctrine would not be extended so as to bind in equity a purchaser taking with notice of a positive covenant which did not run with the land at law. The House of Lords one hundred years later in *Rhone v. Stevens* [sic] [1994] 2 A.C. 310, was invited to overrule that decision, but the rule in the *Austerberry case* was affirmed. However, at least one exception to the rule has been recognised in that a successor in title to a covenantor may be held not to be entitled to take the benefit of a transaction without undertaking the burden imposed by the transaction. The scope and application of that exception are the subject matter of this appeal. …

In *Halsall v. Brizell* land was sold in building plots ... and the owners of the plots ... covenanted that they and their successors in title would pay a due proportion of the expenses of maintenance of the roads, sewers promenade and sea wall... . Upjohn J ... said that it was plain that the successors in title to the covenantors could not be sued on the covenants. However, he continued:

"But it is conceded that it is ancient law that a man cannot take benefit under a deed without subscribing to the obligations thereunder. ...If the defendants did not desire to take the benefit of this deed ... they could not be under any liability to pay the obligations thereunder. ..."

...[In] *Rhone v Stephens* ... [t]he reasoning of Lord Templeman suggests that there are two requirements for the enforceability of a positive covenant against a successor in title to the covenantor. The first is that the condition of discharging the burden must be relevant to the exercise of the rights which enable the benefit to be obtained. In *Rhone v. Stephens* the mutual obligation of support was unrelated to and independent of the covenant to maintain the roof. The second is that the successors in title must have the opportunity to choose whether to take the benefit or having taken it to renounce it, even if only in theory, and thereby to escape the burden and that the successors in title can be deprived of the benefit if they fail to assume the burden. ...

 Alert

Lord Templeman was plainly seeking to restrict, not enlarge, the scope of the exception from the rule that positive covenants affecting freehold land are not directly enforceable except against the original covenantor. Lord Templeman treated *Halsall v. Brizell* as a case where the right to use the estate roads and sewers was conditional on a payment of a due proportion of the maintenance expenses for those facilities. Whilst agreeing with the decision, Lord Templeman made clear that for a burden to be enforceable it must be relevant to the benefit. He said that simply to attach a right to a condition for payment would not render that condition enforceable. Similarly, it is not possible to enforce every burden in a conveyance by depriving the covenantor's successors in title of every benefit which he enjoyed under the conveyance. There must be a correlation between the burden and the benefit which the successor has chosen to take. Lord Templeman plainly rejected the notion that taking a benefit under a conveyance was sufficient to make every burden of the conveyance enforceable. Further, there is no authority to suggest that any benefit obtained by a successor in title, once the property has been transferred to him, to enable the enforcement of a burden under the conveyance is sufficient, even if that benefit was not conferred as of right by the conveyance. In my judgment, it cannot be sufficient that the taking of an incidental benefit should enable the enforcement of a burden against a person who has not himself covenanted to undertake the particular burden. ...I have already pointed out that not only is there no right conferred on the defendant by the ... transfer to use the communal areas but also the plaintiff has no obligation to maintain those areas.

...As I have already pointed out, in *Halsall v. Brizell*, at 182, Upjohn J. was expressing the relevant principle in terms that the successors in title could choose whether or not to take the benefit of the deed. Similarly, in *Rhone v. Stephens*, Lord Templeman in distinguishing *Halsall v. Brizell*, expressed himself in terms which indicated that the successors in title had to have a choice whether to exercise the right or, having taken the right, whether to renounce the benefit. Lord Templeman was not expressing himself in terms that the successors in title had to have a choice whether to acquire the rights at all. ...

It follows that I would dismiss this appeal essentially for the reasons given by the judge. But I cannot forbear to add my voice to the criticisms of the existing law. ...

The Court of Appeal unanimously dismissed the appeal.

Lord Justice Peter Gibson approved of the narrow application of the rule which Lord Templeman had confirmed in *Rhone v Stephens*, based on the earlier case *of Halsall v Brizell*. The burden of a covenant will only run with the land in extremely limited circumstances at common law.

In relation to the running of the benefit of a covenant, there are several rules to comply with at common law in order for the benefit to pass by implication. One of these rules, that the covenant must touch and concern the dominant land, is examined in some detail in the following case.

P & A Swift Investments (a firm) v Combined English Stores Group plc [1989] AC 632

Panel: Lord Keith of Kinkel, Lord Roskill, Lord Templeman, Lord Ackner and Lord Oliver of Aylmerton

Facts: A landlord granted an underlease to a subsidiary company of the defendant (CES). CES acted as guarantor and guaranteed that the undertenant would pay the rent and observe the covenants in the lease. The leasehold reversion was assigned to the claimant. The undertenant failed to pay the rent and went into voluntary liquidation. CES refused to pay the outstanding rent, stating that the benefit of the guarantee covenant had not passed to the claimant, the new landlord. The claimant sued CES for the outstanding rent and the judge in the High Court found in favour of the claimant. CES appealed, arguing that the guarantee covenant did not touch and concern the land, so the benefit had not passed to the claimant. The case was referred to the House of Lords to rule on the meaning of 'touch and concern the land', and whether this particular covenant was one which did touch and concern the land.

LORD OLIVER OF AYLMERTON

...[The] claim to enforce rests upon the common law rule, under which the benefit of the covenant would run with the land if, but only if, the assignee had the legal estate in the land and the covenant was one which "touched and concerned" the land. There is no question but that the first of these conditions is complied with in the instant case, but it is said ... that the covenant of a surety is no more than a covenant to pay a sum of money which is entirely collateral and does not therefore touch and concern the land. ...

In my opinion the question of whether a surety's covenant in a lease touches and concerns the land falls to be determined by the same test ... adopted by Farwell J. in *Rogers v Hosegood* [1900] 2 Ch. 388, 395:

Link

Rogers v Hosegood

"the covenant must either affect the land as regards mode of occupation, or it must be such as per se, and not merely from collateral circumstances, affects the value of the land." ...

Formulations of definitive tests are always dangerous, but it seems to me that, without claiming to expound an exhaustive guide, the following provides a satisfactory working test for whether, in any given case, a covenant touches and concerns the land: (1) the covenant benefits only the reversioner for time being, and if separated from the reversion ceases to be of benefit to the covenantee; (2) the covenant affects the nature, quality, mode of user or value of the land of the reversioner; (3) the covenant is not expressed to be personal (that is to say neither being given only to a specific reversioner nor in respect of the obligations only of a specific tenant); (4) the fact that a covenant is to pay a sum of money will not prevent it from touching and concerning the land so long as the three foregoing conditions are satisfied and the covenant is connected with something to be done on to or in relation to the land.

Alert

...It follows that I would dismiss this appeal.

The House of Lords unanimously dismissed the appeal.

Although the case relates to the running of leasehold covenants, the meaning of 'touch and concern the land' also applies to freehold covenants. In Lord Oliver of Aylmerton's test, the words 'reversion' and 'reversioner' may be replaced by the words 'dominant land' and 'covenantee' respectively.

A further test for whether the benefit runs at common law is that the covenantee must have held a legal estate in the land at the time that the covenant was made, and the successor in title must also hold a legal estate at the time of enforcement. Lord Justice Denning confirms this test in the following case.

Smith and Snipes Hall Farm Limited v River Douglas Catchment Board [1949] 2 KB 500

Panel: Tucker, Somervell and Denning LJJ

Statute: Law of Property Act 1925 s 78

Facts: The defendant, the local drainage board, covenanted with eleven different owners of freehold land situated next to a river that it would widen and repair the banks of the river and maintain those banks in the future to prevent flooding. The landowners agreed that they would, in return, contribute to the costs of repair. One of the covenantees transferred her land to Mr Smith. The transfer agreement included a clause which expressly assigned the benefit of the covenant. Mr Smith orally leased his land on an annual basis to the second claimant. In 1946, the river burst its banks and Mr Smith's/his tenant's land was flooded. The claimants claimed that the repair work had not been carried out properly by the defendant and sued the defendant for damages. The judge at first instance found in favour of the defendant and the claimants appealed to the Court of Appeal.

LORD JUSTICE DENNING

...The damage has been suffered partly by the man who purchased the land, but principally by the tenants, and the question is whether they can sue on the contract. ...

The particular application of the principle with which we are concerned here is the case of covenants made with the owner of the land to which they relate. ...Such covenants are clearly intended, and usually expressed, to be for the benefit of whomsoever should be the owner of the land for the time being; and at common law each successive owner has a sufficient interest to sue because he holds the same estate as the original owner. ...If a successor in title were not allowed to sue it would mean that the covenantor could break his contract with impunity, for it is clear that the original owner, after he has parted with the land, could recover no more than nominal damages for any breach that occurred thereafter. It was always held, however, at common law that, in order that a successor in title should be entitled to sue, he must be of the same estate as the original owner. ...[However] s. 78 of the Law of Property Act, 1925 ... provides that a covenant relating to any land of the covenantee shall be deemed to be made with the covenantee and his successors in title, "and the persons deriving title under him or them" and shall have effect as if such successors "and other persons" were expressed.

The covenant of the catchment board in this case clearly relates to the land of the covenantees. It was a covenant to do work on the land for the benefit of the land. By the statute, therefore, it is to be deemed to be made, not only with the original owner, but also with the purchasers of the land and their tenants as if they were expressed. Now if they were expressed, it would be clear that the covenant was made for their benefit; and they clearly have sufficient interest to entitle them to enforce it because they have suffered the damage. The result is that the plaintiffs come within the principle whereby a person interested can sue on a contract expressly made for his benefit....

In my opinion, therefore, the board are liable to the plaintiffs in damages for breach of covenant. ...I agree, therefore, that the appeal should be allowed.

 Alert

The Court of Appeal unanimously allowed the appeal.

Lord Justice Denning's wide interpretation of the Law of Property Act 1925 (LPA 1925) s 78 allows more parties to enforce the benefit of a covenant at common law than was previously thought prior to 1926. Section 78 may also be used as evidence of the intention of the original parties for the benefit to run – the final requirement for implied passing of the benefit at common law. The effects of section 78 in equity are examined below.

As the rules for the passing of the benefit and burden of freehold covenants at common law were deemed to be inadequate, equity developed rules to assist successors in title wishing to enforce covenants against the party in breach of covenant.

6.2 Equity

Tulk v Moxhay (1848) 2 Ph 774

Panel: Lord Cottenham

Facts: In 1808, Tulk sold land in the centre of Leicester Square (in London) to Elms, who covenanted to "keep and maintain the said piece of ground and square garden, and the iron railing round the same in its then form, and in sufficient and proper repair as a square garden and pleasure ground, in an open state, uncovered with any buildings, in neat and ornamental order". The land in Leicester Square was later sold by Elms to Moxhay, who had notice of the covenant, but declared an intention to build on the land. Tulk sought an injunction to prevent the building, which was granted by the Master of the Rolls. The defendant appealed, stating that the burden of the covenant did not run with the land at law.

LORD COTTENHAM

That this Court has jurisdiction to enforce a contract between the owner of land and his neighbour purchasing a part of it, that the latter shall either use or abstain from using the land purchased in a particular way, is what I never knew disputed. Here there is no question about the contract: the owner of certain houses in the square sells the land adjoining, with a covenant from the purchaser not to use it for any other purpose than as a square garden. And it is now contended, not that the vendee could violate that contract, but that he might sell the piece of land, and that the purchaser from him may violate it without this Court having any power to interfere. If that were so, it would be impossible for an owner of land to sell part of it without incurring the risk of rendering what he retains worthless. It is said that, the covenant being one which does not run with the land, this Court cannot enforce it; but the question is, not whether the covenant runs with the land, but whether a party shall be permitted to use the land in a manner inconsistent with the contract entered into by his vendor, and with notice of which he purchased. ...

That the question does not depend upon whether the covenant runs with the land is evident from this, that if there was a mere agreement and no covenant, this Court would enforce it against a party purchasing with notice of it; for if an equity is attached to the property by the owner, no one purchasing with notice of that equity can stand in a different situation from the party from whom he purchased. ...

 Alert

The appeal was dismissed.

The modern equitable rules relating to the running of the burden of restrictive covenants derive from this case. Originally the rule was that a purchaser who bought servient land with notice of a restrictive covenant affecting the land was bound by that covenant. This has evolved into the equitable rules which apply today.

The following case sets out another equitable rule, namely that the covenant must benefit land belonging to the covenantee.

London County Council v Allen and others [1914] 3 KB 642

Panel: Buckley and Kennedy LJJ and Scrutton J

Facts: A landowner applied to the claimant (London County Council) for planning permission to construct a road on his land. The claimant granted the permission, subject to a covenant by the landowner not to build on the part of his land at the end of the proposed road, in case the claimant itself should decide to carry on constructing a longer road. The claimant did not own any land adjacent to the landowner's land. The landowner transferred his land to the defendant, his wife, who had notice of the covenant, but proceeded to build houses on the land which was the subject of the covenant without the claimant's consent. The claimant sued the defendant for breach of covenant, and the judge at first instance found in favour of the claimant, awarding damages, rather than a mandatory injunction to remove the houses. The defendant appealed to the Court of Appeal.

LORD JUSTICE BUCKLEY

...The plaintiffs at the date of the deed of covenant had no estate or interest in any land adjoining or in any manner affected by the observance or non-observance of the covenant contained in the deed. ...The short proposition is that as [a] matter of law a derivative owner of land, deriving title under a person who has entered into a restrictive covenant concerning the land, is not bound by the covenant even if he took with notice of its existence if the covenantee has no land adjoining or affected by the observance or non-observance of the covenant. I proceed to examine how the law upon this point stands upon the authorities.

...*Tulk v. Moxhay* [(1848) 2 Ph. 774] established that as between the grantor of a restrictive covenant affecting certain land and the owner of adjoining land the covenantee may in equity enforce the covenant against the derivative owner taking with notice. The reasoning of Lord Cottenham's judgment in *Tulk v. Moxhay* [(1848) 2 Ph. 774] is that if an owner of land sells part of it reserving the rest, and takes from his purchaser a covenant that the purchaser shall use or abstain from using the land purchased in a particular way, that covenant (being one for the protection of the land reserved) is enforceable against a sub-purchaser with notice. The reason given is that, if that were not so, it would be impossible for an owner of land to sell part of it without incurring the risk of rendering what he retains worthless. If the vendor has retained no land which can be protected by the restrictive covenant, the basis of the reasoning of the judgment is swept away. ...In the present case we are asked to extend the doctrine of Tulk v. Moxhay [(1848) 2 Ph. 774] so as to affirm that a restrictive covenant can be enforced against a derivative owner taking with notice by a person who never has had or who does not retain any land to be protected by the restrictive covenant in question. In my opinion the doctrine does not extend to that case. ...The doctrine ceases to be applicable when the person seeking to enforce the covenant against the derivative owner has no land to be protected by the negative covenant. ...

 Alert

Upon the authorities, therefore, as a whole I am of opinion that the doctrine in *Tulk v. Moxhay* [(1848) 2 Ph. 774] does not extend to the case in which the covenantee has no land capable of enjoying, as against the land of the covenantor, the benefit of the restrictive covenant. ...Where the covenantee has no land, the derivative owner claiming under the covenantor is bound neither in contract nor by the equitable doctrine which attaches in the case where there is land capable of enjoying the restrictive covenant.

The appeal ... upon the point of law in my opinion succeeds. ...

MR JUSTICE SCRUTTON

The question then is whether it is essential to the doctrine of *Tulk v. Moxhay* [(1848) 2 Ph. 774] that the covenantee should have at the time of the creation of the covenant, and afterwards, land for the benefit of which the covenant is created, in order that the burden of the covenant may bind assigns of the land to which it relates. ...

...I regard it as very regrettable that a public body should be prevented from enforcing a restriction on the use of property imposed for the public benefit against persons who bought the property knowing of the restriction, by the apparently immaterial circumstance that the public body does not own any land in the immediate neighbourhood. But, after a careful consideration of the authorities, I am forced to the view that the later decisions of this Court compel me so to hold. ...

The Court of Appeal allowed the appeal by Mrs Allen.

Although Scrutton J in particular was reluctant to allow the appeal, he was bound by precedent to hold that the covenantee and its successors in title must have an interest in some dominant land at the date of the covenant and at the time of enforcement respectively; the covenant must attach to dominant land.

One of the most debated areas of the law of freehold covenants relates to the running of the benefit of a covenant in equity. The following four cases focus on the different methods of annexing the benefit of a freehold covenant to the dominant land.

Rogers v Hosegood [1900] 2 Ch 388

Panel: Lord Alverstone MR and Rigby and Collins LJJ

Facts: A company of builders (who owned several pieces of land) sold a plot of freehold land to the Duke of Bedford, who covenanted with the sellers not to build more than one residential dwelling on the land and to use the land only as a private residence. The covenant was stated to bind the servient land and was for the benefit of any land belonging to the sellers and their successors in title adjoining or near to the land conveyed. The Duke later bought another plot of land from the sellers, subject to the same covenants.

The sellers sold another plot of their land to a purchaser, Sir John Millais, which was situated close to the Duke of Bedford's land. Sir John Millais was unaware of the covenants entered into by the Duke of Bedford and there was no express assignment of the benefit of the covenants to him. Finally, the sellers transferred the rest of their land to Mr Rogers. On Sir Millais's death, his land passed to the trustees of his will.

The defendant bought the Duke of Bedford's land and proposed to build a block of thirty to forty residential flats on that land. The trustees of Sir Millais's will joined Mr Rogers in suing the defendant for breach of covenant. Mr Justice Farwell at first instance held that claimants could enforce the restrictive covenants as the benefit of the covenants had passed to them. The defendant appealed to the Court of Appeal.

LORD JUSTICE COLLINS

This case raises questions of some difficulty, but we are of [the] opinion that the decision of Farwell J. is right and ought to be affirmed. ...No difficulty arises in this case as to the burden of the covenants. The defendant is the assignee of the covenantor ... and he took with notice of the covenants now sought to be enforced. Nor [have] we any hesitation in accepting the conclusion of Farwell J., that the buildings which the defendant proposes to erect will involve a breach of those covenants. The real and only difficulty arises on the question - whether the benefit of the covenants has passed to the assigns of Sir John Millais as owners of the plot purchased by him... . Here, again, the difficulty is narrowed, because by express declaration on the face of the conveyances ... the benefit of the two covenants in question was intended for all or any of the vendor's lands near to or adjoining the plot sold, and therefore for (among others) the plot of land acquired by Sir John Millais... . Therefore, ... we should agree with [Farwell J] that the benefit of the covenants in question was annexed to and passed to Sir John Millais by the conveyance of the land which he bought... . [I]n equity, just as at law, the first point to be determined is whether the covenant or contract in its inception binds the land. If it does, it is then capable of passing with the land to subsequent assignees; if it does not, it is incapable of passing by mere assignment of the land. The benefit may be annexed to one plot and the burden to another, and when this has been once clearly done the benefit and the burden pass to the respective assignees, subject, in the case of the burden, to proof that the legal estate, if acquired, has been acquired with notice of the covenant. The ... judgment of Hall V.-C. in *Renals v Cowlishaw* [9 Ch. D. 130] supports the same view, nor are the general observations or the decision of the case itself inconsistent with it. There, in the original conveyance which imposed the restrictive covenant, there was no expression, as there is in the present case, that the restriction was intended for the benefit of any part of the estate retained... . These authorities establish the proposition that, when the benefit has been once clearly annexed to one piece [of] land, it passes by assignment of that land, and may be said to run with it, in contemplation as well of equity as of law, without proof of special bargain or representation on the assignment. In such a case it runs, not because the conscience of either party is affected, but because the purchaser has bought something which inhered in or was annexed to the land bought. ...When, as in *Renals v. Cowlishaw* [9 Ch. D. 130], there is no indication in the original conveyance, or in the circumstances attending it, that the burden of the restrictive covenant is imposed for the benefit of the land reserved, or any particular part of it, then it becomes necessary to examine the circumstances under which any part of the land reserved is sold, in order to see whether a benefit, not originally annexed to it, has

Alert

become annexed to it on the sale, so that the purchaser is deemed to have bought it with the land, and this can hardly be the case when the purchaser did not know of the existence of the restrictive covenant. But when, as here, it has been once annexed to the land reserved, then … the presumption must be that it passes on a sale of that land, unless there is something to rebut it, and the purchaser's ignorance of the existence of the covenant does not defeat the presumption. We can find nothing in the conveyance to Sir John Millais in any degree inconsistent with the intention to pass to him the benefit already annexed to the land sold to him. We are of opinion, therefore, that Sir John Millais's assigns are entitled to enforce the restrictive covenant against the defendant, and that his appeal must be dismissed. …

The Court of Appeal unanimously dismissed the appeal.

Lord Justice Collins's judgment is useful in explaining the difference between the effects of the covenants in *Renals v Cowlishaw* (1879) 11 Ch D 866 and *Rogers v Hosegood*. If the benefit of the covenant is expressly annexed to the land at the time of the covenant, it is thereafter permanently attached. If it is not expressly annexed, the successor in title to the dominant land may have to rely on express assignment of the benefit to be able to enforce it. However, it may alternatively be possible to infer from the circumstances that the benefit was annexed to the dominant land at the time of the covenant, as in the following case.

Newton Abbot Cooperative Society Limited v Williamson & Treadgold Limited [1952] Ch 286

Panel: Upjohn J

Facts: Mrs Mardon, the freehold owner of a property known as Devonia, sold another property, Swiss Cottage, to a grocer in 1923. Swiss Cottage was situated opposite Devonia. Mrs Mardon used Devonia as an ironmonger's store. The grocer entered into a restrictive covenant not to use Swiss Cottage for any business relating to ironmongery. When Mrs Mardon died, Devonia vested in her son, who leased Devonia to the claimants for a twenty-one year term and expressly assigned the benefit of the covenant to them. The defendants bought Swiss Cottage and started to use it as an ironmonger's shop. The claimants sued the defendants for breach of covenant, requesting an injunction to stop the breach. An issue arose at court as to whether the land with the benefit of the covenant (Devonia) had been sufficiently described in the conveyance containing the covenant. Counsel for the defendants also argued that the covenant could only be a personal one, as it only benefited Mrs Mardon's business and not her land.

MR JUSTICE UPJOHN

…Mr. Bowles [counsel for the defence] strongly urged that the covenant was taken solely to protect the goodwill of the business carried on at Devonia, that it had no reference to the land itself, and that it was not taken for the benefit of that land; in brief, that it was a covenant in gross incapable of assignment. He urged that taking such a covenant would benefit the business in that an enhanced price could be obtained for the business, but no such enhanced price would be obtained for the land.

...Here he says there was no dominant tenement; the covenant was taken not for the benefit of any land, but for the benefit of the business.

I do not accept this view of the transaction of 1923. In 1923 Mrs. Mardon was carrying on the business of an ironmonger at Devonia. No doubt the covenant was taken for the benefit of that business and to prevent competition therewith, but I see no reason to think ... that that was the sole object of taking the covenant. ...

Mr. Bowles' second point was that, in order that the benefit of the covenant may be assignable, the land for which the benefit of the covenant is taken must in some way be referred to in the conveyance creating the covenant...

I am unable to agree that where a person is suing as an assign of the benefit of the covenant there must necessarily be something in the [deed] containing the covenant to define the land for the benefit of which the covenant was entered into. ...

In my judgment ... the problem which I have to consider is this: First, when Mrs. Mardon took the covenant in 1923, did she retain other lands capable of being benefited by the covenant? The answer is plainly yes. Secondly, was such land "ascertainable" or "certain" in this sense that the existence and situation of the land must be indicated in the conveyance or otherwise shown with reasonable certainty?

Apart from the fact that Mrs. Mardon is described as of Devonia, there is nothing in the conveyance of 1923 to define the land for the benefit of which the restrictive covenant was taken ... but ... I am, in my judgment, entitled to look at the attendant circumstances to see if the land to be benefited is shown "otherwise" with reasonable certainty. That is a question of fact and ... bearing in mind the close juxtaposition of Devonia and the defendants' premises, in my view the only reasonable inference to draw from the circumstances at the time of the conveyance of 1923 was that Mrs. Mardon took the covenant restrictive of the user of the defendants' premises for the benefit of her own business of ironmonger and of her property Devonia where at all material times she was carrying on that business... .

It follows, therefore, in my judgment, that Mrs. Mardon could on any subsequent sale of her land Devonia, if she so chose, as part of the transaction of sale, assign the benefit of the covenant so as to enable the purchaser from her and his assignees of the land and covenant to enforce it against an owner of the defendants' premises taking with notice... .

 Alert

The judge found in favour of the claimant who was granted an injunction to enforce the restrictive covenant.

It is only in rare cases that the annexation of the benefit to the dominant land will be implied from the surrounding circumstances and Upjohn J confirmed that it would be a question of fact in each case. The case is also interesting as it shows that a covenant which affects the business of the dominant landowner may still touch and concern the dominant land.

The final method of annexation of the benefit of a freehold covenant is statutory annexation which is addressed in the following two cases.

Federated Homes Limited v Mill Lodge Properties Limited [1980] 1 WLR 594

Panel: Megaw, Browne and Brightman LJJ

Statute: Law of Property Act 1925 s 78

Facts: Mackenzie Hill Limited (MHL) bought four pieces of land described as the Red Land, the Green Land, the Pink Land (which was not ultimately relevant to the claim as it was sold separately) and the Blue Land. MHL obtained an outline planning permission from the local authority to build 1,250 private residential homes and the planning permission was for the benefit of MHL and its subsidiaries. MHL sold the Blue Land to the defendant (with the benefit of the planning permission), who covenanted in clause 5(iv) of the conveyance not to build at a density of greater than 300 dwellings so as not to reduce the number of properties which MHL could build on its retained land under the planning permission. The retained land was described in the conveyance as "any adjoining or adjacent property retained by" MHL. The Green Land and the Red Land were then transferred to a company called Brandt's. Both areas of land were transferred expressly with the benefit of the covenant entered into by the defendant. Brandt's subsequently transferred the Green Land to the claimant expressly with the benefit of the covenant entered into by the defendant. The Red Land was transferred to another party before being transferred to the claimant, but the benefit of the restrictive covenant was not expressly assigned to the claimant upon transfer of the Red Land.

The defendant constructed 300 houses on the Blue Land. The claimant obtained a new planning permission to build on the Red Land and the Green Land (the previous one having expired). The claimant then discovered that the defendant had obtained another planning permission to build an additional thirty-two houses on the Blue Land. The claimant sued the defendant for breach of covenant, objecting to the defendant's intention to build on the Blue Land at a density of more than 300 houses. The judge at first instance granted an injunction to the claimant so the defendant appealed to the Court of Appeal, pleading that the covenant was personal to MHL and had not therefore run with the Green Land and the Red Land.

LORD JUSTICE BRIGHTMAN

...[The] conveyance contains no express definition of the retained land. There is, however, a reference in clause 2 to "any adjoining or adjacent property retained by the vendor." I read "the retained land" in clause 5(iv) as meaning just that. ...I, therefore, conclude that the retained land means the red and the green land and the small additional areas comprised in the site, other, of course, than the blue and the pink land. ...

I entirely agree with [the judge at first instance] when he said that it is neither necessary nor natural nor sensible to read the covenant as personal to Mackenzie Hill. Generally speaking, the benefit of a contract between businessmen is assignable without mention of assignability unless the contract is of a personal nature, which the restrictive covenant was not. ...

If there were still any doubt, section 78 of the Law of Property Act 1925 , in my view, sets that doubt at rest. For it provides that a covenant relating to any land of the covenantee shall be deemed to have been made with the covenantee and his successors in title, which presupposes assignability. I shall have occasion in due course to examine this section at greater length. ...

Alert

I turn to the question whether the benefit has safely reached the hands of the plaintiff. The green land has no problem, owing to the unbroken chain of assignments. ...However, the judge [at first instance] dealt with both areas of land and I propose to do the same.

An express assignment of the benefit of a covenant is not necessary if the benefit of the covenant is annexed to the land. In that event, the benefit will pass automatically on a conveyance of the land, without express mention, because it is annexed to the land and runs with it. So the issue of annexation is logically the next to be considered. ...

In my judgment the benefit of this covenant was annexed to the retained land, and I think that this is a consequence of section 78 of the Act of 1925... .

[Counsel for the defence] submitted that there were three possible views about section 78. One view, which he described as "the orthodox view" hitherto held, is that it is merely a statutory shorthand for reducing the length of legal documents. A second view, which was the one that [counsel for the defence] was inclined to place in the forefront of his argument, is that the section only applies, or at any rate only achieves annexation, when the land intended to be benefited is signified in the document by express words or necessary implication as the intended beneficiary of the covenant. A third view is that the section applies if the covenant in fact touches and concerns the land of the covenantee, whether that be gleaned from the document itself or from evidence outside the document.

For myself, I reject the narrowest interpretation of section 78, the supposed orthodox view, which seems to me to fly in the face of the wording of the section. Before I express my reasons I will say that I do not find it necessary to choose between the second and third views because, in my opinion, this covenant relates to land of the covenantee on either interpretation of section 78. Clause 5(iv) shows clearly that the covenant is for the protection of the retained land and that land is described ... as "any adjoining or adjacent property retained by the vendor." This formulation is sufficient for annexation purposes: see *Rogers v. Hosegood* [1900] 2 Ch. 388. ...

Link
Rogers v Hosegood

If, as the language of section 78 implies, a covenant relating to land which is restrictive of the user thereof is enforceable at the suit of (1) a successor in title of the covenantee, (2) a person deriving title under the covenantee or under his successors in title, and (3) the owner or occupier of the land intended to be benefited by the covenant, it must, in my view, follow that the covenant runs with the land, because ex hypothesi every successor in title to the land, every derivative proprietor of the land and every other owner and occupier has a right by statute to the covenant. In other words, if the condition precedent of section 78 is satisfied — that is to say, there exists a covenant which touches and concerns the land of the covenantee — that covenant runs with the

Alert

land for the benefit of his successors in title, persons deriving title under him or them and other owners and occupiers. ...

Although the section does not seem to have been extensively used in the course of argument in this type of case, the construction of section 78 which appeals to me appears to be consistent with ... *Smith and Snipes Hall Farm Ltd. v. River Douglas Catchment Board* [1949] 2 K.B. 500. In that case ... the agreement was not expressed to be for the benefit of the landowner's successors in title; and there was no assignment of the benefit of the agreement in favour of the second plaintiff, the tenant. In reliance, as I understand the case, upon section 78 of the Act of 1925, it was held that the second plaintiff was entitled to sue the catchment board for damages for breach of the agreement. It seems to me that that conclusion can only have been reached on the basis that section 78 had the effect of causing the benefit of the agreement to run with the land so as to be capable of being sued upon by the tenant. ...

It was suggested ... that, if this covenant ought to be read as enuring for the benefit of the retained land, it should be read as enuring only for the benefit of the retained land as a whole and not for the benefit of every part of it; with the apparent result that there is no annexation of the benefit to a part of the retained land when any severance takes place. ...

I find the idea of the annexation of a covenant to the whole of the land but not to a part of it a difficult conception fully to grasp. ...I would have thought, if the benefit of a covenant is, on a proper construction of a document, annexed to the land, prima facie it is annexed to every part thereof, unless the contrary clearly appears. ...

 Alert

In the end, I come to the conclusion that section 78 of the Law of Property Act 1925 caused the benefit of the restrictive covenant in question to run with the red land and therefore to be annexed to it, with the result that the plaintiff is able to enforce the covenant against Mill Lodge, not only in its capacity as owner of the green land, but also in its capacity as owner of the red land.

For these reasons I think that the judge reached the correct view on the right of the plaintiff to enforce the covenant, although in part he arrived there by a different route. ...

I would therefore, uphold the injunction and I would dismiss this appeal.

The Court of Appeal unanimously dismissed the appeal.

The case is useful for showing the difference between express assignment of the benefit of a covenant (which was the case with the Green Land) and statutory annexation (which was the case with the Red Land). The judgment has been the subject of criticism because it seems to suggest that the effect of LPA 1925 s 78 cannot be excluded, thereby rendering express annexation and express assignment of the benefit of a covenant redundant. This criticism has been tempered by the decision of *Roake and others v Chadha and another* [1984] 1 WLR 40 and the following case (which describes the reasoning in *Roake v Chadha* in detail).

Crest Nicholson Residential (South) Limited v McAllister [2004] EWCA Civ 410, [2004] 1 WLR 2409

Panel: Auld, Chadwick and Arden LJJ

Facts: Percy and Charles Mitchell sold plots of land to various purchasers. The conveyances of the plots were divided into four different groups as follows: the Arthur conveyances, the Humphreys conveyances, the Roberts conveyances and the Wing conveyance (the groups being based on the names of the purchasers who originally bought the plots). These conveyances all contained restrictive covenants, restricting the use of each plot of land to either "a private dwelling house or for professional purposes" and preventing building unless plans had first been submitted to and approved by the Mitchell brothers or their company. The brothers later died and their company was dissolved.

The Arthur conveyances contained no express words of annexation which annexed the benefit of the covenants to the land retained by the Mitchell brothers. The Humphreys conveyances did contain express words of annexation which annexed the benefit of the covenants to the land retained by the Mitchell brothers. One of the Roberts conveyances contained express words of annexation but the other did not.

The claimant, referred to as Crest Nicholson, became the owner of most of the land conveyed by the Arthur conveyances, the Humphreys conveyances, the Roberts conveyances and the Wing conveyance. This land had by this point been divided up into five plots and five houses and gardens had been constructed on the plots. Crest Nicholson wished to build six further houses in the gardens of these five properties.

Mrs McAllister became the owner of the rest of the land which was conveyed by the Wing conveyance, now known as Newlyn. She objected to the proposed building in the gardens, stating that it would be in breach of the restrictive covenants which benefited her land. Crest Nicholson applied to the court for declarations in relation to two questions: (a) whether the covenants would prevent them from building the six additional houses; and (b) whether the covenant regarding approval of the plans was still enforceable on the death of the original covenantees and the dissolution of their company. Mr Justice Neuberger found at first instance that on the true construction of the covenants, the claimant was prevented from building more than one house on each of the plots of land. The claimant appealed to the Court of Appeal.

LORD JUSTICE CHADWICK

22. It is trite law that, in order to enforce a covenant affecting land, a person (say, A) who is not the original covenantee must show that he is entitled to the benefit of it. Further, if A seeks to enforce the covenant against a person (say, B) who is not the original covenantor, A must show that B has become subject to the burden of the covenant. Absent, on the one hand, an express assignment (or chain of assignments) of the benefit of the covenant and, on the other hand, an express covenant for indemnity (or chain of covenants) from successors of the original covenantor (neither of which is not alleged in this case), A cannot enforce the covenant against B at law. But, since the decision in *Tulk v Moxhay*

(1848) 11 Beavan 571, the covenant may, nevertheless, be enforced in equity if certain conditions are satisfied. In the present case it is not in dispute that, in equity, the burden of the covenants imposed in the Arthur, Humphreys and Roberts conveyances has passed... . The question now raised is whether Mrs McAllister, as the owner of part of the land conveyed by the Wing conveyance, is ... entitled to the benefit of the covenants imposed in the Arthur, Humphreys and Roberts conveyances?

23. The benefit of a covenant may pass in equity (as in law) through a chain of assignments. That is not this case. Or the benefit of a covenant may pass where land has been sold off under a building scheme (which is not now alleged). Absent a chain of assignments or a building scheme, the benefit of a covenant may, nevertheless, pass to the owner for the time being of land to which it has been annexed. ...

24. In relation to covenants imposed in instruments made after 1925 (as were the covenants with which we are concerned in this appeal) the position is governed by the provisions of s 78 of the Law of Property Act 1925 (Benefit of covenants relating to land). ...

29. It is clear that the Court approached the question of annexation in the *Federated Homes* case on the basis that the density covenant was taken for the benefit of retained land which could be identified in the ... conveyance. ...

30. The decision of this Court in the Federated Homes case leaves open the question whether s 78 of the 1925 Act only effects annexation when the land intended to be benefited is described in the instrument itself (by express words or necessary implication, albeit that it may be necessary to have regard to evidence outside the document fully to identify that land) or whether it is enough that it can be shown, from evidence wholly outside the document, that the covenant does in fact touch and concern land of the covenantee which can be identified.

Link

Federated Homes Limited v Mill Lodge Properties Limited

31. It is clear from ... *Rogers v Hosegood* [1900] 2 Ch 388 that it is sufficient for the conveyance to describe the land intended to be benefited in terms which enable it to be identified from other evidence. ...

33. In its later decision in the *Federated Homes* case this Court held that the provisions of s 78 of the 1925 Act had made it unnecessary to state, in the conveyance, that the covenant was to be enforceable by persons deriving title under the covenantee or under his successors in title and the owner or occupier of the land intended to be benefited, or that the covenant was to run with the land intended to be benefited; but there is nothing in that case which suggests that it is no longer necessary that the land which is intended to be benefited should be so defined that it is easily ascertainable. In my view, that requirement ... remains a necessary condition for annexation.

Alert

34. There are, I think, good reasons for that requirement. ...It is obviously desirable that a purchaser of land burdened with a restrictive covenant should be able not only to ascertain, by inspection of the entries on the relevant register, that the

land is so burdened, but also to ascertain the land for which the benefit of the covenant was taken - so that he can identify who can enforce the covenant. That latter object is achieved if the land which is intended to be benefited is defined in the instrument so as to be easily ascertainable. To require a purchaser of land burdened with a restrictive covenant, but where the land for the benefit of which the covenant was taken is not described in the instrument, to make enquiries as to what (if any) land the original covenantee retained at the time of the conveyance and what (if any) of that retained land the covenant did, or might have, "touched and concerned" would be oppressive. It must be kept in mind that (as in the present case) the time at which the enforceability of the covenant becomes an issue may be long after the date of the instrument by which it was imposed. ...

37.   ...[There is] a second question which this Court did not need to address in the *Federated Homes* case: whether the effect of the [sic] s 78 of the Law of Property Act 1925 is displaced by a contrary intention manifested in the instrument itself. But that question was addressed, specifically, in *Roake and others v Chadha and another* [1984] 1 WLR 40, to which I now turn. ...

39.   It was accepted ... that the express words of the covenant appeared to exclude annexation. ...But it was said that, nevertheless, the covenant imposed by the transfer ... had become annexed to the land ... by the operation of s 78 of the 1925 Act. Reliance was placed on the contrast between the language of s 78 and s 79 (Burden of covenants relating to land) of that Act. ...

[I]t was said, the legislature must have intended the provisions of s 78 (Benefit of covenants relating to land) to be mandatory; it must have intended that those provisions could not be excluded by a contrary intention, however clearly expressed.

40.   His Honour Judge Paul Baker QC, sitting as a Judge of the High Court, rejected that submission. After analysing the judgment of Brightman LJ in *Federated Homes Ltd v Mill Lodge Ltd* (supra), and pointing out that no reason of policy had been suggested to explain why s 78 of the 1925 Act should be mandatory, the judge said this, at [1984] 1 WLR 40, 46B-H:

"I am thus far from satisfied that s 78 has the mandatory operation which [counsel] claimed for it. But if one accepts that it is not subject to a contrary intention, I do not consider that it has the effect of annexing the benefit of the covenant in each and every case irrespective of the other express terms of the covenant. ...

The true position as I see it is that even where a covenant is deemed to be made with successors in title as s 78 requires, one still has to construe the covenant as a whole to see whether the benefit of the covenant is annexed. Where one finds, as in the *Federated Homes* case, the covenant is not qualified in any way, annexation may be readily inferred; but where, as in the present case, it is expressly provided:

'this covenant shall not enure for the benefit of any owner or subsequent purchaser ... unless the benefit of this covenant shall be expressly assigned... '

one cannot just ignore these words. One may not be able to exclude the operation of the section in widening the range of the covenantees, but one has to consider the covenant as a whole to determine its true effect. ..."

41. I respectfully agree, first, that it is impossible to identify any reason of policy why a covenantor should not, by express words, be entitled to limit the scope of the obligation which he is undertaking; nor why a covenantee should not be able to accept a covenant for his own benefit on terms that the benefit does not pass automatically to all those to whom he sells on parts of his retained land. ...I can see no reason why, if original covenantor and covenantee make clear their mutual intention in that respect, the legislature should wish to prevent effect being given to that intention.

42. ...In a case where the parties to the instrument make clear their intention that land retained by the covenantee at the time of the conveyance effected by the transfer is to have the benefit of the covenant only for so long as it continues to be in the ownership of the original covenantee, and not after it has been sold on by the original covenantee ... I agree with the judge in *Roake v Chadha* (supra) that, in such a case, it is possible to give full effect to the statute and to the terms of the covenant.

43. This approach to s 78 of the 1925 Act provides, as it seems to me, the answer to the question why, if the legislature did not intend to distinguish between the effect of s 78 (mandatory) and the effect of s 79 (subject to contrary intention), it did not include the words "unless a contrary intention is expressed" in the first of those sections. The answer is that it did not need to. ...If the terms in which the covenant is imposed show - as they did in ... *Roake v Chadha* - that the land of the covenantee intended to be benefited does not include land which may subsequently be sold off by the original covenantee in circumstances where (at the time of that subsequent sale) there is no express assignment of the benefit of the covenant, then the owners and occupiers of the land sold off in those circumstances are not "owners and occupiers for the time being of the land of the covenantee intended to be benefited"; and so are not "successors in title" of the original covenantee for the purposes of s 78(1) in its application to covenants restrictive of the user of land. ...

47. In my view the benefit of the covenants is not annexed to the land now owned by Mrs McAllister... . I reach that conclusion for the following reasons.

48. It seems to me that the effect of the express words of annexation contained in the two Humphreys conveyances and in the second of the Roberts conveyances was to identify the land of the covenantee intended to be benefited, for the purposes of s 78(1) of the Law of Property Act 1925, in terms which excluded land which was in the ownership of the company at the time of the relevant conveyance but which, thereafter, was sold off by the company. ...

50. It seems to me that there is nothing in the first of the Roberts conveyance[s] ... which enables the Court to identify, even with the aid of external evidence to assist general words of description, what land (if any) was intended to be benefited by the covenants. ...In those circumstances s 78 of the Law of Property Act 1925 is of no assistance to Mrs McAllister. She cannot show that she is the owner or occupier of "land of the covenantee intended to be benefited."

51. The position in relation to the land conveyed by the two Arthur conveyances is less obvious. ...There is nothing in that conveyance to show what land (if any) the brothers or their company own in the neighbourhood... . In the case of the second conveyance the plan does show land in the ownership of the company on each side of, and adjoining, the land conveyed. But the adjoining land shown by the plan to be in the ownership of the company does not extend to the land now owned by Mrs McAllister.

52. ...It follows that, in relation to the Arthur conveyances also, s 78 of the Law of Property Act 1925 is of no assistance to Mrs McAllister. She cannot show that she is the owner or occupier of "land of the covenantee intended to be benefited." ...

CONCLUSION

54. I would allow this appeal and ... vary the judge's order so as to declare that the covenants in the ... conveyances ... are not enforceable by Mrs McAllister as the owner of Newlyn.

The Court of Appeal unanimously allowed the appeal by the claimant.

This case, and that of *Roake and others v Chadha and another*, have had the effect of limiting to some extent the wide scope of LPA 1925 s 78 as interpreted in *Federated Homes Limited v Mill Lodge Properties Limited*. It is possible to exclude the effect of LPA 1925 s 78 and it is still necessary to show in the transfer the land which is intended to benefit from the covenant. If this is not done, as in the above case, LPA 1925 s 78 will not annex the benefit of the covenant to the dominant land.

The final case in this chapter is concerned with the extent of remedies awarded for breach of a freehold covenant.

Wrotham Park Estate Co. Limited v Parkside Homes Limited and others [1974] 1 WLR 798

Panel: Brightman J

Facts: The Earl of Strafford sold part of the Wrotham Park Estate to Mr Blake subject to a covenant not to develop the land without first submitting the plans outlining the development to the seller for approval. The covenant was registered on the Land Charges Register as a Class D(ii) land charge. Mr Blake developed most of the land as a housing estate (obtaining the requisite approval of the building plans from the seller) apart from a small triangular area. Mr Blake later sold the triangular piece of land to the Potters Bar Urban District Council who obtained planning permission to build houses on it. The Potters Bar Urban District Council then sold the triangular piece of land to the defendants with the benefit of the planning permission. The defendants started to build houses on the land, but they did not submit plans to the claimant (the successors in title to the dominant land), stating that counsel had informed them that the covenant was unenforceable. The claimant sought an injunction to prevent further building and to remove the houses which had already been constructed in breach of covenant (although the claimant did not apply for interim relief). However, the defendant continued to build and some purchasers bought and moved into the new houses in the meantime.

MR JUSTICE BRIGHTMAN

I turn first to the nature, scope and purpose of the lay-out covenant. In terms it is an absolute prohibition against development for building purposes except in strict accordance with a lay-out plan approved by the vendor... .

The next issue is whether the stipulation in question is enforceable as between the plaintiffs and the defendants or any of them, having regard to the fact that they are respectively the assigns of the original covenantee and the original covenantor. This issue can appropriately be broken down into the questions posed in the judgment in *Marten v. Flight Refuelling Ltd.* [1962] Ch. 115.

(a)   Whether the covenant was entered into for the benefit of any land of the covenantee. The answer to that question is clearly affirmative because the covenant so states.

(b)   Whether that land is sufficiently defined or ascertainable. ...

(c)   Whether the Wrotham Park Estate was and still is capable of being benefited by the stipulations. This is the point against which the defendants concentrated their attack when challenging enforceability. ...

There can be obvious cases where a restrictive covenant clearly is, or clearly is not, of benefit to an estate. Between these two extremes there is inevitably an area where the benefit to the estate is a matter of personal opinion, where responsible and reasonable persons can have divergent views sincerely and reasonably held. ...

 Alert

If a restriction is bargained for at the time of sale with the intention of giving the vendor a protection which he desires for the land he retains, and the restriction is expressed to be imposed for the benefit of the estate so that both sides are apparently accepting that the restriction is of value to the retained land, I think that the validity of the restriction should be upheld so long as an estate owner may reasonably take the view that the restriction remains of value to his estate, and that the restriction should not be discarded merely because others may reasonably argue that the restriction is spent. ...I therefore conclude that the lay-out covenant imposed ... is still capable of benefiting the Wrotham Park Estate or, at any rate, that the contrary has not been proved.

On the issue of enforceability there remains only the question whether the [servient land] is subject to the burden of the restrictive covenant. That question is to be answered affirmatively. The covenant was duly registered in 1935 as a class D (ii) land charge under the Land Charges Act 1925; therefore purchasers took with notice of it and are bound by it.

I must now consider the relief to which the plaintiffs are entitled, that is to say a mandatory injunction or damages ... whether substantial or nominal; or a declaration of the plaintiffs' rights as the sole relief. The plaintiffs made it abundantly clear at the outset of the case that the relief they primarily sought was a mandatory injunction. ...

The plaintiffs concede that they are not entitled to a mandatory injunction "as of course." Every case must depend, essentially, upon its own particular circumstances.

Undoubtedly it is a highly material factor that Parkside, aided and abetted by those who entered into contracts with it, continued building operations in the face of the clear and early protest by the plaintiffs and the issue of proceedings. In such circumstances a defendant proceeds at his own peril... . But even where the defendant has continued in the face of protest or writ, there is no rule that the plaintiff will be granted a mandatory injunction if he succeeds at the trial. ...

One naturally asks why in the present case the plaintiffs did not seek interim relief to prevent the houses being erected before the trial of the action. ...

[Counsel for the claimant] submitted, and I accept, that it is no answer to a claim for a mandatory injunction that the plaintiffs, having issued proceedings, deliberately held their hand and did not seek the assistance of the court for the purpose of preserving the status quo. On the other hand, it is, in my view, equally true that a plaintiff is not entitled "as of course" to have everything pulled down that was built after the issue of the writ. The erection of the houses, whether one likes it or not, is a fait accompli and the houses are now the homes of people. I accept that this particular fait accompli is reversible and could be undone. But I cannot close my eyes to the fact that the houses now exist. It would, in my opinion, be an unpardonable waste of much needed houses to direct that they now be pulled down and I have never had a moment's doubt during the hearing of this case that such an order ought to be refused. No damage of a financial nature has been done to the plaintiffs by the breach of the lay-out stipulation. The plaintiffs' use of the Wrotham Park Estate has not been and will not be impeded. It is totally [unnecessary] to demolish the houses in order to preserve the integrity of the restrictive covenants imposed... . Without hesitation I decline to grant a mandatory injunction. ...

Alert

In the present case I am faced with the problem what damages ought to be awarded to the plaintiffs in the place of mandatory injunctions which would have restored the plaintiffs' rights. If the plaintiffs are merely given a nominal sum, or no sum, in substitution for injunctions, [it] seems to me that justice will manifestly not have been done.

...In my judgment a just substitute for a mandatory injunction would be such a sum of money as might reasonably have been demanded by the plaintiffs from Parkside as a quid pro quo for relaxing the covenant. ...

I think that damages must be assessed in such a case on a basis which is fair and, in all the circumstances, in my judgment a sum equal to five per cent. of Parkside's anticipated profit is the most that is fair. I accordingly award the sum of £2,500 in substitution for mandatory injunctions. ...

The judge did not award an injunction to the claimant but awarded damages instead for breach of covenant by the defendants. The remedy awarded will depend on the facts of the case, but it is evident that it may not be proportionate to award an injunction resulting in the removal of buildings, particularly if the buildings in question are residential accommodation. The judgment is also useful in demonstrating that a covenant can be of benefit to the whole of a piece of land, even where the benefited land is a sizeable estate.

Further Reading

Law Commission Report 'Making Land Work: Easements, Covenants and Profits a Prendre' (Report No. 327)

MacKenzie & Phillips, *Textbook on Land Law*, (15th Edition), Chapter 26

Megarry & Wade, *The Law of Real Property*, (8th Edition), pp 1372 - 1425

Gray & Gray, *Elements of Land Law*, (5th Edition), pp 237-297

7

Mortgages

Topic List

1   Contentious Terms

2   Undue Influence

3   Rights and Duties of the Mortgagee

Introduction

A mortgage is the grant of rights over a property in exchange for a loan. The mortgagor (the borrower) gives the mortgagee (the lender) an interest in his land in order to secure the loan.

The case law on mortgages comprises three main areas: contentious terms contained within the mortgage agreement, undue influence, and the rights and duties of the mortgagee upon the mortgagor's default.

7.1 Contentious Terms

The mortgagor's rights are collectively known as the equity of redemption; this includes the mortgagor's right to redeem the property upon the repayment of the loan. The courts will not allow any clause in a mortgage agreement to be a clog or a fetter on the equity of redemption. In *Biggs v Hoddinott* [1898] 2 Ch 307, the Court of Appeal considered whether a collateral advantage that lasted solely for the duration of the mortgage constituted a clog or fetter on the equity of redemption.

Biggs v Hoddinott [1898] 2 Ch 307

Panel: Lindley MR, Chitty and Collins LJJ

Facts: A pub landlord mortgaged the freehold of a public house to a brewer in exchange for a loan. The landlord covenanted to buy beer only from the brewer for the duration of the mortgage. The mortgage could not be redeemed for five years. After two years the landlord stopped buying the brewer's beer and argued the *solus tie* (or trade tie) was a clog on the equity of redemption.

LINDLEY MR

We have listened to a very ingenious and learned argument with the view of inducing us under pressure to lay down a proposition of law which would be very unfortunate for business men. The proposition contended for comes to this - that while two people are engaged in a mortgage transaction they cannot enter into any other transaction with each other which can possibly benefit the mortgagee, and that any such transaction must be before or after the mortgage, and be independent of it, so that it cannot be said that the mortgagee got any additional benefit from the mortgage transaction. Mr. Farwell did not attempt to uphold this on any rational principle, but relied on authority. Of course, we must follow settled authorities whether we like them or not; but do they support this proposition? *Jennings v. Ward* 2 Vern. 520 was the first case relied upon. That was a redemption suit, and the stipulation which was in question seriously interfered with the redemption of the mortgaged property, and the Master of the Rolls (Sir J. Trevor) decreed redemption without regard to that stipulation. He is reported to have said: "A man shall not have interest for his money, and a collateral advantage besides for the loan of it, or clog the redemption with any by-agreement." That has been understood as meaning exactly what was said, without regard to the circumstances of the case, and has found its way into the text-books as establishing that a mortgagee cannot have principal, interest, and costs, and also some collateral advantage...

The proposition stated in *Jennings v. Ward* 2 Vern. 520 is too wide. If properly guarded it is good law and good sense. A mortgage is regarded as a security for money, and the mortgagor can always redeem on payment of principal, interest, and costs; and no bargain preventing such redemption is valid, nor will unconscionable bargains be enforced. There is no case where collateral advantages have been disallowed which does not come under one of these two heads. To say that to require such a covenant as that now in question is unconscionable is asking us to lay down a proposition which would shock any business man, and we are not driven to it by authority. The proposition laid down by Hargreave J. in *In re Edwards's Estate* 11 Ir. Ch. Rep. 367, that where an onerous contract entered into by a mortgagor with his mortgagee is part of the arrangement for the loan, and is actually inserted in the mortgage deed, it is presumed to be made under pressure, and is not capable of being enforced, goes too far, though the decision of the learned judge was correct; for the stipulation with which he had to deal was unreasonable, and one which ought not to be enforced...

LORD JUSTICE CHITTY

The mortgage here is a mortgage of a public-house for a time certain by publicans to a brewer, effected in the usual way, and it contains a covenant by the mortgagors during the continuance of the security to take all their beer from the mortgagee, and a covenant by the mortgagee to supply it. It is contended that the covenant by the mortgagors is void in equity. The first objection I have to make is that it in no way affects the equity of redemption, for it is not stipulated that damages for breach of the covenant shall be covered by the security, and redemption takes place quite independently of the covenant; so this is not a case where the right to redeem is affected. Equity has always looked upon a mortgage as only a security for money, and here the right of the mortgagors to redeem on payment of principal, interest, and costs is maintained. It has been contended that the principle is established by the authorities that a mortgagee shall not stipulate for any collateral advantage to himself. I think the cases only establish that the mortgagee shall not impose on the mortgagor an unconscionable or oppressive bargain. The present appears to me to be a reasonable trade bargain between two business men who enter into it with their eyes open, and it would be a fanciful doctrine of equity that would set it aside.

 Alert

This case establishes that a collateral advantage that is neither unconscionable, nor repugnant to the right to redeem, nor continues beyond the redemption date will be upheld by the court.

This can be contrasted with *Noakes & Co v Rice* [1902] AC 24. In that case, the House of Lords established that a collateral advantage, such as a *solus tie*, will not normally be permitted to endure beyond the date of redemption.

Noakes & Co v Rice [1902] AC 24

Panel: Earl of Halsbury LC, Lord Macnaghten, Lord Shand, Lord Davey, Lord Brampton, Lord Robertson and Lord Lindley

Facts: The landlord of a free house granted a brewer a mortgage over a leasehold property in exchange for a loan. The landlord covenanted to sell only the brewer's malt liquors. Under the agreement, the covenant would last for the duration of the lease, even once the mortgage had been repaid.

LORD DAVEY

My Lords, there are three doctrines of the Courts of Equity in this country which have been referred to in the course of the argument in this case. The first doctrine to which I refer is expressed in the maxim, "Once a mortgage always a mortgage". The second is that the mortgagee shall not reserve to himself any collateral advantage outside the mortgage contract; and the third is that a provision or stipulation which will have the effect of clogging or fettering the equity of redemption is void.

My Lords, the first maxim presents no difficulty: it is only another way of saying that a mortgage cannot be made irredeemable, and that a provision to that effect is void. In the case of the *Salt v. Marquis of Northampton* [1892] A C 1 the question was whether a certain life policy, the premiums on which were charged against the mortgagor, was comprised in the mortgage security. That question having been decided in the affirmative, it was declared to be redeemable, notwithstanding an express provision to the contrary contained in the deed.

My Lords, the second doctrine to which I refer, namely, that the mortgagee shall not reserve to himself any collateral advantage outside the mortgage contract, was established long ago when the usury laws were in force. The Court of Equity went beyond the usury laws, and set its face against every transaction which tended to usury. It therefore declared void every stipulation by a mortgagee for a collateral advantage which made his total remuneration for the loan indirectly exceed the legal interest. I think it will be found that every case under this head of equity was decided either on this ground, or on the ground that the bargain was oppressive and unconscionable. The abolition of the usury laws has made an alteration in the view the Court should take on this subject, and I agree that a collateral advantage may now be stipulated for by a mortgagee, provided that no unfair advantage be taken by the mortgagee which would render it void or voidable, according to the general principles of equity, and provided that it does not offend against the third doctrine. On these grounds I think the case of *Biggs v. Hoddinott* [1898] 2 Ch. 307 in the Court of Appeal was rightly decided.

The third doctrine to which I have referred is really a corollary from the first, and might be expressed in this form: Once a mortgage always a mortgage and nothing but a mortgage. The meaning of that is that the mortgagee shall not make any stipulation which will prevent a mortgagor, who has paid principal, interest, and costs, from getting back his mortgaged property in the condition in which he parted with it. I do not dissent from the opinion expressed by my noble and learned friend opposite (Lord

Lindley), when Master of the Rolls, in the case of *Santley v. Wilde* [1899] 2 Ch. 474. He says: "A clog or fetter is something which is inconsistent with the idea of security; a clog or fetter is in the nature of a repugnant condition." But I ask, "security" for what? I think it must be security for the principal, interest, and costs, and, I will add, for any advantages in the nature of increased interest or remuneration for the loan which the mortgagee has validly stipulated for during the continuance of the mortgage. There are two elements in the conception of a mortgage: first, security for the money advanced; and, secondly, remuneration for the use of the money. When the mortgage is paid off the security is at an end, and, as the mortgagee is no longer kept out of his money, the remuneration to him for the use of his money is also at an end... The principle is this - that a mortgage must not be converted into something else; and when once you come to the conclusion that a stipulation for the benefit of the mortgagee is part of the mortgage transaction, it is but part of his security, and necessarily comes to an end on the payment off of the loan. In my opinion, every yearly or other recurring payment stipulated for by the mortgagee should be held to be in the nature of interest, and no more payable after the principal is paid off than interest would be. I apprehend a man could not stipulate for the continuance of payment of interest after the principal is paid, and I do not think he can stipulate for any other recurring payment such as a share of profits. Any stipulation to that effect would, in my opinion, be void as a clog or fetter on the equity of redemption...

Now, applying what I have said to the present case, the decision becomes easy. In the first place, I do not think that the respondent's covenant to deal exclusively with the brewers continued after the payment off of the loan and the redemption; and, secondly, if it did, it was an attempt to charge it on the property, and that constituted a clog or fetter which, according to well-established principles, was void.

The previously 'free house' had become a 'tied house' after redemption, thereby losing value. The *solus tie* became void once the loan was repaid, as it devalued the equity of redemption.

In *G. and C. Kreglinger v New Patagonia Meat and Cold Storage Company* [1914] AC 25, the House of Lords considered whether a different type of collateral advantage could form a part of a mortgage agreement.

G. and C. Kreglinger v New Patagonia Meat and Cold Storage Company [1914] AC 25

Panel: Viscount Haldane LC, Earl of Halsbury, Lord Atkinson, Lord Mersey and Lord Parker of Waddington

Facts: Woolbrokers loaned a meat preserve company £10,000. The company mortgaged all its present and future property (a floating charge) to secure the loan. The woolbrokers agreed not to demand repayment until September 1915, as long as interest was paid. The company could pay off the loan at any time, giving one calendar month's notice; it did so in January 1913. The agreement gave the woolbrokers a right of first refusal to buy at market rate all of the company's sheepskins until August 1915.

LORD MERSEY

It is contended that the contract is a mortgage to which the equitable doctrine prohibiting the imposition of a clog on a mortgagor's right to redeem applies, and that, therefore, on payment off of the loan the borrowers are entitled to have back their undertaking freed from any further obligation to sell or deliver sheepskins. Now, whether a transaction is or is not such a mortgage is a question of intention... The obligation to sell sheepskins created by clause 8 of the agreement was to endure in any event until August, 1915. That was the plain intention of both parties to the agreement, and the only effect of applying to the contract the equitable doctrine against clogging the right to redeem would be to defeat that intention and to enable one of the parties to inflict an injustice on the other.

I have nothing to say about the doctrine itself. It seems to me to be like an unruly dog, which, if not securely chained to its own kennel, is prone to wander into places where it ought not to be. Its introduction into the present case would give effect to no equity and would defeat justice...

LORD PARKER OF WADDINGTON

This is the principle underlying the rule against fetters or clogs on the equity of redemption. The rule may be stated thus: The equity which arises on failure to exercise the contractual right cannot be fettered or clogged by any stipulation contained in the mortgage or entered into as part of the mortgage transaction. This rule is equally applicable to all transactions of mortgage, whether the mortgagor is or is not under personal liability to pay the money secured, and whether or not the mortgage is given to secure a loan made at the time of the mortgage or some existing debt of the mortgagee. For example, it would be applicable to a mortgage with a proviso for reconveyance on the payment to the mortgagee by the mortgagor or a third party of moneys owing by such third party to the mortgagee...

My Lords, after the most careful consideration of the authorities I think it is open to this House to hold, and I invite your Lordships to hold, that there is now no rule in equity which precludes a mortgagee, whether the mortgage be made upon the occasion of a loan or otherwise, from stipulating for any collateral advantage, provided such collateral advantage is not either (1.) unfair and unconscionable, or (2.) in the nature of a penalty clogging the equity of redemption, or (3.) inconsistent with or repugnant to the contractual and equitable right to redeem... I doubt whether, even before the repeal of the usury laws, this perfectly fair and businesslike transaction would have been considered a mortgage within any equitable rule or maxim relating to mortgages. The only possible way of deciding whether a transaction is a mortgage within any such rule or maxim is by reference to the intention of the parties. It never was intended by the parties that if the defendant company exercised their right to pay off the loan they should get rid of the option. The option was not in the nature of a penalty, nor was it nor could it ever become inconsistent with or repugnant to any other part of the real bargain within any such rule or maxim. The same is true of the commission payable on the sale of skins as to which the option was not exercised. Under these circumstances it

Alert

> seems to me that the bargain must stand and that the plaintiffs are entitled to the relief they claim.

Here the court allowed a collateral advantage to continue beyond the date of redemption, as the agreement was between two commercial parties of equal bargaining power. It was clearly the parties' intention that the right of first refusal should continue; the right of first refusal was deemed to be an independent transaction, contained in the same document, but created separately from the mortgage.

The court will strike down a redemption date that is so far in the future that it renders the right to redeem illusory. Whether the right to redeem has been rendered illusory is a question of fact and degree. *Knightsbridge Estates Trust Limited v Byrne and Others* [1939] Ch 441 considered previous case law in determining whether the right to redeem had been rendered illusory before making its decision on the instant facts; the Court of Appeal decision cited below was subsequently affirmed by the House of Lords.

Knightsbridge Estates Trust, Limited v Byrne and Others [1939] Ch 441

Panel: Sir Wilfred Greene MR, Scott and Farwell LJJ

Facts: The mortgagor mortgaged a number of properties to secure a loan. The agreement prevented redemption for a 40-year period and stipulated that, in absence of any breach by the mortgagor, the mortgagee would not require payment other than by the stated instalments.

> SIR WILFRED GREENE MR (reading the judgment of the court)
>
> It is indisputable that any provision which hampers redemption after the contractual date for redemption has passed will not be permitted. Further, it is undoubtedly true to say that a right of redemption is a necessary element in a mortgage transaction, and consequently that, where the contractual right of redemption is illusory, equity will grant relief by allowing redemption. This was the point in the case of *Fairclough v. Swan Brewery Co* [1912] A.C 565 decided in the Privy Council, where in a mortgage of a lease of twenty years the contractual right to redeem was postponed until six weeks before the expiration of the lease. The following passage from the judgment explains the reason for that decision [1912] A C 565, 565, 570: "The learned counsel on behalf of the respondents admitted, as he was bound to admit, that a mortgage cannot be made irredeemable. That is plainly forbidden. Is there any difference between forbidding redemption and permitting it, if the permission be a mere pretence? Here the provision for redemption is nugatory."
>
> Moreover, equity may give relief against contractual terms in a mortgage transaction if they are oppressive or unconscionable, and in deciding whether or not a particular transaction falls within this category the length of time for which the contractual right to redeem is postponed may well be an important consideration. In the present case no question of this kind was or could have been raised.
>
> But equity does not reform mortgage transactions because they are unreasonable. It is concerned to see two things - one that the essential requirements of a mortgage transaction are observed, and the other that oppressive or unconscionable terms are

not enforced. Subject to this, it does not, in our opinion, interfere. The question therefore arises whether, in a case where the right of redemption is real and not illusory and there is nothing oppressive or unconscionable in the transaction, there is something in a postponement of the contractual right to redeem, such as we have in the present case, that is inconsistent with the essential requirements of a mortgage transaction? Apart from authority the answer to this question would, in our opinion, be clearly in the negative. Any other answer would place an unfortunate restriction on the liberty of contract of competent parties who are at arm's length - in the present case it would have operated to prevent the respondents obtaining financial terms which for obvious reasons they themselves considered to be most desirable. It would, moreover, lead to highly inequitable results. The remedy sought by the respondents and the only remedy which is said to be open to them is the establishment of a right to redeem at any time on the ground that the postponement of the contractual right to redeem is void. They do not and could not suggest that the contract as a contract is affected, and the result would accordingly be that whereas the respondents would have had from the first the right to redeem at any time, the appellants would have had no right to require payment otherwise than by the specified instalments. Such an outcome to a bargain entered into by business people negotiating at arm's length would indeed be unfortunate, and we should require clear authority before coming to such a conclusion.

The court concluded that the postponement of redemption for 40 years was not a clog or fetter on the equity of redemption. The mortgaged property was freehold and would therefore not be devalued by the postponement. It was an arm's length transaction between two commercial parties. The long redemption period had been used to secure other favourable terms. The court contrasted this to *Fairclough v Swan Brewery Co* [1912] AC 565, where the mortgaged estate was a 17 ½ year lease and redemption was postponed until 6 weeks before the expiry of the lease. On the facts of that case, the postponement was deemed a clog on the equity of redemption.

If a mortgage includes an option for the mortgagee to purchase the mortgaged property, the option will be struck down as a clog on the equity of redemption. The court has been frequently asked to determine whether an option to purchase is a part of a mortgage transaction, or is in fact an independent transaction. If an option to purchase the property is deemed to be an independent transaction, it will be upheld; if it is deemed to be a part of the mortgage transaction, it will be struck down. In *Jones v Morgan* [2001] EWCA Civ 995, (2001) 82 P&CR D36, the Court of Appeal considered some of the leading authorities in this area.

Jones v Morgan [2001] EWCA Civ 995, [2001] 82 P&CR D36

Panel: Lord Phillips MR, Pill and Chadwick LJJ

Facts: In 1994 Morgan and his brother (the mortgagors) took out a loan from Jones (the mortgagee) to fund the redevelopment of their farm to turn it into a nursing home. This project was eventually abandoned. In 1997, the brothers decided to sell part of the land; they refinanced the original mortgage with Jones at this time.

LORD JUSTICE CHADWICK

Lord Parker had observed that the maxims "Once a mortgage, always a mortgage", or "A mortgage cannot be made irredeemable", were of little assistance where the court was faced with a new or doubtful case. He said this:

"[Those maxims] obviously beg the question, always of great importance, whether the particular transaction which the court has to consider is, in fact, a mortgage or not and, if they be acted on without a careful consideration of the equitable considerations on which they are based, can only, like Bacon's idols of the market place, lead to misconception and error."

The principles which I derive from those passages, so far as material to the present appeal, may be summarised as follows: (i) there is a rule that a mortgagee cannot as a term of the mortgage enter into a contract to purchase, or stipulate for an option to purchase, any part of or interest in the mortgaged property; (ii) the foundation of the rule is that a contract to purchase, or an option to purchase, any part of or interest in the mortgaged property, is repugnant to or inconsistent with the transaction of mortgage of which it forms part, and so must be rejected; (iii) the reason why the contract or option to purchase is repugnant to or inconsistent with the mortgage transaction is that it cannot stand with the contractual proviso for redemption or with the equitable right to redeem – the proviso for redemption (and, where the contractual date for redemption is past, the equitable right to redeem) requires the mortgagee to reconvey the mortgaged property to the mortgagor in the state in which it had been conveyed to him at the time of the mortgage; and (iv) it is essential, in any case to which the rule is said to apply, to consider whether or not the transaction is, in substance, a transaction of mortgage...

In *Reeve v Lisle* [1902] AC 461 the facts were more complex. In April 1896 the plaintiffs agreed to lend £5,000 to the defendant to be secured by a ship mortgage (which was executed in July of that year). If at any time during the period of two years the plaintiffs should elect to enter into partnership with the defendant, they would relieve the defendant of liability for payment of the mortgage money, and would transfer the ship, free of the mortgage, so that it could form part of the capital of the partnership. The plaintiffs did not exercise their right to enter into partnership within the two years, but the loan of £5,000 remained outstanding. A further mortgage was executed, as additional security, in June 1898. In July 1898 the parties entered into a further agreement, which, after referring to the existing mortgages, the fact that the monies were outstanding and a request from the defendant for further time for payment, provided that the plaintiffs should have the right, for a further five years, to enter into partnership with the defendant, in which case the same consequences would follow as had been agreed in the April 1896 agreement. In February 1900 the plaintiffs sought to exercise the right to enter into partnership with the defendant. The defendant resisted, on the basis that the right granted by the July 1898 agreement was in the nature of a clog on the right to redeem the mortgage made in June of that year. The Court of Appeal, reversing Mr Justice Buckley on the facts, held that the June 1898 mortgage and the July 1898 agreement were separate and distinct transactions. On that basis there was nothing objectionable in the grant of an option over the mortgaged property in the July agreement. Lord Justice Vaughan Williams explained the position in the following passage, at [1902] 1 Ch 53, 71:

"I do not understand the defendant's counsel to dispute that it is competent for a mortgagee to enter into an agreement to purchase from the mortgagor his equity of redemption. The only objection to such an agreement is, that it must not be part and parcel of the original loan or mortgage bargain. The mortgagee cannot, at the moment when he is lending his money and taking his security, enter into an agreement the effect of which would be that the mortgagor would have no equity of redemption. But there is nothing to prevent that being done which in substance and fact is subsequent to and independent of the original bargain."

The argument in the House of Lords was limited to the question whether the mortgage of June 1898 and the agreement of July 1898 were, in reality, one and the same transaction. The House of Lords rejected that contention. As Lord Macnaghten put it, at [1902] AC 461, 464:

"Notwithstanding the very able and ingenious argument by [counsel for the appellant] to prove that the purpose of this document [the July 1898 agreement] was really consolidation and rearrangement of the mortgages, in my opinion it was nothing of the kind."

There is a passage in the speech of Lord Lindley to the same effect, at page 465:

"In point of fact, the real transaction was not taking a mortgage security for 5000l. or getting a better security than they had. The real transaction [in July 1898] was that the mortgagees were bargaining for a share in the partnership on certain terms."

The case is authority, on its facts, for the proposition set out in the headnote:

"A mortgagor and a mortgagee may, by a separate and independent transaction subsequent to the mortgage, make a valid agreement which gives the mortgagee the option of purchasing the mortgaged property, and thus may have the effect of depriving the mortgagor of his right to redeem."...

 Alert

In *Samuel v Jarrah Timber Corporation* [1904] AC 323 the appellant advanced £5000 to the respondent company upon the security of £30,000 mortgage debenture stock of the company upon terms that he should have the option to purchase the whole or any part of that stock at 40%. at any time within twelve months. The company sought to repay the advance within the period of twelve months, whereupon the appellant claimed to purchase the whole of the stock at the agreed price. The company brought a redemption action, seeking a declaration that the option was void. The House of Lords (the Earl of Halsbury, Lord Chancellor, Lord Macnaghten and Lord Lindley), upholding Mr Justice Kekewich and the Court of Appeal, held that company was entitled to the declaration which it sought. Lord Halsbury and Lord Macnaghten reached that conclusion with obvious reluctance. Lord Lindley affirmed that the doctrine "Once a mortgage, always a mortgage" was not confined to deeds creating legal mortgages; it applied to all mortgage transactions. He went on, at page 329, to say this:

"The doctrine ... means that no contract between a mortgagor and a mortgagee made at the time of the mortgage and as part of the mortgage transaction, or, in other words, as one of the terms of the loan, can be valid if it prevents the mortgagor from getting back his property on paying off what is due on his security. Any bargain which has that effect is invalid, and is inconsistent with the transaction being a mortgage. This principle is fatal to the appellant's contention if the transaction under consideration is a mortgage transaction, as I am of opinion it clearly is."...

In my view the principle which prevents a mortgagee from stipulating for an interest in the mortgaged property at the time of the mortgage does have application in the circumstances of the present case, notwithstanding that the stipulation was contained in the 1997 agreement rather than in the 1994 mortgage. There are two reasons which lead me to that conclusion. First, it seems to me artificial to regard the 1997 agreement as being, in substance, independent of the 1994 mortgage transaction. It is, I think, important to have in mind that the genesis of clause 2 of the 1997 agreement was the assurance given to the appellant on 6 June 1994. The judge took the view that that assurance was spent when Mr Will Morgan abandoned the plan to develop the farmhouse at West Hall Farm as a nursing home. Whether or not that would be correct if the assurance were otherwise enforceable as a contract, the true position was that the appellant sought – and the respondents were content to concede – the inclusion of clause 2 in the 1997 agreement because that gave effect, in the context of the new plan to develop the farmhouse as residential flats, to the understanding which had been reached in 1994. It was, throughout, the intention of the parties to the mortgage transaction that the appellant should have a share of the development. The 1997 agreement sought to give effect to that intention.

Second, the 1997 agreement constituted a variation of the contractual terms upon which the respondents were entitled to redeem the mortgaged property. Prior to that agreement, the position was that they were entitled to redeem the mortgage upon payment off of the whole of the principal and interest then secured. On redemption they would get back the whole of the mortgaged property free from any incumbrance created by or at the time of the mortgage. The effect of the 1997 agreement was that they were entitled to redeem part of the mortgaged property – that is to say, the part that was to be sold to Mr Lougher – on payment of an amount equal to the price which they were to receive from the purchaser; and they were entitled to redeem the remainder of the mortgaged property – that is to say the Retained Lands – on payment of an amount equal to the balance of the principal and interest then outstanding, and further interest accruing thereafter. In substance, the effect of the 1997 agreement was to convert what had been a single, indivisible, mortgage loan into two distinct mortgage loans. It seems to me that there is no reason why the principle which prevents a mortgagee from stipulating for an interest in the mortgaged property should not apply to a transaction which has that effect. Plainly the principle would apply if the transaction in 1997 had taken the form of a payment off of the whole of the secured loan, a discharge of the existing mortgage, and a re-lending of the difference between the amount of the secured loan and the moneys to be received from the purchaser upon the security of a mortgage of the Retained Lands. Although different in form, the 1997 transaction was identical in substance.

Thus, where an option is linked to a mortgage agreement, the option will be void as it prevents the equitable right to redeem by the mortgagor.

The courts have also considered whether unusually high rates of interest are unfair and unconscionable (and therefore unenforceable), rather than simply unreasonable; they will consider the circumstances on a case by case basis.

Cityland and Property (Holdings) Ltd v Dabrah [1968] Ch 166

Panel: Goff J

Facts: The defendant was the plaintiff's tenant for 11 years. Upon the expiry of the lease, the plaintiff offered to sell the property to the defendant. The defendant took a loan from and granted a mortgage to the plaintiff in order to fund the purchase. The interest rate was not clearly stated in the mortgage agreement, but it was calculated to have been 19 per cent per annum based on the division of the premium into instalments. The premium amounted to 57 per cent of the value of the loan and it became payable in its entirety upon default.

MR JUSTICE GOFF

It follows... that the defendant cannot succeed merely because this is a collateral advantage, but he can succeed if - and only if - on the evidence, the bonus in this case was, to use the language of Lord Parker, "unfair and unconscionable," or, to use the language used in Halsbury's Laws of England, "unreasonable"; and I therefore have to determine whether it was or was not. In doing that, I have to consider all the circumstances. Unlike the facts in *Kreglinger v. New Patagonia Meat & Cold Storage Co. Ltd* [1914] A.C. 25 this was not a bargain between two large trading concerns. It was the case of a man who was buying his house and a man who was obviously of limited means because he was unable to find more than £600 towards the purchase, whereas, in evidence filed for another purpose, the plaintiffs have stated that all the other persons who had purchased property from them had been able themselves to finance or to arrange finance for the purchases. The premium which was added to the loan was, as I understand, no less than 57 per cent of the amount of the loan. I do not think it is really open to the plaintiffs to justify this premium as being in lieu of interest because they claim interest on the aggregate of the loan and the premium: but even if it should be, then, taking the mortgage as a six-year mortgage - and, of course, they bound themselves not to call it in within that time if the instalments were duly paid - it would still represent interest at 19 per cent., which is out of all proportion to any investment rates prevailing at the time. Moreover, it was expressly provided by the charge that, on default, the whole should immediately become due...

Reasonableness, fairness and conscionability depend upon all the circumstances, and, in my judgment, I am entitled to weigh as a factor that, on default, the premium could become payable forthwith, and I am told that the effect of that would be, on the facts, to make interest in effect 38 per cent.

I have further to bear in mind that this was not an unsecured loan: a security was being offered with a reasonable margin, not, it is true, a one-third/two-thirds margin as one usually expects in trustee investments, but still the defendant provided £600 and there was that margin in the property to secure the plaintiffs. I think they would have been entitled to charge a higher rate of interest than the normal market rate, or a reasonable premium comparable therewith, but nothing like the extent of 19 per cent looked at as an interest rate, or 57 per cent looked at as a capital sum, and it must be borne in mind that this premium was so large that it forthwith destroyed the whole equity and made it a completely deficient security. If default were made, and all that had been secured was the principal and interest, it was likely that on any exercise of the plaintiffs' powers as mortgagees, there would be a surplus for the mortgagor, but this premium destroyed any possibility of that, and it also made the security which was offered deficient.

For these reasons, in my judgment this was not reasonable, and, on the equity as now defined in *Kreglinger v. New Patagonia Meat & Cold Storage Co. Ltd* [1914] A.C. 25 I can and ought to interfere....

This was a mortgage upon security, and upon security in which there was a reasonable margin of equity for the protection of the plaintiffs as mortgagees. In my judgment, therefore, all that the plaintiffs are entitled to enforce is the amount outstanding in respect of principal and interest, after bringing into account the payments which have been made...

It remains only to say something on the rate of interest. When the plaintiffs were claiming interest on the aggregate of the loan and the premium, they suggested 5 per cent, and the defendant has embraced that. But I think that is too low a rate. If one is charging interest on the actual loan, one ought at least to give market rates and possibly, in the circumstances of this case, somewhat more.

After hearing submissions, Goff J replaced the 19 per cent interest rate with 7 per cent. In reaching his decision that the interest rate was unconscionable, he emphasised the inequality of bargaining power. The court is much less likely to intervene where both parties are commercial enterprises with equally strong bargaining positions. This was demonstrated in *Multiservice Bookbinding Ltd and Others v Marden* [1979] Ch 84.

Multiservice Bookbinding Ltd and Others v Marden [1979] Ch 84

Panel: Browne-Wilkinson J

Facts: The plaintiffs granted a mortgage on their business premises to the defendant in return for a loan of £36,000. The mortgage included the following terms: (1) interest at 2 per cent above bank rate; (2) the loan could not be redeemed for 10 years; (3) the capital and interest repayments would be index-linked to the exchange rate of the Swiss franc. The pound subsequently depreciated and the repayments rose dramatically. The plaintiffs argued that the clause index-linking the repayments to the Swiss franc was unconscionable.

MR JUSTICE BROWNE-WILKINSON

I... approach the second point on the basis that, in order to be freed from the necessity to comply with all the terms of the mortgage, the plaintiffs must show that the bargain, or some of its terms, was unfair and unconscionable: it is not enough to show that, in the eyes of the court, it was unreasonable. In my judgment a bargain cannot be unfair and unconscionable unless one of the parties to it has imposed the objectionable terms in a morally reprehensible manner, that is to say, in a way which affects his conscience.

The classic example of an unconscionable bargain is where advantage has been taken of a young, inexperienced or ignorant person to introduce a term which no sensible well-advised person or party would have accepted. But I do not think the categories of unconscionable bargains are limited: the court can and should intervene where a bargain has been procured by unfair means.

Mr. Nugee submitted that a borrower was, in the normal case, in an unequal bargaining position vis-à-vis the lender and that the care taken by the courts of equity to protect borrowers... was reflected in a general rule that, except in the case of two large equally powerful institutions, any unreasonable term would be "unconscionable" within Lord Parker's test. I cannot accept this. In my judgment there is no such special rule applicable to contracts of loan which requires one to treat a bargain as having been unfairly made even where it is demonstrated that no unfair advantage has been taken of the borrower. No decision illustrating Mr. Nugee's principle was cited. However, if, as in the *Cityland* case [1968] Ch 166, there is an unusual or unreasonable stipulation the reason for which is not explained, it may well be that in the absence of any explanation, the court will assume that unfair advantage has been taken of the borrower. In considering all the facts, it will often be the case that the borrower's need for the money was far more pressing than the lenders need to lend: if this proves to be the case, then circumstances exist in which an unfair advantage could have been taken. It does not necessarily follow that what could have been done has been done: whether or not an unfair advantage has in fact been taken depends on the facts of each case.

Applying those principles to this case, first I do not think it is right to treat the "Swiss franc uplift" element in the capital-repayments as being in any sense a premium or collateral advantage. In my judgment a lender of money is entitled to insure that he is repaid the real value of his loan and if he introduces a term which so provides, he is not stipulating for anything beyond the repayment of principal. I do not think equity would have struck down clause 6 as a collateral advantage even before the repeal of the usury laws. The decision in *Booth v. Salvation Army Building Association Ltd.* (1897) 14 T.L.R. 3, turned on quite different considerations. It is in my opinion correctly explained by Professor Waldock in his Law of Mortgages, 2nd ed. (1950), p. 182 as a decision that any additional sum expressed to be payable on redemption or default is not recoverable since it is a clog on the equity of redemption.

Secondly, considering the mortgage bargain as a whole, in my judgment there was no great inequality of bargaining power as between the plaintiffs and the defendant. The

Link

Mr Justice Browne-Wilkinson refers to Lord Parker's judgment in *G&C Kreglinger v New Patagonia Meat & Cold Storage Co Ltd.*

plaintiff company was a small but prosperous company in need of cash to enable it to expand: if it did not like the terms offered it could have refused them without being made insolvent or, as in the *Cityland* case [1968] Ch. 166, losing its home. The defendant had £40,000 to lend, but only, as he explained to the plaintiffs, if its real value was preserved. The defendant is not a professional moneylender and there is no evidence of any sharp practice of any kind by him. The borrowers were represented by independent solicitors of repute. Therefore the background does not give rise to any pre-supposition that the defendant took an unfair advantage of the plaintiffs.

Mr. Nugee's main case is based on the terms of the mortgage itself. He points to the facts that (1) the defendant's principal and interest is fully inflation proofed (2) that interest is payable at two per cent. above minimum lending rate and (3) that interest is payable on the whole £36,000 throughout the term of the loan. He says that although any one of these provisions by itself might not be objectionable, when all these are joined in one mortgage they are together "unfair and unconscionable". He adds further subsidiary points, amongst them that it is impossible to know the sum required for redemption when notice to redeem has to be given; that interest is payable in advance; that no days of grace were allowed for paying the instalments of capital and any expenses incurred by the lender are charged on the property and therefore under clause 6 subject to the Swiss franc uplift even though incurred long after 1966. He also contends that if there were capitalised arrears of interest, the Swiss franc uplift would be applied twice: once when the arrears are capitalised and again when the capitalised sum is paid: in my opinion this is not the true construction of the mortgage.

However, Mr. Nugee's other points amount to a formidable list and if it were relevant I would be of the view that the terms were unreasonable judged by the standards which the court would adopt if it had to settle the terms of a mortgage. In particular I consider that it was unreasonable both for the debt to be inflation proofed by reference to the Swiss franc and at the same time to provide for a rate of interest two per cent. above bank rate - a rate which reflects at least in part the unstable state of the pound sterling. On top of this interest on the whole sum advanced was to be paid throughout the term. The defendant made a hard bargain. But the test is not reasonableness. The parties made a bargain which the plaintiffs, who are businessmen, went into with their eyes open, with the benefit of independent advice, without any compelling necessity to accept a loan on these terms and without any sharp practice by the defendant. I cannot see that there was anything unfair or oppressive or morally reprehensible in such a bargain entered into in such circumstances. The need for the defendant to invest his money in a way which preserved its real purchasing power provides an adequate explanation of all the terms of the mortgage, except the provision which would apply the Swiss franc uplift to expenses defrayed in, say 1975, for which there can be no possible justification. It is common ground that this was not an intended result - and therefore it cannot reflect on the morality of the defendant's behaviour - and the defendant has stated that he would not apply the Swiss franc uplift to moneys other than the principal and interest. It is not necessary for me, therefore, to decide whether clause 6 would be permitted to apply to such expenditure.

Mr Justice Browne-Wilkinson judged that the interest rate, including the index-linking to the Swiss franc, was not unconscionable. In contrast to *Cityland and Property (Holdings) Ltd v Dabrah*, the parties were of equal bargaining power. The lender was not a money lender by trade, and there was no question of sharp practice. It was simply a hard bargain.

There are also statutory provisions to protect borrowers from unusually high rates of interest. The Consumer Credit Act 2006, the Financial Services and Markets Act 2000 and the Unfair Terms in Consumer Contract Regulations 1999 all provide further protection to borrowers (although note that from 26 April 2014 regulation of the consumer credit legislation passed to the Financial Conduct Authority). Case judgments in relation to these Acts have approached the issue of unfair interest rates in a comparable manner.

Link
See Contract Law Case Book

7.2 Undue Influence

Where more than one person has an interest in a property, lenders must be careful that there is no undue influence asserted by one of the owners upon the other before they agree to grant a mortgage. If the court decides the bank was put on enquiry regarding undue influence, it will be bound by the interest of the person who was subject to undue influence. *Barclays Bank plc v O'Brien and Another* [1994] 1 AC 180 considered when a lender is put on enquiry.

Barclays Bank plc v O'Brien and Another [1994] 1 AC 180

Panel: Lord Templeman, Lord Lowry, Lord Browne-Wilkinson, Lord Slynn of Hadley and Lord Woolf

Facts: A husband and wife held the legal title to the matrimonial home. The husband arranged a mortgage of the property to raise capital for a company in which he, but not his wife, had an interest. The husband told the wife the loan was for a fixed amount (£60,000) for three weeks only. In fact, the husband guaranteed the company's debt (up to £135,000). The Bank drafted the mortgage agreement and told the Branch staff to inform the wife about the content and to advise her to seek independent legal advice before signing. When the wife attended the bank, she signed the agreement without reading it; she was not advised to seek independent legal advice and did not have the document explained to her. When the husband subsequently failed to make the repayments, the bank sought possession of the property.

LORD BROWNE-WILKINSON

In my judgment, if the doctrine of notice is properly applied, there is no need for the introduction of a special equity in these types of cases. A wife who has been induced to stand as a surety for her husband's debts by his undue influence, misrepresentation or some other legal wrong has an equity as against him to set aside that transaction. Under the ordinary principles of equity, her right to set aside that transaction will be enforceable against third parties (e.g. against a creditor) if either the husband was acting as the third party's agent or the third party had actual or constructive notice of the facts giving rise to her equity. Although there may be cases where, without artificiality, it can properly be held that the husband was acting as the agent of the creditor in procuring the wife to stand as surety, such cases will be of very rare occurrence. The key to the problem is to identify the circumstances in which the creditor will be taken to have had notice of the wife's equity to set aside the transaction.

The doctrine of notice lies at the heart of equity. Given that there are two innocent parties, each enjoying rights, the earlier right prevails against the later right if the acquirer of the later right knows of the earlier right (actual notice) or would have discovered it had he taken proper steps (constructive notice). In particular, if the party asserting that he takes free of the earlier rights of another knows of certain facts which put him on inquiry as to the possible existence of the rights of that other and he fails to make such inquiry or take such other steps as are reasonable to verify whether such earlier right does or does not exist, he will have constructive notice of the earlier right and take subject to it. Therefore where a wife has agreed to stand surety for her husband's debts as a result of undue influence or misrepresentation, the creditor will take subject to the wife's equity to set aside the transaction if the circumstances are such as to put the creditor on inquiry as to the circumstances in which she agreed to stand surety...

Therefore in my judgment a creditor is put on inquiry when a wife offers to stand surety for her husband's debts by the combination of two factors: (a) the transaction is on its face not to the financial advantage of the wife; and (b) there is a substantial risk in transactions of that kind that, in procuring the wife to act as surety, the husband has committed a legal or equitable wrong that entitles the wife to set aside the transaction.

It follow that unless the creditor who is put on inquiry takes reasonable steps to satisfy himself that the wife's agreement to stand surety has been properly obtained, the creditor will have constructive notice of the wife's rights...

But in my judgment the creditor, in order to avoid being fixed with constructive notice, can reasonably be expected to take steps to bring home to the wife the risk she is running by standing as surety and to advise her to take independent advice. As to past transactions, it will depend on the facts of each case whether the steps taken by the creditor satisfy this test. However for the future in my judgment a creditor will have satisfied these requirements if it insists that the wife attend a private meeting (in the absence of the husband) with a representative of the creditor at which she is told of the extent of her liability as surety, warned of the risk she is running and urged to take independent legal advice. If these steps are taken in my judgment the creditor will have taken such reasonable steps as are necessary to preclude a subsequent claim that it had constructive notice of the wife's rights. I should make it clear that I have been considering the ordinary case where the creditor knows only that the wife is to stand surety for her husband's debts. I would not exclude exceptional cases where a creditor has knowledge of further facts which render the presence of undue influence not only possible but probable. In such cases, the creditor to be safe will have to insist that the wife is separately advised...

I have hitherto dealt only with the position where a wife stands surety for her husband's debts. But in my judgment the same principles are applicable to all other cases where there is an emotional relationship between cohabitees. The "tenderness" shown by the law to married women is not based on the marriage ceremony but reflects the underlying risk of one cohabitee exploiting the emotional involvement and trust of the other. Now that unmarried cohabitation, whether heterosexual or homosexual, is widespread in our society, the law should recognise this. Legal wives are not the only group which are now exposed to the emotional pressure of cohabitation. Therefore if, but only if, the creditor is aware that the surety is cohabiting with the principal debtor, in my judgment the same principles should apply to them as apply to husband and wife...

I can therefore summarise my views as follows. Where one cohabitee has entered into an obligation to stand as surety for the debts of the other cohabitee and the creditor is aware that they are cohabitees: (1) the surety obligation will be valid and enforceable by the creditor unless the suretyship was procured by the undue influence, misrepresentation or other legal wrong of the principal debtor; (2) if there has been undue influence, misrepresentation or other legal wrong by the principal debtor, unless the creditor has taken reasonable steps to satisfy himself that the surety entered into the obligation freely and in knowledge of the true facts, the creditor will be unable to enforce the surety obligation because he will be fixed with constructive notice of the surety's right to set aside the transaction; (3) unless there are special exceptional circumstances, a creditor will have taken such reasonable steps to avoid being fixed with constructive notice if the creditor warns the surety (at a meeting not attended by the principal debtor) of the amount of her potential liability and of the risks involved and advises the surety to take independent legal advice.

 Alert

In *Royal Bank of Scotland v Etridge (No 2) and Other Appeals* [2001] UKHL 44, [2002] 2 AC 773, the House of Lords provided clear guidance on the precautionary steps a bank should take to ensure they take the property free from constructive notice of undue influence.

Royal Bank of Scotland v Etridge (No 2) and Other Appeals [2001] UKHL 44, [2002] 2 AC 773

Panel: Lord Bingham of Cornhill, Lord Nicholls of Birkenhead, Lord Clyde, Lord Hobhouse of Woodborough, Lord Scott of Foscote

Facts: This case dealt with eight separate appeals. In seven of these appeals, a wife had agreed to mortgage her interest to a bank, as security for a loan to benefit her husband. In each case, the bank had understood the wife to have sought legal advice. In each case, the wife claimed to have been subject to undue influence.

LORD NICHOLLS OF BIRKENHEAD

The problem has arisen in the context of wives guaranteeing payment of their husband's business debts. In recent years judge after judge has grappled with the baffling question whether a wife's guarantee of her husband's bank overdraft, together with a charge on her share of the matrimonial home, was a transaction manifestly to her disadvantage.

In a narrow sense, such a transaction plainly ('manifestly') is disadvantageous to the wife. She undertakes a serious financial obligation, and in return she personally receives nothing. But that would be to take an unrealistically blinkered view of such a transaction. Unlike the relationship of solicitor and client or medical adviser and patient, in the case of husband and wife there are inherent reasons why such a transaction may well be for her benefit. Ordinarily, the fortunes of husband and wife are bound up together. If the husband's business is the source of the family income, the wife has a lively interest in doing what she can to support the business. A wife's affection and self-interest run hand-in-hand in inclining her to join with her husband in charging the matrimonial home, usually a jointly-owned asset, to obtain the financial facilities needed by the business. The finance may be needed to start a new business, or expand a promising business, or rescue an ailing business...

If the freedom of home-owners to make economic use of their homes is not to be frustrated, a bank must be able to have confidence that a wife's signature of the necessary guarantee and charge will be as binding upon her as is the signature of anyone else on documents which he or she may sign. Otherwise banks will not be willing to lend money on the security of a jointly owned house or flat.

At the same time, the high degree of trust and confidence and emotional interdependence which normally characterises a marriage relationship provides scope for abuse. One party may take advantage of the other's vulnerability. Unhappily, such abuse does occur. Further, it is all too easy for a husband, anxious or even desperate for bank finance, to misstate the position in some particular or to mislead the wife, wittingly or unwittingly, in some other way. The law would be seriously defective if it did not recognise these realities...

In *O'Brien* the House considered the circumstances in which a bank, or other creditor, is 'put on inquiry.' Strictly this is a misnomer. As already noted, a bank is not required to make inquiries. But it will be convenient to use the terminology which has now become accepted in this context. The House set a low level for the threshold which must be crossed before a bank is put on inquiry. For practical reasons the level is set much lower than is required to satisfy a court that, failing contrary evidence, the court may infer that the transaction was procured by undue influence. Lord Browne-Wilkinson said ([1994] 1 AC 180, 196):

'Therefore in my judgment a creditor in put on inquiry when a wife offers to stand surety for her husband's debts by the combination of two factors: (a) the transaction is on its face not to the financial advantage of the wife; and (b) there is a substantial risk in transactions of that kind that, in procuring the wife to act as surety, the husband has committed a legal or equitable wrong that entitles the wife to set aside the transaction.'

In my view, this passage, read in context, is to be taken to mean, quite simply, that a bank is put on inquiry whenever a wife offers to stand surety for her husband's debts...

The position is likewise if the husband stands surety for his wife's debts. Similarly, in the case of unmarried couples, whether heterosexual or homosexual, where the bank is aware of the relationship: see Lord Browne-Wilkinson in *O'Brien*'s case, at p 198. Cohabitation is not essential. The Court of Appeal rightly so decided in *Massey v Midland Bank Plc* [1995] 1 All ER 929: see Steyn LJ, at p 933.

As to the type of transactions where a bank is put on inquiry, the case where a wife becomes surety for her husband's debts is, in this context, a straightforward case. The bank is put on inquiry. On the other side of the line is the case where money is being advanced, or has been advanced, to husband and wife jointly. In such a case the bank is not put on inquiry, unless the bank is aware the loan is being made for the husband's purposes, as distinct from their joint purposes. That was decided in *CIBC Mortgages Plc v Pitt* [1994] 1 AC 200 ...

The principal area of controversy on these appeals concerns the steps a bank should take when it has been put on inquiry. In *O'Brien* Lord Browne-Wilkinson, at [1994] 1 AC 180, 196-197, said that a bank can reasonably be expected to take steps to bring home to the wife the risk she is running by standing as surety and to advise her to take independent advice. That test is applicable to past transactions. All the cases now before your Lordships' House fall into this category. For the future a bank satisfies these requirements if it insists that the wife attend a private meeting with a representative of the bank at which she is told of the extent of her liability as surety, warned of the risk she is running and urged to take independent legal advice. In exceptional cases the bank, to be safe, has to insist that the wife is separately advised...

The furthest a bank can be expected to go is to take reasonable steps to satisfy itself that the wife has had brought home to her, in a meaningful way, the practical implications of the proposed transaction. This does not wholly eliminate the risk of undue influence or misrepresentation. But it does mean that a wife enters into a transaction with her eyes open so far as the basic elements of the transaction are concerned...

Thus, in the present type of case it is not for the solicitor to veto the transaction by declining to confirm to the bank that he has explained the documents to the wife and the risks she is taking upon herself. If the solicitor considers the transaction is not in the wife's best interests, he will give reasoned advice to the wife to that effect. But at the end of the day the decision on whether to proceed is the decision of the client, not the solicitor. A wife is not to be precluded from entering into a financially unwise transaction if, for her own reasons, she wishes to do so...

When an instruction to this effect is forthcoming, the content of the advice required from a solicitor before giving the confirmation sought by the bank will, inevitably, depend upon the circumstances of the case. Typically, the advice a solicitor can be expected to give should cover the following matters as the core minimum. (1) He will need to explain the nature of the documents and the practical consequences these will have for the wife if she signs them. She could lose her home if her husband's business does not prosper. Her home may be her only substantial asset, as well as the family's home. She could be made bankrupt. (2) He will need to point out the seriousness of the risks involved. The wife should be told the purpose of the proposed new facility, the amount and principal terms of the new facility, and that the bank might increase the amount of the facility, or change its terms, or grant a new facility, without reference to her. She should be told the amount of her liability under her guarantee. The solicitor should discuss the wife's financial means, including her understanding of the value of the property being charged. The solicitor should discuss whether the wife or her husband has any other assets out of which repayment could be made if the husband's business should fail. These matters are relevant to the seriousness of the risks involved. (3) The solicitor will need to state clearly that the wife has a choice. The decision is hers and hers alone. Explanation of the choice facing the wife will call for some discussion of the present financial position, including the amount of the husband's present indebtedness, and the amount of his current overdraft facility. (4) The solicitor should check whether the wife wishes to proceed. She should be asked whether she is content that the solicitor should write to the bank confirming he has explained to her the nature of the documents and the practical implications they may have for her, or whether, for instance, she would prefer him to negotiate with the bank on the terms of the transaction. Matters for negotiation could include the sequence in which the various securities will be called upon or a specific or lower limit to her liabilities. The solicitor should not give any confirmation to the bank without the wife's authority.

The solicitor's discussion with the wife should take place at a face-to-face meeting, in the absence of the husband. It goes without saying that the solicitor's explanations should be couched in suitably non-technical language. It also goes without saying that the solicitor's task is an important one. It is not a formality...

In the *O'Brien* case the House was concerned with formulating a fair and practical solution to problems occurring when a creditor obtains a security from a guarantor whose sexual relationship with the debtor gives rise to a heightened risk of undue influence. But the law does not regard sexual relationships as standing in some special category of their own so far as undue influence is concerned. Sexual relationships are no more than one type of relationship in which an individual may acquire influence over another individual. The *O'Brien* decision cannot sensibly be regarded as confined to sexual relationships, although these are likely to be its main field of application at present. What is appropriate for sexual relationships ought, in principle, to be appropriate also for other relationships where trust and confidence are likely to exist.

The House of Lords has clearly defined the duties and responsibilities of lenders and has outlined a very clear procedure for banks to follow to ensure they are not fixed with constructive notice of undue influence.

7.3 Rights and Duties of the Mortgagee

There is a wealth of case law dealing with the rights and duties of the mortgagee upon default by the mortgagor. Upon default, a mortgagee will ordinarily seek to take possession and then sell the property. The mortgagee can take possession with a court order or by self-help. The Administration of Justice Act 1970 s 36 provides the mortgagor with some protection if the mortgagee seeks a court order prior to taking possession of a dwelling house. The question arose whether this statutory protection prevented mortgagees from pursuing self-help in future.

Ropaigealach v Barclays Bank plc [2000] QB 263

Panel: Henry, Chadwick and Clarke LJJ

Statutes: Administration of Justice Act 1970 s 36, Criminal Law Act 1977 s 6

Facts: The mortgagee had taken possession by self-help (without obtaining a court order). The mortgagor argued that it could not be Parliament's intention only to provide protection to mortgagors where mortgagees sought court orders; the issue of the appeal was whether the mortgagee had been entitled to take possession without first obtaining a court order.

LORD JUSTICE CHADWICK

Mr. Ropaigealach relies on section 36 of the Administration of Justice Act 1970. The section is in these terms, in so far as material:

[Section 36 was set out and Chadwick LJ continued.]

For the purposes of those provisions "dwelling-house" includes any building or part thereof which is used as a dwelling; and "mortgagor" and "mortgagee" includes any person having title under the original mortgagor or mortgagee - see section 39(1) of the Act of 1970...

I find it impossible to be satisfied that Parliament must have intended, when enacting section 36 of the Act of 1970, that the mortgagee's common law right to take possession by virtue of his estate should only be exercisable with the assistance of the court. In my view, the only conclusion as to parliamentary intention that this court can properly reach is that which can be derived from the circumstances in which the section was enacted, the statutory context in which it appears and the language which was used. All point in the same direction. Parliament was concerned with the problem which had arisen following *Birmingham Citizens Permanent Building Society v. Caunt* [1962] Ch. 883; it intended to restore the position to what it had been thought to be before that decision; and it did not address its mind to the question whether the mortgagor required protection against the mortgagee who took possession without the assistance of the court. It is impossible to be sure what course Parliament would have thought it appropriate to adopt, in 1970, if it had identified and addressed that question. It is impossible to be sure that Parliament did not intend (or would not have intended, if it had addressed its mind to the question) to leave the position as it was in that regard. It is not irrelevant that, at the date at which the Act of 1970 was enacted, the mortgagor who was in occupation had the protection - subsequently replaced in a different and, perhaps, more limited form by section 6 of the Criminal Law Act 1977 - afforded by the Forcible Entry Acts 1381-1623. It is because it is impossible to be sure that Parliament cannot have intended to leave the position as it was - but must have intended that the mortgagee should only be entitled to exercise his common law right to possession with the assistance of the court - that it cannot be appropriate to embark on an investigation whether the words which have been used are capable of some other construction than that which they naturally bear.

Thus, the protection afforded to the mortgagor by these statutory provisions applies only where the mortgagee seek a court order; it does not apply where a mortgagee takes possession by self-help, which was confirmed by the court as an alternative available to lenders seeking to take possession. Nonetheless, where a mortgagee takes possession by self-help, the court has discretion to grant a short adjournment to give the mortgagor an opportunity to pay off his debt (*Birmingham Citizens Permanent BS v Caunt and Another* [1962] Ch 883).

Once the mortgagee has obtained possession and moves to sell the property, he remains under a duty of care to the mortgagor. The right of the mortgagee to sell the property is governed by the Law of Property Act 1925 ss 101 and 103. The precise nature and extent of the mortgagee's duty upon such a sale to the mortgagor was discussed in *Silven Properties Ltd and another v Royal Bank of Scotland plc and others* [2004] 4 All ER 484.

Silven Properties Ltd and another v Royal Bank of Scotland plc and others [2004] 4 All ER 484

Panel: Aldous and Tuckey LJJ and Lightman J

Facts: The mortgagor had defaulted. The mortgagee's agent, in selling the property, started applications for planning permission with a view to increasing the value of the property sold. The agent subsequently decided not to proceed with the applications and sold immediately. The mortgagor claimed the agent was under an obligation to proceed with the applications and sell the property at the best obtainable price.

MR JUSTICE LIGHTMAN

A mortgagee has no duty at any time to exercise his powers as mortgagee to sell, to take possession or to appoint a receiver and preserve the security or its value or to realise his security. He is entitled to remain totally passive. If the mortgagee takes possession, he becomes the manager of the charged property: see *Kendle v Melsom* (1998) 193 CLR 46 at 64. He thereby assumes a duty to take reasonable care of the property secured: see *Downsview Nominees Ltd v First City Corp Ltd* [1993] 3 All ER 626 at 637 per Lord Templeman; and this requires him to be active in protecting and exploiting the security, maximising the return, but without taking undue risks: see *Palk v Mortgage Services Funding plc* [1993] 2 All ER 481 at 486 per Nicholls V-C.

A mortgagee 'is not a trustee of the power of sale for the mortgagor'. This time-honoured expression can be traced back at least as far as Jessel MR in *Nash v Eads* (1880) 25 Sol Jo 95. In default of provision to the contrary in the mortgage, the power is conferred upon the mortgagee by way of bargain by the mortgagor for his own benefit and he has an unfettered discretion to sell when he likes to achieve repayment of the debt which he is owed: see *Cuckmere Brick Co Ltd v Mutual Finance Ltd* [1971] 2 All ER 633 at 646–647. A mortgagee is at all times free to consult his own interests alone whether and when to exercise his power of sale. The most recent authoritative restatement of this principle is to be found in *Raja (administratrix of the estate of Raja (decd)) v Austin Gray (a firm)* [2002] EWCA Civ 1965 at [55], [2003] Lloyd's Rep PN 126 at [55] per Peter Gibson LJ. The mortgagee's decision is not constrained by reason of the fact that the exercise or non-exercise of the power will occasion loss or damage to the mortgagor: see *China and South Sea Bank Ltd v Tan* [1989] 3 All ER 839. It does not matter that the time may be unpropitious and that by waiting a higher price could be obtained: he is not bound to postpone in the hope of obtaining a better price: see *Tse Kwong Lam v Wong Chit Sen* [1983] 3 All ER 54 at 59...

The mortgagee is entitled to sell the mortgaged property as it is. He is under no obligation to improve it or increase its value. There is no obligation to take any such pre-marketing steps to increase the value of the property as is suggested by the claimants. The claimants submitted that this principle could not stand with the decision of the Privy Council in *McHugh v Union Bank of Canada* [1913] AC 299. Lord Moulton in that case held (at 312) that, if a mortgagee does proceed with a sale of property which is unsaleable as it stands, a duty of care may be imposed on him when taking the necessary steps to render the mortgaged property saleable. The mortgage in that case was of horses, which the mortgagee needed to drive to market if he was to sell them. The mortgagee was held to owe to the mortgagor a duty to take proper care of them whilst driving them to market. The duty imposed on the mortgagee was to take care to preserve, not increase, the value of the security. The decision accordingly affords no support for the claimants' case.

The mortgagee is free (in his own interest as well as that of the mortgagor) to investigate whether and how he can 'unlock' the potential for an increase in value of the property mortgaged (eg by an application for planning permission or the grant of a lease) and indeed (going further) he can proceed with such an application or grant. But he is likewise free at any time to halt his efforts and proceed instead immediately with a sale. By commencing on this path the mortgagee does not in any way preclude himself from calling a halt at will: he does not assume any such obligation of care to the mortgagor in respect of its continuance as the claimants contend. If however the mortgagee is to seek to charge to the mortgagor the costs of the exercise which he has undertaken of obtaining planning permission or a lessee, subject to any applicable terms of the mortgage, the mortgagee may only be entitled to do so if he acted reasonably in incurring those costs and fairly balanced the costs of the exercise against the potential benefits taking fully into account the possibility that he might at any moment 'pull the plug' on these efforts and the consequences for the mortgagor if he did so.

If the mortgagor requires protection in any of these respects, whether by imposing further duties on the mortgagee or limitations on his rights and powers, he must insist upon them when the bargain is made and upon the inclusion of protective provisions in the mortgage. In the absence of such protective provisions, the mortgagee is entitled to rest on the terms of the mortgage and (save where statute otherwise requires) the court must give effect to them. The one method available to the mortgagor to prevent the mortgagee exercising the rights conferred upon him by the mortgagee is to redeem the mortgage. If he redeems, there can be no need or justification for recourse by the mortgagee to the power of sale to achieve repayment of the debt due to him secured by the mortgage.

When and if the mortgagee does exercise the power of sale, he comes under a duty in equity (and not tort) to the mortgagor (and all others interested in the equity of redemption) to take reasonable precautions to obtain 'the fair' or 'the true market' value of or the 'proper price' for the mortgaged property at the date of the sale, and not (as the claimants submitted) the date of the decision to sell. If the period of time between the dates of the decision to sell and of the sale is short, there may be no difference in value between the two dates and indeed in many (if not most cases) this may be readily assumed. But where there is a period of delay, the difference in date could prove significant. The mortgagee is not entitled to act in a way which unfairly prejudices the mortgagor by selling hastily at a knock-down price sufficient to pay off his debt: see *Palk's case* [1993] 2 All ER 481 at 486–487. He must take proper care whether by fairly and properly exposing the property to the market or otherwise to obtain the best price reasonably obtainable at the date of sale. The remedy for breach of this equitable duty is not common law damages, but an order that the mortgagee account to the mortgagor and all others interested in the equity of redemption, not just for what he actually received, but for what he should have received: see the *Standard Chartered Bank* case [1982] 3 All ER 938 at 942.

In our judgment there can accordingly be no duty on the part of a mortgagee, as suggested by the claimants, to postpone exercising the power of sale until after the further pursuit (let alone the outcome) of an application for planning permission or the grant of a lease of the mortgaged property, though the outcome of the application and the effect of the grant of the lease may be to increase the market value of the mortgaged property and price obtained on sale. A mortgagee is entitled to sell the property in the condition in which it stands without investing money or time in increasing its likely sale value. He is entitled to discontinue efforts already undertaken to increase their likely sale value in favour of such a sale. A mortgagee is under a duty to take reasonable care to obtain a sale price which reflects the added value available on the grant of planning permission and the grant of a lease of a vacant property and (as a means of achieving this end) to ensure that the potential is brought to the notice of prospective purchasers and accordingly taken into account in their offers: see the *Cuckmere* case. But that is the limit of his duty.

Thus, a mortgagee has a wide discretion in deciding how and when to dispose of a property. The most significant duty is to take reasonable care to obtain a proper price for the property; there are no further obligations to postpone sale or make improvements.

Further Reading

MacKenzie & Phillips *Textbook on Land Law*, (15th Edition), Oxford University Press, pp 451-473

Gray & Gray *Elements of Land Law,* (5th Edition), Oxford University Press, pp 716-746, 756-797

Bright, Susan, 'Attacking Unfair Mortgage Terms', LQR 1999 pp 360-365

Pawlowski, Mark, 'Insolvency – Ordering a Sale of the Family Home', Conv. 2007 Jan/Feb 78-87

8

Easements

Topic List

1   Is the Right Capable of Being an Easement?

2   Does the Right Accommodate the Dominant Tenement?

3   Does the Right Claimed amount to Exclusive Possession?

4   Has the Right been Acquired as an Easement?

Introduction

An easement is a proprietary right to use someone else's land. It is an interest, rather than an estate in land, because the extent of user conferred by an easement falls short of a right to possess the land. Classic examples of easements include rights of way, drainage, parking and storage.

As it is a proprietary right, an easement can be enforced 'in rem', by action for recovery of the use of the land itself. It is enforceable not simply against the grantor, but also against a third party, a new owner of the servient land. So, if a right to park on a neighbour's land is obstructed, it is important to decide whether the right to park exists as an easement or simply as a personal right. If it is an easement, action can be taken to remove the obstruction so that the right to park on the land can be exercised. This is what is meant by enforcing the right 'in rem'. The action may also be taken against a third party, the current owner of the servient land, even though he or she may not have been the original party to the arrangement.

Because an easement is a very powerful right it is not surprising that there are very strict rules for deciding when a right is enforceable as an easement. The rules fall into two broad categories. First, the right must be capable, in principle, of being an easement. Second, there are rules which must be complied with in order to determine whether the particular right has been properly acquired. Only then can the easement be fully enforceable. There are many different ways of acquiring an easement, either expressly or by implication.

8.1 Is the Right Capable of Being an Easement?

The seminal case on whether a right is capable of being an easement is *In Re Ellenborough Park* [1956] Ch 131. Lord Evershed set out the four essential characteristics which must be present before a right can be said to be capable of being an easement.

In Re Ellenborough Park [1956] Ch 131

Panel: Evershed MR, Birkett and Romer LJJ

Facts: Land around Ellenborough Park was developed for housing. The conveyances of the individual plots included the following right: "...full enjoyment at all times hereafter in common with the other persons to whom such easements may be granted of the pleasure ground set out and made in front of the said plot of land...in the centre of the square called Ellenborough Park...". During the Second World War the park was requisitioned and the War Office paid compensation. The question was whether the purchasers of the plots and their successors in title had a legal easement to use the park. If they did, then the fact that the park had been requisitioned meant that they had lost a legal right for which compensation should be paid.

Lord Evershed first of all stated that if the house owners were to have an enforceable legal interest it must have the characteristics of an easement. He set these out quoting Dr Cheshire's *Modern Real Property*, (7th Edition), then went on to examine two, more complicated, characteristics in detail:

EVERSHED MR

They [the essential characteristics of an easement] are (1) there must be a dominant and a servient tenement: (2) an easement must "accommodate" the dominant tenement: (3) dominant and servient owners must be different persons, and (4) a right over land cannot amount to an easement, unless it is capable of forming the subject-matter of a grant.

...Two of the four may be disregarded for present purposes, namely, the first and the third. If the garden or park is, as it is alleged to be, the servient tenement in the present case, then it is undoubtedly distinct from the alleged dominant tenements, namely, the freeholds of the several houses whose owners claim to exercise the rights. It is equally clear that if these lands respectively constitute the servient and dominant tenements then they are owned by different persons. The argument in the case is found, accordingly, to turn upon the meaning and application to the circumstances of the present case of the second and fourth conditions; that is, first, whether the alleged easement can be said in truth to "accommodate" the dominant tenement - in other words, whether there exists the required "connexion" between the one and the other: and, secondly, whether the right alleged is "capable of forming the subject-matter of a grant." The exact significance of this fourth and last condition is, at first sight perhaps, not entirely clear. As between the original parties to the "grant," it is not in doubt that rights of this kind would be capable of taking effect by way of contract or licence. But for the purposes of the present case, as the arguments made clear, the cognate questions involved under this condition are: whether the rights purported to be given are expressed in terms of too wide and vague a character; whether, if and so far as effective, such rights would amount to rights of joint occupation or would substantially deprive the park owners of proprietorship or legal possession; whether, if and so far as effective, such rights constitute mere rights of recreation, possessing no quality of utility or benefit; and on such grounds cannot quality [sic] as easements.

It was contended by the appellant that the right amounted to *jus spatiandi*, or a right to wander at large over a servient tenement, which is not recognised by English law. Evershed MR then looked closely at the exact wording of the rights granted, before concluding:

Although we are now anticipating to some extent the question which arises under the fourth of Dr. Cheshire's conditions, it seems to us, as a matter of construction, that the use contemplated and granted was the use of the park as a garden, the proprietorship of which (and of the produce of which) remained vested in the vendors and their successors. The enjoyment contemplated was the enjoyment of the vendors' ornamental garden in its physical state as such - the right, that is to say, of walking on or over those parts provided for such purpose, that is, pathways and (subject to restrictions in the ordinary course in the interest of the grass) the lawns; to rest in or upon the seats or other places provided; and, if certain parts were set apart for particular recreations such as tennis or bowls, to use those parts for those purposes, subject again, in the ordinary course, to the provisions made for their regulation; but not to trample at will all over the park, to cut or pluck the flowers or shrubs, or to interfere in the laying out or upkeep of the park. Such use or enjoyment is, we think, a common and clearly understood conception, analogous to the use and enjoyment conferred upon members of the public, when they are open to the public, of parks or gardens such as St. James's Park, Kew Gardens or the Gardens of Lincoln's Inn Fields.

He then considered the meaning of 'accommodates the dominant tenement'.

We pass, accordingly, to a consideration of the first of Dr. Cheshire's conditions - that of the accommodation of the alleged dominant tenements by the rights as we have interpreted them. For it was one of the main submissions by Mr. Cross on behalf of the appellant that the right of full enjoyment of the park, granted to the purchaser by the conveyance of December 23, 1864, was insufficiently connected with the enjoyment of the property conveyed, in that it did not subserve some use which was to be made of that property; and that such a right accordingly could not exist in law as an easement. ...We think it unnecessary to review the authorities in which the principle has been applied; for the effect of the decisions is stated with accuracy in Dr. Cheshire's Modern Real Property, 7th ed., at p. 457. After pointing out that "one of the fundamental principles concerning easements is that they must be not only appurtenant to a dominant tenement, but also connected with the normal enjoyment of the dominant tenement" and referring to certain citations in support of that proposition the author proceeded: "We may expand the statement of the principle thus: a right enjoyed by one over the land of another does not possess the status of an easement unless it accommodates and serves the dominant tenement, and is reasonably necessary for the better enjoyment of that tenement, for if it has no necessary connexion therewith, although it confers an advantage upon the owner and renders his ownership of the land more valuable, it is not an easement at all, but a mere contractual right personal to and only enforceable between the two contracting parties."

 Alert

He then applied this test to the facts and concluded that the right to use the park in this case did accommodate the dominant tenement.

It is clear that the right did, in some degree, enhance the value of the property, and this consideration cannot be dismissed as wholly irrelevant. It is, of course, a point to be noted; but we agree with Mr. Cross's submission that it is in no way decisive of the problem; it is not sufficient to show that the right increased the value of the property conveyed, unless it is also shown that it was connected with the normal enjoyment of that property. It appears to us that the question whether or not this connexion exists is primarily one of fact, and depends largely on the nature of the alleged dominant tenement and the nature of the right granted. As to the former, it was in the contemplation of the parties to the conveyance of 1864 that the property conveyed should be used for residential and not commercial purposes. That appears from the conveyance itself, and the covenant by the purchaser already quoted, that the dwelling-

 Alert

house, etc., which he bound himself to build should not "be occupied or used as an open or exposed shop or for any purpose of trade or commerce other than a lodging-house or private school or seminary" without the vendor's written consent.... As to the nature of the right granted, the conveyance of 1864 shows that the park was to be kept and maintained as a pleasure ground or ornamental garden, and that it was contemplated that it should at all times be kept in good order and condition and well stocked with plants and shrubs; and the vendors covenanted that they would not at any time thereafter erect or permit to be erected any dwelling-house or other building (except a grotto, bower, summer-house, flower-stand, fountain, music-stand or other ornamental erection) within or on any part of the pleasure ground. On these facts Mr. Cross submitted that the requisite connexion between the right to use the park and the normal enjoyment of the houses which were built around it or near it had not been established. He likened the position to a right granted to the purchaser of a house to use the Zoological Gardens free of charge or to attend Lord's Cricket Ground without payment. Such a right would undoubtedly, he said, increase the value of the property conveyed but could not run with it at law as an easement, because there was no sufficient nexus between the enjoyment of the right and the use of the house. It is probably true, we think, that in neither of Mr. Cross's illustrations would the supposed right constitute an easement, for it would be wholly extraneous to, and independent of, the use of a house as a house, namely, as a place in which the householder and his family live and make their home; and it is for this reason that the analogy which Mr. Cross sought to establish between his illustrations and the present case cannot, in our opinion, be supported. A much closer analogy, as it seems to us, is the case of a man selling the freehold of part of his house and granting to the purchaser, his heirs and assigns, the right, appurtenant to such part, to use the garden in common with the vendor and his assigns. In such a case, the test of connexion, or accommodation, would be amply satisfied; for just as the use of a garden undoubtedly enhances, and is connected with, the normal enjoyment of the house to which it belongs, so also would the right granted, in the case supposed, be closely connected with the use and enjoyment of the part of the premises sold. Such, we think, is in substance the position in the present case. The park became a communal garden for the benefit and enjoyment of those whose houses adjoined it or were in its close proximity. Its flower beds, lawns and walks were calculated to afford all the amenities which it is the purpose of the garden of a house to provide; and, apart from the fact that these amenities extended to a number of householders, instead of being confined to one (which on this aspect of the case is immaterial), we can see no difference in principle between Ellenborough Park and a garden in the ordinary signification of that word. It is the collective garden of the neighbouring houses, to whose use it was dedicated by the owners of the estate and as such amply satisfied, in our judgment, the requirement of connexion with the dominant tenements to which it is appurtenant.

The most complex characteristic of an easement is that it must be capable of lying in grant. Evershed MR reiterated what this meant and explained why he thought each part of the test was satisfied.

We turn next to Dr. Cheshire's fourth condition for an easement - that the right must be capable of forming the subject-matter of a grant. As we have earlier stated, satisfaction of the condition in the present case depends on a consideration of the questions whether the right conferred is too wide and vague, whether it is inconsistent with the proprietorship or possession of the alleged servient owners, and whether it is a mere right of recreation without utility or benefit.

To the first of these questions the interpretation which we have given to the typical deed provides, in our judgment, the answer; for we have construed the right conferred as being both well defined and commonly understood. In these essential respects the right may be said to be distinct from the indefinite and unregulated privilege which, we think, would ordinarily be understood by the Latin term "jus spatiandi," a privilege of wandering at will over all and every part of another's field or park, and which, though easily intelligible as the subject-matter of a personal licence, is something substantially different from the subject-matter of the grant in question, namely, the provision for a limited number of houses in a uniform crescent of one single large but private garden.

Our interpretation of the deed also provides, we think, the answer to the second question; for the right conferred no more amounts to a joint occupation of the park with its owners, no more excludes the proprietorship or possession of the latter, than a right of way granted through a passage, or than the use by the public of the gardens of Lincoln's Inn Fields (to take one of our former examples) amount to joint occupation of that garden with the London County Council, or involve an inconsistency with the possession or proprietorship of the council as lessees.

Evershed MR said that *Copeland v Greenhalf* [1952] Ch 488 (discussed below), where the right claimed was too intense to be capable of being an easement, was not relevant to the facts of this case. He then went on to consider the final aspect of 'lying in grant'. It was argued that as the right amounted to a *jus spatiandi* it was merely a right of recreation and amusement and not therefore capable of being an easement. Evershed MR disagreed. He regarded the right claimed as more than a *jus spatiandi* and considered it to be analogous to a right already judicially recognised in the case of *Duncan v Louch* (1845) 6 QB 904.

Link
See *Copeland v Greenhalf*

We do not think that the right to use a garden of the character with which we are concerned in this case can be called one of mere recreation and amusement... . No doubt a garden is a pleasure - on high authority, it is the purest of pleasures - but, in our judgment, it is not a right having no quality either of utility or benefit as those words should be understood. The right here in suit is, for reasons already given, one appurtenant to the surrounding houses as such, and constitutes a beneficial attribute of residence in a house as ordinarily understood. Its use for the purposes, not only of exercise and rest but also for such domestic purposes as were suggested in argument - for example, for taking out small children in perambulators or otherwise - is not fairly to be described as one of mere recreation or amusement, and is clearly beneficial to the premises to which it is attached... . In a sense, no doubt, such a right includes something of a jus spatiandi, inasmuch as it involves the principle of wandering at will round each part of the garden, except of course, such parts as comprise flower beds, or are laid out for some other purpose, which renders walking impossible or unsuitable. We doubt, nevertheless, whether the right to use and enjoy a garden in this manner can with accuracy be said to constitute a mere *jus spatiandi*. Wandering at large is of the essence of such a right and constitutes the main purpose for which it exists. A private garden, on the other hand, is an attribute of the ordinary enjoyment of the residence to which it is attached, and the right of wandering in it is but one method of enjoying it. On the assumption, however, that the right now in question does constitute a jus spatiandi, or that it is analogous thereto, it becomes necessary to consider whether the right, which is in question in these proceedings, is, for that reason, incapable of ranking in law as an easement.

Evershed MR rejected *obiter dicta* in *International Tea Stores v Hobbs* [1903] 2 Ch 165 and *A-G v Antrobus* [1905] 2 Ch 188, which suggested that *jus spatiandi* could not be recognised as legal rights. He agreed with the judge in *Duncan v Louch*, a case which was not cited to the court in either of those cases.

Duncan v. Louch ... is authoritative in favour of the recognition by our law as an easement of a right closely comparable to that now in question which, if it involves in some sense a jus spatiandi, is nevertheless properly annexed and appurtenant to a defined hereditament.

The court held that the right met all of the criteria for existing as an easement.

8.2 Does the Right Accommodate the Dominant Tenement?

There is wide scope for argument as to whether a particular right does indeed 'accommodate the dominant tenement' or whether it simply benefits a particular person or business.

Hill v Tupper (1863) 2 H&C 121

Panel: Pollock CB, Martin and Bramwell BB

Facts: Hill ran a boat hire business from his leased premises on the bank of the Basingstoke Canal. In the lease, granted by the Basingstoke Canal Navigation Company, he was granted 'sole and exclusive right or liberty to put or use boats on the said canal, and let the same for the purpose of pleasure only.' He claimed that the right was an easement, and that Tupper had interfered with his easement by putting his own boats on the canal. The court held that Hill did not have an easement: the right claimed could not possibly be an easement as it simply benefited Hill personally, not the dominant land itself.

POLLOCK CB

... The case of *Ackroyd v Smith* (10 CB 164) expressly decided that it is not competent to create rights unconnected with the use and enjoyment of land, and annex them to it so as to constitute a property in the grantee. This grant merely operates as a licence or

Alert

covenant on the part of the grantors, and is binding on them as between themselves and the grantee, but gives him no right of action in his own name for any infringement of the supposed exclusive right.

BARON MARTIN

[Baron Martin warned against relaxing the rules to admit this type of right as an easement, and continued.]

This grant is perfectly valid as between the plaintiff and the canal Company; but in order to support this action, the plaintiff must establish that such an estate or interest vested in him that the act of the defendant amounted to an eviction. None of the cases cited are at all analogous to this, and some authority must be produced before we can hold that such a right can be created. To admit the right would lead to the creation of an infinite variety of interests in land, and an indefinite increase of possible estates.

By contrast, in *Moody v Steggles* (1879) LR 12 ChD 261, a right which benefited a business was held also to benefit the dominant tenement itself.

Moody v Steggles (1879) LR 12 ChD 261

Panel: Fry J

Facts: Harriet Moody owned a pub in Newmarket. The pub was down a narrow alleyway and could not be seen from the High Street. For more than forty years, a sign for the pub had hung on Steggles' property which faced the High Street. When Steggles removed the sign because it creaked, Moody claimed the right to hang the sign existed as an easement and sought an injunction. This was granted. Although the right benefited the pub business, it was held to benefit the land too as the business was so closely connected to the land.

MR JUSTICE FRY

... It is said that the easement in question relates, not to the tenement, but to the business of the occupant of the tenement, and that therefore I cannot tie the easement to the house. It appears to me that that argument is of too refined a nature to prevail, and for this reason, that the house can only be used by an occupant, and that the occupant only uses the house for the business which he pursues, and therefore in some manner (direct or indirect) an easement is more or less connected with the mode in which the occupant of the house uses it.

 Alert

8.3 Does the Right Claimed amount to Exclusive Possession?

A right is not capable of being an easement if the use of the servient land is too extensive and in effect amounts to exclusive possession. As the cases show, the law on the test for what is 'too extensive' is still developing.

Copeland v Greenhalf [1952] Ch 488

Panel: Upjohn J

Facts: Greenhalf ran a business as a wheelwright. He claimed he had a right to store vehicles awaiting repair and collection by customers on Copeland's land, and that this right existed as an easement acquired by long use. Copeland was granted an injunction ordering Greenhalf to remove the vehicles. The judge acknowledged that a right of storage could, in principle, exist as an easement which benefited land and not simply the claimant's business. However, he said that the right claimed in this particular case was not an easement as the use was too extensive to constitute an easement. It amounted to an ouster of the servient owner from the beneficial enjoyment of her land. The test formulated by Upjohn J is known as 'the ouster principle'.

MR JUSTICE UPJOHN

I think that the right claimed goes wholly outside any normal idea of an easement, that is, the right of the owner or the occupier of a dominant tenement over a servient tenement. This claim (to which no closely related authority has been referred to me) really amounts to a claim to a joint user of the land by the defendant. Practically, the defendant is claiming the whole beneficial user of the strip of land on the south-east side of the track there; he can leave as many or as few lorries there as he likes for as long as he likes; he may enter on it by himself, his servants and agents to do repair work thereon. In my judgment, that is not a claim which can be established as an easement. It is virtually a claim to possession of the servient tenement, if necessary to the exclusion of the owner; or, at any rate, to a joint user, and no authority has been cited to me which would justify the conclusion that a right of this wide and undefined nature can be the proper subject-matter of an easement. It seems to me that to succeed, this claim must amount to a successful claim of possession by reason of long adverse possession.

 Alert

It must be noted that Upjohn J was not referred to the Court of Appeal decision in *Wright v Macadam* [1949] 2 KB 744 (discussed below) which held that an apparently exclusive right to store coal in a small shed was capable of being an easement. In *Moncrieff v Jamieson* [2007] UKHL 42 (also discussed below) Lord Scott and Lord Neuberger make extensive comments about this, thereby casting doubt on the ouster principle formulated in *Copeland v Greenhalf*.

The question of the appropriate test to be applied has been the subject of much debate, especially where the right claimed is a right to park. It is clear that a right to park in one of a number of designated spaces may exist as an easement. Problems arise where the right is to park in a defined space. Can this exist as an easement, or is the use too great to amount to an easement?

The ouster principle was applied in *Batchelor v Marlow* [2003] 1 WLR 764.

Batchelor v Marlow [2003] 1 WLR 764

Panel: Henry, Tucker and Kay LJJ

Facts: Mr Batchelor sought a declaration that Marlow's right to park on a strip of his land could not exist as an easement because, relying on *Copeland v Greenhalf*, it amounted to exclusive possession of the land. The court held that the test for deciding whether there was exclusive possession was whether the right would deprive the servient owner of any reasonable use of his land. This was a matter of fact and degree in each case. In this particular instance the right was a right to park up to six cars from 8.30am until 6pm each weekday. This user was held to be too excessive to be an easement as it effectively prevented the servient owner from reasonable enjoyment of the land.

LORD JUSTICE TUCKEY

In dealing with the point at issue on this appeal the deputy judge [at first instance] simply said, at p 190:

"I consider that the exclusive right to park six cars during normal business hours on Mondays to Fridays in connection with the business carried on [by the defendants] is capable of subsisting as an easement ... In my judgment, such a right, being limited as it is in time, does not, as a matter of degree, amount to such exclusion of the plaintiff and his predecessors in title as to preclude it subsisting as an easement".

Earlier in his judgment he referred to the authorities and accepted that the question he had to answer was one of degree. This followed the approach adopted by Judge Paul Baker QC in *London and Blenheim Estates Ltd v Ladbroke Retail Parks Ltd* [1992] 1 WLR 1278, 1288 who, after reviewing the earlier authorities on car parking, said:

"The essential question is one of degree. If the right granted in relation to the area over which it is to be exercisable is such that it would leave the servient owner without any reasonable use of his land, whether for parking or anything else, it could not be an easement though it might be some larger or different grant."

Lord Justice Tuckey disagreed with the finding of the judge at first instance:

Does an exclusive right to park six cars for 9½ hours every day of the working week leave the plaintiff without any reasonable use of his land, whether for parking or anything else?

Miss Williamson [counsel for the landowner] emphasised the fact that the right asserted is exclusive of all others, including the plaintiff. Car parking over the whole of the land is highly intrusive because no other use can be made of it when cars are parked on it. In practice it prevents the plaintiff from making any use of his land and makes his ownership of it illusory. Not so, said Mr West [counsel for the defendant]. Mathematically the defendants only have use of the land for 47½ hours per week, whereas the plaintiff has 120½ hours. He suggested various uses which the plaintiff could make of the land. He could sell it to the defendants or charge them for using it outside business hours, if that is what they wanted. Outside those hours he could park on the land himself or charge others for doing so. He would be able to concrete over the surface of the land without interfering with the right.

I think these suggestions demonstrate the difficulties which Mr West faces. Sale to the defendants would amount to a recognition that the rights they asserted had given them in practice a beneficial interest and no doubt the price would reflect this fact. The plaintiff could of course park himself at night or the weekends but the commercial scope for getting others to pay for doing so must be very limited indeed. I cannot see how the plaintiff would benefit from concreting over the land, although this would certainly enhance the defendants' right.

If one asks the simple question: "Would the plaintiff have any reasonable use of the land for parking?" the answer, I think, must be "No". He has no use at all during the whole of the time that parking space is likely to be needed. But if one asks the question whether the plaintiff has any reasonable use of the land for any other purpose, the answer is even clearer. His right to use his land is curtailed altogether for intermittent periods throughout the week. Such a restriction would, I think, make his ownership of the land illusory.

A different test was proposed in *Moncrieff v Jamieson* [2007] 1 WLR 2620, although this is a Scottish case and therefore of persuasive authority only. Lord Scott in his opinion emphasised the similarities between the Scottish law of servitudes and the English law of easements, and made an extensive survey of the English authorities.

Moncrieff v Jamieson [2007] 1 WLR 2620

Panel: Lord Hope of Craighead, Lord Scott of Foscote, Lord Rodger of Earlsferry, Lord Mance and Lord Neuberger of Abbotsbury

Facts: Moncrieff owned property called Da Store on the seashore, at the foot of a steep cliff on Shetland. There was a right of access across Jamieson's land from the main road to the top of the cliff above the property. It was not disputed that Moncrieff and his visitors had ancillary rights to turn vehicles and to stop temporarily for deliveries and so on. What *was* disputed was whether they had the right to park on Jamieson's land at the top of the cliff, referred to as 'the pink land'. The court held that it was possible to imply a right of parking as ancillary to a right of access, and that the parking was not too extensive to be an easement.

LORD SCOTT OF FOSCOTE

Lord Scott reviewed the English authorities on exclusive possession, as he saw no difference between the common law in England relating to easements and the common law in Scotland relating to servitudes. He dismissed the 'ouster' or 'reasonable use' test of *Copeland v Greenhalf* and *Batchelor v Marlow* and instead formulated a new test based on possession and control.

It has been argued that the rights of parking claimed by the pursuers in respect of the pink land deprive the defenders of any reasonable use of that land, are therefore inconsistent with their ownership of the pink land and should not be recognised as servitudal rights in rem that can bind them and their successors in title. This is the so-called "ouster" principle to which I have already referred. ...

Every servitude or easement will bar some ordinary use of the servient land. For example, a right of way prevents all manner of ordinary uses of the land over which the road passes. The servient owner cannot plough up the road. He cannot grow cabbages on it or use it for basketball practice. A viaduct carrying water across the servient land to the dominant land will prevent the same things. Every servitude prevents any use of the servient land, whether ordinary or otherwise, that would interfere with the reasonable exercise of the servitude.... There will always be some such use that is prevented.

 Alert

Lord Scott drew a distinction between exclusive possession by the dominant owner, and sole user for a limited purpose:

In *Wright v Macadam* [1949] 2 KB 744, the Court of Appeal had to consider whether the right to use a coal shed could exist as an easement and held that it could: see per Jenkins LJ, at p 752. It has been suggested that the case may have turned on whether the claimant had sole use of the coal shed, but it is difficult to see any difference in principle between a case in which the dominant owner has sole use of a patch of ground for storage purposes, eg a coal shed, and a case in which the dominant owner is the only user of a strip of road for access purposes or of a viaduct for the passage of water. Sole user, as a concept, is quite different from, and fundamentally inferior to, exclusive possession. Sole use of a coal shed for the storage of coal does not prevent the servient owner from using the shed for any purposes of his own that do not interfere with the dominant owner's reasonable use for the storage of coal. The dominant owner entitled to a servitude of way or for the passage of water along a viaduct does not have possession of the land over which the road or the viaduct passes. If the coal shed door had been locked with only the dominant owner possessing a key and entry by the servient owner barred, so that the dominant owner would have been in possession and control of the shed, I would have regarded it as arguable that the right granted was inconsistent with the servient owner's ownership and inconsistent with the nature of a servitude or an easement. But sole use for a limited purpose is not, in my opinion, inconsistent with the servient owner's retention of possession and control or inconsistent with the nature of an easement. This conclusion is supported by Lord Evershed MR's remarks in In re Ellenborough Park [1956] Ch 131, 176 where the issue was whether the right to use a communal garden could take effect as an easement. He said that:

 Alert

"the right conferred no more amounts to a joint occupation of the park with its owners, no more excludes the proprietorship or possession of the latter, than a right of way granted through a passage, or than the use by the public of the gardens of Lincoln's Inn Fields... amount to joint occupation of that garden with the London County Council, or involve an inconsistency with the possession or proprietorship of the council as lessees."

Lord Scott then turned his attention to the parking cases which turned on the application of the 'ouster principle':

Copeland v Greenhalf [1952] Ch 488, a case that goes the other way [to *Wright v Macadam*], was a case in which a prescriptive easement to use a strip of land by the side of a private roadway for depositing vehicles and for other purposes connected with a wheelwright's business had been claimed. Upjohn J, at p498, rejected the claim on the ground that:

"Practically, the defendant is claiming the whole beneficial user of the strip of land... It is virtually a claim to possession of the servient tenement, if necessary to the exclusion of the owner..."

There may be arguments as to whether the facts of the case justified those remarks but, for my part, I would accept that if they did Upjohn J was right to reject the easement claim and to require the defendant, if he was to succeed in resisting the plaintiff's claim to remove him from the land, to establish a title by adverse possession.

It has often been commented that *Wright v Macadam* was not cited to Upjohn J and the possible inconsistency between the two cases was addressed by Judge Paul Baker QC in *London & Blenheim Estates Ltd v Ladbroke Retail Parks Ltd* [1992] 1 WLR 1278 where a right of parking had been claimed. He commented, at p 1286, that the question whether the right to park that had been claimed was consistent with the nature of an easement was one of degree: "A small coal shed in a large property is one thing. The exclusive use of a large part of the alleged servient tenement is another." I think, with respect, that this attempt to reconcile the two authorities was addressing the wrong point. The servient land in relation to a servitude or easement is surely the land over which the servitude or easement is enjoyed, not the totality of the surrounding land of which the servient owner happens to be the owner. If there is an easement of way over a 100-yard roadway on a 1,000-acre estate, or an easement to use for storage a small shed on the estate access to which is gained via the 100-yard roadway, it would be fairly meaningless in relation to either easement to speak of the whole estate as the servient land. Would the right of way and the storage right fail to qualify as easements if the whole estate bar the actual land over which the roadway ran and on which the shed stood, with or without a narrow surrounding strip, were sold? How could it be open to the servient owner to destroy easements by such a stratagem? In my opinion such a stratagem would fail. It would fail because the servient land was never the whole estate but was the land over which the roadway ran and on which the shed stood. Provided the servient land was land of which the servient owner was in possession, the rights of way and of storage would continue, in my opinion, to qualify as easements.

Link
back to
*Copeland v
Greenhalf*

Applying his comments set out above, Lord Scott explains that he feels that the 'reasonable use' test, sometimes called the 'ouster principle', is the wrong test.

Link
See *Batchelor v
Marlow*

In my respectful opinion the test formulated in the *London & Blenheim Estates* case [1992] 1 WLR 1278 and applied by the Court of Appeal in *Batchelor v Marlow* [2003] 1 WLR 764, a test that would reject the claim to an easement if its exercise would leave the servient owner with no "reasonable use" to which he could put the servient land, needs some qualification. It is impossible to assert that there would be no use that could be made by an owner of land over which he had granted parking rights.

He could, for example, build above or under the parking area. He could place advertising hoardings on the walls. Other possible uses can be conjured up. And by what yardstick is it to be decided whether the residual uses of the servient land available to its owner are "reasonable" or sufficient to save his ownership from being "illusory"? It is not the uncertainty of the test that, in my opinion, is the main problem. It is the test itself. I do not see why a landowner should not grant rights of a servitudal character over his land to any extent that he wishes. The claim in Batchelor v Marlow for an easement to park cars was a prescriptive claim based on over 20 years of that use of the strip of land. There is no difference between the characteristics of an easement that can be acquired by grant and the characteristics of an easement that can be acquired by prescription. If an easement can be created by grant it can be acquired by prescription and I can think of no reason why, if an area of land can accommodate nine cars, the owner of the land should not grant an easement to park nine cars on the land. The servient owner would remain the owner of the land and in possession and control of it. The dominant owner would have the right to station up to nine cars there and, of course, to have access to his nine cars. How could it be said that the law would recognise an easement allowing the dominant owner to park five cars or six or seven or eight but not nine? I would, for my part, reject the test that asks whether the servient owner is left with any reasonable use of his land, and substitute for it a test which asks whether the servient owner retains possession and, subject to the reasonable exercise of the right in question, control of the servient land.

If, which as at present advised I regard as doubtful, *Batchelor v Marlow* was correctly decided, I can see some force in the defenders' arguments regarding the pink land. The use that the servient owner can still make of the pink land, if two cars are parked there, is very limited. But it is the servient owner, not the pursuers, who is in possession and control of the pink land and entitled to remain so. The pursuers are entitled to do nothing with the pink land other than park vehicles on it, while the defenders are entitled to do what they like with the pink land provided they do not interfere with the pursuers' right to park two cars there. For the reasons I have given I regard the "ouster" principle as inapplicable to this case.

Link

See Alexander Hill-Smith's article in the Further Reading list

LORD NEUBERGER OF ABBOTSBURY

Lord Neuberger examined the cases on the ouster principle and emphasised the inconsistency in its application depending on whether the right was to park in one of several spaces or simply in one defined space. He had doubts about Lord Scott's test, but was reluctant to formulate one of his own.

The decision of Upjohn J in *Copeland v Greenhalf* [1952] Ch 488 has been relied on in England to support the contention that the right to park cannot be an easement. In that case, Upjohn J held that the right claimed in that case could not be an easement because "Practically, the defendant is claiming the whole beneficial user" of the land in question: see at p 498. This is consistent with what Lopes LJ said in *Reilly v Booth* (1890) 44 Ch D 12, 26, namely that an easement could not give "exclusive and unrestricted use of a piece of land". Similarly in *Grigsby v Melville* [1972] 1 WLR

1355, Brightman J intimated that he considered, without having to decide, that an effectively exclusive right to use a cellar for storage could not have been an easement.

At least on the basis of the authorities to which we have been referred, the case law of England ... and of Scotland seem to me, at least so far, to have marched together on this issue. ...

In my judgment, the grant of a right to park a single vehicle anywhere on a servient tenement which is large enough to hold, say, twenty vehicles, must be capable of being a servitude or an easement. In such a case, there is no specific place where the vehicle is to be parked, so that there is no specific area from which the servient owner can be said to be excluded. ...

It was on this basis that Judge Paul Baker QC held that the right to park granted in *London & Blenheim Estates Ltd v Ladbroke Retail Parks Ltd* [1992] 1 WLR 1278 was a valid easement. He said, at p 1286, that "The matter must be one of degree. A small coal shed in a large property is one thing. The exclusive use of a large part of the alleged servient tenement is another".

A somewhat similar test was applied in *Batchelor v Marlow* [2003] 1 WLR 764, where the Court of Appeal held that a right to park vehicles for 9½ hours a day was not an easement because it left "the servient owner without any reasonable use of his land whether for parking or anything else", and that it thereby rendered "his ownership of the land illusory".

Accordingly, it seems to me that, on the pursuers' case, a right to park could only be prevented from being a servitude or an easement if it resulted in the servient owner either being effectively excluded from the whole of the land in question or being left without any reasonable use of that land.

If the right to park a vehicle in an area that can hold 20 vehicles is capable of being a servitude or an easement, then it would logically follow that the same conclusion should apply to an area that can hold two vehicles. On that basis, it can be said to be somewhat contrary to common sense that the arrangement is debarred from being a servitude or an easement simply because the parties have chosen to identify a precise space in the area, over which the right is to be exercised, and the space is just big enough to hold the vehicle. Also, presumably on the pursuers' case, such a right would indeed be capable of being a servitude or an easement if the servient owner had the right to change the location of the precise space within the area from time to time.

At least as at present advised, I am not satisfied that a right is prevented from being a servitude or an easement simply because the right granted would involve the servient owner being effectively excluded from the property. In this connection, the Privy Council in *Attorney General of Southern Nigeria v John Holt & Co (Liverpool) Ltd* [1915] AC 599 , 617 appears to have held that a right to store materials on land could be an easement although it involved the dominant owner enjoying an "exclusive" right to enjoy the property concerned. Citing *Dyce v Hay* in support, the Privy Council immediately went on to observe that, in considering arguments as to whether a right could be an easement "The law must adapt itself to the conditions of modern society and trade". Further, the Court of Appeal in *Wright v Macadam* [1949] 2 KB 744 held that an apparently exclusive right to store coal in a small shed was capable of being an easement. Neither case was cited to Upjohn J in *Copeland v Greenhalf*. ...

Accordingly, I see considerable force in the views expressed by Lord Scott in paras 57 and 59 of his opinion, to the effect that a right can be an easement notwithstanding that the dominant owner effectively enjoys exclusive occupation, on the basis that the essential requirement is that the servient owner retains possession and control. If that were the right test, then it seems likely that *Batchelor v Marlow* [2003] 1 WLR 764 was wrongly decided. However, unless it is necessary to decide the point to dispose of this appeal, I consider that it would be dangerous to try and identify [what] degree of ouster is required to disqualify a right from constituting a servitude or easement, given the very limited argument your Lordships have received on the topic.

 Alert

It is unclear how the law will develop in this area. Recent cases give no clear indication of whether the traditional 'ouster/reasonable use' test or the new 'possession and control' test proposed by Lord Scott in *Moncrieff v Jamieson* will be favoured, or indeed whether another test is needed. See, for example, the slightly confused test applied in *Kettel & Ors v Bloomfold Ltd* [2012] EWHC 1422.

 Link

See Allyson Colby's article in the Further Reading list

The Law Commission Report No 327 'Making Land Work: Easements, Covenants and Profits a Prendre', published 8 June 2011, puts forward a number of recommended reforms to the law of easements. The Law Commission recognised in this report, that post *Moncrieff* the effect of the 'ouster principle', and the point at which it prevents an easement from being valid, is now unclear and that this lack of clarity puts many valuable parking rights at risk. Furthermore, in making any reforms to this test, the Commission emphasised the need to ensure that easements, as mere interests in land, remain mutually exclusive from possessory rights in land. One must be able to determine whether a particular right is a lease or freehold on the one hand, or an easement on the other.

Consequently, the Commission was clear that if a dominant owner is granted exclusive possession of the land, then it cannot be an easement (although it may be a lease or a freehold). However, it also felt that the ouster principle should be abolished:

'An easement that stops short of exclusive possession, even if it deprives the owner of much of the use of his land, or indeed of all reasonable use of it, is valid. The effect of this would be to reverse, for the future, the decision in Batchelor v Marlow, for example, and therefore to validate a potentially wide range of parking easements. In particular, easements that confer an 'exclusive right to park' would be clearly valid, provided that the servient owner can access the land (to however limited an extent).' (paras 3.188 – 3.211).

8.4 Has the Right been Acquired as an Easement?

8.4.1 Easements acquired by express reservation

The most obvious way of creating an easement is expressly, either by way of grant or reservation. An easement is created by express grant where one owner specifically allows another to use his land in some way. A reservation occurs when one owner sells or leases part of his land and keeps back or 'reserves' an easement for the benefit of the land retained, in the transfer deed or lease. A reservation is strictly construed against the person reserving the right, as he is in a position to reserve exactly what he needs at the time of the sale or lease. To interpret the right any more widely would in effect derogate from the grant of the estate he has made to the buyer or tenant in the transfer deed or lease.

Link

See comments on derogation from grant in *Wheeldon v Burrows*, below

Cordell v Second Clanfield Properties Limited [1969] 2 Ch 9

Panel: Megarry J

Facts: Cordell sold development land to Second Clanfield Properties Limited, and retained land adjacent to it. In the transfer deed, Cordell reserved a right of way over any estate roads to be constructed on the land sold. When Second Clanfield started to build a bungalow on the part of the land adjacent to Cordell's reserved land, Cordell sought a declaration that he was entitled to a right of way 28 feet wide at all times and for all purposes over it. He also sought injunctions to prevent further building.

The injunctions were refused on the basis that a reservation of a right is to be strictly construed against the person reserving it. If Cordell needed such an extensive right of way he should have reserved it specifically in the transfer deed. The court rejected the argument that the right should be treated as a grant by the transferee, because interpreting it in that way would mean that it should be construed against the transferee/grantor and thus in favour of the person actually reserving.

MR JUSTICE MEGARRY

If there were in situ an estate road which gave the plaintiff the desired access, then no doubt the conveyance would give him the right to use it and the other estate roads. But there is no such connecting road, other than the 12-ft. way which the plaintiff disdains; and the plaintiff must conjure out of the conveyance some obligation on the defendant company either to construct such a road for the plaintiff or to permit the plaintiff to construct such a road for himself.

... I hold that in this case the reservation should be construed against the vendor, that is, against the plaintiff. So construed, it seems to me quite impossible to read it as imposing on the defendant company an obligation either to construct a road such as the plaintiff claims or to permit the plaintiff to do so. I may add that where a vendor wishes to retain for himself some right over the land that he has conveyed, a rule that

Alert

requires him to ensure that the words inserted are ample enough to give him what he wants seems to me to be bottomed in practical common sense.

8.4.2 Easements acquired impliedly

As well as being granted or reserved expressly, it is possible for easements to be created impliedly by a number of methods: by common intention of the parties at the time of the grant; under the rule in *Wheeldon v Burrows*; and under the Law of Property Act 1925 (LPA 1925) s 62.

Note that the Law Commission, in its 2011 report, regards s62 LPA 1925 as a method of express, rather than implied, acquisition. This is because, in its view, the operation of s62 deems a conveyance to have included a right amongst its express terms. Further, it differs from implied acquisition as it operates neutrally, without regard to intention or necessity.

8.4.2.1 Implied by the common intention of the parties

Wong v Beaumont Properties Limited [1965] 1 QB 173

Panel: Lord Denning MR, Pearson and Salmon LJJ

Facts: Wong had a lease of a basement restaurant. He was not the original Tenant. Beaumont Properties Limited was the freeholder and the successor-in-title to the original Landlord. The lease contained Tenant's covenants to keep the premises as a restaurant; to comply with health regulations and to eliminate all cooking smells from the premises. From the beginning, although the original parties did not appreciate this, it was not possible to comply with these covenants without the use of a ventilation system on the Landlord's adjoining land. Beaumont refused Wong's request to install such a system. Wong sought a declaration that he was entitled to enter the Landlord's adjoining premises to install and use a ventilation system.

The court granted the declaration sought.

LORD DENNING MR

The question is: Has the plaintiff a right to put up this duct without the landlords' consent? If he is to have any right at all, it must be by way of easement and not merely by way of implied contract. He is not the original lessee, nor are the defendants the original lessors. Each is a successor in title. As between them, a right of this kind, if it exists at all, must be by way of an easement. In particular, an easement of necessity. The law on the matter was stated by Lord Parker of Waddington in *Pwllbach Colliery Co. Ltd. v. Woodman*, 12 where he said, 13 omitting immaterial words, "The law will readily imply the grant or reservation of such easements as may be necessary to give effect to the common intention of the parties to a grant of real property, with reference to the manner or purposes in and for which the land granted ... is to be used. But it is essential for this purpose that the parties should intend that the subject of the grant ... should be used in some definite and particular manner. It is not enough that the subject

 Alert

of the grant ... should be intended to be used in a manner which may or may not involve this definite and particular use." That is the principle which underlies all easements of necessity. If you go back to Rolle's Abridgment you will find it stated in this way: "If I have a field inclosed by my own land on all sides, and I alien this close to another, he shall have a way to this close over my land, as incident to the grant; for otherwise he cannot have any benefit by the grant."

I would apply those principles here. Here was the grant of a lease to the lessee for the very purpose of carrying on a restaurant business. It was to be a popular restaurant, and it was to be developed and extended. There was a covenant not to cause any nuisance; and to control and eliminate all smells; and to comply with the Food Hygiene Regulations. That was "a definite and particular manner" in which the business had to be conducted. It could not be carried on in that manner at all unless a ventilation system was installed by a duct of this kind. In these circumstances it seems to me that, if the business is to be carried on at all - if, in the words of Rolle's Abridgment, the lessee is to "have any benefit by the grant" at all - he must of necessity be able to put a ventilation duct up the wall. It may be that in Blackaby's [the original tenant] time it would not have needed such a large duct as is now needed in the plaintiff's time. But nevertheless a duct of some kind would have had to be put up the wall. The plaintiff may need a bigger one. But that does not matter. A man who has a right to an easement can use it in any proper way, so long as he does not substantially increase the burden on the servient tenement. In this case a bigger duct will not substantially increase the burden.

There is one point in which this case goes further than the earlier cases which have been cited. It is this. It was not realised by the parties, at the time of the lease, that this duct would be necessary. But it was in fact necessary from the very beginning. That seems to me sufficient to bring the principle into play. In order to use this place as a restaurant, there must be implied an easement, by the necessity of the case, to carry a duct up this wall. The county court judge so held. He granted a declaration. I agree with him.

In his judgment extracted above, Lord Denning refers to the easement being an 'easement of necessity'. Although there is some overlap, acquisition by 'necessity' and by the 'common intention of the parties' are arguably distinct means of creating easements.

8.4.2.2 Implied under the rule in *Wheeldon v Burrows*

This rule sets out the circumstances in which easements may be impliedly acquired where land is originally in one single ownership and part of it is sold off, or leased for the first time.

Wheeldon v Burrows (1879) LR 12 ChD 31

Panel: Thesiger, James and Baggally LJJ

Facts: Tetley owned a plot of land and sold part to Wheeldon in January 1876, but did not expressly reserve any rights in the transfer for the benefit of the land retained.

A month later he sold the remaining part to Burrows. The land sold to Burrows had a workshop on it, lit by natural light through three windows. When Wheeldon's widow started to build on her land, Burrows claimed he had a right to light which was impliedly reserved by the January conveyance. The Court of Appeal held that there was no easement, on the basis that to imply one into the January conveyance would have been to derogate from Tetley's original grant to Wheeldon. In order for Burrows to claim an easement of light, he would have to show that such a right had been reserved for the benefit of the retained land in the January conveyance. Lord Justice Thesiger made some important *obiter* statements explaining the circumstances in which a right could have passed by implied grant, as opposed to reservation, in this case. These statements, although *obiter*, have become known as the rule in *Wheeldon v Burrows*.

LORD JUSTICE THESIGER

… I think that two propositions may be stated as what I may call the general rules governing cases of this kind. The first of these rules is, that on the grant by the owner of a tenement of part of that tenement as it is then used and enjoyed, there will pass to the grantee all those continuous and apparent easements (by which, of course, I mean quasi easements), or, in other words, all those easements which are necessary to the reasonable enjoyment of the property granted, and which have been and are at the time of the grant used by the owners of the entirety for the benefit of the part granted. The second proposition is that, if the grantor intends to reserve any right over the tenement granted, it is his duty to reserve it expressly in the grant. Those are the general rules governing cases of this kind, but the second of those rules is subject to certain exceptions. One of those exceptions is the well-known exception which attaches to cases of what are called ways of necessity; and I do not dispute for a moment that there may be, and probably are, certain other exceptions… .

Both of the general rules which I have mentioned are founded upon a maxim which is as well established by authority as it is consonant to reason and common sense, viz., that a grantor shall not derogate from his grant. It has been argued before us that there is no distinction between what has been called an implied grant and what is attempted to be established under the name of an implied reservation; and that such a distinction between the implied grant and the implied reservation is a mere modern invention, and one which runs contrary, not only to the general practice upon which land has been bought and sold for a considerable time, but also to authorities which are said to be clear and distinct upon the matter. So far, however, from that distinction being one which was laid down for the first time by and which is to be attributed to Lord Westbury in *Suffield v. Brown*, it appears to me that it has existed almost as far back as we can trace the law upon the subject… .

Alert

Link

See explanation on express reservations earlier in this chapter.

Lord Justice Thesiger then surveyed the authorities on the point before endorsing the distinction between implied grant and implied reservation. He suggested that, as a general rule based on the principle of non-derogation from grant, easements may only be created by implied grant. He did however acknowledge that it was not impossible for an easement to be created by implied reservation, although not under the 'rule in

Wheeldon v Burrows'. However, the Law Commission in its report of 2011 paras 3.25–30, says that it ought to be immaterial whether the implied easement under *Wheeldon v Burrows* would take effect by grant or reservation, because the primary purpose of the principle is to generate an easement in a transaction where the need for an express easement has been overlooked. It takes the view that the rule in *Wheeldon v Burrows* should also operate to imply a reservation. As yet, the courts have not acted upon this suggestion by the Law Commission.

The exact meaning of 'necessary for the reasonable enjoyment of [dominant] land' required by *Wheeldon v Burrows* was considered in *Borman v Griffith* [1930] 1 Ch 493.

Borman v Griffith [1930] 1 Ch 493

Panel: Maugham J

Facts: In 1923 a landowner entered into a contract with Borman to grant a seven-year lease of a house within a large park. The only access to the house was over a drive leading to a larger property, The Hall. The landowner agreed to construct an alternative access to the house, but it was not robust enough for the heavy vehicles and the volume of traffic in connection with Borman's trade as a poultry dealer. In 1926 the landowner granted a 14-year lease of The Hall to Griffith. Griffith put up a wire fence preventing Borman from using the main drive. Borman claimed that he had an easement to use the main drive. The court held that he did have an easement. The court held that an easement had been acquired under the rule in *Wheeldon v Burrows*.

MR JUSTICE MAUGHAM

In my view, the principles laid down in such cases as *Wheeldon v. Burrows*; *Brown v. Alabaster*; and *Nicholls v. Nicholls* are applicable. Without going through all those cases in detail, I may state the principle as follows - namely, that where, as in the present case, two properties belonging to a single owner and about to be granted are separated by a common road, or where a plainly visible road exists over the one for the apparent use of the other, and that road is necessary for the reasonable enjoyment of the property, a right to use the road will pass with the quasi-dominant tenement, unless by the terms of the contract that right is excluded: and in my opinion, if the present position were that the plaintiff was claiming against the lessor specific performance of the agreement of October 10, 1923, he would be entitled to be given a right of way for all reasonable purposes along the drive, including the part that passes the farm on the way to the orchard.

It is true that the easement, or, rather, quasi-easement, is not continuous. But the authorities are sufficient to show that a grantor of property, in circumstances where an obvious, i.e., visible and made road is necessary for the reasonable enjoyment of the property by the grantee, must be taken prima facie to have intended to grant a right to use it.

It would therefore appear that 'necessary' in the context of 'necessary for the reasonable enjoyment' should be interpreted widely and not as absolute 'necessity'. In this instance, there was an alternative access but nonetheless, taking into account the user of the dominant land, the right was deemed necessary for the reasonable enjoyment of the dominant land. 'Necessary' here would appear simply to mean any right which 'enhances' the dominant land. By way of contrast, there was also an alternative access in *Wheeler v JJ Saunders Limited* [1996] Ch D 31. In that case, the court held that there was no easement implied under the rule in *Wheeldon v Burrows*. One reason for that decision was that the access claimed as an easement was not 'necessary' in any sense, as the alternative was equally convenient and therefore the right claimed did not enhance the dominant land.

8.4.2.3 Implied under the Law of Property Act 1925 s 62

The LPA 1925 s 62 has two functions. First, it has what may be termed the 'normal' function of passing the benefit of *existing* easements in conveyances of the dominant land without any specific words being needed. Second, it operates as a method of creating a new easement impliedly.

Wright v Macadam [1949] 2 KB 744

Panel: Tucker, Singleton and Jenkins LJJ

Statutes: Law of Property Act 1925 ss 54(2) and 62

Facts: In 1940, Macadam let a flat to Mrs Wright. She occupied it on a weekly tenancy. From 1941 onwards, with Macadam's permission, she stored her coal in a shed in Macadam's garden. She was granted a one-year tenancy in 1943 but the lease contained no reference to the right to use the shed. When Macadam asked for payment for the use of the shed, Mrs Wright refused. Macadam stopped her from using the shed, and Mrs Wright sought an injunction to restrain interference with her right which she argued she held as an easement. The court granted the injunction and held that the right passed to Mrs Wright as a full easement under s 62, on the grant of the lease in 1943.

LORD JUSTICE JENKINS

Lord Justice Jenkins examined the wording of s 62 in detail and concluded that s 62 requires 'a conveyance' to imply the easement into. Lord Justice Jenkins interpreted 'conveyance' as being a document which creates a legal estate. Here, a legal lease was created even though it was not by deed, as LPA 1925 s 54(2) applied, meaning that even though the lease was created informally, it operated as a legal lease creating a legal estate.

The question in the present case, therefore, is whether the right to use the coal shed was at the date of the letting of August 28, 1943, a liberty, privilege, easement, right or advantage appertaining or reputed to appertain, to the land, or any part thereof, or, at the time of the conveyance, demised, occupied or enjoyed with the land - that is the flat - or any part thereof. It is enough for the plaintiffs' purposes if they can bring the right claimed within the widest part of the sub-section - that is to say, if they can show that the right was at the time of the material letting demised, occupied or enjoyed with the flat or any part thereof.

 Alert

The judge then looked at the authorities on the Conveyancing Act s 6, which was the precursor to s 62 and used those authorities to conclude:

> There is, therefore, ample authority for the proposition that a right in fact enjoyed with property will pass on a conveyance of the property by virtue of the grant to be read into it under s. 62, even although down to the date of the conveyance the right was exercised by permission only, and therefore was in that sense precarious.
>
> ...It is necessary to keep clearly in mind the distinction between "precariousness" in the sense in which it is used in relation to quasi rights of that description, and precariousness of title as used in relation to a permissively exercised right. For the purposes of s. 62, it is only necessary that the right should be one capable of being granted at law, or, in other words, a right known to the law. If it is a right of that description it matters not, as the *International Tea Stores* case shows, that it has been in fact enjoyed by permission only. The reason for that is clear, for, on the assumption that the right is included or imported into the parcels of the conveyance by virtue of s. 62, the grant under the conveyance supplies what one may call the defect in title, and substitutes a new title based on the grant.

Alert

After looking at all the authorities he stated:

> I think those are all the cases to which I can usefully refer, and applying the principles deducible from them to the present case one finds, I think, this. First of all, on the evidence the coal shed was used by Mrs. Wright by the permission of Mr. Macadam, but *International Tea Stores Co. v. Hobbs* shows that that does not prevent s. 62 from applying, because permissive as the right may have been it was in fact enjoyed.
>
> Next, the right was, as I understand it, a right to use the coal shed in question for the purpose of storing such coal as might be required for the domestic purposes of the flat. In my judgment that is a right or easement which the law will clearly recognize, and it is a right or easement of a kind which could readily be included in a lease or conveyance by the insertion of appropriate words in the parcels. This, therefore, is not a case in which a title to a right unknown to the law is claimed by virtue of s. 62. Nor is it a case in which it can be said to have been in the contemplation of the parties that the enjoyment of the right should be purely temporary. No limit was set as to the time during which the coal shed could continue to be used. Mr. Macadam simply gave his permission; that permission was acted on; and the use of the coal shed in fact went on down to August 28, 1943, and thereafter down to 1947. Therefore, applying to the facts of the present case the principles which seem to be deducible from the authorities, the conclusion to which I have come is that the right to use the coal shed was at the date of the letting of August 28, 1943, a right enjoyed with the top floor flat within the meaning of s. 62 of the Law of Property Act, 1925 , with the result that (as no contrary intention was expressed in the document) the right in question must be regarded as having passed by virtue of that letting, just as it would have passed if it had been mentioned in express terms in cl. 1, which sets out the subject-matter of the lease.

The exact circumstances in which s 62 applies to create an easement impliedly were considered in *Sovmots Investments Limited v Secretary of State for the Environment* [1979] AC 144.

Sovmots Investments Limited v Secretary of State for the Environment [1979] AC 144

Panel: Lord Wilberforce, Lord Edmund-Davies, Lord Fraser of Tullybenton, Lord Russell of Killowen and Lord Keith of Kinkel

Statute: Law of Property Act 1925 s 62

Facts: In 1960, Greater London Council granted to Sovmots a 150-year lease of Centre Point, which was an office complex with maisonettes above. The maisonettes were never occupied or sublet separately. In 1972 there was a severe housing shortage, and the Council for the London Borough of Camden compulsorily purchased the maisonettes. The compulsory purchase order did not include certain ancillary rights such as easements for gas, electricity and water for the benefit of the maisonettes. The Council claimed that these passed, by virtue of either the rule in *Wheeldon v Burrows* or the LPA 1925 s 62, into the deed by which the maisonettes were conveyed to the Council. The court held that *Wheeldon v Burrows* did not apply as it related only to voluntary conveyances and not to conveyances made pursuant to compulsory purchase orders. Further, s 62 did not operate in this situation as it required diversity of occupation or ownership of the dominant and servient tenements prior to the conveyance into which the easements were to be implied.

LORD WILBERFORCE

It is common ground between the appellants and the respondents that if Camden cannot under the compulsory purchase order acquire the ancillary rights over the appellants' property which are necessary if the maisonettes, when severed in ownership from the rest of Centre Point, are to be used as dwellings, then the Secretary of State could not confirm the order and it must be quashed. So the question is whether these ancillary rights can be acquired. ...

The main argument before the inspector and in the courts below was that in this case and under the compulsory purchase order as made no specific power to require the creation of ancillary rights was necessary because these would pass to the acquiring authority under either, or both, of the first rule in *Wheeldon v. Burrows* (1879) 12 Ch.D. 31 ("the rule") or of section 62 of the Law of Property Act 1925. Under the rule (I apologise for the reminder but the expression of the rule is important)

"on the grant by the owner of a tenement of part of that tenement *as it is then used and enjoyed*, there will pass to the grantee all those continuous and apparent easements (by which, of course, I mean quasi-easements), or, in other words, all those easements which are necessary to the reasonable enjoyment of the property granted, and *which have been and are at the time of the grant* used by the owners of the entirety for the benefit of the part granted" (see *per* Thesiger L.J., at p. 49, my emphasis).

Under section 62 a conveyance of land operates to convey with the land all ways, watercourses, liberties, privileges, easements, rights, and advantages whatsoever, appertaining or reputed to appertain to the land, or any part thereof, or, at the time of conveyance, demised, occupied or enjoyed with, or reputed or known as part or parcel or appurtenant to the land or any part thereof.

My Lords, there are very comprehensive expressions here, but it does not take much analysis to see that they have no relevance to the situation under consideration.

The rule is a rule of intention, based on the proposition that a man may not derogate from his grant. He cannot grant or agree to grant land and at the same time deny to his grantee what is at the time of the grant obviously necessary for its reasonable enjoyment. To apply this to a case where a public authority is taking from an owner his land without his will is to stand the rule on its head: it means substituting for the intention of a reasonable voluntary grantor the unilateral, opposed, intention of the acquirer.

Moreover, ... for the rule to apply there must be actual, and apparent, use and enjoyment at the time of the grant. But no such use or enjoyment had, at Centre Point, taken place at all.

Equally, section 62 does not fit this case. The reason is that when land is under one ownership one cannot speak in any intelligible sense of rights, or privileges, or easements being exercised over one part for the benefit of another. Whatever the owner does, he does as owner and, until a separation occurs, of ownership or at least of occupation, the condition for the existence of rights, etc., does not exist: see *Bolton v. Bolton* (1879) 11 Ch.D. 968 , 970 per Fry J. and *Long v. Gowlett* [1923] 2 Ch. 177, 189, 198, in my opinion a correct decision.

A separation of ownership, in a case like the present, will arise on conveyance of one of the parts (e.g. the maisonettes), but this separation cannot be projected back to the stage of the compulsory purchase order so as, by anticipation to bring into existence rights not existing in fact.

Links

See the Harpum and Smith articles in the Further Reading section

The requirement of prior diversity of ownership or occupation in *Sovmots* has been doubted in *P&S Platt v Crouch* [2004] 1 P&CR 18.

P&S Platt Limited v Crouch [2004] 1 P&CR 18

Panel: Peter Gibson, Dyson and Longmore LJJ

Statutes: Law of Property Act 192 s 62

Facts: The Crouch family owned riverside properties in the Norfolk Broads comprising a hotel and house within the hotel grounds. They also owned an island in the river with a bungalow on it. The hotel guests enjoyed exclusive use of the river moorings on the island and the hotel trade generated from the availability of the river moorings was considerable. P&S Platt Limited, the claimant, bought the hotel in 2001, and took an option to buy the house and bungalow. The option was not exercised. The claimant alleged that the rights to enjoy the river moorings passed for the benefit of the hotel in the conveyance to the claimant by virtue of s 62 and the rule in *Wheeldon v Burrows*.

The court held that the rights passed as easements under s 62 even though there was no prior diversity of ownership or occupation as required by the *Sovmots* case. Lord Justice Peter Gibson looked at the case of *Birmingham, Dudley and District Banking Co v Ross* (1888) 38 ChD 295, which he called 'the *Birmingham* case', to see what the intention of the parties was at the time of the sale. The defendants argued that it was not the intention of the parties that the rights should pass, and that s 62 should be excluded from the transfer impliedly, as the circumstances were such that it could not have intended the rights to pass.

LORD JUSTICE PETER GIBSON

Jenkins L.J.'s proposition extracted from the Birmingham case was applied by this court in *Hair v Gillman* [2000] 3 E.G.L.R. 76 G. In Megarry and Wade, The Law of Real Property 6th ed. (2001) para. 18–115 under the heading "Contrary Intention" it is stated:

"Section 62 applies 'only if and as far as a contrary intention is not expressed in the conveyance' .... But the section is also subject to any contrary intention which may be implied from circumstances existing at the time of the grant. If, for example, the plot sold and the plot retained are both subject to a building scheme, the purchaser of a house standing on the plot sold will not be able to prevent the plot retained from being built upon so as to diminish his light; for the light was enjoyed 'under such circumstances as to show that there could be no expectation of its continuance.'"

The authority given for the last sentence is the Birmingham case at 307 per Cotton L.J. A similar comment based on the Birmingham case is made in Emmet on Title para.17.076. ...

After considering the circumstances of the case, the judge rejected the arguments that the parties did not intend the mooring rights to pass for the benefit of the hotel:

> To my mind the evidence is clear that the rights in question did appertain to and were reputed to appertain to and were enjoyed with the hotel, being part of the hotel business and advertised as such and enjoyed by the hotel guests. The rights were continuous and apparent, and so it matters not that prior to the sale of the hotel there was no prior diversity of occupation of the dominant and servient tenancies. Accordingly, I reach the conclusion that s.62 operated to convert the rights into full easements... .

Alert

Thus it appears that prior diversity of ownership or occupation is not necessary, provided that the right is 'continuous and apparent'. This decision was cited as good law in the recent case of *Alford v Hannaford* [2011] EWCA Civ 1099.

The Law Commission, in its 2011 report, recognised that as well as conveying with the land existing easements appurtenant to it, the current operation of s62 has two further effects. First, it can transform leasehold easements into freehold ones. This upgrading effect was considered acceptable by the Commission and it was recommended that it

Link

See *Sovmots* and *Platt v Crouch*

should continue. The second, however, was recommended to be abolished, namely the effect of transforming precarious permissions into proprietary rights i.e. easements (see paras 3.52-70).

Further Reading

Megarry and Wade, *The Law of Real Property*, (7th Edition), Sweet & Maxwell 2008, pp 1207-1207 and pp 1240-1258

Law Commission Report No. 327 'Making Land Work: Easements, Covenants and Profits a Prendre'

Colby, A., 'Easing Into a Defined Space', 2009 *EG* 100

Harpum, C., 'Easements and Centre Point: Old Problems Resolved in a Novel Setting', 1977 *Conv* 415

Hill-Smith, A., 'Rights of Parking and the Ouster Principle after Batchelor v Marlow', 2007 *Conv* 71

Smith, P., Centre Point: Faulty Towers and Shaky Foundations, 1978 *Conv* 449

Lu Xu 'Easement of car parking: the ouster principle is out but problems may aggravate', 2012 *Conv* 4, 291-306

Part III

The Landlord and Tenant Relationship

9

Essential Characteristics of the Leasehold Relationship

Topic List

1   Essential Characteristics of a Lease

2   Intention To Create Legal Relations

3   Service Occupancies

4   Commercial Arrangements

Introduction

A lease which is properly created is a proprietary right in land. It must be distinguished from a licence, which is merely a personal right and cannot therefore be enforced against a third party. The essential characteristics of a lease were set out in *Street v Mountford* [1985] AC 809 by Lord Templeman. There must be a certain term, whether fixed or periodic, and exclusive possession. The cases in this chapter focus on the meaning of 'exclusive possession' and the way in which courts identify whether it exists: by looking at the underlying substance of the arrangement rather than at any express wording or the stated intentions of the parties. The problems involved in identifying exclusive possession are further complicated when there is more than one occupant, or where the premises are commercial rather than residential. Even where there is found to be certainty of term and exclusive possession, there may be circumstances in which there is still found to be no lease: for example, where there is an employer/employee relationship, or where there is no intention to create legal relations. Many of these cases are based on claims under the Rent Acts, which are now of limited significance. However, the question of whether an arrangement is a lease or simply a licence is still important for business arrangements. It is also crucial for residential arrangements, where the Landlord and Tenant Act 1985 may affect repair covenants if those covenants are contained in a lease rather than a licence (see Chapter 10).

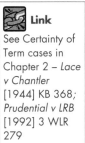

Link

See Certainty of Term cases in Chapter 2 – *Lace v Chantler* [1944] KB 368; *Prudential v LRB* [1992] 3 WLR 279

9.1 Essential Characteristics of a Lease

9.1.1 Exclusive possession as the defining characteristic

Street v Mountford [1985] AC 809

Panel: Lord Scarman, Lord Keith of Kinkel, Lord Bridge of Harwich, Lord Brightman and Lord Templeman

Facts: In March 1983 Mr Street granted to Mrs Mountford the right to occupy rooms at St Clements Gardens, Boscombe, for £37 per week. The parties entered into a written agreement in which the arrangement was described throughout as a 'licence'; the payment was called a 'licence fee' and Mr Street reserved the right to enter the rooms at any time for any reasonable purpose. A declaration in the agreement signed by Mrs Mountford stated: 'I understand and accept that a licence in the above form does not and is not intended to give me a tenancy protected under the Rent Acts'.

Mrs Mountford registered a fair rent under the Rent Acts in respect of the premises. The House of Lords considered whether there was a tenancy, in which case the fair rent was correctly registered; or whether the arrangement was simply a licence not protected by the Rent Acts.

LORD TEMPLEMAN

The traditional view that the grant of exclusive possession for a term at a rent creates a tenancy is consistent with the elevation of a tenancy into an estate in land. The tenant possessing exclusive possession is able to exercise the rights of an owner of land, which is in the real sense his land albeit temporarily and subject to certain restrictions. A tenant armed with exclusive possession can keep out strangers and keep out the landlord unless the landlord is exercising limited rights reserved to him by the tenancy agreement to enter and view and repair. A licensee lacking exclusive possession can in no sense call the land his own and cannot be said to own any estate in the land. The licence does not create an estate in the land to which it relates but only makes an act lawful which would otherwise be unlawful… .

In the case of residential accommodation there is no difficulty in deciding whether the grant confers exclusive possession. An occupier of residential accommodation at a rent for a term is either a lodger or a tenant. The occupier is a lodger if the landlord provides attendance or services which require the landlord or his servants to exercise unrestricted access to and use of the premises. A lodger is entitled to live in the premises but cannot call the place his own. In *Allan v Liverpool Overseers* (1874) L.R. 9 Q.B. 180, 191-192 Blackburn J. said:

'A lodger in a house, although he has the exclusive use of rooms in the house, in the sense that nobody else is to be there, and though his goods are stowed there, yet he is not in exclusive occupation in that sense, because the landlord is there for the purpose of being able, as landlords commonly do in the case of lodgings, to have his own servants to look after the house and the furniture, and has retained to himself the occupation, though he has agreed to give the exclusive enjoyment of the occupation to the lodger.'

If on the other hand residential accommodation is granted for a term at a rent with exclusive possession, the landlord providing neither attendance nor services, the grant is a tenancy; any express reservation to the landlord of limited rights to enter and view the state of the premises and to repair and maintain the premises only serves to emphasise the fact that the grantee is entitled to exclusive possession and is a tenant. In the present case it is conceded that Mrs. Mountford is entitled to exclusive possession and is not a lodger. Mr. Street provided neither attendance nor services and only reserved the limited rights of inspection and maintenance and the like set forth in clause 3 of the agreement. On the traditional view of the matter, Mrs. Mountford not being a lodger must be a tenant.

Alert

Mr Street conceded that Mrs Mountford had exclusive possession of the rooms, but he argued that it was clear from the document that both parties had intended to create a licence, not a lease. Lord Templeman stated that it is the underlying substance of the agreement which determines its effect. The label or the words used simply indicate the apparent intention of the parties rather than the true effect of the document.

Both parties enjoyed freedom to contract or not to contract and both parties exercised that freedom by contracting on the terms set forth in the written agreement and on no other terms. But the consequences in law of the agreement, once concluded, can only be determined by consideration of the effect of the agreement. If the agreement satisfied all the requirements of a tenancy, then the agreement produced a tenancy and the parties cannot alter the effect of the agreement by insisting that they only created a licence. The manufacture of a five-pronged implement for manual digging results in a fork even if the manufacturer, unfamiliar with the English language, insists that he intended to make and has made a spade. …

Alert

… It may fairly be said that the circumstances negative any intention to create a mere licence. Words alone do not suffice. Parties cannot turn a tenancy into a licence merely by calling it one. The circumstances and the conduct of the parties show that what was intended was that the occupier should be granted exclusive possession at a rent for a term with a corresponding interest in the land which created a tenancy.

Link

See *Norris v Checksfield* [1991] 1 WLR 1241; *RPS v County* (1985) 276 EG 1038; *Facchini v Bryson* [1952] 1 TLR 1386

Lord Templeman stated clearly that exclusive possession is the key characteristic of a lease: without it, a lease simply cannot exist. However he did acknowledge that exclusive possession is, of itself, not conclusive. An occupier who has exclusive possession may nevertheless simply be a licensee if he has a service occupancy, or if the parties have no intention to create legal relations.

My Lords, the only intention which is relevant is the intention demonstrated by the agreement to grant exclusive possession for a term at a rent. Sometimes it may be difficult to discover whether, on the true construction of an agreement, exclusive possession is conferred. Sometimes it may appear from the surrounding circumstances that there was no intention to create legal relationships. Sometimes it may appear from the surrounding circumstances that the right to exclusive possession is referable to a legal relationship other than a tenancy. Legal relationships to which the grant of exclusive possession might be referable and which would or might negative the grant of an estate or interest in the land include occupancy under a contract for the sale of the land, occupancy pursuant to a contract of employment or occupancy referable to the holding of an office. But where as in the present case the only circumstances are that residential accommodation is offered and accepted with exclusive possession for a term at a rent, the result is a tenancy.

Alert

Westminster City Council v Clarke [1992] AC 288

Panel: Lord Bridge of Harwich, Lord Templeman, Lord Griffiths, Lord Ackner and Lord Lowry

Facts: Westminster City Council owned houses which were used by the council as a hostel for homeless, single men with problems such as alcoholism and drug addiction. Many of them had been evicted from ordinary residential accommodation, or discharged from prison or hospital. The hostel was intended to be a temporary home, where the occupants could undergo supervised treatment and rehabilitation before moving on to permanent, independent living arrangements. Clarke had signed an agreement called a 'licence to occupy' in which he acknowledged that he had no exclusive possession and that the Council could change his room or require him to share at any time. The Council sought to terminate the arrangement after complaints about Clarke's behaviour. He claimed he was a tenant and as such had statutory protection from eviction under the Housing Act 1985. The House of Lords looked at the reality of the arrangement and concluded that there genuinely was a licence in the circumstances.

LORD TEMPLEMAN

In the circumstances of the present case I consider that the council legitimately and effectively retained for themselves possession of room E and that Mr. Clarke was only a licensee with rights corresponding to the rights of a lodger. In reaching this conclusion I take into account the object of the council, namely the provision of accommodation for vulnerable homeless persons, the necessity for the council to retain possession of all the rooms in order to make and administer arrangements for the suitable accommodation of all the occupiers and the need for the council to retain possession of every room not only in the interests of the council as the owners of the terrace but also for the purpose of providing for the occupiers supervision and assistance. For many obvious reasons it was highly undesirable for the council to grant to any occupier of a room exclusive possession which obstructed the use by the council of all the rooms of the hostel in the interests of every occupier. By the terms of the licence to occupy Mr. Clarke was not entitled to any particular room, he could be required to share with any other person as required by the council and he was only entitled to 'occupy accommodation in common with the council whose representative may enter the accommodation at any time.' It is accepted that these provisions of the licence to occupy were inserted to enable the council to discharge its responsibilities to the vulnerable persons accommodated at the Cambridge Street terrace and were not inserted for the purpose of enabling the council to avoid the creation of a secure tenancy. The conditions of occupancy support the view that Mr. Clarke was not in exclusive occupation of room E. He was expressly limited in his enjoyment of any accommodation provided for him. He was forbidden to entertain visitors without the approval of the council staff and was bound to comply with the council's warden or other staff in charge of the hostel. These limitations confirmed that the council retained possession of all the rooms of the hostel in order to supervise and control the activities of the occupiers, including Mr. Clarke. Although Mr. Clarke physically occupied room E he did not enjoy possession exclusively of the council.

This is a very special case which depends on the peculiar nature of the hostel maintained by the council, the use of the hostel by the council, the totality, immediacy, and objectives of the powers exercisable by the council and the restrictions imposed on Mr. Clarke. The decision in this case will not allow a landlord, private or public, to free himself from the Rent Acts or from the restrictions of a secure tenancy merely by adopting or adapting the language of the licence to occupy. The provisions of the licence to occupy and the circumstances in which that licence was granted and continued lead to the conclusion that Mr. Clarke has never enjoyed that exclusive possession which he claims.

Bruton v London & Quadrant Housing Trust [2000] 1 AC 406

Panel: Lord Slynn of Hadley, Lord Jauncey of Tullichettle, Lord Hoffmann, Lord Hope of Craighead and Lord Hobhouse of Woodborough

Facts: Lambeth Council owned a block of flats in Brixton. In 1986 it granted a licence of the block to London and Quadrant Housing Trust, which was a charity providing short-term accommodation for the homeless and others in need. The Trust in turn entered into an agreement with Mr Bruton in 1989 allowing him to occupy one of the flats. The agreement clearly stated that it created a temporary licence only, that the Trust held the premises on a licence, and that the Trust had a right to enter the flat. Mr Bruton claimed that the Trust was in breach of its implied repairing obligations under the Landlord and Tenant Act 1985 s 11. Those repairing obligations only apply to leases, not to licences. Mr Bruton therefore sought to argue that he had a lease of the premises. The House of Lords reversed the decision of the Court of Appeal and held that, although the Trust itself had no legal estate in the land, it had nevertheless granted a lease to Mr Bruton.

LORD HOFFMANN

Did this agreement create a "lease" or "tenancy" within the meaning of the Landlord and Tenant Act 1985 or any other legislation which refers to a lease or tenancy? The decision of this House in Street v. Mountford [1985] A.C. 809 is authority for the proposition that a "lease" or "tenancy" is a contractually binding agreement, not referable to any other relationship between the parties, by which one person gives another the right to exclusive occupation of land for a fixed or renewable period or periods of time, usually in return for a periodic payment in money. An agreement having these characteristics creates a relationship of landlord and tenant to which the common law or statute may then attach various incidents. The fact that the parties use language more appropriate to a different kind of agreement, such as a licence, is irrelevant if upon its true construction it has the identifying characteristics of a lease. The meaning of the agreement, for example, as to the extent of the possession which it grants, depend upon the intention of the parties, objectively ascertained by reference to the language and relevant background. The decision of your Lordships' House in *Westminster City Council v. Clarke* [1992] 2 A.C. 288 is a good example of the importance of background in deciding whether the agreement grants exclusive possession or not. But the classification of the agreement as a lease does not depend upon any intention additional to that expressed in the choice of terms. It is simply a question of characterising the terms which the parties have agreed. This is a question of law.

 Alert

In this case, it seems to me that the agreement, construed against the relevant background, plainly gave Mr. Bruton a right to exclusive possession. There is nothing to suggest that he was to share possession with the trust, the council or anyone else. The trust did not retain such control over the premises as was inconsistent with Mr. Bruton having exclusive possession, as was the case in *Westminster City Council v. Clarke* [1992] 2 A.C. 288. The only rights which it reserved were for itself and the council to enter at certain times and for limited purposes. As Lord Templeman said in

Street v. Mountford [1985] A.C. 809, 818, such an express reservation "only serves to emphasise the fact that the grantee is entitled to exclusive possession and is a tenant." Nor was there any other relationship between the parties to which Mr. Bruton's exclusive possession could be referable.

Mr. Henderson, who appeared for the trust, submitted that there were "special circumstances" in this case which enabled one to construe the agreement as a licence despite the presence of all the characteristics identified in *Street v. Mountford* [1985] A.C. 809. These circumstances were that the trust was a responsible landlord performing socially valuable functions, it had agreed with the council not to grant tenancies, Mr. Bruton had agreed that he was not to have a tenancy and the trust had no estate out of which it could grant one.

In my opinion none of these circumstances can make an agreement to grant exclusive possession something other than a tenancy. ... I consider that the agreement between the trust and Mr. Bruton was a lease within the meaning of section 11 of the Landlord and Tenant Act 1985.

My Lords, in my opinion, that is the end of the matter. ...

This is a radical decision in that it ignores the crucial prerequisite for granting a lease, that the landlord must have an estate in land.

9.1.2 Devices to defeat exclusive possession

Aslan v Murphy [1990] 1 WLR 766

Panel: Lord Donaldson of Lymingtom MR, Butler-Sloss and Stuart-Smith LJJ

Facts: Aslan owned a property and granted to Murphy a right to occupy a tiny basement room. The written agreement signed by them was labelled 'Licence'. It contained the following provisions: a statement that the licensor was not willing to grant the licensee exclusive possession of any part of the room; a reservation of the rights for the licensor to use the room in common with the licensee and any other licensees who may be permitted to use it, and to decide the position of the furniture in the room. The right to occupy was strictly limited and excluded the hours of 10.30am until midday each day and the licensor retained the keys and reserved a right of entry at all times for the provision of services. When the landowner claimed possession, Murphy argued that the agreement was a sham, that he had exclusive possession and thus a lease.

LORD DONALDSON OF LYMINGTON MR

General principles

The status of a tenant is essentially different from that of a lodger and owners of property are free to make accommodation available on either basis. Which basis applies in any particular case depends upon what was the true bargain between the parties. It is the ascertainment of that true bargain which lies at the heart of the problem.

Labelling

The labels which parties agree to attach to themselves or to their agreements are never conclusive and in this particular field, in which there is enormous pressure on the homeless to agree to any label which will facilitate the obtaining of accommodation, they give no guidance at all. As Lord Templeman said in *Street v. Mountford* [1985] A.C. 809, 819:

"The manufacture of a five-pronged implement for manual digging results in a fork even if the manufacturer, unfamiliar with the English language, insists that he intended to make and has made a spade."

Exclusive or non-exclusive occupation

This is the touchstone by which the "spade" of tenancy falls to be distinguished from the "fork" of lodging. In this context it is necessary to consider the rights and duties of the person making the accommodation available ("the owner") and the rights of other occupiers. The occupier has in the end to be a tenant or a lodger. He cannot be both. But there is a spectrum of exclusivity ranging from the occupier of a detached property under a full repairing lease, who is without doubt a tenant, to the overnight occupier of a hotel bedroom who, however up-market the hotel, is without doubt a lodger. The dividing line — the sorting of the forks from the spades — will not necessarily or even usually depend upon a single factor, but upon a combination of factors.

Pretences

Quite apart from labelling, parties may succumb to the temptation to agree to pretend to have particular rights and duties which are not in fact any part of the true bargain. Prima facie, the parties must be taken to mean what they say, but given the pressures on both parties to pretend, albeit for different reasons, the courts would be acting unrealistically if they did not keep a weather eye open for pretences, taking due account of how the parties have acted in performance of their apparent bargain. This identification and exposure of such pretences does not necessarily lead to the conclusion that their agreement is a sham, but only to the conclusion that the terms of the true bargain are not wholly the same as those of the bargain appearing on the face of the agreement.

 Alert

The judge at first instance had analysed the agreement at its face value, in accordance with the approach of the Court of Appeal in *AG Securities v Vaughan* and *Antoniades v Villiers* to find that the agreement was a licence. Lord Donaldson MR here applied the reasoning of the House of Lords in the *AG Securities v Vaughan* and *Antoniades v Villiers* to find that the agreement was a sham:

 **Link**
See *AG Securities v Vaughan* and *Antoniades v Villiers* [1990] 1 AC 417

The judge was, of course, quite right to approach the matter on this basis that it is not a crime, nor is it contrary to public policy, for a property owner to license occupiers to occupy a property on terms which do not give rise to a tenancy. Where he went wrong was in considering whether the whole agreement was a sham and, having concluded that it was not, giving effect to its terms, i.e. taking it throughout at face value. What he should have done, and I am sure would have done if he had known of the House of Lords approach to the problem, was to consider whether the whole agreement was a sham and, if it was not, whether in the light of the factual situation the provisions for sharing the room and those depriving the defendant of the right to occupy it for 90 minutes out of each 24 hours were part of the true bargain between the parties or were pretences. Both provisions were wholly unrealistic and were clearly pretences.

His Lordship then turned to the question of the retention of the keys to see whether he could uphold the lower court's finding that there was a licence on that basis.

Provisions as to keys, if not a pretence which they often are, do not have any magic in themselves. It is not a requirement of a tenancy that the occupier shall have exclusive possession of the keys to the property. What matters is what underlies the provisions as to keys. Why does the owner want a key, want to prevent keys being issued to the friends of the occupier or want to prevent the lock being changed?

 Alert

A landlord may well need a key in order that he may be able to enter quickly in the event of emergency: fire, burst pipes or whatever. He may need a key to enable him or those authorised by him to read meters or to do repairs which are his responsibility. None of these underlying reasons would of themselves indicate that the true bargain between the parties was such that the occupier was in law a lodger. On the other hand, if the true bargain is that the owner will provide genuine services which can only be provided by having keys, such as frequent cleaning, daily bed-making, the provision of clean linen at regular intervals and the like, there are materials from which it is possible to infer that the occupier is a lodger rather than a tenant. But the inference arises not from the provisions as to keys, but from the reason why those provisions formed part of the bargain.

Marchant v Charters [1977] 1 WLR 1181

Panel: Lord Denning MR, Orr and Waller LJJ

Facts: Anne Marchant owned a house in Clapham Common which consisted of seven furnished bedsits with cooking facilities. The rooms were cleaned daily and the linen changed every week. The occupants shared bathroom facilities. George Charters occupied one of the bedsits. He applied to register a fair rent under the Rent Acts. Marchant then served a notice to quit and claimed possession. Charters claimed that he had a tenancy of the room, which was protected by the Rent Acts. Lord Denning MR said although the room was let as a separate dwelling, the level of services which were provided was too substantial to support the finding of a tenancy. The arrangement was a licence.

LORD DENNING MR

Gathering the cases together, what does it come to? What is the test to see whether the occupier of one room in a house is a tenant or a licensee? It does not depend on whether he or she has exclusive possession or not. It does not depend on whether the room is furnished or not. It does not depend on whether the occupation is permanent or temporary. It does not depend on the label which the parties put upon it. All these are factors which may influence the decision but none of them is conclusive. All the circumstances have to be worked out. Eventually the answer depends on the nature and quality of the occupancy. Was it intended that the occupier should have a stake in the room or did he have only permission for himself personally to occupy the room, whether under a contract or not? In which case he is a licensee.

He elaborated on what might constitute sufficient 'attendance' and 'services' to defeat a lease:

The word "attendance" was much considered by the House of Lords in *Palser v. Grinling* [1948] A.C. 291. Viscount Simon said, at pp. 310–311, that attendance meant "service personal to the tenant provided by the landlord ... for the benefit or convenience of the individual tenant in his use or enjoyment" of the room. It does not include services in regard to the common parts, such as cleaning the common staircase, or the porter at the bottom. Applying that test, it is quite plain that the attendance here included these services: each day the room was cleaned, each day the rubbish was removed, and each week the dirty linen was removed and clean linen was supplied in its place. The fact that Mr. Charters may have refused it on some occasions does not affect the matter.

9.1.3 Exclusive possession and multiple occupancy

AG Securities v Vaughan and Others; Antoniades v Villiers and Another [1990] AC 417

Panel: Lord Bridge of Harwich, Lord Templeman, Lord Ackner, Lord Oliver of Aylmerton and Lord Jauncey of Tullichettle

Facts: Two appeals on the same point of law were heard together in the House of Lords. *AG Securities v Vaughan* is referred to by their Lordships as 'the first appeal' and involved the occupants of a large flat with four bedrooms and spacious shared accommodation comprising a lounge, sitting room, kitchen and bathroom. The occupants, at least at first, did not know each other. They all signed separate agreements setting out the terms of their occupancy; the agreements contained different monthly payments and began at different times. The landowner reserved a right to introduce others to share the flat, up to a maximum of four people. By contrast, in *Antoniades v Villiers*, referred to in the opinions as 'the second appeal', the accommodation comprised a small attic flat with a bedroom, sitting room, kitchen and bathroom. Mr Villiers and Miss Bridger had been looking for somewhere to live together for several months. When they viewed the flat, they asked for a double bed to be provided. They signed separate agreements which were identical, including the level of payments. The agreements reserved a right for the landowner to introduce others to share, and indeed to share the premises himself with the occupants. They also contained acknowledgements that the occupants did not have exclusive possession, that the agreements constituted a licence and that the agreements would be terminated if the parties married.

The Court of Appeal had held that the first arrangement amounted to a lease and that the second created two licences. In the House of Lords, those decisions were reversed. Their Lordships made some points which were of a general nature, applicable to both appeals.

LORD TEMPLEMAN

Since parties to an agreement cannot contract out of the Rent Acts, a document expressed in the language of a licence must nevertheless be examined and construed by the court in order to decide whether the rights and obligations enjoyed and imposed create a licence or a tenancy. A person seeking residential accommodation may sign a document couched in any language in order to obtain shelter. Since parties to an agreement cannot contract out of the Rent Acts, the grant of a tenancy to two persons jointly cannot be concealed, accidentally or by design, by the creation of two documents in the form of licences. Two persons seeking residential accommodation may sign any number of documents in order to obtain joint shelter. In considering one or more documents for the purpose of deciding whether a tenancy has been created, the court must consider the surrounding circumstances including any relationship between the prospective occupiers, the course of negotiations and the nature and extent of the accommodation and the intended and actual mode of occupation of the accommodation. If the owner of a one-bedroomed flat granted a licence to a husband to occupy the flat provided he shared the flat with his wife and nobody else and granted a similar licence to the wife provided she shared the flat with the husband and nobody else, the court would be bound to consider the effect of both documents together. If the licence to the husband required him to pay a licence fee of £50 per month and the licence to the wife required her to pay a further licence fee of £50 per month, the two documents read together in the light of the property to be occupied and the obvious intended mode of occupation would confer exclusive occupation on the husband and wife jointly and a tenancy at the rent of £100.

 Alert

Landlords dislike the Rent Acts and wish to enjoy the benefits of letting property without the burden of the restrictions imposed by the Acts. Landlords believe that the Rent Acts unfairly interfere with freedom of contract and exacerbate the housing shortage. Tenants on the other hand believe that the Acts are a necessary protection against the exploitation of people who do not own the freehold or long leases of their homes. The court lacks the knowledge and the power to form any judgment on these arguments which fall to be considered and determined by Parliament. The duty of the court is to enforce the Acts and in so doing to observe one principle which is inherent in the Acts and has been long recognised, the principle that parties cannot contract out of the Acts.

The enjoyment of exclusive occupation for a term in consideration of periodical payments creates a tenancy, save in exceptional circumstances not relevant to these appeals: ...

If, under an agreement, the owner of residential accommodation provides services or attendance and retains possession for that purpose the occupier is a lodger and the agreement creates a licence. Under an agreement for the exclusive occupation of a room or rooms consisting of a dwelling for periodic payments then, save in the exceptional circumstances mentioned in *Street v. Mountford* [1985] A.C. 809, 826-827, a single occupier, if he is not a lodger, must be a tenant. The agreement may provide, expressly or by implication, power for the owner to enter the dwelling to inspect or repair but if the occupier is entitled to the use and enjoyment of the dwelling and is not a lodger he is in exclusive occupation and the agreement creates a tenancy.

Where residential accommodation is occupied by two or more persons the occupiers may be licensees or tenants of the whole or each occupier may be a separate tenant of part. In the present appeals the only question raised is whether the occupiers are licensees or tenants of the whole.

 Alert

LORD OLIVER OF AYLMERTON

The critical question, however, in every case is not simply how the arrangement is presented to the outside world in the relevant documentation, but what is the true nature of the arrangement. The decision of this House in *Street v. Mountford* [1985] A.C. 809 established quite clearly that if the true legal effect of the arrangement entered into is that the occupier of residential property has exclusive possession of the property for an ascertainable period in return for periodical money payments, a tenancy is created, whatever the label the parties may have chosen to attach to it. Where, as in that case, the circumstances show that the occupant is the only occupier realistically contemplated and the premises are inherently suitable only for single occupation, there is, generally, very little difficulty. Such an occupier normally has exclusive possession, as indeed she did in *Street v. Mountford*, where such possession was conceded, unless the owner retains control and unrestricted access for the purpose of providing attendance and services. As my noble and learned friend, Lord Templeman, observed in that case, the occupier in those circumstances is either a lodger or a tenant. Where, however, the premises are such as, by their nature, to lend themselves to multiple occupation and they are in fact occupied in common by a number of persons under different individual agreements with the owner, more difficult problems arise. These two appeals, at different ends of the scale, are illustrations of such problems.

 Alert

Having made general points applicable to both appeals, their Lordships then turned their attention to the individual cases. All began by considering *AG Securities v Vaughan*:

LORD BRIDGE OF HARWICH

The four respondents acquired their contractual rights to occupy the flat in question and undertook their relevant obligations by separate agreements with the appellants made at different times and on different terms. These rights and obligations having initially been several, I do not understand by what legal alchemy they could ever become joint. Each occupant had a contractual right, enforceable against the appellants, to prevent the number of persons permitted to occupy the flat at any one time exceeding four. But this did not give them exclusive possession of the kind which is distinctive of a leasehold interest. Having no estate in land, they could not sue in trespass. Their remedy against intruders would have been to persuade the appellants to sue as plaintiffs or to join the appellants as defendants by way of enforcement of their contractual rights.

The arrangement seems to have been a sensible and realistic one to provide accommodation for a shifting population of individuals who were genuinely prepared to share the flat with others introduced from time to time who would, at least initially, be strangers to them. There was no artificiality in the contracts concluded to give effect to this arrangement. On the contrary, it seems to me, with respect to the majority of the Court of Appeal, to require the highest degree of artificiality to force these contracts into the mould of a joint tenancy.

 Alert

LORD TEMPLEMAN

If the company granted exclusive possession of the flat to one single occupier or to two or more occupiers jointly in consideration of periodical payments, the grant would create a tenancy of the flat. If the company granted exclusive possession of one bedroom to four different occupiers with joint use of the lounge, sitting-room, kitchen and bathroom, each of the four grants would create a tenancy of one bedroom. ...

The Court of Appeal, ante p. 422C, (Fox and Mustill L.JJ., Sir George Waller dissenting), concluded that the four respondents were jointly entitled to exclusive occupation of the flat. I am unable to agree. If a landlord who owns a three-bedroom flat enters into three separate independent tenancies with three independent tenants each of whom is entitled to one bedroom and to share the common parts, then the three tenants, if they agree, can exclude anyone else from the flat. But they do not enjoy exclusive occupation of the flat jointly under the terms of their tenancies. In the present case, if the four respondents had been jointly entitled to exclusive occupation of the flat then, on the death of one of the respondents, the remaining three would be entitled to joint and exclusive occupation. But, in fact, on the death of one respondent the remaining three would not be entitled to joint and exclusive occupation of the flat. They could not exclude a fourth person nominated by the company. I would allow the appeal.

LORD OLIVER OF AYLMERTON

There is no question but that the agreements with which the appeal is concerned reflect the true bargain between the parties. It is the purpose and intention of both parties to each agreement that it should confer an individual right on the licensee named, that he should be liable only for the payment which he had undertaken, and that his agreement should be capable of termination without reference to the agreements with other persons occupying the flat. The judge found that the agreements were not shams and that each of the four occupants had arrived independently of one another and not as a group. His finding was that there was never a group of persons coming to the flat altogether. ... The only questions are those of the effect of each agreement vis-à-vis the individual licensee and whether the agreements collectively had the effect of creating a joint tenancy among the occupants of the premises for the time being by virtue of their having between them exclusive possession of the premises.

Taking first, by way of example, the position of the first occupier to be let into the premises on the terms of one of these agreements, it is, in my judgment, quite unarguable, once any question of sham is out of the way, that he has an estate in the premises which entitles him to exclusive possession. His right, which is, by definition, a right to share use and occupation with such other persons not exceeding three in number as the licensor shall introduce from time to time, is clearly inconsistent with any exclusive possession in him alone even though he may be the only person in physical occupation at a particular time. He has no legal title which will permit him to exclude other persons to whom the licensor may choose to grant the privilege of entry. That must equally apply to the additional licensees who join him. None of them has individually nor have they collectively the right or power lawfully to exclude a further nominee of the licensor within the prescribed maximum.

I pause to note that it has never been contended that any individual occupier has a tenancy of a particular room in the flat with a right to use the remainder of the flat in common with the tenants of other rooms. I can envisage that as a possibility in cases of arrangements of this kind if the facts support the marking out with the landlord's concurrence of a particular room as the exclusive domain of a particular individual. But to support that there would, I think, have to be proved the grant of an indentifiable part of the flat and that simply does not fit with the system described in the evidence of the instant case.

Their Lordships then considered the specific situation in *Antoniades v Villiers*:

LORD TEMPLEMAN

In the first appeal the four agreements were independent of one another. In the second appeal the two agreements were interdependent. Both would have been signed or neither. The two agreements must therefore be read together. Mr. Villiers and Miss Bridger applied to rent the flat jointly and sought and enjoyed joint and exclusive occupation of the whole of the flat. They shared the rights and the obligations imposed by the terms of their occupation. They acquired joint and exclusive occupation of the flat in consideration of periodical payments and they therefore acquired a tenancy jointly. Mr. Antoniades required each of them, Mr. Villiers and Miss Bridger, to agree to pay one half of each aggregate periodical payment, but this circumstance cannot convert a tenancy into a licence. A tenancy remains a tenancy even though the landlord may choose to require each of two joint tenants to agree expressly to pay one half of the rent. The tenancy conferred on Mr. Villiers and Miss Bridger the right to occupy the whole flat as their dwelling. Clause 16 reserved to Mr. Antoniades the power at any time to go into occupation of the flat jointly with Mr. Villiers and Miss Bridger. The exercise of that power would at common law put an end to the exclusive occupation of the flat by Mr. Villiers and Miss Bridger, terminate the tenancy of Mr. Villiers and Miss Bridger, and convert Mr. Villiers and Miss Bridger into licensees. But the powers reserved to Mr. Antoniades by clause 16 cannot be lawfully exercised because they are inconsistent with the provisions of the Rent Acts.

When Mr. Antoniades entered into the agreements dated 9 February 1985 with Mr. Villiers and Miss Bridger and when Mr. Antoniades allowed Mr. Villiers and Miss

Alert

Bridger to occupy the flat, it is clear from the negotiations which had taken place, from the surrounding circumstances, and from subsequent events, that Mr. Antoniades did not intend in February 1985, immediately or contemporaneously, to share occupation or to authorise any other person to deprive Mr. Villiers and Miss Bridger of exclusive occupation of the flat. Clause 16, if genuine, was a reservation by a landlord of a power at some time during the currency of the tenancy to share occupation with the tenant. The exclusive occupation of the tenant coupled with the payment of rent created a tenancy which at common law could be terminated and converted into a licence as soon as the landlord exercised his power to share occupation. But under the Rent Acts, if a contractual tenancy is terminated, the Acts protect the occupiers from eviction.

...

In the second appeal now under consideration, there was, in my opinion, the grant of a joint tenancy for the following reasons. (1) The applicants for the flat applied to rent the flat jointly and to enjoy exclusive occupation. (2) The landlord allowed the applicants jointly to enjoy exclusive occupation and accepted rent. A tenancy was created. (3) The power reserved to the landlord to deprive the applicants of exclusive occupation was inconsistent with the provisions of the Rent Acts. (4) Moreover in all the circumstances the power which the landlord insisted upon to deprive the applicants of exclusive occupation was a pretence only intended to deprive the applicants of the protection of the Rent Acts.

LORD OLIVER OF AYLMERTON

There is an air of total unreality about these documents read as separate and individual licences in the light of the circumstance that the appellants were together seeking a flat as a quasi-matrimonial home. A separate licensee does not realistically assume responsibility for all repairs and all outgoings. Nor in the circumstances can any realistic significance be given to clauses 16 and 17 of the document. It cannot realistically have been contemplated that the respondent would either himself use or occupy any part of the flat or put some other person in to share accommodation specifically adapted for the occupation by a couple living together. These clauses cannot be considered as seriously intended to have any practical operation or to serve any purpose apart from the purely technical one of seeking to avoid the ordinary legal consequences attendant upon letting the appellants into possession at a monthly rent. The unreality is enhanced by the reservation of the right of eviction without court order, which cannot seriously have been thought to be effective, and by the accompanying agreement not to get married, which can only have been designed to prevent a situation arising in which it would be quite impossible to argue that the "licensees" were enjoying separate rights of occupation.

... Though subsequent conduct is irrelevant as an aid to construction, it is certainly admissible as evidence on the question of whether the documents were or were not genuine documents giving effect to the parties' true intentions. Broadly what is said by Mr. Colyer is that nobody acquainted with the circumstances in which the parties had come together and with the physical lay-out and size of the premises could seriously have imagined that the clauses in the licence which, on the face of them, contemplate

Alert

the respondent and an apparently limitless number of other persons moving in to share the whole of the available accommodation, including the bedroom, with what, to all intents and purposes, was a married couple committed to paying £174 a month in advance, were anything other than a smoke-screen; and the fact the respondent, who might be assumed to want to make the maximum profit out of the premises, never sought to introduce anyone else is at least some indication that that is exactly what it was. Adopting the definition of a sham formulated by Purchas L.J. in *Hadjiloucas v. Crean* [1988] 1 W.L.R. 1006, 1013, Mr. Colyer submits that the licences clearly incorporate clauses by which neither party intended to be bound and which were obviously a smoke-screen to cover the real intentions of both contracting parties. ...

If the real transaction was, as the judge found, one under which the appellants became joint tenants with exclusive possession, on the footing that the two agreements are to be construed together, then it would follow that they were together jointly and severally responsible for the whole rent. It would equally follow that they could effectively exclude the respondent and his nominees.

His Lordship agreed with the finding of the original judgment that there was in fact exclusive possession and a lease.

The next case is very similar in facts to *Antoniades v Villiers*.

Mikeover Limited v Brady [1989] 3 All ER 618

Panel: Slade LJ and Anthony Lincoln J

Facts: Mikeover Limited owned a small flat which was advertised as a flat for two people to share. Mr Brady and Miss Guile entered into two separate but identical 'licence agreements' and each paid a deposit. Once they were in occupation, as Miss Guile had a bank account and Mr Brady did not, it was convenient for her to write a cheque for the full 'licence fee' and Mr Brady reimbursed her. Miss Guile left in early 1986. Mikeover Limited returned her deposit, and although Brady offered to pay the full amount of the combined licence fee, this was refused and he continued only to pay his half. When Mikeover Limited served one month's notice to quit on Brady, he claimed he had a lease protected by the Rent Acts.

LORD JUSTICE SLADE

We look first at the circumstances which constituted the background to the agreements (the "matrix" of the transaction). At all material times, as the judge found, the flat comprised a front room which had a cooker and refrigerator in it, and a back room which had a sink in it. In addition, there were a bathroom and lavatory in the attic. This accommodation and these facilities were to be available to the people who were to occupy the top floor flat. While the defendant's evidence was that there were two divans in the front room when he first came to the flat, Mr. Ferster's evidence was that each of the two main rooms had a single divan in it. Though the judge made no finding on this latter point, and made no finding that Mr. Ferster was aware of any intention there may have been on the part of the defendant and Miss Guile to live together in a quasi-matrimonial relationship, the lay-out of the flat was such that it was clearly only suitable for occupation by persons who were personally acceptable to one another. In this context Mr. Andrew Nicol, on behalf of the defendant, naturally laid some stress on the position of the sink in one room and the cooker in the other. And, indeed, the plaintiffs clearly wished and contemplated that it would be occupied by two friends because he had advertised it as a flat for two people to share.

Furthermore, an important feature of the matrix to the defendant's agreement was the contemporaneous execution of an agreement with Miss Guile in identical form. Whether or not it is correct to classify these two agreements as "inter-dependent," as Mr. Nicol described them in argument, it is, in our judgment, quite plain that one must construe the provisions of the defendant's agreement having full regard to the fact that Miss Guile had just executed or was about to execute an agreement in identical form (and vice versa).

The judge then examined the words of the agreement against that background:

On the face of Clause 1 of the agreements in the present case, though the right to use the rooms given to each "Licensee" is merely a right to use them in common with others "who *have been* granted the like right" (*i.e.* Miss Guile in the case of the defendant's agreement and the defendant in the case of her agreement), their right is not qualified by any obligation to share such use with any others who may be granted such right *in the future. Inclusio unius exclusio alterius.*

... If they wished to reserve the right to impose on the defendant or Miss Guile a substitute co-occupant during the currency of the agreements, it was, in our judgment, incumbent on the plaintiffs to do so in much clearer terms.

It follows that, in our judgment, the defendant's agreement on its true construction conferred on him the *right* (by Clause 1) to exclusive occupation of the flat in common only with Miss Guile during its currency. Clause 2(4) is to be read simply as imposing on him a corresponding *obligation* not to impede the use of the rooms, etc., by Miss Guile during the currency of the term. Thus it is not necessary or relevant to consider the alternative argument of the defendant's counsel to the effect that, in so far as the agreement purported to reserve to the plaintiffs the right to impose on the defendant a substitute co-occupier in place of Miss Guile, it was a "sham."

The judge acknowledged that there were many similarities with *Antoniades v Villiers*, but that there were significant additional points in the agreements in *Antoniades v Villiers* which enabled him to distinguish it:

In *Antoniades v. Villiers*, therefore, unlike the present case, there was no doubt that the wording of the agreements purported to reserve to the landlord the right to share the accommodation with the couple, either himself or by introducing one or more persons to use the flat with them. If the provisions reserving this right had been seriously intended by the parties to have practical application, this would have eliminated any possibility of the couple being able to sustain a claim to be tenants, since their occupation would have lacked the feature of joint exclusive possession which would have been required for this purpose: ...

It is, however, well settled that four unities must be present for the creation of a joint tenancy, namely the unities of possession, interest, title and time: (see *Megarry & Wade The Law of Real Property* (5th ed. 1984) pp. 419 *et seq.*). In the present case there is no dispute that the two agreements of June 6, 1984 operated to confer on the defendant and Miss Guile unity of possession and title. Likewise, there was unity of time in that each of their interests arose simultaneously and was expressed to endure for six months. The dispute concerns unity of interest. The general principle, as stated in Megarry & Wade at p. 420 is that "the interest of each joint tenant is the same in extent, nature and duration, for in theory of law they hold but one estate." "Interest" in this context must, in our judgment, include the bundle of rights and obligations representing that interest. The difficulty, from the defendant's point of view, is that the two agreements instead of imposing a joint liability on him and Miss Guile to pay a deposit of £80 and monthly payments of £173.32, on their face, imposed on each of them individual and separate obligations to pay only a deposit of £40 and monthly payments of only £86.66. On the face of it, the absence of joint obligations of payment were inconsistent with the existence of a joint tenancy.

The judge did not accept any arguments that the agreements were interdependent and that any wording to the contrary was a sham. The parties genuinely made their own payments and Mikeover Limited refused to accept a double payment from Mr Brady when Miss Guile had left.

... Every case where the question of lease or licence arises must depend on its own facts. All we need say is that in our view and on the judge's findings, on the particular facts of the present case, no sham device or artificial transaction is involved. At first sight it appeared to us that the employment of two forms of agreement, rather than one, had an air of artificiality about it. However, once it is accepted that the monetary obligations of each licensee were genuinely intended to be entirely independent from those of the other, it seems to us that this course was understandable, even though not essential, and is not fairly open to criticism. We have already accepted that each agreement has to be construed in the light of the other. However, we do not accept Mr. Nicol's submission that they were "interdependent". While each had to be read with the other, each was perfectly capable of being operated on its own.

The court held that the arrangement on its true construction was a licence. Although there was exclusive possession, there was no unity of interest: the financial obligations were not intended or regarded as joint obligations; the separate licence agreements, unlike in *Antoniades v Villiers,* were not interdependent and did not create a lease.

9.2 Intention To Create Legal Relations

Facchini v Bryson [1952] 1 TLR 1386

Panel: Somervell and Denning LJJ

Facts: An employer allowed his assistant to occupy a house under an agreement which specifically stated that it did not create a tenancy. The assistant had exclusive possession in return for a weekly payment. He did not occupy as a service occupant.

The Court of Appeal held that there was a tenancy, and Denning LJ set out the circumstances in which an intention to create a tenancy can be negated. The stated intentions of the parties are irrelevant.

 Link

See Service Occupancy cases – *Norris v Checksfield; Royal Philanthropic v County* below

LORD JUSTICE DENNING

In all the cases where an occupier has been held to be a licensee there has been something in the circumstances, such as a family arrangement, an act of friendship or generosity, or such like, to negative any intention to create a tenancy. ... In the present case, however, there are no special circumstances.

Nunn v Dalrymple [1990] 59 P&CR 231

Panel: O'Connor and Stocker LJJ

Facts: Robert Chapman was the leaseholder of a large farm which included a dwelling on part of the estate, North Lodge. His son Guy arranged for Guy's parents-in-law, the Dalrymples, to give up their council house and live in North Lodge, while they renovated it. They paid regular payments in the nature of rent. Nine years later, Robert Chapman sold the lease of the farm to Nunn, who served notice to quit on the Dalrymples. They argued that the notice was ineffective as they had a lease and were tenants, with security of tenure. The judge at first instance held that this was a family arrangement, there was no intention to create legal relations and therefore there was no tenancy. The Court of Appeal held that the fact that a family relationship exists between the parties does not necessarily mean that there is simply a licence.

LORD JUSTICE STOCKER

The judge summarised the submission of counsel for the Dalrymples that five factors supported the argument that there was an intention to create legal relations: the importance of the agreement to the parties; acts, such as substantial renovation work, done by the Dalrymples in reliance on it; the precise terms of the arrangement, including payment of rent, which gave rise to an enforceable obligation; the lack of any elements of generosity; and other relevant conduct. He continued:

The proposition that it is possible, even where there is exclusive occupation coupled with rent, to negative the conclusion of a tenancy by reason of family relationship does not itself mean that because of the family relationship that conclusion is negatived. There is nothing that I am aware of or has been referred to me to indicate that because family relations exist between a landlord and a tenant the resulting relationship is necessarily not one of landlord and tenant. One relative can of course become the landlord of another, and the mere fact of that relationship is not itself conclusive.

For the reasons that I have endeavoured to give, I think that this was a case in which the learned judge was not entitled to tip the balance against what would otherwise be the natural assumption of the existence of a tenancy by reason of exclusive occupation coupled with rent because of the relationship which existed in this case.

He allowed the appeal and O'Connor LJ agreed:

LORD JUSTICE O'CONNOR

The exception of a family relationship is a sustainable one, and therefore one has to look and see in some detail as to what part the family relationship played in the occupancy by the Dalrymples of the lodge. Of course, there is no doubt whatever that they would never have gone there but for the fact that their daughter was married to the farmer, but that is not good enough. It is not sufficient, and it seems to me that the learned judge, apart from not appreciating the effect of the evidence, as has been pointed out, did not pay sufficient attention to the importance of the change of house which was being made by the Dalrymples. He recorded that they had been living in a council house for a great many years, but it does not seem to have occurred to him that he had to throw that into the scales in considering just what part the family relationship was playing. Here we have a case not of people who were homeless and being offered a home, but who were living in a council house. They had their grown-up son living with them. Everybody was in employment and there was no need for them in one sense to move house. When an important decision like that is to be taken one looks to see what happens in the beginning and, again, the learned judge records in his notes of evidence that Mrs. Dalrymple, when she had spoken to her daughter and son-in-law, said to Mr. Chapman, "We want to rent the lodge," and nowhere does the judge say that he did not believe her or that she was unreliable as a witness.

So that, from the word go, it seems to me that what was intended was a commercial relationship and, when you find that, then one would need some evidence—which, for my part, I do not find in the present case—to set it aside and say, nevertheless, the parties did not intend to create the relationship of landlord and tenant.

I would allow this appeal.

9.3 Service Occupancies

Norris v Checksfield [1991] 1 WLR 1241

Panel: Balcombe, Woolf and Staughton LJJ

Facts: Checksfield worked for Norris as a mechanic. He was allowed to live in a bungalow next to his workplace, on condition that he would apply for a licence to enable him to become a coach driver for Norris, who felt that it was advantageous for Checksfield to be near to the depot so that he could carry out any urgent driving work. Checksfield signed an agreement before he moved in. It included a clause acknowledging that he occupied the premises on licence which would terminate if the employment terminated. Checksfield had exclusive possession of the premises. When it came to light that he had been banned from driving, he was sacked and Norris claimed possession of the premises. The judge at first instance granted the order on the basis that Checksfield occupied the premises under a service licence which ended with the employment. Checksfield appealed to the Court of Appeal and his appeal was dismissed.

LORD JUSTICE WOOLF

In relation to the thorny issue as to when an employee is a licensee and not a tenant of premises belonging to his employer which he is allowed to occupy, Mr. Seaward, who appeared on behalf of the employee, was prepared to accept Mr. Zeidman's submission on behalf of the employer. Mr. Zeidman submitted that an employee can be a licensee, although his occupation of the premises is not *necessary* for the purposes of the employment, if he is genuinely *required* to occupy the premises for the *better performance* of his duties. In my judgment this submission accurately reflects the law. We have been referred to a number of authorities which set out different tests.

The judge referred to *Glasgow Corporation v Johnstone* [1965] AC 609 and continued:

Lord Reid was ... of the opinion that it would be sufficient if the employee's occupation was of "material assistance" to his employment. It need not be "*necessary*" for his employment. The same view was taken by Lord Evershed and Lord Hodson. Lord Guest stated the position which must exist for there to be a licence in the following terms, at p. 629:

"The residence must be ancillary to the duties which the servant has to perform (*Smith v. Seghill Overseers*) or, put in another way, the requirement must be with a view to the more efficient performance of the servant's duties (*Fox v. Dalby* (1874) L.R. 10 C.P. 285)."

As Mr. Seaward correctly submitted, it would not suffice if the occupation was a "fringe benefit" or merely an inducement to encourage the employee to work better. Unless the occupation fulfilled this test, the fact that the employee had exclusive possession and paid rent would almost inevitably establish a service tenancy: see generally *Street v. Mountford* [1985] A.C. 809 and *A.G. Securities v. Vaughan* [1990] 1 A.C. 417, 459, *per* Lord Templeman.

If in this case, as was contemplated, when the employee went into occupation he had obtained a P.S.V. licence and had changed the nature of his job so that he became a coach driver, the judge would undoubtedly have been entitled to regard the employee as a licensee. He would then have entered into occupation under a document which described the relationship in terms of a licence and the occupation would be beneficial to the employee's employment on the judge's findings. His occupation would enable him to assist his employer in cases of emergency or on short notice.

However Mr. Seaward submitted that the employment situation which has to be considered is that which existed in fact at the time the licence was entered into. Not the situation which might exist in the future. The situation which existed at the time the licence was entered into was that the employee's occupation of the premises was irrelevant to his employment as a semi-skilled mechanic. In that employment he was not required to assist with emergencies and he could perform the work equally as well from the lodgings at which he was previously living or indeed from any other address which was within travelling distance to his place of work. Occupation was beneficial to the employee but not beneficial to his employment.

There is no previous decision of the courts which directly conflicts with Mr. Seaward's approach. However, I have no hesitation in coming to the conclusion that notwithstanding this argument the judge was entitled to come to the conclusion that the employee was a licensee. Although the employee was unable to obtain the necessary P.S.V. licence to drive coaches, he was on the judge's finding only allowed into occupation on the basis that he would obtain the necessary qualifications and work as a coach driver. In my judgment it would not be sensible, unless compelled to do so, to restrict an employer's ability to grant a licence to situations where the employment which would be benefited by the employee taking up occupation commenced simultaneously with or prior to the occupation of the premises. There may be many circumstances where it would be desirable for the employee to take up occupation before the relevant work commenced. What is required is that there should be a sufficient factual nexus between the commencement of the occupation of the premises and the employment which would benefit from that occupation. If for some reason it becomes apparent that the employee is not going to be able to fulfil the requirements of that employment within a reasonable time, then the position may be different. However, if the situation is one where it is contemplated, as was the position here, that the employee would, within a reasonable time, be able to take up the relevant employment, that will suffice. The fact that the employee during the interval may be performing some other duties which are not affected by the occupation of the premises does not prevent a licence coming into existence.

 Alert

Royal Philanthropic Society v County [1986] 18 HLR 83

Panel: Fox LJ and Waterhouse J

Facts: Mr County worked as a school houseparent. The Royal Philanthropic Society owned the school land and a house about two miles away. At first, Mr County was given accommodation within the school building, but when he was due to be married, he asked for family accommodation and was offered the house. When his employment with the school ended, he refused to vacate the house and was served with notice to quit. The court at first instance, hearing the matter before the decision in *Street v Mountford*, granted the order for possession. The Court of Appeal, applying *Street v Mountford*, allowed Mr County's appeal.

LORD JUSTICE FOX

In the present case there clearly was a rent. Mr. County, by the letter of September 30, was told to agree a rent; that was done, and it was deducted from his salary. And, it is in our view, clear that the grant was for a term (which may have been yearly or monthly, it does not matter which for present purposes). Further, it is not in dispute that Mr. County had exclusive possession. It follows, in our view, that he was a tenant. He plainly was not a lodger; no services were provided, and the landlord did not retain unrestricted access to the premises or otherwise have exclusive possession of them.

"Henceforth" it is stated in *Street v. Mountford* at page 827 "the courts which deal with these problems will, save in exceptional circumstances, only be concerned to inquire whether, as a result of an agreement relating to residential accommodation, the occupier is a lodger or a tenant." We see no reason for regarding the circumstances of this case as exceptional. The parties certainly intended to enter into a legal relationship in the sense that Mr. County was obviously intended to have some rights in return for his payments; it is a question of determining what the rights were. Mr. County, it is true, accepted in his evidence that if he had thought about it he would have expected that he would have to leave the house if he left the job. But that does not affect the question of tenancy or no tenancy. The employment, it seems to us, is only material if there is a true service occupancy, i.e. where the servant requires the premises for the better performance of his duties as a servant, which is not suggested to be the case. But in such a case the importance of the service element is that the possession and occupation is regarded by law as that of the master. That is not the present case at all. The present case more clearly resembles Facchini v. Bryson [1952] T.L.R. 1386.

 Alert

9.4 Commercial Arrangements

Dresden Estates Limited v Collinson (1988) 55 P&CR 47

Panel: Lloyd and Glidewell LJJ

Facts: Dresden Estates Limited and Collinson entered into an agreement allowing Collinson to occupy a workshop and store owned by Dresden. The agreement was labelled 'Licence' and the parties referred to throughout as 'Licensor' and 'Licensee'; it was expressed to be personal to Collinson and not to constitute any tenancy. Dresden reserved the right to require Collinson to move into other premises owned by Dresden on giving notice. At first instance it was held that Collinson had a tenancy which attracted the protection of the Landlord and Tenant Act 1954. Dresden's appeal was allowed.

LORD JUSTICE GLIDEWELL

... Although one has to look at all the circumstances, certainly the most important factor is that of exclusive possession. Did the agreement give Mr. Collinson an exclusive right to the possession of the premises which he occupied? Secondly, *Street v. Mountford*, as I have said, was concerned with residential premises. Mr. Coveney conceded that there was no material difference, at least for present purposes, between the law applicable to residential premises and the law applicable to business premises. As a broad, general proposition that may be right, but I am not sure that his concession may not have gone too far in this respect, that the attributes of residential premises and business premises are often quite different. ...

The judge then quoted from *Halsbury's Laws of England* to summarise the law in this area: the key consideration is the intention of the parties, ascertained from all relevant provisions and circumstances. He then turned to the agreement itself:

... Clause 2 of the agreement ... contains a number of provisions which are wholly appropriate to and some of which are certainly indicative of this agreement creating a tenancy. In particular, as counsel pointed out, the agreement by which Mr. Collinson permitted Dresden Estates Ltd. to enter with workmen and contractors to carry out any work on the premises or adjoining premises is one which would not be necessary, if this agreement constituted a mere licence, not reserving exclusive possession to Mr. Collinson. But the provisions of that clause seem to me to be in conflict with many of the provisions of clause 4, and the real difficulty in this case, and the difficulty that confronted the learned judge, is to resolve that conflict. To my mind, the opening words of clause 4—"This licence is personal to the Licensees and the Licensees shall not transfer this interest in the same in any manner whatsoever"—cannot be disregarded and are of importance.

What is even more important is to decide what clause 4(b) and also clause 4(f) mean. Clause 4(b) is the clause that starts by saying in terms: "This Licence confers no exclusive right for the Licensees to use and occupy the premises." It then goes on to give Dresden Estates Ltd. The right:

'... from time to time on giving the Required Notice to require [Mr. Collinson] to transfer his occupation to other premises within [Dresden's] adjoining property.'

Clause 4(f) entitles Dresden Estates Ltd. by giving the required notice to increase the licence fee to such amount as the notice may specify. Both those clauses, if they have their apparent meaning, are inconsistent with there being a tenancy. You cannot have a tenancy granting exclusive possession of particular premises, subject to a provision that the landlord can require the tenant to move to somewhere else. The landlord can only do that by terminating the tenancy and creating a new one in other premises. So, too, with regard to the rent and licence fee. It is axiomatic that unless there is a rent review clause a landlord cannot for the duration of the tenancy alter the rent unilaterally. All he can do is to terminate the tenancy and then enter into a new agreement for the letting of the same premises at a new rent. Of course, the whole thing can be done by agreement. The tenancy agreement itself cannot give a landlord the power to alter a rent unilaterally.

Mr. Rank says that this agreement, properly read, does not. All that it really does is to say that the landlord (Dresden Estates Ltd.) can, if he wishes to require Mr. Collinson to move to some other part of the total premises or if he wishes to raise rent shall give notice to terminate. He claims that the phrase the "Required Notice" in the definition clause of the agreement means "notice to terminate."

Mr. Coveney argues, I think correctly, that that is not so. This agreement carefully defines the phrase "the Required Notice" simply in relation to the length of notice— "Not less than three months' notice in writing to be served before the first day of any month." It then uses the phrase in relation to three different concepts: giving notice to terminate the agreement; giving notice to move out of the particular premises, and move to other accommodation; and giving notice to increase the rent. Mr. Coveney says (and I conclude that he is right in this), that this agreement entitles Dresden Estates Ltd. to take either of those other steps unilaterally. The remedy which Mr. Collinson had, if he did not like it, being himself then to serve three months' notice to terminate, as the agreement provided that he could.

If, as I believe, that is right, then clauses 4(b) and 4(f) militate very strongly against this agreement creating a tenancy. I should say that there is some difficulty in Mr. Rank's way, because it is difficult to see how clause 4(b) could allow Dresden Estates Ltd. to require Mr. Collinson to move to some other part of the wider premises which was wholly unsuitable for him. Mr. Coveney says, and I think he is right, that clause 4(b) must be read as relating to alternative premises that were reasonably comparable and reasonably suitable. But that comment apart, those two clauses do seem to me to permit what Dresden Estates Ltd. wish to achieve to take place within the context of the agreement and without terminating. If that is so, Mr. Coveney argues that it means that there is strong evidence that Mr. Collinson did not have exclusive possession of these premises during the period of the agreement, because he could be required to go out of these premises while the agreement subsisted and go into other premises.

That argument, I think, is right; and though it does conflict with clause 2, I think, on balance the considerations set out in clause 4, added to the express terms of the agreement which refer to it time and again as "a licence," outweigh the considerations based upon clause 2. ...

... I want to make it clear that, for my part, my decision is based upon the particular facts of this agreement, it is not intended to be read and should not be read as laying down any guidelines for the future going outside agreements containing these unusual provisions. Subject to that, as I say, I would allow the appeal.

Esso Petroleum Co Ltd v Fumegrange Ltd and others [1994] 2 EGLR 90

Panel: Neill and Saville LJJ and Sir Christopher Slade

Facts: Esso and Fumegrange entered into three agreements allowing Fumegrange to occupy two service stations: a partnership licence agreement to use Esso's land and fixtures and fittings for three years; a shop franchise agreement and a car wash agreement. The licence agreement included a provision whereby Fumegrange permitted Esso to inspect Fumegrange's business documents and books; to inspect the premises to ensure compliance with Esso's 'operating standards'; to alter the layout and décor of the station; and to make further alterations and additions. When Fumegrange fell behind with their payments, Esso was granted possession of the premises. Fumegrange appealed to the Court of Appeal. The appeal was dismissed.

LORD JUSTICE NEILL

In the present case, we are concerned with commercial premises. There is no dispute as to the correct test to be applied. The question is whether on the proper construction of the licence agreements exclusive possession of the service stations was granted to Fumegrange.

It will be convenient to deal first with the submission that the provisions in these agreements, and in particular para 22 in the seventh schedule to the licence agreements, were sham provisions designed to disguise the true nature of the contract.

Like the judge, I am quite unable to accept the submission that any of these provisions was a sham or that any argument to that effect can properly be advanced. Counsel for Esso took us through the agreements relating to Brookside Service Station and explained the commercial justification for the several provisions. I found these explanations convincing and I was satisfied that the suggestion of pretence or sham was without foundation.

I come, therefore, to the question of construction.

I have found it to be of assistance to study the provisions of all three agreements relating to Brookside Service Station as well as the terms of the manual. These documents have to be read as a whole if one is to reach a clear conclusion as to the true relationship between the parties and the nature of Fumegrange's occupation.

Para 22 of the seventh schedule to the licence agreement provides a useful starting point. The paragraph referred to "Esso's right of possession and control of the service station" and required Fumegrange not to impede in any way the exercise of that right. It is to be noted that para 22(1) is in very similar terms to clause 19 of the first schedule to the agreement, which was considered by the Court of Appeal in *Shell-Mex & BP Ltd v Manchester Garages Ltd* [1971] 1 WLR 612. It is further to be noted that, though Lord Templeman in *Street v Mountford* (*supra*) rejected Lord Denning's conclusion in the *Shell-Mex* case that exclusive possession was no longer decisive, it does not appear that any doubt was thrown on the correctness of the *Shell-Mex* decision or on the fact that the Court of Appeal attached great importance to the fact that in clause 19 "the right of possession and control of the premises" was stated to be a right of the oil company.

In the present case, however, para 22 does not stand alone. I have set out most of the provisions to which I attach particular importance which demonstrate the degree of control exercised by Esso over the premises and the way in which it was conducted. Esso can make alterations on the premises; it can install a car wash (as was in fact done at Brookside); and it can change the layout of the shop.

The rights and powers of Esso have to be looked at together and cumulatively. I have come to the conclusion that these rights and powers are quite inconsistent with an exclusive right to possession of the service stations being vested in Fumegrange. The degree of physical control over the premises is very significant. In addition, account is to be taken of the degree of control over the conduct of the business at the service station.

Further Reading

Megarry and Wade, *The Law of Real Property*, (8th Edition), Sweet & Maxwell 2012, pp 750-762

Chappelle, D, *Land Law*, (8th Edition), Pearson Longman 2008, pp 250-262 and pp 264-268

Bright, S, Leases, Exclusive Possession and Estates, 2000 *LQR 7*

Baker, P V, Exclusive Possession Determined, 1989 *LQR 165*

Pawlowski, M, The Bruton Tenancy – Clarity or More Confusion? 2005 *Conv 262*

Waite, A J, Leases and Licences: The True Distinguishing Test, 1987 *MLR 226*

10

Covenants between a Landlord and Tenant

Topic List

1   Implied Covenants in Leases
2   The Running of Covenants
3   The Old Rules
4   The New Rules

Introduction

A lease will include many express obligations, or express covenants, on the part of landlords and tenants. In addition, statute imposes implied obligations on landlords and tenants. The Landlord and Tenant Act 1985 (LTA 1985) section 11 imposes an implied covenant on the landlord to keep in repair, amongst other things, the structure and exterior of certain leasehold property. This implied covenant applies to short leases of residential property, and it overrides any express covenant by the tenant to do repairs. Consequently, there has been much case law addressing what constitutes a part of the structure and exterior of a property.

10.1 Implied Covenants in Leases

Irvine v Moran [1991] 1 EGLR 261

Panel: Recorder Forbes QC

Statutes: Landlord and Tenant Act 1985 s 11; Housing Act 1961 s 32

Facts: A landlord brought an action against a tenant for failing to comply with express repair and decoration covenants in the lease. The court considered whether the repairs concerned the structure and exterior of the property, in which case they were covered by Housing Act 1961 (HA 1961) s 32 (the predecessor of LTA 1985 s 11), making the landlord responsible for the repairs, or whether the duty to repair lay with the tenant under the express covenant.

RECORDER FORBES QC

Preliminary issue no 1 has directed my attention to determining to what extent certain aspects of the demised premises can be said to be either part of the structure of the dwelling-house or part of the exterior of the dwelling-house, because it is in relation to the structure and exterior of the dwelling-house that the landlord's implied repairing covenants arise. Also, it is to certain specified installations in the dwelling-house that his obligations are addressed by the section. I am asked to consider in particular the garage, the gates, the driveway, the gardens, the grounds, the windows and so forth, the internal plaster and door furniture. I am asked to give a ruling in relation to those as a matter of law. The preliminary issue also asks me to rule upon the landlord's implied covenants without limiting my ruling to those items, although those are the ones of prime concern to the parties. It is of interest, and somewhat surprising, that there is very little authority on this matter at all and so I have to decide this preliminary issue without significant assistance from the authorities.

The first thing that I have to address my mind to is what is meant by section 32(1)(a) as keeping in repair the structure and exterior of the dwelling-house. I think that Mr Brock is correct in his submission, and I so hold, that the word "structure" in subsection (1)(a) should not be construed in isolation but should be construed as part and parcel of the overall expression "the structure of the dwelling-house" as distinct from "the exterior of the dwelling-house". .... The structure of the dwelling-house is something less than the overall dwelling-house itself and the exterior of the dwelling-house is also something less than the overall dwelling-house itself. Of course, the difficulty that is posed is deciding to what more limited aspects of the overall dwelling-house the word "structure" is addressed. I have come to the view that the structure of the dwelling-house consists of those elements of the overall dwelling-house which give it its essential appearance, stability and shape. The expression does not extend to the many and various ways in which the dwelling-house will be fitted out, equipped, decorated and generally made to be habitable...

[I]n order to be part of the structure of the dwelling-house a particular element must be a material or significant element in the overall construction. To some extent, in every case there will be a degree of fact to be gone into to decide whether something is or is not part of the structure of the dwelling-house. It is not easy to think of an overall explanation of the meaning of those words which will be applicable in every case and I deliberately decline to attempt such a definition...

I see no reason at this stage not to follow the natural approach and say that a separate garage and separate gates do not ordinarily, in my judgment, form part of the dwelling-house...

I therefore turn to internal wall plaster and door furniture. As I have said, section 32(1)(a) and the words "structure of the dwelling-house" mean something less than the dwelling-house overall and are limited to the essential material elements that go to make up the structure of the dwelling-house. It seems to me that internal wall plaster is more in the nature of a decorative finish and is not part of the essential material elements which go to make up the structure of the dwelling-house. I therefore hold that internal wall plaster and, for the same reason, the door furniture do not form part of the structure of the dwelling-house, bearing in mind I have held that those words mean something less than the overall construction.

Windows pose a slightly different problem. I have some hesitation about this, but bearing in mind that one is talking about a dwelling-house, and rejecting as I do the suggestion that one should use "load-bearing" as the only touchstone to determining what is the structure of the dwelling-house in its essential material elements, I have come to the conclusion that windows do form part of the structure of the dwelling-house. My conclusion might be different if one were talking about windows in, let us say, an agricultural building. The essential material elements may change, depending on the nature and use of the building in question. In the case of a dwelling-house, it seems to me that an essential and material element in a dwelling-house, using ordinary common sense and an application of the words "structure of the dwelling-house" without limiting them to a concept such as "load-bearing", must include the external windows and doors. Therefore, I hold that windows themselves, the window frames and the sashes do form part of the structure. It follows that, since these are sash windows, it would be invidious to separate the cords from the sashes and the essential furniture from the frames. So, in my judgment, the windows including the sashes, the cords, the frames and the furniture are part of the structure of the dwelling-house...

Alert

The issue that has to be determined is to what extent the tenant's covenants to paint and decorate the exterior of the dwelling-house and other relevant installations, such as radiators, remain wholly or partially in effect on a true construction of section 32(1). This preliminary issue is directed at elements in the claim where the plaintiff has conceded that the element is within section 32(1) and is thus subject to the landlord's covenants to repair. The plaintiff submits that notwithstanding the landlord's covenants to repair and notwithstanding the "non-effect" of the tenant's covenants to put in repair, deliver up in repair, to paint, to point or render, and so forth, there is still a liability on the part of the tenant to paint and decorate elements of the building which are the subject-matter of the landlord's repairing covenants, because of clauses 2(iv) and (v) of the lease. The submission is that the painting and decoration of the exterior of the dwelling-house and other relevant installations is purely decorative and does not involve any "keeping in repair". In my judgment, so far as the exterior of the dwelling-house is concerned, the tenant's obligation to paint and decorate has been eliminated by section 32(1) of the Act. It seems to me that painting and decorating the exterior of the dwelling-house must inevitably and invariably involve a degree of protection against the elements and against the processes of rot and the like. Inevitably it is part and parcel of the process of keeping the exterior of the dwelling-house in repair. There are aesthetic benefits and pleasure to be gained from a high state of decorative order, but in my judgment, once I am satisfied that the obligation that would otherwise be imposed on the tenant by the express terms of the tenancy involves a degree of keeping in repair the exterior of the dwelling-house, then the tenant's obligation is subsumed into the landlord's implied obligations under the Act.

Note that the part of the judgment relating to internal plaster has been held to be incorrect by the case of *Grand v Gill* [2011] EWCA Civ 554 in which the Court of Appeal held that internal plaster does form part of the structure for the purposes of LTA 1985 s 11.

Recorder Forbes QC held that an external garage is not a part of the structure and exterior, as it was not part of the essential appearance, stability and shape of the dwelling. Windows, by contrast, are on balance a part of the structure and exterior. Where there is an express covenant by the tenant to decorate a part of the exterior, it will be overridden by the landlord's implied obligation to repair the structure and exterior of a property under statute. In this case, the landlord was therefore liable for the repair to the window.

The extent of the implied covenant of the landlord to repair the structure and exterior of a property under statute was further considered in *Hopwood v Cannock Chase District Council* [1975] 1 All ER 796.

Hopwood v Cannock Chase District Council **[1975] 1 All ER 796**

Panel: Cairns, Stephenson LJJ and Brightman J

Statute: Housing Act 1961 s 32

Facts: A tenant brought an action for damages against the landlord for personal injury. The tenant occupied a property with a rear garden under a lease; the lease was subject to the HA 1961 s 32. The rear garden incorporated paved and concrete areas. The garden led onto an alley; the alley did not form the main access to the property. The paved area was approximately 4 cm lower than the concrete area. The tenant tripped on the uneven surface and sustained an injury.

LORD JUSTICE CAIRNS

[Cairns LJ discussed the reasoning of deputy Judge Lewis in the lower court.]

In reaching his decision [that the paved and concrete areas did not form a part of the structure and exterior of the property], he founded himself on the only reported case as far as we know that has been decided under this provision; it is the decision of the Court of Appeal in *Brown v Liverpool Corp* [1969] 3 All ER 1345. That was a case in which the house had a path running to steps which went up to the road, the house being at a lower level than the road, and the plaintiff met with an accident on those steps. The question was whether the landlords had a duty under s 32 to keep those steps in repair, and the question that had to be considered in that case, as in this one, was: did they form part of the structure or exterior of the building?

Danckwerts LJ, giving the first judgment, first easily reached the conclusion that they did not form part of the structure and then went on in this way (at 1346):

'On the other hand it seems to me equally clear that the 7 feet of flagstones and the steps up do form part of the exterior of the dwelling-house. They are attached in that manner to the house for the purpose of access to this dwelling-house, and they are part of the dwelling-house which is necessary for the purpose of anybody who wishes to live in the dwelling-house enjoying that privilege. If they have not means of access of some sort they could not get there, and these are simply the means of access. The steps are an outside structure, and therefore, it seems to me that they are plainly part of the building, and, therefore, the covenant implied by s. 32 of the Act of 1961 fits and applies to the obligations of the landlords in this case'.

Salmon LJ agreed; he said (at 1346):

'I do not think that this case is by any means free from difficulty, or, indeed, from doubt. I do not wish to lay down any general principle of law or any general proposition as to the construction of the Housing Act 1961, or as to the meaning of the words "building" or "dwelling-house". I base my judgment on the particular facts of this case.'

Then, after referring to the main facts and quoting s 32(5) of the 1961 Act he went on (at 1346):

'In the particular circumstances of this case I think it proper to regard the house, with the short concrete path and steps leading to it, as being one unit. Together they formed one building and were, therefore, "the dwelling-house". It is conceded by the defendant corporation that the steps and the path were demised with the house. It seems to me that the path and steps must be an integral part of the building, otherwise it would be impossible for the building to be used as a dwelling-house for it would have no access. On that narrow ground I think that the judgment of the learned county court judge can be supported. I also think that an alternative way of putting the matter would be to say that, on the facts here, that short concrete path and those four steps were part of the exterior of the dwelling-house. Whichever way it is put—whether it is put in that way or whether one says that, looking at the facts, the path, steps and house are all part of the building which was let as a private dwelling-house—it would follow that the plaintiff is entitled to succeed.'

Sachs LJ, after quoting s 32(5), said (at 1347):

'For my part I have no doubt but that, as counsel for the plaintiff has correctly conceded, the definition given to 'the dwelling-house' was intended to and does exclude from the ambit of the landlord's liability those parts of the demise that are not part of the building itself. In particular, to my mind, there would normally be excluded from the ambit of those liabilities a garden or a pond, and likewise the fences round or a gate leading to such a garden or pond. Similarly, there would normally be excluded the steps leading into the garden from a road ... The question, accordingly, is whether, in this particular case, the 7 feet approach with the steps at the end of it really was part of the exterior of the terrace building or whether that 7 feet pathway and the steps down into it were simply part of a means of traversing a garden. That seems to me— as, indeed counsel for the plaintiff rightly contended—to be a question of degree, and a very close run thing at that.'

Then, after quoting a clause of the conditions of tenancy, he said (at 1347, 1348):

'In the end, however, I have come to the conclusion that the learned county court judge adopted the right approach and did treat this question as one of degree and fact. He referred specifically to the point that this concrete path was "only 7 feet long", and it seems to me that on the evidence he was entitled to come to the conclusion which he reached on this question of fact, i.e., that in all the circumstances the steps formed part of the building.'

One matter on which all three members of the court founded their judgments was that in that case the path and steps formed an essential part of the means of access to the house, in that it was the only way in. In this case that certainly was not so; the ordinary means of access to the house was from the front of the house and to my mind it is very doubtful whether this yard could be regarded as a means of access to the house at all. It is true that there was a way out from one side of the yard, apparently into an alley or lance, this house being at the end of the terrace of houses; and there was also a way through from the yard into the corresponding yard of the adjoining house. But that is very far from saying, as could be said in *Brown's* case, that it was necessary to the house as the means of access to it.

Alert

Accordingly the court held that the paved and concrete areas did not form a part of the exterior of the property, as it was not an essential means of access to the house. Consequently, the landlord was not under an implied obligation to repair.

The tenant is also subject to certain implied covenants. There is, for example, an implied obligation on the tenant to use the property in a tenant-like manner. *Warren v Keen* [1954] 1 QB 15 considered the nature and extent of this implied obligation.

Warren v Keen [1954] 1 QB 15

Panel: Somervell, Denning and Romer LJJ

Facts: A landlord let a property on a weekly tenancy. The property suffered some disrepair, including discolouration below windows, cracked rendering and a leak in the boiler. The issue arose as to whether the tenant has used the property in a tenant-like manner.

LORD JUSTICE DENNING

Apart from express contract, a tenant owes no duty to the landlord to keep the premises in repair. The only duty of the tenant is to use the premises in a husbandlike, or what is the same thing, a tenantlike manner. That is how it was put by Sir Vicary Gibbs C.J. in *Horsefall v. Mather* Holt NP 7 and by Scrutton L.J. and Atkin L.J. in *Marsden v. Edward Heyes Ld* [1927] 2 KB 7, 8. But what does "to use the premises in a tenantlike manner" mean? It can, I think, best be shown by some illustrations. The tenant must take proper care of the place. He must, if he is going away for the winter, turn off the water and empty the boiler. He must clean the chimneys, when necessary, and also the windows. He must mend the electric light when it fuses. He must unstop the sink when it is blocked by his waste. In short, he must do the little jobs about the place which a reasonable tenant would do. In addition, he must, of course, not damage the house, wilfully or negligently; and he must see that his family and guests do not damage it: and if they do, he must repair it. But apart from such things, if the house falls into disrepair through fair wear and tear or lapse of time, or for any reason not caused by him, then the tenant is not liable to repair it.

The landlord sought to put upon the tenant a higher obligation. She said that the duty of the tenant was to keep the premises wind and water tight and to make fair and tenantable repairs thereto. ... I do not think that is a correct statement of the obligation. ...

I think that the expression "wind and water tight" is of doubtful value and should be avoided. It is better to keep to the simple obligation "to use the premises in a tenantlike manner."

Take the second branch, "to make fair and tenantable repairs." Lord Kenyon used the expression in *Ferguson v Anon* (1798) 2 Esp. 590. which is only reported by Espinasse, who was notoriously defective. It is said that he only heard half of what went on and reported the other half. If you read the whole sentence used by Lord Kenyon, however, it is clear that he was only referring to cases where a tenant does damage himself, such as breaking the windows or the doors. Then, of course, he must repair them. The sentence, used by Lord Kenyon, was explained by Bankes LJ in *Marsden v Heyes* [1927] 2 KB 1 by saying that if a tenant commits waste - that is, if he commits voluntary waste by doing damage himself - he must do such repairs to the premises as will enable them to exclude wind and water.

Thus where a property falls into disrepair by reasonable wear and tear or by the passage of time, a tenant will not be under an implied obligation to make any repairs.

 Alert

A tenant is under an obligation to use the property in a tenant-like manner, and where a failure to do so leads to disrepair, a tenant will be liable to make the repairs.

Where a lease contains an express covenant for the tenant to keep the property in repair, he cannot be held liable for such extensive work that it amounts to renewal. *Brew Bros Ltd v Snax (Ross) Ltd* [1970] 1 QB 612 looked at the leading authorities on this issue and considered the extent of the obligation on a tenant where there is an express covenant for the tenant to keep the property in repair.

Brew Bros Ltd v Snax (Ross) Ltd [1970] 1 QB 612

Panel: Harman, Sachs and Phillimore LJJ

Facts: The freeholder granted the tenants a 14-year lease; the lease included an express covenant by the tenants to repair the premises. Owing to seepage of water from a long-defective drain, a wall of the property tilted. This caused nuisance to the neighbour, who eventually brought an action for damages against both the landlord and the tenant. The cost of the repairs was estimated at £8000 and the value of the property after the work had been completed was estimated between £7500 and £9000. The landlord denied any liability under the terms of the lease.

LORD JUSTICE HARMAN

Proudfoot v Hart (1890) 25 Q.B.D. 42 clearly shows that a covenant to repair and keep in repair covers the obligation to put in repair: ... Lord Esher MR said, at p 50:

"What is the true construction of a tenant's contract to keep and deliver up premises in 'tenantable repair'? Now, it is not an express term of that contract that the premises should be put into tenantable repair, and it may therefore be argued that, where it is conceded, as it is in this case, that the premises were out of tenantable repair when the tenancy began, the tenant is not bound to put them into tenantable repair, but is only bound to keep them in the same repair as they were in when he became the tenant of them. But it has been decided - and, I think, rightly decided - that, where the premises are not in repair when the tenant takes them, he must put them into repair in order to discharge his obligation under a contract to keep and deliver them up in repair. If the premises are out of repair at any time during the tenancy the landlord is entitled to say to the tenant, 'you have now broken your contract to keep them in repair'; and if they were out of repair at the end of the tenancy he is entitled to say, 'you have broken your contract to deliver them up in repair.' I am of opinion that under a contract to keep the premises in tenantable repair and leave them in tenantable repair, the obligation of the tenant, if the premises are not in tenantable repair when the tenancy begins, is to put them into, keep them in, and deliver them up in tenantable repair"...

The leading case is *Lurcott v Wakely & Wheeler* [1911] 1 KB 905. There the front external wall of a house had to be taken down in compliance with a demolition order and was so taken down and rebuilt by the plaintiff landlord, who sued the defendant lessees under a repairing covenant and succeeded. The dangerous condition of the wall was due to old age... Finally, in *Lurcott v Wakely & Wheeler*, Cozens-Hardy MR said, at p 914:

"… we are driven to ask in this particular case, and in every case of this kind, Is what has happened of such a nature that it can fairly be said that the character of the subject-matter of the demise, or part of the demise, in question has been changed? Is it something which goes to the whole, or substantially the whole, or is it simply an injury to a portion, a subsidiary portion, to use Buckley L.J.'s phrase, of the demised property? In this case the view taken by the official referee and the Divisional Court is the view which commends itself to me, that this portion of the wall, 24 feet in front, is merely a subsidiary portion of the demised premises, the restoration of this wall leaving the rest of the building, which goes back more than 100 feet, untouched. The restoration of this wall will not change the character or nature of the building, and I am unable to say that the question differs in any way from that which we should have had to consider if by reason of the elements and lapse of time, say, some rafters in the roof had become rotten, and a corner of the roof gave way so that the water came in. It seems to me that we should be narrowing in a most dangerous way the limit and extent of these covenants if we did not hold that the defendants were liable under covenants framed as these are to make good the cost of repairing this wall in the only sense in which it can be repaired, namely, by rebuilding it according to the requirements of the county council."… Finally, Buckley L.J. said, at p 924:

"Repair is restoration by renewal or replacement of subsidiary parts of a whole. Renewal, as distinguished from repair, is reconstruction of the entirety, meaning by the entirety not necessarily the whole but substantially the whole subject-matter under discussion. I agree that if repair of the whole subject-matter has become impossible a covenant to repair does not carry an obligation to renew or replace. … But if that which I have said is accurate, it follows that the question of repair is in every case one of degree, and the test is whether the act to be done is one which in substance is the renewal or replacement of defective parts, or the renewal or replacement of substantially the whole."

 Alert

In *Lister v Lane & Nesham* [1893] 2 Q.B. 212 the house fell down and the landlords sought to recover from the tenants the costs of rebuilding it. The headnote in that case reads as follows:

"The plaintiffs granted to the defendants a lease of a house in Lambeth, containing a covenant by the lessees that they would 'when and where and as often as occasion shall require, well, sufficiently, and substantially, repair, uphold, sustain, maintain, amend and keep' the demised premises, and the same 'so well and substantially repaired, upheld, sustained, maintained, amended and kept,' at the end of the term yield up to the lessors. Before the end of the term one of the walls of the house was bulging out, and after the end of the term the house was condemned by the district surveyor as a dangerous structure and was pulled down. The plaintiffs sought to recover from the defendants the cost of rebuilding the house. The evidence showed that the foundation of the house was a timber platform, which rested on a boggy or muddy soil. The bulging of the wall was caused by the rotting of the timber. The house was at least 100 years old, and possibly much older. The solid gravel was 17 feet below the surface of the mud. There was evidence that the wall might have been repaired during the term by means of underpinning. Held, that the defect having been caused by the natural operation of time and the elements upon a house the original construction of which was faulty, the defendants were not under their covenant liable to make it good."

You are not to hand back to your landlord a different thing from that which he demised to you: for instance, in *Pembery v. Lamdin* [1940] 2 All E.R. 434, the property had no damp-course and the tenant was held not liable to put one in...

LORD JUSTICE PHILLIMORE

I do not think that it is right to look at each component part of the claim and to say in regard to each item whether it is properly to be called repair or otherwise. The essence of the tenants' case here is that these landlords less than 18 months after letting the premises were requiring work to remedy defects which existed at the date of the lease at a cost which would be about equal to that of rebuilding the premises as new. After all, the judge had found that the estimate of just under £8,000 to make the premises safe was acceptable but had added that he was satisfied that the flank wall would have to be pulled down and rebuilt on new foundations. This must surely have added largely to the £8,000 figure.

Megaw J had of course specifically held that with the exception of the foundation to the flank wall the underpinning of the other two main walls of the premises would be necessary to render the building safe in accordance with the Pynford report and the notice of dilapidations served by the landlords.

I agree with the judge, who concluded after reviewing the authorities and particularly the observations of Lord Esher M.R. in *Lister v Lane & Nesham* [1893] 2 Q.B. 212, 216 and those of Buckley L.J. in *Lurcott v Wakely & Wheeler* [1911] 1 K.B. 905, 924, that the vital question in each case is whether the total work to be done can properly be described as repair since it involves no more than renewal or replacement of defective parts, or whether it is in effect renewal or replacement of substantially the whole. It is, as Megaw J held, a question of degree in each case. It is well established that a tenant is not liable to produce a different thing from that which he took when he entered into the lease or to remedy the results of bad design. On what basis, then, where a house is doomed at the time he leases it, is he to be required substantially to rebuild it so as to hand back to his landlord something which is in fact quite different from what he took? Does it matter whether it is falling down because of old age, bad design, or past neglect, and, if so, why?

In my judgment, the work which these tenants were required to perform and to pay for went far beyond what any reasonable person would have contemplated under the word "repair." This was well on the renewal side of the line. If I had to decide this case on the basis that the tenants had only to perform the work which has been actually performed by the landlords I would have taken the same view - this went beyond repair!

Suppose some busybody had said to these parties when signing the contract: "You realise, of course, that it might be necessary within 18 months to spend between £8,000 and £9,000 to render this building safe. If that happened, would you both

> regard that as repair?" I suspect that even a landlord (unless utterly unreasonable) would have replied: "Of course not."

In *Brew Brothers v Snax Ltd* the tenant was not held liable for the repairs, in spite of the comprehensive express repair covenant, as the scale of the work far exceeded mere repair, and in fact constituted renewal of the property.

There are, of course, many leasehold covenants that do not concern repair. A common covenant concerns assignment or subletting. It is common for a tenant to covenant not to assign or sublet without the landlord's consent; this is known as a 'qualified covenant'. The Landlord and Tenant Act 1927 s 19(1) states that in respect of a qualified covenant a landlord may not unreasonably withhold consent. In *International Drilling Fluids Ltd v Louisville Investments (Uxbridge) Ltd* [1986] Ch 513, the court considered in what circumstances it would be reasonable for a landlord to refuse consent.

International Drilling Fluids Ltd v Louisville Investments (Uxbridge) Ltd [1986] Ch 513

Panel: Fox, Mustill and Balcombe LJJ

Facts: A 30-year lease was granted containing a covenant by the tenant not to assign the lease without the landlord's consent. After 13 years, the current tenant sought to assign the lease, but the landlord refused consent on the grounds that the proposed use of the property (as serviced offices) would have a negative effect on the value of the freehold reversion. At first instance, the landlord was held to have unreasonably refused consent to the assignment; the landlord appealed.

LORD JUSTICE BALCOMBE

From the authorities I deduce the following propositions of law.

1. The purpose of a covenant against assignment without the consent of the landlord, such consent not to be unreasonably withheld, is to protect the lessor from having his premises used or occupied in an undesirable way, or by an undesirable tenant or assignee ...

2. As a corollary to the first proposition, a landlord is not entitled to refuse his consent to an assignment on grounds which have nothing whatever to do with the relationship of landlord and tenant in regard to the subject matter of the lease: see *Houlder Brothers & Co. Ltd. v. Gibbs*, a decision which (despite some criticism) is binding on this court: *Bickel v. Duke of Westminster* [1977] Q.B. 517. A recent example of a case where the landlord's consent was unreasonably withheld because the refusal was designed to achieve a collateral purpose unconnected with the terms of the lease is *Bromley Park Garden Estates Ltd. v. Moss* [1982] 1 W.L.R. 1019.

3. The onus of proving that consent has been unreasonably withheld is on the tenant: see *Shanly v. Ward* (1913) 29 T.L.R. 714 and *Pimms Ltd. v. Tallow Chandlers Company* [1964] 2 Q.B. 547, 564. [Note that the burden of proof

has now moved to the landlord to prove that his refusal of consent was reasonable under the Landlord and Tenant Act 1988.]

4. It is not necessary for the landlord to prove that the conclusions which led him to refuse consent were justified, if they were conclusions which might be reached by a reasonable man in the circumstances: *Pimms Ltd. v. Tallow Chandlers Company* [1964] 2 Q.B. 547, 564.

5. It may be reasonable for the landlord to refuse his consent to an assignment on the ground of the purpose for which the proposed assignee intends to use the premises, even though that purpose is not forbidden by the lease: see *Bates v. Donaldson* [1896] 2 Q.B. 241, 244.

6. There is a divergence of authority on the question, in considering whether the landlord's refusal of consent is reasonable, whether it is permissible to have regard to the consequences to the tenant if consent to the proposed assignment is withheld. ...

[I]n my judgment, the judge reached the right decision. Although he did not expressly mention the disproportionate harm to the tenants if the landlords were entitled to refuse consent to the assignment, compared with the minimum disadvantage which he clearly considered the landlords would suffer by a diminution in the paper value of the reversion - "paper value" because he was satisfied there was no prospect of the landlords wishing to realise the reversion - he clearly recognised the curious results to which the landlords' arguments, based solely upon a consideration of their own interests, could lead. As he said in his judgment:

"It seems to me that, if Mr Lewison is right, the more substantial the lessee, the more easily the landlord would be able to justify a refusal of consent to an assignment, since unless the proposed assignee's covenant was as strong as the assignor's, a reasonable man might form the view that the market would consider the reversion less attractive if the lease were vested in the proposed assignee than if it were vested in the assignor. To take the matter to extremes, if a lease was made in favour of a government department it would be unassignable except to another government department; for... the market would prefer to have the government as the lessee, whether the premises were being used as serviced offices or not, even if they were standing empty, rather than a company, however strong its covenant."

In my judgment, the gross unfairness to the tenants of the example postulated by the judge strengthens the arguments in favour, in an appropriate case of which the instant case is one, of it being unreasonable for the landlord not to consider the detriment to the tenant if consent is refused, where the detriment is extreme and disproportionate to the benefit to the landlord.

I am also satisfied that the judge could, and should, have had regard to the fact that the proposed serviced office user was within the only form of user permitted by the lease. I have already stated the proposition of law, derived from the cases, that it may be reasonable for the landlord to refuse his consent to an assignment on the grounds of the proposed user, even though that proposed user is permitted by the lease. But it does not follow from that that, in all circumstances, it will be reasonable for the landlord to object to a proposed user which is not forbidden by the lease...

There is all the difference in the world between the case where the user clause prohibits only certain types of use, so that the tenant is free to use the property in any other way, and the case where (as here) only one specific type of use is permitted. In my judgment, in that type of case it is not reasonable for the landlord to refuse consent to an assignment on the grounds of the proposed user (being within the only specific type of use), where the result will be that the property is left vacant and where (as here) the landlord is fully secured for payment of the rent.

The landlord's refusal was deemed unreasonable as the detriment to the tenant was disproportionate to the benefit to the landlord. In addition, the reason for refusal affected neither the landlord in his capacity as landlord, nor the tenant in his capacity as tenant.

10.2 The Running of Covenants

When the leasehold or the freehold reversion is assigned, it is necessary to consider who will be liable under the tenant and landlord covenants. If the landlord assigns the freehold reversion, will the original landlord or his assignee be liable for any breach of a landlord covenant? Likewise, if the tenant assigns his lease, will the original tenant or his assignee be liable for any breach of a tenant covenant? The liability of the parties is affected by when the lease was granted; liability of the parties under leases granted prior to 1996 are governed by 'the old rules' and liability of the parties under leases granted in or after 1996 are governed by 'the new rules'.

10.3 The Old Rules

Under the old rules, the original landlord and the original tenant remain liable for the duration of the lease under the doctrine of privity of contract and the operation of the Law of Property Act 1925 (LPA 1925) s 79. This means that the original parties to a lease can be sued even when they have assigned their interest. *Stuart and Others v Joy and Another* [1904] 1 KB 362 considered the continuing liability of a landlord after he had assigned the reversion.

Stuart and Others v Joy and Another [1904] 1 KB 362

Panel: Earl of Halsbury LC, Lord Alverstone CJ and Cozens-Hardy LJ

Facts: The lease contained a landlord covenant to repair parts of the property, including millstones. The freehold reversion was assigned. The tenant sought to have the millstones put in repair. The court considered whether the original landlord remained liable under landlord covenants after the assignment of the reversion.

LORD JUSTICE COZENS-HARDY

It was strenuously argued... that no liability can now be enforced against the lessors, inasmuch as they have assigned the reversion, the effect of which was to shift the obligation from the lessors to the assignees... In every case the express covenants entered into by the lessor with the lessee, or by the lessee with the lessor, remain unaffected. The consequence of holding that a landlord can escape from all liability upon his express covenants in the lease by assigning to a pauper would be alarming. In my opinion, the position of the lessor with respect to covenants running with the reversion is now precisely similar to the position of the lessee with respect to covenants running with the lease. In neither case is liability extinguished by assignment. No authority contrary to this view has been called to our attention, but the very point was raised before the Privy Council in *Eccles v Mills* [1898] AC 360. That case was ultimately decided on the ground that the covenant in question by the testator, who was the lessor, did not run with the reversion; but the arguments and the judgment dealt with the case also on the alternative view, which had been adopted in the Court below, that the covenant did run with the reversion; and Lord Macnaghten says (at p 371): "Whatever liability the statute threw on the specific devisees as assignees of the reversion, that they were bound to bear as between themselves and the lessee. But the testator's estate was also liable." This dictum, though not necessary for the decision of the case, strongly supports the view which, apart from authority, I have expressed. For these reasons I think that the lessees and the assignees of the lease, as co-plaintiffs, can maintain the present action against the lessors for breach of the covenant to obey the award.

Under the old rules, the original landlord remains liable after assignment of the freehold reversion. Similarly, the original tenant remains liable after the assignment of the leasehold under *Thursby v Plant* (1690) 1 Saund 230. Both the original parties retain the burden of covenants for the duration of the lease. However, as the original party will no longer have control of the premises and cannot therefore comply with an injunction, for example, the remedy will be confined to an award of damages.

Under the LPA 1925 s 142, the burden of a landlord covenant passes to the successor upon assignment of the freehold reversion, in so far as the covenant has reference to the subject matter of the lease. Under s 141, the benefit of a landlord covenant similarly passes. In *Re King, Robinson v Gray* [1963] Ch 459, the court considered whether the original landlord still retained the benefit of covenant for the period prior to assignment, and whether the original landlord therefore could still bring an action for a breach by the tenant prior to the assignment of the reversion.

Re King, Robinson v Gray [1963] Ch 459

Panel: Lord Denning MR, Upjohn and Diplock LJJ

Statute: LPA 1925 s 141

Facts: The case concerned the lease of a factory premises in Bethnal Green. The tenant entered into covenants to keep the property in repair, to insure the property against damage by fire and, in the event of a fire, to use the money claimed on the insurance to repair the property. The property was largely destroyed by a fire, a claim was made on the insurance but the property could not be rebuilt owing to wartime restrictions. The property was subsequently subject to a compulsory purchase order and the freehold and the leasehold were assigned. The issue arose whether the original landlord (and his successor in title) retained the benefit of the repair and insurance covenants prior to the assignment of the freehold reversion.

LORD JUSTICE DIPLOCK

We are here concerned with covenants in a lease (1) to keep premises in repair during the term, and (2) to reinstate after damage by fire. These covenants overlap. I need not rehearse the relevant facts. The main and short question in the case is: Can the assignor of the reversion to the lease sue the tenant for breaches of these covenants committed before the date of the assignment where the assignment itself contains no express provision about the matter? The answer, I emphasise at the outset, depends upon the true construction of section 141 of the Law of Property Act, 1925...

Where the reversion to a lease is assigned after breach by the tenant of a repairing covenant, there are mathematically only four possible answers to the question: Who is entitled to sue the tenant for damages for the breach? namely, (1) the assignor of the reversion, (2) the assignee of the reversion, (3) both, and (4) neither. The third and fourth possibilities would not be easy to reconcile with a just and rational system of law...

Diplock LJ discussed the lack of authority on the point in issue and continued:

I, therefore, approach the question unassisted, and I hope unconfused, by authority, as a simple question of the meaning of section 141 of the Law of Property Act, 1925, which reads as follows: "(1) Rent reserved by a lease, and the benefit of every covenant or provision therein contained, having reference to the subject-matter thereof, and on the lessee's part to be observed or performed, and every condition of re-entry and other condition therein contained, shall be annexed and incident to and shall go with the reversionary estate in the land, or in any part thereof, immediately expectant on the term granted by the lease, notwithstanding severance of that reversionary estate, and without prejudice to any liability affecting a covenantor or his estate. (2) Any such rent, covenant or provision shall be capable of being recovered, received, enforced, and taken advantage of, by the person from time to time entitled, subject to the term, to the income of the whole or any part, as the case may require, of the land leased. (3) Where that person becomes entitled by conveyance or otherwise, such rent, covenant or provision may be recovered, received, enforced or taken advantage of by him notwithstanding that he becomes so entitled after the condition of re-entry or forfeiture has become enforceable, but this sub-section does not render enforceable any condition of re-entry or other condition waived or released before such person becomes entitled as aforesaid. (4) This section applies to leases made before or after the commencement of this Act, but does not affect the operation of - (a) any severance of the reversionary estate; or (b) any acquisition by conveyance or otherwise of the right to receive or enforce any rent covenant or provision; effected before the commencement of this Act."

The "benefit" of a covenant to keep premises in repair or to reinstate them after fire is (as is apparent from subsection (2)) the right to enforce the covenant by exercising such remedies for its breach as are expressly provided by the lease, for example, by forfeiture or entry to execute the repairs and recover their cost, or as are available at common law, namely, by suing for damages for breach. By subsection (1) this right to enforce the covenant in question is not only to be "annexed and incident to" the reversionary estate in the land, but also is to "go with" that reversionary estate. The expression "go with" must be intended to add something to the concept involved in the expression "annexed and incident to" and in my view connotes the transfer of the right to enforce the covenant from the assignor to the assignee with the consequent cessation of the right to the assignor to enforce the covenant against the tenant. Such remedies as the assignor was entitled to exercise in respect of existing breaches of covenant by the tenant become vested in, and exercisable by, the assignee. This view of the meaning of subsection (1) is confirmed by subsection (3) which makes it clear that the assignee can exercise the remedies available under the terms of the lease or at common law in respect of breaches committed before the date of assignment of the reversion, for it is only in respect of such breaches that "the condition of re-entry or forfeiture" can have become enforceable before the assignee became entitled to the reversion.

Looked at purely as a matter of the meaning of the words used in section 141 of the Law of Property Act, 1925, I take the view that the effect of this section is that after the assignment of the reversion to a lease, the assignee alone is entitled to sue the tenant for breaches of covenants contained in the lease whether such breaches occurred before or after the date of the assignment of the reversion. The effect of the section so construed is to enact a simple, rational and just rule of law. The measure of damages for breach of a covenant in a lease which runs with the land - the only kind of covenant with which the section is concerned - is the diminution in the value of the reversion consequent upon the breach and is sustained by the person entitled to the reversion. If upon an assignment of the reversion the benefit of such covenants, including the right to exercise remedies in respect of existing breaches, is transferred from the assignor to the assignee, justice is done to all three parties concerned. The assignor suffers no loss, for the sale price of the reversion will take account of the value of the rights of action or other remedies against the tenant for antecedent breaches of covenant which are transferred to the assignee; the assignee will be able to enforce these remedies against the tenant; the tenant will remain liable for the diminution in value of the reversion caused by his breaches of covenant whenever committed. Any other solution would lead to complication and injustice, particularly where there is a continuing covenant to keep in repair which, as in the present case, overlaps a covenant to reinstate within a limited time. What would be the tenant's position if the assignor could sue for breaches committed before the date of the assignment of the reversion? If the tenant put the premises into repair after the date of the assignment, either voluntarily or under threat of forfeiture by the assignee, what would happen to the assignor's right of action for lack of repair before the assignment and what would be the measure of damages? If the assignor sued the tenant after the assignment and recovered damages representing the diminution in value of the reversion at the date of the breach or breaches relied upon, could the assignee nevertheless subsequently enforce a forfeiture for failure to put

 Alert

the premises into repair or bring an action against the tenant and recover a similar measure of damages? I need not set out the permutations and combinations of complications and injustices which would result. They seem to me strongly to confirm the construction of section 141 of the Law of Property Act, 1925, to which a consideration of its language had already led me. On this issue, therefore, I would allow this appeal.

Upon the assignment of the freehold reversion under the old rules, the original landlord loses all benefit of covenants contained in the lease. The original landlord cannot, consequently, bring an action for breaches that occurred prior to the assignment of the reversion, unless his assignee is willing to act as an agent and bring an action on his predecessor's behalf.

Under the principle of continuing liability, the original tenant retains the burden after the assignment of the lease, as discussed previously. In *Arlesford Trading Co Ltd v Servansingh* [1971] 3 All ER 113, the question arose whether an assignee of the freehold reversion was able to bring an action against the original tenant after the assignment of the lease, even though the assignee of the freehold reversion had never shared privity of contract or privity of estate with the original tenant.

Arlesford Trading Co Ltd v Servansingh **[1971] 3 All ER 113**

Panel: Russell and Phillimore LJJ and Lyell J

Facts: The lease included a tenant covenant to pay rent with which the original tenant failed to comply. The tenant assigned his lease and the landlord subsequently assigned the freehold reversion. The question arose as to whether the landlord's assignee could enforce the covenant against the original tenant.

LORD JUSTICE RUSSELL

Now it has been established in this court that an assignee of the reversion can claim, against the lessee, arrears of rent accrued prior to the assignment, and to re-enter on the ground of the failure to have paid such arrears; this is by force of s 141 of the Law of Property Act 1925: see *London and County (A & D) Ltd v Wilfred Sportsman Ltd (Greenwoods (Hosiers and Outfitters) Ltd, third party)* [1970] 3 WLR 418. In that case, however, the claim to re-enter and forfeit the lease was against the original lessee (and his chargee). It is pointed out that in the present case the defendant assigned his lease before the reversion was assigned to the plaintiffs and that there has never been privity of estate between the plaintiffs and the defendant, contrary to what appears from the note of the judgment to have been the judge's view. But it is argued for the plaintiffs that an original lessee remains at all times liable under the lessee's covenants throughout the lease, and the assignment of the reversion does not automatically release him from that liability. This argument is in our judgment correct; so that if there is no special feature in this case the plaintiffs undoubtedly have a right as assignee of the reversion, and with it of the benefit of the lessee's covenants for rent etc to sue for arrears of rent.

Was there a special feature which denies the plaintiffs the right to sue the defendant?... It was manifestly the intention that the lease should be assigned 'clean', so to speak, of any liability for those three unpaid instalments. Equally, the plaintiffs could not have asserted against the assignee of the term...the failure in the payment of those three instalments. But does it follow from that that the postponed obligation of the defendant to pay those three instalments no longer had sufficiently the quality of an obligation to pay rent etc under the lease to enable the assignee of the reversion to assert against the defendant that the benefit of that obligation was assigned together with the reversion? In our judgment the answer is in the negative. The obligation on the defendant remained on him in his capacity as lessee under the lease, and the ability to enforce against him passed with the reversion to the plaintiffs.

In our judgment accordingly the appeal fails.

The landlord's assignee had neither privity of contract, nor of estate with the original tenant, but he was able to enforce the covenant against the original tenant. The LPA 1925 s 141 is deemed to assign the entire benefit of covenants to a new landlord, effectively creating privity of contract between the original tenant and the assignee of the reversion.

The passing of the burdens and benefits of covenants to a tenant's assignee under the old rules is dealt with in *Spencer's Case* [1558-1774] All ER Rep 68.

Spencer's Case (1582) 5 Coke Reports 16a

Panel: Wray CJ, Gawdy J and other judges

Facts: A tenant covenanted to build a brick wall on the leased property. The court considered whether the tenant's assignee was subject to this covenant.

JUDGMENT

...after many arguments at the Bar, the case was excellently argued and debated by the Justices at the Bench: and in this case these points were unanimously resolved by Sir Christopher Wray, Chief Justice, Sir Thomas Gawdy, and the whole Court. And many differences taken and agreed concerning express covenants, and covenants in law, and which of them run with the land, and which of them are collateral, and do not go with the land, and where the assignee shall be bound without naming him, and where not; and where he shall not be bound although he be expressly named, and where not.

1. When the covenant extends to a thing *in esse*, parcel of the demise, the thing to be done by force of the covenant is *quodammodo* annexed and appurtenant to the thing demised, and shall go with the land, and shall bind the assignee although he be not bound by express words: but when the covenant extends to a thing which is not in being at the time of the demise made, it cannot be appurtenant or annexed to the thing which hath no being: as if the lessee covenants to repair the houses demised to him during the term, that is parcel of the contract, and extends to the support of the thing demised, and therefore is *quodammodo* annexed appurtenant to houses, and shall bind the assignee

although he be not bound expressly by the covenant: but in the case at Bar, the covenant concerns a thing which was not *in esse* at the time of the demise made, but to be newly built after, and therefore shall bind the covenantor, his executors, or administrators, and not the assignee, for the law will not annex the covenant to a thing which hath no being.

2.   It was resolved that in this case, if the lessee had covenanted for him and his assigns, that they would make a new wall upon some part of the thing demised, that for as much as it is to be done upon the land demised, that it should bind the assignee; for although the covenant doth extend to a thing to be newly made, yet it is to be made upon the thing demised, and the assignee is to take the benefit of it, and therefore shall bind the assignee by express words. So on the other side, if a warranty be made to one, his heirs and assigns, by express words, the assignee shall take benefit of it, and shall have a *warrantia chartæ* , F. N. B. 135. & 9 E. 2. Garr' de Charters 30. 36 E. 3. Garr. 1. 4 H. 8. Dyer 1. But although the covenant be for him and his assigns, yet if the thing to be done be merely collateral to the land, and doth not touch or concern the thing demised in any sort, there the assignee shall not be charged. As if the lessee covenants for him and his assigns to build a house upon the land of the lessor which is no parcel of the demise, or to pay any collateral sum to the lessor, or to a stranger, it shall not bind the assignee, because it is merely collateral, and in no manner touches or concerns the thing that was demised, or that is assigned over; and therefore in such case the assignee of the thing demised cannot be charged with it, no more than any other stranger.

The assignee was deemed not to be subject to the covenant. This case introduced four requirements that must be satisfied in order for the burden or benefit of a covenant to pass to a tenant's assignee: (1) the covenant must touch and concern the land, (2) there must be a legal lease, (3) which has been legally assigned and (4) there must be privity of estate between the parties. Only when these four requirements have been met, does the burden or benefit of a covenant contained in a lease pass to the tenant's assignee under the old rules. Some of these requirements were further considered in *Purchase v Lichfield Brewery Company* [1915] 1 KB 184.

Purchase v Lichfield Brewery Company [1915] 1 KB 184

Panel: Horridge and Lush JJ

Facts: The landlord granted a lease in writing, but not by deed, to the tenant. As it was not made by deed, the lease was equitable rather than legal. The tenant granted a mortgage of the lease to a third party and assigned the lease to the mortgagee as security for the loan. The tenant failed to pay rent and the issue arose whether the landlord could enforce the rent covenant against the mortgagee as the tenant's assignee.

MR JUSTICE LUSH

The only point which the county court judge decided was that the present case was governed by *Williams v Bosanquet* 1 Brod & B 238. In my view that case does not apply. The lease in question there was under seal. It was assigned by deed to mortgagees. That was a valid assignment. The only question was whether the mortgagees, not having taken possession, were bound by the covenants in the lease. It was held that they were bound. In this case there was no lease under seal. No term was created as between lessor and lessee. Therefore the question decided in *Williams v Bosanquet* does not arise in this case. Consequently the judgment of the county court judge cannot stand on the grounds on which he has based it.

Then can the judgment be supported on other grounds? I do not think it is necessary to say how the case might have stood if the defendants had ever taken possession. They are liable, if at all, on the principle of *Walsh v Lonsdale* 21 Ch D 9. In that case the tenant was in possession under the agreement. In the present case the defendants never did take possession. The agreement contained a provision against assigning. The defendants were only mortgagees. It does not follow from *Walsh v Lonsdale* that a Court of Equity would decree specific performance against mere mortgagees who only took an assignment by way of security. In my opinion it would leave the parties to their position at law. Accordingly the matter stands thus: A tenant under an agreement, whose only title to call himself a lessee depends on his right to specific performance of the agreement, assigns his right to assignees. The assignees never had a term vested in them because no term was ever created; therefore there was never privity of estate. They never went into possession or were recognized by the landlord; therefore there was never privity of contract. It is impossible that specific performance of a contract can be decreed against a person with whom there is neither privity of contract nor privity of estate. Therefore these assignees are not liable to perform the terms of the agreement and this appeal must be allowed.

In this case, there was neither privity of estate between the landlord and the mortgagee (as assignee), nor a legal lease. Therefore, the burden of the covenant was not enforceable against the mortgagee.

The formalities required for the benefit or burden to pass under *Spencer's Case* were further clarified by Denning LJ in *Boyer v Worbey* [1953] 1 QB 234.

Boyer v Worbey [1953] 1 QB 234

Panel: Evershed MR, Denning and Romer LJJ

Facts: A tenant occupied a property first under a short lease and then under a periodic tenancy, which is a legal lease. The tenant was subject to a covenant to pay £40 towards redecoration upon quitting the property. The tenant assigned the lease to the defendant. The defendant subsequently left without paying the amount and the landlord brought an action to recover the sum.

LORD JUSTICE DENNING

There is no valid reason nowadays why the doctrine of covenants running with the land - or with the reversion should not apply equally to agreements under hand as to covenants under seal; and I think we should so hold, not only in the case of agreements for more than three years which need the intervention of equity to perfect them, but also in the case of agreements for three years or less which do not.

Denning LJ hereby established that the requirements for the burden or benefit of a covenant to pass to a tenant's assignee under *Spencer's Case* can be met without a deed, as long as there exists a legal lease which is then legally assigned. On the facts of the case, the burden of the informal legal lease had therefore passed. Further *obiter dicta*, suggesting that the burden of an equitable lease can also pass, has not been followed.

The requirement that a covenant touches and concerns the land as set out in *Spencer's Case* [1558-1774] All ER Rep 68 was further considered in *Hua Chiao Commercial Bank Ltd v Chiaphua Industries Ltd* [1987] AC 99.

Hua Chiao Commercial Bank Ltd v Chiaphua Industries Ltd [1987] AC 99

Panel: Lord Bridge of Harwich, Lord Brandon of Oakbrook, Lord Oliver of Aylmerton, Lord Goff of Chieveley and Sir Ivor Richardson

Facts: The tenant entered into a covenant to pay the landlord a security deposit, which the landlord covenanted to repay at the end of the lease if there had been no breach by the tenant of the leasehold covenants. The landlord granted a mortgage over the freehold and then defaulted; the bank took possession of the property. The tenant committed no breach of any tenant covenant for the duration of the lease. At the end of the lease, the tenant claimed the return of the deposit. The court considered whether the landlord's covenant touched and concerned the land, and whether the burden would therefore pass to the bank with the reversion.

LORD OLIVER OF AYLMERTON delivered the advice of the board.

There is a considerable measure of common ground between the parties. It is not in dispute that the bank constitutes, by assignment, "the landlord" for the purposes of the lease. Equally it is not in dispute that the test of whether the original landlord's covenant to return the amount of the deposit is enforceable against a successor in title is the same as it would be if the lease had been a lease of land in England, that is to say, whether the covenant is one "entered into by a lessor with reference to the subject matter of the lease" or, to use the common law terminology, whether it is a covenant which "touches and concerns the land." Nor is there any disagreement about the formulation of the test for determining whether any given covenant touches or concerns the land. Their Lordships have been referred to and are content to adopt the following passage from *Cheshire and Burn's Modern Law of Real Property*, 13th ed (1982), pp 430-431:

"If the covenant has direct reference to the land, if it lays down something which is to be done or is not to be done upon the land, or, and perhaps this is the clearest way of

Alert

describing the test, if it affects the landlord in his normal capacity as landlord or the tenant in his normal capacity as tenant, it may be said to touch and concern the land.

"Lord Russell CJ in *Horsey Estate Ltd v Steiger* [1899] 2 QB 79, 89 said: 'The true principle is that no covenant or condition which affects merely the person, and which does not affect the nature, quality, or value of the thing demised or the mode of using or enjoying the thing demised, runs with the land;' and Bayley J at an earlier date asserted the same principle in *Congleton Corporation v Pattison* (1808) 10 East 130, 138: 'In order to bind the assignee, the covenant must either affect the land itself during the term, such as those which regard the mode of occupation, or it must be such as per se, and not merely from collateral circumstances, affects the value of the land at the end of the term.'

"If a simple test is desired for ascertaining into which category a covenant falls, it is suggested that the proper inquiry should be whether the covenant affects either the landlord qua landlord or the tenant qua tenant. A covenant may very well have reference to the land, but, unless it is reasonably incidental to the relation of landlord and tenant, it cannot be said to touch and concern the land so as to be capable of running therewith or with the reversion."

...To say that the obligation to "return" the amount of the deposit is "inextricably bound up with" covenants which touch and concern the land in the sense in which the expression was used by McMullin V.P. in the instant case - i.e. that, in order to determine whether or not the obligation to pay could have arisen against anyone, it would be necessary to survey the other covenants - does not, in their Lordships' view, answer the critical question of whether it itself touches and concerns the land. It certainly does not per se affect the nature quality or value of the land either during or at the end of the term. It does not per se affect the mode of using or enjoying that which is demised. And to ask whether it affects the landlord qua landlord or the tenant qua tenant is an exercise which begs the question. It does so only if it runs with the reversion or with the land respectively. There is not, on any conceivable construction of the clause, anything which either divests the original tenant of his contractual right to receive back after assignment the deposit which he has paid or which entitles an assignee from him to claim the benefit of the sum to the exclusion of his assignor; and, plainly, the money cannot be repaid more than once. Equally, there is not on any conceivable construction anything in the clause which entitles the assignee of the reversion to take over from his assignor the benefit of the sum deposited or which obliges the assignee, in enforcing the covenants against the tenant for the time being, to give credit for money which he himself has never received and to which he has no claim. Whilst it is true that the deposit is paid to the original payee because it is security for the performance of contractual obligations assumed throughout the term by the payer and because the payee is the party with whom the contract is entered into, it is, in their Lordships' view, more realistic to regard the obligation as one entered into with the landlord qua payee rather than qua landlord. By demanding and receiving this security, he assumes the obligation of any mortgagee to repay on the stipulated condition and that obligation remains, as between himself and the original payer, throughout the period of the lease, even though neither party may, when the condition is fulfilled, have any further interest in the land demised. The nature of the obligation is simply that of an obligation to repay money which has been received and it is neither necessary nor logical, simply because the conditions of repayment relate to the performance of covenants in a lease, that the transfer of the reversion should create in the transferee an additional and co-extensive obligation to pay money which he has never received and in which he never had any interest or that the assignment of the term should vest in the assignee the right to receive a sum which he has never paid.

The covenant by a landlord to refund the deposit guaranteeing the fulfilment of tenant covenants was not deemed to touch and concern the land, as it affected neither the landlord in his capacity as landlord, nor the tenant in his capacity as tenant. Therefore the bank as the landlord's successor in title did not have the burden of the covenant to repay.

Thus, upon assignment of an old lease, the burden passes to the assignee if the requirements of *Spencer's Case* are satisfied. The assignee is liable for his own breaches, but not for those of his predecessor. Similarly, an assignee will no longer be liable once he himself assigns the lease, as he will no longer have privity of estate. He will, however, remain liable for breaches after assignment, if he has entered into direct covenants with the landlord.

Estates Gazette Ltd v Benjamin Restaurants Ltd and another [1995] 1 All ER 129

Panel: Nourse, Hirst and Saville LJJ

Facts: The original tenant assigned the lease to the defendant. The defendant later assigned the lease again. The landlord consented to the assignment, on condition that the defendant and his assignee entered into direct covenants with the landlord promising the continued fulfilment of the covenants contained in the lease. The defendant's assignee later breached the tenant covenants in the lease. The assignee and the original tenant were insolvent, so the landlord sought to enforce the covenants against the defendant. The defendant's assignee is referred to as the first defendant in the judgment. The defendant is referred to as 'the second defendant' in the judgment.

LORD JUSTICE NOURSE

Two obligations were assumed by the first defendant in cl 2 of the licence [to assign]. The first was to pay the rents reserved by the lease at the time and in manner therein provided for. The rents reserved by the lease were those for whose payment provision was made by the reddendum. The reddendum provided for the payment 'during the said term hereby granted' of the yearly rent of £4,500 (subject to review). Thus the first defendant became bound to pay the rents payable during the whole of the term.

The second obligation assumed by the first defendant was to observe and perform all the covenants on the lessee's part and the conditions contained in the lease. It is clear that 'the lessee' here includes the person or persons in whom the term may from time to time be vested. One of the lessee's covenants is that contained in cl 2(1): 'To pay the rent hereinbefore reserved at the times and in manner aforesaid.' So, by an identical process of construction, the first defendant became doubly bound to pay the rents payable during the whole of the term.

Shortly stated, the obligation assumed by the second defendant in cl 3(1) of the licence was to ensure that the first defendant would perform the obligations imposed on it by cl 2. In all material respects the wording of the two provisions was identical. So the second defendant became bound to pay the rents payable during the whole of the term, if and in so far as they were not paid by the first defendant.

The defendant was held liable, owing to the direct covenants he had entered into with the landlord. It is common for landlords to refuse consent to the assignment of an old lease, unless the tenant agrees to enter into direct covenants in this manner.

Where a party is held liable for an assignee's breach, he is likely to want to recover his losses. He may seek to enforce an indemnity covenant against his successor, or, if he has been pursued for a fixed sum, he may seek to claim an overriding lease under the Landlord and Tenant (Covenants) Act 1995 (LTCA 1995) s 19. Alternatively, he may seek to recover his losses directly from the party in breach under the rule in *Moule v Garrett and others* (1872) LR 7 Exch 101.

Moule v Garrett and others (1872) LR 7 Exch 101

Panel: Cockburn CJ, Willes, Blackburn, Mellor, Brett and Grove JJ

Facts: The original tenant had assigned the lease to a party, who in turn assigned to the defendant. The defendant failed to comply with a covenant in the lease to keep the property in repair. The original tenant was held liable for this breach and sought to recover his losses directly from the defendant.

COCKBURN CJ

I am of opinion that the judgment of the Court of Exchequer is right, and that it must be affirmed. The defendants are the ultimate assignees of a lease, and the plaintiff, who is suing them for indemnity against the consequence of a breach of a covenant contained in that lease, is the original lessee. There is no doubt that the breach of covenant is one in respect of which the defendants, as such assignees, are liable to the lessor, and that they have acquired by virtue of mesne assignments the same estate which the plaintiff originally took. And I think that taking this estate from the assignee of the plaintiff, their own immediate assignor, they must be taken to have acquired it, subject to the discharge of all the liabilities which the possession of that estate imposed on them under the terms of the original lease, not merely as regards the immediate assignor, but as regards the original lessee.

Another ground on which the judgment below may be upheld, and, as I think, a preferable one, is that, the premises which are the subject of the lease being in the possession of the defendants as ultimate assignees, they were the parties whose duty it was to perform the covenants which were to be performed upon and in respect of those premises. It was their immediate duty to keep in repair, and by their default the lessee, though he had parted with the estate, became liable to make good to the lessor the conditions of the lease. The damage therefore arises through their default, and the general proposition applicable to such a case as the present is, that where one person is compelled to pay damages by the legal default of another, he is entitled to recover from the person by whose default the damage was occasioned the sum so paid...

 Alert

Whether the liability is put on the ground of an implied contract, or of an obligation imposed by law, is a matter of indifference: it is such a duty as the law will enforce. The lessee has been compelled to make good an omission to repair, which has arisen entirely from the default of the defendants, and the defendants are therefore liable to reimburse him.

Consequently where a party is held liable for the breach of a leasehold covenant by another, he may recover the losses directly from the party in breach.

10.4 The New Rules

Under the new rules, case law is less significant; the majority of relevant law can be found in the LT(C)A 1995 (although the rule in *Moule v Garrett* applies to old and new leases alike). LT(C)A 1995 s 3 states that the benefit and burden of all landlord and tenant covenants pass upon assignment, unless they are expressed to be personal. *BHP Petroleum Great Britain Ltd v Chesterfield Properties Ltd and another* [2002] Ch 194 considered the effect of this change in the law.

BHP Petroleum Great Britain Ltd v Chesterfield Properties Ltd and another **[2002] Ch 194**

Panel: Judge and Jonathan Parker LJJ and Bodey J

Facts: A landlord assigned the freehold reversion. The tenant claimed the original landlord remained liable for covenant to a remedy defect in the property demised by the lease, on the grounds that it was expressed to be a personal covenant in the lease.

LORD JUSTICE JONATHAN PARKER giving the judgment of the court.

Clause 12.5 of the agreement is headed "General provisions". Clause 12.5.1 provides as follows:

"12.5.1. For the avoidance of doubt: 12.5.1.1 the tenant acknowledges that the obligations on the part of the landlord contained in this clause 12 are personal obligations of Chesterfield Properties plc and the tenant acknowledges and confirms that the tenant shall have no claim of any nature whatsoever against the landlords successors in title to the demised premises arising out of or otherwise in connection with the obligations on the part of the landlord contained in this clause 12; 12.5.1.2 the benefit of the provisions contained in this clause 12 shall enure for the tenants successors in title and the tenant and the tenants successors in title shall be entitled to assign the benefit of the provisions contained in this clause 12 to each subsequent assignee of the lease but not otherwise." ...

Jonathan Parker LJ then turned to the LTCA 1995:

Section 3 is entitled "Transmission of benefit and burden of covenants". It provides as follows (so far as material):

"(1) The benefit and burden of all landlord and tenant covenants of a tenancy—(a) shall be annexed and incident to the whole, and to each and every part, of the premises demised by the tenancy and of the reversion in them, and (b) shall in accordance with this section pass on an assignment of the whole or any part of those premises or of the reversion in them...

"(6) Nothing in this section shall operate—(a) in the case of a covenant which (in whatever terms) is expressed to be personal to any person, to make the covenant enforceable by or (as the case may be) against any other person" ...

Sections 5 to 8 inclusive are headed "Release of covenants on assignment". Section 5 applies where a tenant assigns premises demised to him under a tenancy. Section 5(2) provides as follows (so far as material): "If the tenant assigns the whole of the premises demised to him, he—(a) is released from the tenant covenants of the tenancy, and (b) ceases to be entitled to the benefit of the landlord covenants of the tenancy, as from the assignment."

Section 6 applies where a landlord assigns the reversion in the premises subject to the tenancy. Section 6(2) provides as follows: "If the landlord assigns the reversion in the whole of the premises of which he is the landlord—(a) he may apply to be released from the landlord covenants of the tenancy in accordance with section 8; and (b) if he is so released from all of those covenants, he ceases to be entitled to the benefit of the tenant covenants of the tenancy as from the assignment."...

Section 8 lays down the procedure for seeking release from a covenant under section 6...

It follows that in our judgment Chesterfield's obligations in clause 12 of the agreement, being expressed to be personal to Chesterfield, are not "landlord covenants" within the meaning of the 1995 Act, and that the [section 8] notice was accordingly ineffective to release Chesterfield from such obligations...

Nor can we see anything in the 1995 Act to fetter the freedom of contracting parties to place a contractual limit on the transmissibility of the benefit or burden of obligations under a tenancy. On the contrary, that no such fetter was intended by Parliament is clearly demonstrated, in our judgment, by section 3(6)(a) (quoted earlier).

The court held that the original landlord remained liable as the covenant was personal. Under the new law, the only exception to the rule that the benefit and burden will always pass is where the covenant is expressed to be personal. If the covenant is not expressed to be personal, the burden and benefit will pass under LT(C)A 1995 s 3. The original tenant is released from liability under LT(C)A 1995 s 5. The original landlord must apply to the tenant for release from liability under LT(C)A 1995 ss 6 and 8.

Further Reading

Megarry & Wade, *The Law of Real Property*, (8ᵗʰ Edition) Sweet & Maxwell, pp 20-001 – 20-130

Williamson, H, The best way to deal with a nasty surprise, *Estates Gazette* 2006, 0605, 267

Woolhouse, B, Don't paint over the cracks, *Estates Gazette* 2008, EG 2008, 0843, 190 –191

11

Termination of Leases and Extending Business Tenancies

Topic List

1   Termination of Leases by Forfeiture
2   Extending Business Tenancies

Introduction

A lease may come to an end in a number of different ways. For example, the parties may agree to terminate it, the lease may naturally come to an end or it may be forfeited.

11.1 Termination of Leases by Forfeiture

If a tenant breaches a covenant contained in a lease, a landlord may exercise his right to forfeit the lease. The procedure for forfeiting the lease will depend upon whether the tenant is in breach of a covenant to pay rent or another covenant.

The following case relates to the granting of relief from forfeiture to a tenant who is in breach of a covenant to pay rent.

Gill and another v Lewis and another [1956] 2 QB 1

Panel: Singleton, Jenkins and Hodson LJJ

Statute: Common Law Procedure Act 1852 (CLPA 1852) ss 210, 211 and 212

Facts: The claimants, Mr Gill and Miss Bradshaw, were the personal representatives of Mrs Cole, the deceased landlord, who had granted leases of two houses to Mr Lewis and Mr Wright as joint tenants. Mr Lewis and Mr Wright regularly failed to pay the rent due under the leases so the claimants decided to terminate the leases, issuing writs claiming possession of the properties and the amounts due. Mr Lewis was unable to appear in court as he was in prison for indecent assault (which had occurred in one of the two houses). The defendants paid some of the arrears into court just before the judgment was granted by the court and the rest (including the costs) after the judgment was granted. The defendants then applied for relief from forfeiture under the CLPA 1852 s 212. Relief was granted by the judge at first instance and the claimants appealed to the Court of Appeal.

LORD JUSTICE JENKINS

...As grounds on which ... relief should have been refused by the judge in the present case, [counsel for the claimants] relied, in effect, on three matters. The first was the previous history of the difficulties which the landlords had experienced in extracting the rent from the defendants; the second was the elusive habits of the defendants, which led to difficulties of service; and the third was the defendant Lewis's conviction of the two acts of indecent assault, committed actually upon a part of the demised premises. ...

The provisions of the Common Law Procedure Act, 1852, to which I need refer are these. Section 210 provides ... that a landlord is to have a right to re-enter when there is a half-year's rent in arrear; and then it goes on to stipulate that any claim to relief ... which a tenant desires to make must be made within six months after execution of the judgment in respect of which relief is sought. ...

Section 211 is to the effect that relief is not to be granted except upon payment of everything that is due to the landlord for rent in arrear and costs. ...

Section 212 ... is in these terms: "If the tenant or his assignee do or shall, at any time before the trial ... pay into the court ... all the rent and arrears, together with the costs, then and in such case all further proceedings on the said ejectment shall cease and be discontinued"...

By way of illustration of the manner in which the jurisdiction to grant relief from forfeiture for non-payment of rent has been exercised by the courts [counsel for the claimants] referred us to *Stanhope v. Haworth* [(1886) 3 T.L.R. 34.] in which an order had been made for possession for non-payment of rent, and the premises were a colliery. Relief was applied for towards the end of the period of six months allowed by section 210 of the Act of 1852. It was held that the parties had so altered their position in the meantime that it would be inequitable to grant relief. It appears that in the meantime the landlord had let other people into possession and had made arrangements with them for the working of the colliery, and a considerable amount of money had been spent on the footing that the lease was at an end. ...

It will be observed that in that case the landlord and those dealing with him had altered their position on the footing that the lease to the party seeking relief was at an end, and they had been led to do that because the tenant had waited until almost the end of the period of six months allowed to him before he claimed relief. So that case shows that where parties have altered their position in the meantime, and in particular where the rights of third parties have intervened, relief ought not to be granted where the effect of it would be to defeat the new rights of third parties or be unfair to the landlord having regard to the way in which he has altered his position. ...

[I]n my view, save in exceptional circumstances, the function of the court in exercising [its] equitable jurisdiction is to grant relief when all that is due for rent and costs has been paid up, and (in general) to disregard any other causes of complaint that the landlord may have against the tenant. ...

 Alert

But there may be very exceptional cases in which the conduct of the tenants has been such as, in effect, to disqualify them from coming to the court and claiming any relief or assistance whatever. The kind of case I have in mind is that of a tenant falling into arrear with the rent of premises which he was notoriously using as a disorderly house: it seems to me that in a case of that sort if the landlord brought an action for possession for non-payment of rent and the tenant applied to the court for relief, the court, on being apprised that the premises were being consistently used for immoral purposes, would decline to give the tenant any relief or assistance which would in any way further his use or allow the continuance of his use of the house for those immoral purposes. ...

I cannot, however, find any facts in the present case approaching the exceptional state of affairs I have in mind. ...

We are left as the sole reason for refusing relief the fact of the two acts of indecent assault committed by the defendant Lewis... . This is the aspect of the case which has occasioned me most difficulty, but, in my view, that matter is not in itself enough to justify the court in refusing relief. ...

I am therefore of opinion that no such exceptional case is here made out as to justify the court in refusing relief on payment or tender of the whole of the amount due. Accordingly, if the matter depends on the equitable jurisdiction to give relief, I think that the defendants are entitled to succeed in this appeal. ...

The Court of Appeal unanimously dismissed the claimants' appeal.

The case demonstrates that if a tenant pays all the rent arrears owed and any costs, it is generally not difficult to obtain relief from forfeiture. If a tenant is able to pay all that is owing, it would usually be inequitable not to grant relief. Exceptional circumstances, where relief should not be granted, tend to arise infrequently. The case cited in the judgment (*Stanhope v Haworth* (1886) 3 TLR 34) demonstrates that the grant of a new lease to a third party after either court proceedings or peaceable re-entry would be the most common reason to deny relief to a tenant.

The remainder of the cases on the termination of leases by forfeiture all relate to the contentious area of breach of covenants other than those relating to the payment of rent.

Rugby School (Governors) v Tannahill [1935] 1 KB 87

Panel: Greer, Maugham and Roche LJJ

Statute: Law of Property Act 1925 (LPA 1925) s 146

Facts: The claimant landlord owned a property in Great Ormond Street in London. They granted a lease of the property to Mr Reason, who later assigned the lease (with the consent of the landlord) to Ms Tannahill, the defendant. The lease contained a covenant by the tenant not to use the property for illegal or immoral purposes, which the tenant breached by using the property for prostitution, for which she was convicted. The landlord served a notice on her terminating the lease in accordance with the LPA 1925 s 146(1). The s 146 notice did not require her to remedy the breach or to provide compensation to the landlord. The tenant stopped using the property for prostitution. She argued that the s 146 notice was invalid as it did not require her to remedy the breach or to pay compensation to the landlord. The judge at first instance found in favour of the claimant and held that the notice was valid. The defendant appealed to the Court of Appeal.

LORD JUSTICE GREER

...The question depends upon whether or not the notice which was served upon her by the plaintiffs sufficiently complies with the requirements of s. 146, sub-s. 1 of the Law of Property Act, 1925...

The covenant, the breach of which is complained of, expressly forbids the tenant to permit the premises to be used for such [an immoral] purpose. ...In those circumstances the plaintiffs were entitled to obtain possession of the premises unless they failed to comply with the terms of s. 146 of the Law of Property Act, 1925. ...

The first point is, whether this particular breach is capable of remedy. In my judgment [the judge at first instance] was right in coming to the conclusion that it was not. ... [I]n some cases where the immediate ceasing of that which is complained of, together with an undertaking against any further breach, it might be said that the breach was capable of remedy. This particular breach, however - conducting the premises, or permitting them to be conducted, as a house of ill-fame - is one which in my judgment was not remedied by merely stopping this user. I cannot conceive how a breach of this kind can be remedied. The result of committing the breach would be known all over the neighbourhood and seriously affect the value of the premises. Even a money payment together with the cessation of the improper use of the house could not be a remedy. Taking the view as I do that this breach was incapable of remedy, it was unnecessary to require in the notice that the defendant should remedy the breach.

The further question is whether the absence of any statement in the notice requiring compensation in money in respect of the breach is fatal to the validity of the notice. As to that ... the plaintiffs were under no obligation to require compensation in money. ...Supposing the lessor does not want compensation, is the notice to be held bad because he does not ask for it? There is no sense in that. ...The appeal must be dismissed.

The Court of Appeal unanimously dismissed the defendant's appeal. As well as taking the view that breach of an 'immoral use' covenant was incapable of remedy, this judgment is also of note in confirming that there is no necessity for the notice to request compensation, if compensation is not required.

Although Greer LJ did not think that the breach of an illegal or immoral use covenant was capable of remedy in the 1930s, more recent case law has been more flexible in its approach and it now seems that it depends on the facts of the case as to whether an illegal or immoral use covenant is capable of remedy, as per Harman J in *Van Haarlam v Kasner* (1992) 64 P & CR 214.

One breach of covenant which is still held to be incapable of remedy is addressed in the following case.

Scala House & District Property Co. Limited v Forbes and others [1974] QB 575

Panel: Russell and James LJJ and Plowman J

Statute: LPA 1925 s 146

Facts: A landlord granted a lease to a tenant, which contained a covenant on the part of the tenant not to assign, sublet or part with possession of the property without the landlord's consent. The landlord reserved a right to forfeit the lease in case of breach of covenant. The lease was assigned to Mr Forbes, the defendant, with the landlord's consent. The defendant used the premises as a restaurant. He wanted the second and third defendants to manage the restaurant but the written agreement entered into by the three defendants (which was supposed to be a management agreement) created a sublease. Mr Forbes was therefore in breach of the lease as he had not sought the landlord's consent to sublet. The claimant bought the freehold reversion to the property (the previous landlord having not been aware that there was a breach of covenant) and shortly afterwards served a s 146 notice on the defendants, terminating the lease for breach of the alienation covenant. The s 146 notice stated that the defendants had to remedy the breach. The judge at first instance held that the breach was capable of remedy and that allowing the defendants only 14 days to remedy the breach before re-possessing the property was not a reasonable time to do so, therefore he refused to allow the landlord to terminate the lease. The claimant appealed to the Court of Appeal.

LORD JUSTICE RUSSELL

…Now the first question for decision is whether this breach of covenant is capable of remedy under section 146 of the Law of Property Act 1925. If it was capable of remedy, then at once there is the question whether the period of 14 days before issue of the writ was sufficient. If it was not capable of remedy I should have thought it obvious that 14 days was sufficient. …

So the first question is whether a breach of covenant such as is involved in the present case is capable of remedy. If it is capable of remedy, and is remedied in reasonable time, the lessor is unable to prove that a condition precedent to his ability to seek to forfeit by action or otherwise has been fulfilled. Here at once is a problem. An unlawful subletting is a breach once and for all. The subterm has been created.

I turn to the authorities. …*Rugby School (Governors) v. Tannahill* [1935] 1 K.B. 87 was a case of user by the lessee for immoral purposes contrary to covenant in the lease sought to be forfeited. …[T]his court expressed the view that breach of negative covenants might be capable of remedy, but not this one, on the ground that the stigma attaching to the premises would not be removed by mere cesser of the immoral user. …It might perhaps be argued that reliance by this court on the "stigma" point suggests that it was considered that a wrongful user in breach wholly in the past, without continuing adverse effect, would not entitle the lessor to seek to forfeit at all. …

In *Hoffmann v. Fineberg* [1949] Ch. 245 (Harman J.), the lessee, in breach of user covenants, allowed the premises to be used for illegal gambling, for which there were convictions. The section 146 notice did not call for the breach to be remedied. It is not clear whether the illegal user continued at the date of the notice. Again the decision was based on the "stigma" aspect as making the breach incapable of remedy within a reasonable time. Harman J. said, at p. 257: "… on the facts of this case this is a breach where mere cesser is no remedy." …

In summary upon the cases we have therefore a number of cases of user of premises in breach of covenant in which the decision that the breach is not capable of remedy has gone upon the "stigma" point, without considering whether a short answer might be … that it was ex hypothesi incapable of remedy… . But whatever may be the position in user breach cases, which are of a continuing nature, there is no authority, … to suggest that the creation of a subterm in breach of covenant is capable of remedy. …

I come to the conclusion that breach by an unlawful subletting is not capable of remedy at all. ...The subterm has been effectively created subject only to risks of forfeiture: it is a complete breach once for all: it is not in any sense a continuing breach. ...

I stress again that where there has been an unlawful subletting which has determined (and which has not been waived) there has been a breach which at common law entitles the lessor to re-enter: nothing can be done to remedy that breach: the expiry of the subterm has not annulled or remedied the breach: in such case the lessor plainly need not, in his section 146 notice, call upon the lessee to remedy the breach which is not capable of remedy... .

Accordingly, I would allow the appeal but grant relief from forfeiture to the lessee.

The Court of Appeal allowed the landlord's appeal and held that the notice was valid, but they nevertheless granted relief from forfeiture to the first tenant as the sublease had been terminated.

This case remains the authority for the fact that a breach of covenant against assignment or subletting without the landlord's consent is incapable of remedy, although it has been the subject of further discussion in two cases referred to below.

It is interesting to note in the above case that, although the covenant was held to be incapable of remedy, relief from forfeiture was still granted to Mr Forbes.

The following three cases all relate to the drafting of the s 146 notice and the question of which breaches of covenant are capable of remedy.

Expert Clothing Service & Sales Limited v Hillgate House Limited and another [1986] Ch 340

Panel: O'Connor and Slade LJJ and Bristow J

Statute: LPA 1925 s 146

Facts: The claimant landlord granted a twenty-five-year lease to the defendant tenant. The defendant obtained the landlord's consent to convert the premises into a gym and health club (although the defendant later decided that the property was too small to convert into a health club). The lease contained an express forfeiture clause. In the first year of the lease, the defendant failed to pay the rent and the claimant re-possessed the property. The defendant obtained relief from forfeiture subject to a variation to the lease that the defendant had to (a) notify the claimant whether it was going to convert the property into an office or a gym, (b) substantially complete the alterations by 28 September 1982 and (c) fully complete the alterations as soon as reasonably possible after that date. No works were carried out to the property and the claimant refused to accept the rent due on the next quarter date. The claimant's solicitor served a s 146 notice on the defendant. The s 146 notice specified that the defendant was in breach of the covenant to carry out the alterations by the necessary date (and additionally, a covenant to serve notice on the landlord that the lease had been charged to a mortgagee) and stated that the breaches were incapable of remedy. The claimant brought proceedings to obtain possession of the property. The defendant claimed relief from forfeiture. The judge at first instance held that the breach of the alterations covenant was incapable of remedy and he granted an order for possession in favour of the claimant. The defendant appealed to the Court of Appeal, arguing that the breaches were capable of remedy and that the s 146 notice was therefore invalid.

LORD JUSTICE SLADE

...[T]he first question which ... falls to be considered by us is whether those breaches are "capable of remedy" within the meaning of section 146(1) of the Law of Property Act 1925. This is a question of crucial importance for it is common ground that, if they are both capable of remedy in this sense, the section 146 notice, which asserted that they were irremediable and gave the first defendant no opportunity to remedy them, must have been a wholly invalid notice.

...In a case where the breach is "capable of remedy" within the meaning of the section, the principal object of the notice procedure provided for by section 146(1), as I read it, is to afford the lessee two opportunities before the lessor actually proceeds to enforce his right of re-entry, namely (1) the opportunity to remedy the breach within a reasonable time after service of the notice, and (2) the opportunity to apply to the court for relief from forfeiture. In a case where the breach is not "capable of remedy," there is clearly no point in affording the first of these two opportunities; the object of the notice procedure is thus simply to give the lessee the opportunity to apply for relief.

Unfortunately the authorities give only limited guidance as to what breaches are "capable of remedy" within the meaning of the section. ...

[I]n the *Scala House case* [1974] Q.B. 575 this court was addressing its mind solely to the once and for all breach of a negative covenant. ...While the *Scala House* decision is, of course, authority binding on this court for the proposition that the breach of a negative covenant not to assign, underlet or part with possession is never "capable of remedy," it is not, in my judgment, authority for the proposition that the once and for all breach of a positive covenant is never capable of remedy.

Mr. Neuberger, on behalf of the defendants, did not feel able to go so far ... that the breach of a positive covenant is always capable of remedy. He accepted, for example, that the breach of a covenant to insure might be incapable of remedy at a time when the premises had already been burnt down. Another example might be the breach of a positive covenant which in the event would be only capable of being fully performed, if at all, after the expiration of the relevant term.

Nevertheless, I would, for my part, accept Mr. Neuberger's submission that the breach of a positive covenant (whether it be a continuing breach or a once and for all breach) will ordinarily be capable of remedy. As Bristow J. pointed out in the course of argument, the concept of capability of remedy for the purpose of section 146 must surely be directed to the question whether the harm that has been done to the landlord by the relevant breach is for practicable purposes capable of being retrieved. In the ordinary case, the breach of a promise to do something by a certain time can for practical purposes be remedied by the thing being done, even out of time. For these reasons I reject the plaintiffs' argument that the breach of the covenant to reconstruct by

 Alert

28 September 1982 was not capable of remedy merely because it was not a continuing breach. ...

The judgment of Maugham L.J. in the *Rugby School case* [1935] 1 K.B. 87, 93 and other judicial dicta indicate that if a breach is to be "capable of remedy" at all within the meaning of section 146, it must be capable of remedy within a "reasonable time." ...In the present case, it was submitted, what was a reasonable time was a question of fact. In deciding that the breach of the covenant to reconstruct was not capable of remedy within a reasonable time, the judge [at first instance] expressed himself as "having regard to the facts as I have found them." ...

I accept that a section 146 notice need not require the tenant to remedy the breach if it is not capable of remedy within a reasonable time after service of the notice: see, for example, the *Rugby School case* [1935] 1 K.B. 87, 93...

However, in my opinion, in considering whether or not remedy within a reasonable time is possible, a crucial distinction ... falls to be drawn between breaches of negative user covenants, such as those under consideration in the *Rugby School* [case] ... and breaches of positive covenants. ...[W]here the relevant breaches consisted of allowing premises to be used as a brothel, even full compliance with the covenant within a reasonable time and for a reasonable time would not have remedied the breach. ...

[M]ere cesser by the tenant of the offending use within a reasonable period and for a reasonable period of time could not have remedied the breaches because it could not have removed the stigma which they had caused to attach to the premises. The harm had been irretrievably done. ...

In contrast with breaches of negative user covenants, the breach of a positive covenant to do something (such as to decorate or build) can ordinarily, for practical purposes, be remedied by the thing being actually done if a reasonable time for its performance (running from the service of the section 146 notice) is duly allowed by the landlord following such service and the tenant duly does it within such time.

...An important purpose of the section 146 procedure is to give even tenants who have hitherto lacked the will or the means to comply with their obligations one last chance to summon up that will or find the necessary means before the landlord re-enters. ...

In my judgment, on the remediability issue, the ultimate question for the court was this: if the section 146 notice had required the lessee to remedy the breach and the lessors had then allowed a reasonable time to elapse to enable the lessee fully to comply with the relevant covenant, would such compliance, coupled with the payment of any appropriate monetary compensation, have effectively remedied the harm which the lessors had suffered or were likely to suffer from the breach? If, but only if, the answer to this question was "No," would the failure of the section 146 notice to require remedy of the breach have been justifiable. In *Rugby School (Governors) v. Tannahill* [1935] 1 K.B. 87 ... and *Hoffmann v. Fineberg* [1949] Ch. 245 the answer to this question plainly would have been "No." In the present case, however, for the reasons already stated, I think the answer to it must have been "Yes." ...

 Alert

In the result, I would allow this appeal on the basis that ... the plaintiffs' section 146 notice was invalid because the relevant breaches were capable of remedy. ...

The Court of Appeal unanimously allowed the defendant's appeal.

This case highlights the importance of drafting the s 146 notice correctly and also established the test for assessing whether a breach of covenant is capable or incapable of remedy. These same issues were addressed in the following Court of Appeal case.

Savva and Savva v Hussein (1997) 73 P & CR 150

Panel: Staughton and Aldous LJJ and Sir John May

Statute: LPA 1925 s 146

Facts: The claimant landlords granted a lease of commercial premises used as a café and minicab firm to the defendant tenant. The lease contained several covenants which the tenant breached. The tenant erected a sign in breach of the covenant not to put up any signs other than one particular sign that was permitted under the terms of the lease. The tenant also carried out various alterations (including installing a flue passing through the roof of the property) in breach of the covenant not to make alterations without the prior written consent of the landlord. The landlords served a s 146 notice on the tenants, forfeiting the lease for breach of covenant. The s 146 notice did not require the breaches of covenant to be remedied. The tenant counter-claimed due to a failure by the landlord to keep the walls and the roof of the property in repair. The judge at first instance dismissed the claim for forfeiture and held that the landlords were in breach of their repair covenant. The landlords appealed to the Court of Appeal.

LORD JUSTICE STAUGHTON

...In this case the question is whether the breaches, if there were breaches, were capable of remedy. ...

It is established law in this court that the breach of a covenant not to assign without consent cannot be remedied. That was decided in *Scala House & District Property Co. Ltd v. Forbes* [[1974] Q.B. 575]. ...

In my judgment, except in a case of breach of a covenant not to assign without consent, the question is: whether the remedy referred to is the process of restoring the situation to what it would have been if the covenant had never been broken, or whether it is sufficient that the mischief resulting from a breach of the covenant can be removed. When something has been done without consent, it is not possible to restore the matter wholly to the situation which it was in before the breach. ...That is not to my mind what is meant by a remedy, it is a remedy if the mischief caused by the breach can be removed. In the case of a covenant not to make alterations without consent or not to display signs without consent, if there is a breach of that, the mischief can be removed by removing the signs or restoring the property to the state it was in before the alterations.

 Alert

I would hold that all the breaches complained of in this case were capable of remedy. It follows that the notice under section 146 should have required them to be remedied.

> ...In those circumstances there is no question of forfeiture here. There is, I suppose, still a claim for damages for breach of covenant, or there may be. ...

The Court of Appeal unanimously dismissed the appeal.

The main difference between this case and that of *Expert Clothing Service & Sales Limited v Hillgate House Limited and another* is that the former deals with breaches of negative covenants whereas the latter deals with a breach of a positive covenant. However, the test to apply is the same for both types of covenant: is the harm or mischief caused by the breach capable of remedy?

A recent case which examined afresh the intricacies of drafting a s 146 notice is the following Court of Appeal case.

Akici v LR Butlin Limited [2005] EWCA Civ 1296, [2006] 1 WLR 201

Panel: Mummery and Neuberger LJJ

Statute: LPA 1925 s 146

Facts: A landlord granted a lease of a commercial unit to a tenant. The lease contained an alienation covenant by the tenant (clause 4.18) not to 'assign equitably assign underlet or part with possession of a part of the demised premises nor to hold the whole or any part of the demised premises on trust for another nor to share possession of the whole or any part of the demised premises nor to part with possession of the whole of the demised premises'. The landlord reserved a right to forfeit the lease in case of breach of covenant. The freehold reversion was transferred to the defendant. The lease was assigned to the claimant.

Mr Akici (the claimant) allowed a company (Deka Limited), solely owned by Mr Gultekin, to trade from the property in the business of preparing and selling pizzas. On finding out that Deka Limited was trading from the property, the defendant's solicitors sent an enquiry to find out why but they did not receive a satisfactory reply. The defendant's solicitors served a s 146 notice on Mr Akici terminating the lease for breach of the alienation covenant. One of the paragraphs in the notice was drafted as follows: "This covenant has been broken and the particular breach complained of is the assignment or alternatively subletting or alternatively parting with possession of the premises without the landlord's consent. You have assigned, sublet or parted with possession to Deka Ltd."

Mr Akici maintained that he had not breached the covenant. A few months later, he became the sole owner of Deka Limited. The defendant then peaceably re-entered the property during the night and changed the locks. Mr Akici applied to the court for relief from forfeiture. The judge at first instance held that Mr Akici had effectively shared possession of the property with Deka Limited and that although the s 146 notice did not specify sharing of possession of the property as a breach, the notice could be construed in that way and the landlord could therefore rely on it as a valid notice. He also held that the breach was incapable of remedy and the re-entry by the landlord was lawful. Relief from forfeiture was refused. The claimant appealed to the Court of Appeal.

LORD JUSTICE NEUBERGER

17. The central questions are the extent and meaning of the covenants in cl 4.18.1 of the lease not to "part with possession" of part of the premises, not to "share possession" of the whole or any part of the premises, and not to "part [with] possession" of the whole of the premises without consent.

...

38. ...[I]t is perfectly possible for a lessee to permit a company, in which he has an interest, to occupy the demised premises for the purpose of its business, without parting with possession of those premises to that company. ...

39. ...[W]here the person prima facie entitled to possession, in this case Mr Akici, is alleged to have parted with possession to an entity which is admittedly in occupation, the ultimate question is whether he has effectively ceded possession to that other entity.

...

42. ...[I]t appears to me that the [judge at first instance] was right to conclude that Mr Akici had not parted with possession of the premises to the company.

43. The potentially more difficult question is whether Mr Akici had shared possession of the premises with the company. ...

44. Did Mr Akici retain possession in himself alone and merely permit the company to occupy the premises, or did the company share possession with Mr Akici? If the former, then there was no sharing of possession; if the latter, there was.

45. ...I take the view that, on the facts found by the [judge at first instance] in this case, he would have been entitled to conclude that there was a sharing of possession.

46. The fact that the company was not directed or owned by Mr Akici, at least until 10 August, and the degree to which the company exercised control over the premises was such ... to conclude that the company enjoyed a degree of control over the premises which amounted to its having possession (albeit non-exclusive). ...

47. In my judgment, looking at all the facts in this case, there was evidence ... that Mr Akici had shared possession of the premises with the company.

WAS THE S 146 NOTICE VALID?

48. ...[T]he s 146 Notice upon which Butlins relied alleged that the particular breach complained of was assigning, underletting or parting with possession of the premises. There was no express allegation of sharing possession. ...

...

50. The simple point made on behalf of Mr Akici is that the s 146 notice in the present case does not "specify . . . the particular breach complained of", in that the only breach (or at least the only relevant breach) which has been established against him is sharing possession, whereas the notice specifies assigning, sub-letting or parting with possession.

...

52. ...The notice quotes Clause 4.18, which includes covenants not to assign, not to sublet, not to part with possession, and not to share possession, and then goes on to allege the breach complained of, which is assigning, subletting or parting with possession. On any rational approach, it seems to me that a reasonable recipient of the notice would have understood that sharing of possession was not being complained of. Although included in the clause of the lease which was quoted, it was excluded from the list of breaches complained of. To put the point another way, Clause 4.18 of the lease quite clearly distinguishes between parting with possession and sharing possession, and the relevant breach of covenant alleged in the notice was parting with possession, and no mention was made of sharing possession. ...

54. ...[T]he notice has to comply with the requirements of s 146(1) of the 1925 Act, and if, as appears pretty plainly to be the case, it does not specify the right breach, then nothing ... can save it.

 Alert

55. ...[I]f, on its true construction, the s 146 notice did not specify sharing possession as a breach complained of, it can be said with considerable force that it neither informed the recipient of the breach complained of, nor indicated to him whether, and if so how, he must remedy any breach. ...

64. ...[I]t seems to me that the proper approach to the question of whether or not a breach is capable of remedy should be practical rather than technical. ...

65. In principle, I would have thought that the great majority of breaches of covenant should be capable of remedy, in the same way as repairing or most user covenant breaches. Even where stopping, or putting right, the breach may leave the lessors out of pocket for some reason, it does not seem to me that there is any problem in concluding that the breach is remediable. ...

66. I consider that it would follow, as a matter of both principle and practicality, that breaches of covenants involving parting with or sharing possession should be capable of remedy. ...

67. So far as the authorities are concerned, it appears to me that ... there are two types of breach of covenant which are as a matter of principle incapable of remedy. The first is a covenant against subletting: that is the effect of the reasoning of this court in Scala House. ...In terms of principle ... this is, I think, based on the proposition that one cannot, as it were, uncreate an underlease. It therefore appears to me that it should very probably follow that the general assumption that an unlawful assignment also constitutes an irremediable breach is correct. ...

 **Link**
See *Scala House & District Property Co Limited v Forbes and others*

68. The other type of breach of covenant which is incapable of remedy is a breach involving illegal or immoral use: see *Rugby School (Governors) v Tannahill* [1935] 1 KB 87, [1934]... . This has been justified on the basis of illegal or immoral user fixing the premises with some sort of irremovable "stigma", which results in the breach being incapable of remedy. Especially in the light of the provision for damages in s 146, it is not entirely easy to justify this, particularly as it does not appear to apply where the lessee himself does not know of the illegal or immoral user, see *Glass v Kencakes* [1966] 1 QB 611... . However, in terms of policy, there is force in the view that a lessee, who has used premises for an illegal or immoral purpose, should not be able to avoid the risk of forfeiture simply by ceasing that use on being given notice of it, particularly as relief from forfeiture would still be available. ...

...

73. In these circumstances, it appears to me that ... a breach of covenant against parting with possession or sharing possession, falling short of creating or transferring of legal interest, are breaches of covenant which are capable of remedy within the meaning of s 146. ...

 Alert

88. It follows that my conclusions are:

    i)   Clause 4.18.1 of the lease precludes the lessee parting with, or sharing, possession ... ;

    ii)   In this case, the Judge was entitled to conclude that the lessee had shared possession with, and had not parted with possession to, the company;

    iii) The s 146 notice did not allege that the lessee was sharing, as opposed to parting with, possession, and therefore was ineffective to support the lessors' re-entry;

    iv)   The breach of the covenant against sharing possession was capable of remedy; ...

89. Mr Akici's appeal must therefore be allowed, in the light of my conclusions in sub-paragraphs 88(ii) and (iii) above. It may appear to a neutral observer that Mr Akici has had a lucky escape from a difficult situation which was, to a significant extent, of his own making.

The Court of Appeal unanimously allowed the appeal.

Although the case focuses on the subtleties of the alienation covenant in question and the precise breach committed by the tenant, the decision is helpful in clarifying the need for a correctly worded s 146 notice, and the current state of the law relating to the breaches of covenant which are considered to be capable of remedy.

The final case to examine in relation to termination by forfeiture is the following House of Lords case which focuses on the granting of relief to a tenant from forfeiture where the forfeiture is for breach of a covenant other than a covenant to pay rent.

Billson and others v Residential Apartments Limited [1992] 1 AC 494

Panel: Lord Keith of Kinkel, Lord Templeman, Lord Oliver of Aylmerton, Lord Goff of Chieveley and Lord Jauncey of Tullichettle

Statute: LPA 1925 s 146

Facts: A landlord granted a lease of a property in London to a tenant which contained a covenant by the tenant not to carry out alterations to the property without the prior written consent of the landlord. The landlord reserved a right to forfeit the lease in case of breach of covenant. The freehold reversion was transferred to the claimants and the lease was assigned to the defendants. The defendant tenants carried out major alterations to the property without obtaining consent from the claimants. The claimants served a s 146 notice requiring the defendants to remedy the breach of covenant, but the defendants continued their building works. Two weeks later, the claimants peaceably re-entered the property when it was vacant at 6am, changed the locks and fixed a notice to the property stating that the lease had been forfeited. On the same day, the defendants' builders broke into the property and re-took possession. The claimants brought a claim for possession of the property as the defendants had failed to comply with the s 146 notice and remedy the breach within a reasonable period. The defendants counterclaimed for relief against forfeiture under s 146(2). The judge at first instance held that he could not grant relief from forfeiture as the landlord had already taken possession of the property, so ordered the defendants to deliver up the property. This decision was upheld by the Court of Appeal. The defendants appealed to the House of Lords.

LORD TEMPLEMAN

...By the common law, when a tenant commits a breach of covenant and the lease contains a proviso for forfeiture, the landlord at his option may either waive the breach or determine the lease. In order to exercise his option to determine the lease the landlord must either re-enter the premises in conformity with the proviso or must issue and serve a writ claiming possession. The bringing of an action to recover possession is equivalent to an entry for the forfeiture. ...

Section 146(1) prevents the landlord from enforcing a right of re-entry or forfeiture by action or otherwise so that the landlord cannot determine the lease by issuing and serving a writ or by re-entering the premises until the tenant has failed within a reasonable time to remedy the breach and make reasonable compensation. Section 146(2) enables the tenant to apply to the court for relief where the landlord "is proceeding, by action or otherwise" to enforce his right of re-entry or forfeiture. If the landlord "is proceeding" to determine the lease by issuing and serving a writ, the tenant may apply for relief after the writ has been served. If the landlord "is proceeding" to determine the lease by re-entering into possession, the tenant may apply for relief after the landlord has re-entered. ...

The tenant may apply for relief where the landlord is "proceeding, by action or otherwise" to enforce his rights. The tenant may apply for relief where the landlord is "proceeding" by action and also where the landlord is proceeding "otherwise" than by action. This can only mean that the tenant may apply for relief where the landlord is proceeding to forfeit by re-entry after the expiry of a section 146 notice. ...

Parliament cannot have intended that if the landlord employs the civilised method of determining the lease by issuing and serving a writ, then the tenant will be entitled to apply for relief, but if the landlord employs the dubious and dangerous method of determining the lease by re-entering the premises, then the tenant will be debarred from applying for relief.

Alert

The right conferred by section 146(2) on a tenant to apply for relief against forfeiture may without violence to the language, be construed as a right to apply "where a lessor *proceeds*, by action or otherwise" to enforce a right of re-entry. So construed, section 146(2) enables the tenant to apply for relief whenever and however the landlord claims that the lease has been determined for breach of covenant. I have no doubt that this was the object and intention and is the effect of section 146.

...I accept that it is now settled law that a tenant cannot apply for relief after the landlord has recovered judgment for possession and has re-entered in reliance on that judgment. But I do not accept that any court has deprived or is entitled to deprive a tenant of any right to apply for relief if the landlord proceeds to forfeit otherwise than by an action instituted for that purpose. ...

The results of section 146 and the authorities are as follows. A tenant may apply for appropriate declarations and for relief from forfeiture under section 146(2) after the issue of a section 146 notice but he is not prejudiced if he does not do so. A tenant cannot apply for relief after a landlord has forfeited a lease by issuing and serving a writ, has recovered judgment and has entered into possession pursuant to that judgment. If the judgment is set aside or successfully appealed the tenant will be able to apply for relief in the landlord's action but the court in deciding whether to grant relief will take into account any consequences of the original order and repossession and the delay of the tenant. A tenant may apply for relief after a landlord has forfeited by re-entry without first obtaining a court order for that purpose but the court in deciding whether to grant relief will take into account all the circumstances, including delay, on the part of the tenant. Any past judicial observations which might suggest that a tenant is debarred from applying for relief after the landlord has re-entered without first obtaining a court order for that purpose are not to be so construed.

Alert

I would therefore allow the appeal and set aside the orders of the trial judge and the Court of Appeal. ...

The House of Lords unanimously allowed the defendant's appeal.

Lord Templeman has set out clearly the circumstances in which the tenant may apply for relief after a s 146 notice has been served on him, depending on whether the landlord has used court proceedings or peaceable re-entry. The judicial dislike of peaceable re-entry as a method of forfeiture is apparent from Lord Templeman's judgment. If a landlord is going to forfeit a lease, following the issue of a s146 notice, using this method rather than obtaining a court order, the tenant may still apply for relief within a reasonable time after the landlord's peaceable re-entry. This is in contrast to the finality of an executed court order, where no further relief application is available.

11.2 Extending Business Tenancies

If a lease comes to an end because the term has naturally expired, there are opportunities for a tenant to remain in the property and request a new lease from the landlord. This is provided for in different statutes depending on whether the tenant is in occupation of residential or commercial premises. The procedure for obtaining a statutory renewal of a business tenancy is set out in the Landlord and Tenant Act 1954 (LTA 1954) and the main issues to be resolved are the meanings of 'occupation' and 'business' as s 23(1) provides that it is only tenants who occupy premises for the purpose of a business who may receive the protection of the LTA 1954.

When a tenant wishes to renew a business tenancy at the end of the term of the lease, this will only be possible if the tenant occupies the premises for the purpose of a business in accordance with the LTA 1954. The meaning of 'occupation' is examined in the following case.

Graysim Holdings Limited v P. & O. Property Holdings Limited [1996] AC 329

Panel: Lord Mackay of Clashfern LC, Lord Goff of Chieveley, Lord Jauncey of Tullichettle, Lord Lloyd of Berwick and Lord Nicholls of Birkenhead

Statute: Landlord and Tenant Act 1954 ss 23(1), 25 and 30(1)

Facts: The landlord (the defendant) granted a lease of a market hall, known as Wallasey Market, to the tenant (the claimant, a market operator). The tenant built 35 stalls in the market hall (which each had a blind and a padlock for security) and sub-leased each stall to stallholders, who paid rent on a weekly basis. The tenant provided facilities and services to its sub-tenants. In the last twelve months of the term of the headlease, the landlord served a section 25 notice on the tenant to terminate the headlease, which stated that any application to the court for a new tenancy would be opposed by the landlord under the LTA 1954 s 30(1). The tenant served a counter-notice (as was required by the statute at that time) as it did not want to give up possession of the market hall and so sought a new lease. The judge at first instance held that the tenant did not occupy the market hall for the purposes of its business within the LTA 1954 s 23(1) and was therefore not entitled to a new lease. The tenant appealed to the Court of Appeal which allowed the appeal. The landlord appealed to the House of Lords.

LORD NICHOLLS OF BIRKENHEAD

My Lords, this case concerns the statutory protection afforded to business tenants by Part II of the Landlord and Tenant Act 1954. The primary object of this legislation was to enable tenants occupying property for business purposes to obtain new tenancies. The basic statutory structure is straightforward. Part II of the Act applies to any tenancy where the demised property is, or includes, premises "which are occupied by the tenant and are so occupied for the purposes of a business carried on by him:" section 23(1). ...

The property comprised in the new tenancy, however, will not necessarily include all the property comprised in the business tenancy. The tenant is entitled only to a new tenancy of "the holding:" section 32(1). "The holding" means, in short, all the property comprised in the business tenancy except any part not "occupied" by the tenant or his employees: section 23(3). ...

[T]he distinction between the holding and the property comprised in a business tenancy lies at the heart of this case. Although a business tenancy may include property not occupied by the tenant, property not occupied by him or his employees is excluded from the holding and, accordingly, it is not property in respect of which the tenant is entitled to obtain a new tenancy or to recover compensation.

...[F]irst I must consider a feature central to the statutory structure: the requirement that the property must be "occupied" by the tenant. ...

In Part II of the Act of 1954 "occupied" and "occupied for the purposes of a business carried on by him" are expressions employed as the means of identifying whether a tenancy is a business tenancy and whether the property is part of the holding and qualifies for inclusion in the grant of a new tenancy. In this context "occupied" points to some business activity by the tenant on the property in question. The Act seeks to protect the tenant in his continuing use of the property for the purposes of that activity. Thus the word carries a connotation of some physical use of the property by the tenant for the purposes of his business. ...

A further element is introduced into the problem when the business of one person consists of permitting others to use his property for their business purposes... . In some circumstances the landowner will remain in occupation of the whole... . At the other extreme are cases where the landowner permits another to enter and carry on his business there to the exclusion of the landowner. ...

When a landowner permits another to use his property for business purposes, the question whether the landowner is sufficiently excluded, and the other is sufficiently present, for the latter to be regarded as the occupier in place of the former is a question of degree. It is, moreover, a question of fact in the sense that the answer depends upon the facts of the particular case. ...The types of property, and the possible uses of property, vary so widely that there can be no hard and fast rules. The degree of presence and exclusion required to constitute occupation, and the acts needed to evince presence and exclusion, must always depend upon the nature of the premises,

 Alert

the use to which they are being put, and the rights enjoyed or exercised by the persons in question. ...

The question is whether it is possible for a landlord and tenant both to occupy the same property for the purposes of Part II at the same time. ...

I am unable to accept that a tenant of a business tenancy can sublet part of the property to a business subtenant on terms which would have the legal result that thereafter the sublet property would form the holding of the subtenant's business tenancy and yet, at the same time, remain part of the holding of the tenant's business tenancy. ...

Assume [a] tenant carries on a business of letting office accommodation. He acquires the tenancy of a building, sublets all the space usable as offices and retains only the common parts and the necessary boiler rooms and other service accommodation. The tenant remains in occupation of these retained parts of the building, for the purposes of his office letting business.

This situation was addressed by the Court of Appeal in *Bagettes Ltd. v. G.P. Estates Ltd.* [1956] Ch. 290. There the sublettings were of unfurnished residential flats, but the same principle is applicable to sublettings for business purposes. The court held that in such a case the tenancy is not a business tenancy and, accordingly, the tenant is not entitled to a new tenancy of the whole building or of the retained parts.

The reasoning can be summarised as follows. The tenant is not in occupation of the sublet flats, so he is not entitled to a new tenancy of the flats. ...As to the retained parts of the building, the tenant remains in occupation of these. But a new tenancy of the retained parts could not be used by the tenant to carry on a business of managing and servicing the sublet accommodation because the tenant will have ceased to be the landlord of the subtenants. ...Once the flats are gone, the business for the purpose of which the tenant occupied the retained parts will be gone also. ...

The fundamental difficulty confronting Graysim can be stated shortly. It is common ground that the traders' tenancies were business tenancies. ...For the reason given earlier, I do not see how, consistently with this, the units can also be occupied by Graysim for the purposes of its business. ...

If it is correct that at the termination of its tenancy Graysim was not in occupation of the units, the conclusion which must follow inescapably is that, although Graysim occupied the retained parts, there was no holding in respect of which Graysim could claim a new tenancy or compensation. That must follow because, once the units are excluded from its tenancy, Graysim can no longer carry on its business of operating Wallasey Market.

...The conclusion follows ineluctably from the facts (1) that the business conducted by Graysim on the retained parts consisted of making accommodation and facilities available to the traders in return for rents for use of the units and (2) that when the reversion to the units vested in P. & O., Graysim would no longer receive any rents. ...In order to carry on its business of running Wallasey Market, Graysim needed both the reversion to the traders' tenancies and the retained parts of the hall. The latter, by themselves, were useless to Graysim. Once the reversions went, their business in this market had gone. ...

Part II of the Act of 1954 ... looks through to the occupying tenants, here the traders, and affords them statutory protection, not their landlord. Intermediate landlords, not themselves in occupation, are not within the class of persons the Act was seeking to protect.

I would allow this appeal. ...

The House of Lords unanimously allowed the landlord's appeal.

Lord Templeman states clearly that it is a question of fact whether a tenant is in occupation of the premises for the purposes of the LTA 1954; however, it is apparent that an intermediate landlord cannot generally expect the same protection from the LTA 1954 as his occupying tenant, as the Act is intended to protect whoever is in occupation of the premises at the relevant time.

A tenant also needs to occupy 'business premises' to receive the protection of the LTA 1954. The meaning of 'business premises' is the subject of the final case in this chapter.

Wright v Mortimer [1996] 28 HLR 719

Panel: Beldam and Waite LJJ

Statute: Landlord and Tenant Act 1954 ss 23(1) and 25

Facts: Mr Wright was the tenant of a ground floor and basement maisonette at 48 Northumberland Place, London. Eighteen years after the lease was granted, Mr Mortimer became the freehold owner of the property and Mr Wright's landlord. A year later, the landlord served a section 25 notice on the tenant to bring the lease to an end, stating that Mr Wright was occupying the property for the purposes of his profession. Mr Wright was an art historian who carried out some of his work at the flat (mainly writing), but the majority of his work, including organising exhibitions, advising private clients and lecturing, took place elsewhere. At trial, the issue arose as to whether Mr Wright's lease was a business tenancy, regulated by LTA 1954, or a residential tenancy. The judge at first instance held that Mr Wright was a tenant under the Rent Act 1977 and was therefore subject to the rules relating to residential tenancies not business tenancies. Mr Mortimer appealed to the Court of Appeal.

LORD JUSTICE BELDAM

...The judge [at first instance] found that Mr Wright's work consisted broadly of four categories. First, the organisation of exhibitions. Secondly, private client work. Thirdly, writing. Finally, lecturing. ...[T]his work, generally speaking, was mostly done away from 48 Northumberland Place... . Virtually all the administrative arrangements were carried out away from the flat ... but some correspondence might go to 48 Northumberland Place. ...

The second category was described as private client work ... and none of this took place at 48 Northumberland Place. ...

The third category of work, writing, took place at 48 Northumberland Place. The writing was not wholly carried out there ... but he thought that about 30 per cent of his work as a writer took place at Northumberland Place. ...

The fourth category of work was lecturing. Mr Wright gives about three or four lectures a year. They were given away from the flat... .

Having considered the four types of activity carried on by Mr Wright ... he then turned to the layout of No 48. He found that there was no office in No 48; there was no photo-copier or fax machine. ...The front space was entirely devoted as a sitting room and the rear was used as a study. ...

The judge ... reminded himself of the guidance given as to the correct test to apply in determining whether the property comprised in the tenancy is, or includes, premises which are occupied by the tenant for the purpose of a business carried on by him ... set out in the judgment of this Court in *Cheryl Investments v. Saldanha* [1978] 1 W.L.R. 1329. ...

In summary he said the question he had to ask himself was, were the activities on the premises more than merely incidental to the residential occupation... .

 Alert

Another way of posing the same question was whether the business activity was part of the reason or purpose, aim or object, of the tenant in occupying the premises. ...

First, he said that he had taken into account the way in which Mr Wright had become attached to this flat ... and that his aim and object ... was, and always remained, to use the flat as his residence or home. ...

The judge went on to consider whether Mr Wright's occupation as a writer ... was inconsistent with his use of the flat as a residence. ...

He then considered the question of degree. He said that he thought it would have been the reaction of any informed person with knowledge of Mr Wright's way of life that he was not carrying on a business at the flat. ...

Finally, at page 17 of his very careful judgment, the judge said:

"Having considered all the facts in detail I have concluded that business activities were never part of Mr Wright's aim and object in occupying the flat. The business activities were incidental to Mr Wright's purpose which was throughout and still remains that of occupying the flat as his home." ...

Viewed overall, I can detect no error in the judge's approach to the case. ...

Accordingly I would refuse leave.

The Court of Appeal unanimously dismissed the appeal, holding that Mr Wright was a residential tenant, whose tenancy would not be protected by the LTA 1954.

The definition of business has been interpreted very widely in case law, but where the property is used partly for business and partly for residential use, the test to apply is whether the business use is significant, or, as held in this case, incidental to the use of the property as a residential home.

Further Reading

MacKenzie & Phillips, *Textbook on Land Law*, (15th Edition), Chapter 10

Megarry & Wade, *The Law of Real Property*, (8th Edition), pp 810-848, 1006-1019

Gray & Gray, *Elements of Land Law*, (5th Edition), pp 469-510, 587-589

Cheshire and Burn, *Modern Law of Real Property*, (17th Edition), pp 273-293, 329, 377-385

Part IV

Co-ownership of Land
Under a Trust

12

Legal Principles Governing Trusts of Land

Topic List

1   Severance of a Beneficial Joint Tenancy
2   Severance by Notice in Writing under the LPA s 36(2)
3   Severance by 'Other Acts or Things'
4   Disputes Relating to Co-owned Property

Introduction

Whenever land is held by more than one person, a statutory trust is automatically imposed on the co-owners. The Law of Property Act 1925 (LPA 1925) imposed a 'trust for sale' thereby giving the trustees a duty to sell, but with the power to postpone sale. The Trusts of Land and Appointment of Trustees Act 1996 (TLATA) brought land ownership into line with modern life and changed the trust for sale into a trust of land, recognising that property ownership now involves a desire to retain land rather than viewing it as a commodity to be traded. The trust of land has the effect of separating the legal and equitable (beneficial) titles and while these may be owned by the same people, for example, when husband and wife own their home jointly at law and in equity, this frequently is not the case. It is important to know on what basis co-owners hold the equitable title as this is where the value lies. While the legal owners must hold as joint tenants for ease of dealing with buyers and mortgagees, the equitable owners may hold as joint tenants or tenants in common as best suits them. There are strict rules for assessing whether a joint tenancy or a tenancy in common exists, and for changing a joint tenancy into a tenancy in common by the process known as 'severance'.

12.1 Severance of a Beneficial Joint Tenancy

Although co-owners may initially hold the beneficial title as joint tenants, that situation may change. Any co-owner can 'sever' his or her beneficial joint tenancy by any one of a variety of methods. After severance he or she will hold a distinct share as a tenant in common. The size of that share will be an equal share depending on the number of equitable joint tenants, for example it will be a half share if there are two or a third share if there are three, and so on. The size of that person's initial contribution to the price is irrelevant, as is the motive or reason for severing.

Goodman v Gallant [1986] Fam 106

Panel: Slade and Purchas LJJ and Sir Roualeyn Cumming-Bruce

Facts: Mr Goodman bought a house in 1960 in his sole name. The conveyance contained an express declaration that he held the property for himself and his wife as beneficial joint tenants. In 1971 Mr Goodman left, and Mrs Goodman began to live with Mr Gallant. Together, they bought Mr Goodman's interest, expressly declaring that they held the legal estate upon trusts for themselves as beneficial joint tenants. When Mr Gallant left her, Mrs Goodman severed the joint tenancy, and claimed a 75 per cent interest in the house.

LORD JUSTICE SLADE

In a case where the legal estate in property is conveyed to two or more persons as joint tenants, but neither the conveyance nor any other written document contains any express declaration of trust concerning the beneficial interests in the property (as would be required for an express declaration of this nature by virtue of section 53(1)(b) of the

Law of Property Act 1925), the way is open for persons claiming a beneficial interest in it or its proceeds of sale to rely on the doctrine of "resulting, implied or constructive trusts"... . If, however, the relevant conveyance contains an express declaration of trust which comprehensively declares the beneficial interests in the property or its proceeds of sale, there is no room for the application of the doctrine of resulting implied or constructive trusts unless and until the conveyance is set aside or rectified; until that event the declaration contained in the document speaks for itself.

Citing *Wilson v Wilson* [1963] 1 WLR 601 his Lordship said that the express declaration of joint tenancy was conclusive. He emphasised that where there are more than two beneficial joint tenants, an equal share would still result on severance:

...Quite apart from authority, it seems to us that it is of the very nature of a joint tenancy that, upon a severance, each takes an equal aliquot share according to the number of joint tenants. *Halsbury's Laws of England*, 4th ed., vol. 39 (1982), p 349, para. 529, which is headed "Nature of joint tenants' interests begins with the words:

"Each joint tenant has an identical interest in the whole land and every part of it. The title of each arises by the same act. The interest of each is the same in extent, nature and duration." Note 2 to this passage begins:

"Until severance, each has the whole, but upon severance each has an aliquot part (a half or less) according to the number of joint tenants..."

The note then points out that severance can only now take effect in respect of the beneficial interests.

Despite claiming a 75 per cent share, Mrs Goodman was awarded 50 per cent, which was a proportionate share, bearing in mind that there were two beneficial joint tenants before severance.

12.2 Severance by Notice in Writing under s36(2) LPA 1925

One way of severing a beneficial joint tenancy is by notice in writing pursuant to the LPA s 36(2). There is no specific form, but the 'writing' must show an immediate and irrevocable intention to sever.

In re Draper's Conveyance [1969] 1 Ch 486

Panel: Plowman J

Statute: Law of Property Act 1925 s 36(2)

Facts: In 1951 Mr and Mrs Porter bought a house from Mr Draper as beneficial joint tenants. In 1965 Mrs Porter issued divorce proceedings in the course of which she applied to the court for an order under the Married Women's Property Act 1882 s 17 that the house be sold and the proceeds split equally. The order was made, but Mr Porter died intestate before the house was sold. Mrs Porter asked the court for a declaration as to whether she held the property for herself absolutely by survivorship or whether the joint tenancy had been severed during Mr Porter's lifetime under s 36(2). The judge held that the summons under s 17 amounted to notice in writing which severed the joint tenancy. Mrs Porter therefore held the property on trust for herself and Mr Porter's estate in equal shares.

MR JUSTICE PLOWMAN

Mr. Cooke [acting for the beneficiaries of Mr Porter's estate]… submits that the summons to which I have already referred, although not signed, amounted to a notice in writing on the part of the wife that she desired to sever the joint tenancy in equity. I say "although not signed by the wife or by anybody on her behalf" because there is no requirement in the subsection of a signature.

Dealing with the matter there, and ignoring for a moment certain matters which were submitted by Mr. McCulloch [on behalf of Mrs Porter], it seems to me that Mr. Cooke's submissions are right whether they are based on the new provision in section 36(2) of the Law of Property Act, 1925, or whether they are based on the old law which applied to severing a joint tenancy in the case of a personal estate. It seems to me that that summons, coupled with the affidavit in support of it, clearly evinced an intention on the part of the wife that she wished the property to be sold and the proceeds distributed, a half to her and a half to the husband, and if that is right then it seems to me that that is wholly inconsistent with the notion that a beneficial joint tenancy in that property is to continue, and therefore, apart from these objections to which I will refer in a moment, I feel little doubt that *in one way or the other* [italics added] this joint tenancy was severed in equity before the end of February, 1966, as a result of the summons which was served on the husband and as a result of what the wife stated in her affidavit in support of the summons.

Link

See also *Harris v Goddard* and *Nielsen-Jones v Fedden* below

It is unclear exactly on what basis the judge found that the joint tenancy had been severed. The judge did not make it clear whether it was the summons or the affidavit in support which constituted 'notice in writing'; or whether the commencement of proceedings amounted to a 'unilateral act operating on a share'.

Harris v Goddard [1983] 1 WLR 1203

Panel: Lawton, Kerr and Dillon LJJ

Statute: Law of Property Act 1925 s 36(2)

Facts: Mr and Mrs Harris bought a property in 1978 as joint tenants at law and in equity. In 1979 Mrs Harris issued divorce proceedings which included a request "that such order may be made by way of transfer of property and/or settlement of property and/or variation of the settlement in respect of the former matrimonial home…and otherwise as may be just." Just before the divorce hearing, Mr Harris was seriously injured in a car accident and he died in 1981. His executors were his children from his first marriage. They sought a declaration that the beneficial joint tenancy had been severed by notice in writing under s 36(2) and that they took their father's half share.

The court distinguished *In re Draper's Conveyance* and found that the joint tenancy had not been severed.

LORD JUSTICE LAWTON

 Alert

When a notice in writing of a desire to sever is served pursuant to section 36 (2) it takes effect forthwith. It follows that a desire to sever must evince an intention to bring about the wanted result immediately. A notice in writing which expresses a desire to bring about the wanted result at some time in the future is not, in my judgment, a notice in writing within section 36 (2). Further the notice must be one which shows an intent to bring about the consequences set out in section 36 (2), namely, that the net proceeds of the statutory trust for sale "shall be held upon the trusts which would have been requisite for giving effect to the beneficial interests if there had been an actual severance."

...Paragraph 3 of the prayer to the petition does no more than invite the court to consider at some future time whether to exercise its jurisdiction under section 24 of the [Matrimonial Causes] Act of 1973, and if it does, to do so in one or more of three different ways. Orders under section 24 (1) (a) and (b) could bring co-ownership to an end by ways other than by severance. It follows, in my judgment, that paragraph 3 of the prayer of the petition did not operate as a notice in writing to sever the joint tenancy in equity. This tenancy had not been severed when Mr. Harris died with the consequence that Mrs. Harris is entitled to the whole of the fund held by the first and second defendants as trustees. I wish to stress that all I am saying is that paragraph 3 in the petition under consideration in this case did not operate as a notice of severance. Perhaps this case should be a cautionary tale for those who draft divorce petitions when the spouses hold property as joint tenants in equity. The decision of Plowman J. in *In re Draper's Conveyance* [1969] 1 Ch 486 is an example of how starting legal proceedings can sever a joint tenancy. ...

 Alert

Plowman J. adjudged that the summons and the affidavit together effected a severance during the lifetime of the husband. I agree that it did; but it is not clear from the judgment whether the judge regarded the summons or the affidavit or both as notices in writing or whether the service of the summons and the filing of the affidavit were acts which were effectual to sever the joint tenancy. I do not share the doubts about the correctness of this judgment on this point which Walton J. expressed in *Nielsen-Jones v Fedden* [1975] Ch 222.

12.2.1 Service of notice in writing

In addition to showing the requisite intention, the notice must, according to the LPA 1925 be properly 'given' to, or served on, all other joint tenants. If it is posted, the rules in the LPA 1925 ss 196(3) and (4) apply.

In re 88 Berkeley Road [1971] Ch 648

Panel: Plowman J

Statute: Law of Property Act 1925 s 36(2) and s 196(4)

Facts: Miss Elridge and Miss Goodwin owned 88 Berkeley Road as beneficial joint tenants. Miss Goodwin was a friend of Miss Elridge's mother. All three had lived together, and Miss Elridge and Miss Goodwin continued to do so after the mother's death. When Miss Elridge announced she was shortly to be married, Miss Goodwin, who was a generation older and likely to die first, decided to sever the beneficial joint tenancy. Miss Goodwin's solicitors sent a notice of severance by recorded delivery to the property. When it was delivered, Miss Elridge had gone to work and Miss Goodwin signed for the letter. Miss Elridge, or Mrs Rickwood as she became, knew nothing about the notice until she found a draft of it amongst Miss Goodwin's papers after her death. Mrs Rickwood applied for a declaration that the notice was of no effect and that she was entitled to the whole property by survivorship. The court examined the rules on what constitutes effective service of a notice under s 36(2).

MR JUSTICE PLOWMAN

I must come now to certain questions of law that have been argued. It is submitted on behalf of the defendants [the executor and residuary legatee of Miss Goodwin's estate] that even if the plaintiff did not actually receive the notice of severance, nevertheless she must conclusively be presumed to have done so...

[The judge then quoted s 36(2) and s 196(4) in full.]

...In my view, the words "... if that letter is not returned through the post office undelivered" refer to the ordinary case of the Post Office being unable to effect delivery at the address on the letter for some reason or other, such as that the addressee has gone away or the house is shut or empty. It does not, in my judgment, apply to a case like the present where the letter has in fact been delivered by the postman at the address to which it was sent.

Alert

The third submission which Mr. Bramall [for the plaintiff] made was to this effect, that where a section in an Act of Parliament is potentially creating an unjust situation, as would be the case here if the notice is to be taken as having been received by the plaintiff although she never received it, then the Act ought to be construed strictly, and that that involves strict proof that the relevant document - the letter containing the notice of severance, in this case - was in fact served, and Mr. Bramall pointed out that Mr. Bender, who was an assistant solicitor in the firm of solicitors who were Miss Goodwin's solicitors at this time and who was responsible for dealing with this matter, could not actually prove putting the notice of severance in the envelope with the covering letter before it was sent. In my judgment, the onus of proof on the defendants here is no higher than proof that, on the balance of probabilities, that was done; and I feel no difficulty in reaching the conclusion that, on the balance of probabilities, it was in fact done.

For those reasons, I cannot accept Mr. Bramall's submissions on section 196 (4).

... In those circumstances, and with some regret having regard to my findings of fact, I feel bound to conclude that the notice of severance, even though never received by the plaintiff, was in fact sufficiently served for the purposes of section 36 (2) of the Law of

Property Act 1925 with the consequence that the joint tenancy was severed during the lifetime of Miss Goodwin.

Kinch v Bullard [1999] 1 WLR 423

Panel: Neuberger J

Statute: Law of Property Act 1925 ss 36(2) and 196(3)

Facts: Mr and Mrs Johnson were beneficial joint tenants of their home, but their relationship had deteriorated. Mrs Johnson was terminally ill and, to prevent her interest in the property passing by survivorship to her husband on her death, she wanted to sever the joint tenancy in equity. The notice was sent by her solicitors by ordinary post on 3rd August 1995. The husband suffered a serious heart attack on 5th August and was in hospital when the letter arrived. Mrs Johnson had subsequently changed her mind about severance, perhaps because it was now likely that her husband would die before her, and therefore destroyed the letter when it was delivered. Mr Johnson died before his wife. The plaintiffs were his executors and claimed that they were entitled to a half share in the property as the notice of severance had been validly served in accordance with the statutory requirements.

MR JUSTICE NEUBERGER

In light of the provisions of section 36(2) of the Act of 1925, the question as to whether or not the joint tenancy was severed depends on whether Mrs. Johnson "gave" the notice to Mr. Johnson. As a matter of ordinary language, at least on the assumptions I am currently making, the notice was not "given" to Mr. Johnson, because he never received it. In order to justify the contention that the notice was in fact given to Mr. Johnson, the plaintiffs rely on section 196 of the Act of 1925. ...

The judge then went on to cite sections 196(3) and (4) in full. He dismissed the defendants' argument that s 196(3) and (4) must be read together: service does not have to be by registered post:

As a matter of ordinary language, section 196(3) provides that service of a notice "at the last-known place of abode or business" of the addressee is good service, and there is no suggestion that it matters how that service is effected, i.e. whether it is by the giver of the notice, his agent, courier service, ordinary post, recorded delivery or registered post, or some other method. Provided that it can be established that, irrespective of the identity of the person who delivered the notice to a particular address, it was delivered to that address, then the notice has been validly served at that address, provided that it is the addressee's last-known abode or place of business.

 Alert

Section 196(4) is a separate and additional provision. It provides, in the first place, that if a notice is served by registered post or recorded delivery, then, even if it can be shown not actually to have been delivered at the relevant premises, the notice will none the less be deemed to have been served at the premises, unless returned undelivered.

He said that if s 196(3) had been complied with it was irrelevant that Mr Johnson had not seen the notice:

It appears to me that the natural meaning of section 196(3) is that, if a notice can be shown to have been left at the last-known abode or place of business of the addressee, then that constitutes good service, even if the addressee does not actually receive it. Although frequently cited as conclusive authority on the point, there is room for argument that In re 88, Berkeley Road, N.W. 9 [1971] Ch. 648 does not actually establish this proposition. Although the passage in the judgment of Plowman J. at pp. 652– 653 appears to be in point, it was actually concerned with section 196(4), because the notice in that case was served by recorded delivery (see p. 651b) and therefore the case is at least arguably distinguishable. ... It is hard to see why the reasoning of Plowman J. should not apply to section 196(3) as much as to section 196(4).

He then dealt with the fact that Mrs Johnson had changed her mind by the time the notice was served, and whether it was possible to revoke a notice on that basis:

... The function of the relevant part of section 36(2) is to instruct any joint tenant who desires to sever the joint tenancy how to do it: he is to give the appropriate notice (or do such other things as are prescribed by the section). Clear words would be required, in my judgment, before a provision such as section 36(2) could be construed as requiring the court to inquire into the state of mind of the sender of the notice. Once the sender has served the requisite notice, the deed is done and cannot be undone. ...

I reach this conclusion based on the proper construction of section 36(2). However, it appears to me that it is also correct as a matter of policy. If it were possible for a notice of severance or any other notice to be ineffective because, between the sender putting it in the post and the addressee receiving it, the sender changed his mind, it would be inconvenient and potentially unfair. The addressee would not be able to rely confidently upon a notice after it had been received, because he might subsequently be faced with the argument that the sender had changed his mind after sending it and before its receipt. ... I am inclined to think that the position would be different if, before the notice was "given," the sender had informed the addressee that he wished to revoke it. In such a case, it appears to me that the notice would have been withdrawn before it had been "given".

He concluded that the notice had been validly served and explained why the rules should be strictly applied:

So far as convenience is concerned, I consider that, if section 196(3) is satisfied once it is shown that the relevant document was bona fide delivered to the last-known place of abode or business of the addressee, then, although it might lead to an unfair result in an exceptional case, the law is at least simple and clear. On the other hand, if the court starts implying exceptions into the clear and simple statutory procedure, confusion and uncertainty could result. ...

[Section 196] could not be relied on by the sender of a notice as an engine of fraud. The very purpose of serving a notice is to convey information, with legal consequences, on the addressee: it cannot be right that the sender of a notice can take positive steps to ensure that the notice does not come to the attention of the addressee, after it has

 Link
to the Percival article in the Further Reading section

been statutorily deemed to have been served, and then fall back on the statute to allege that service has none the less been effected. ...

12.3 Severance by 'Other Acts or Things'

Before 1926 a joint tenancy in personal property (including leaseholds) could be severed in several ways, set out in *Williams v Hensman* (1861) 1 J&H 546. The LPA 1925 s 36(2) added the notice in writing as a new method and confirmed that 'other acts or things as would in the case of personal estate have been effectual to sever the tenancy in equity' were equally applicable to real property, thus continuing the principles of *Williams v Hensman*.

Williams v Hensman (1861) 1 J&H 546

Panel: Sir W Page-Wood V-C

Facts: The case concerned money in the estate of Sarah Creak who had left it on trust for her eight children. Five of them authorised the trustee to invest the fund in a mortgage. In considering whether their interests had been severed so as to create a tenancy in common, the Vice-Chancellor set out the ways in which a joint tenancy in personalty could be severed.

SIR W PAGE-WOOD V-C

A joint-tenancy may be severed in three ways: in the first place, an act of any one of the persons interested operating upon his own share may create a severance as to that share. The right of each joint-tenant is a right by survivorship only in the event of no severance having taken place of the share which is claimed under the *jus accrescendi*. Each one is at liberty to dispose of his own interest in such manner as to sever it from the joint fund— losing, of course, at the same time, his own right of survivorship. Secondly, a joint-tenancy may be severed by mutual agreement. And, in the third place, there may be a severance by any course of dealing sufficient to intimate that the interests of all were mutually treated as constituting a tenancy in common. When the severance depends on an inference of this kind without any express act of severance, it will not suffice to rely on an intention, with respect to the particular share, declared only behind the backs of the other persons interested. You must find in this class of cases a course of dealing by which the shares of all the parties to the contest have been effected... .

12.3.1 Severance by mutual agreement and mutual conduct

Nielsen-Jones v Fedden and Others [1975] Ch 222

Panel: Walton J

Facts: Mr and Mrs Todd were legal and beneficial joint tenants of their home. Mrs Todd and the children moved out, but Mr Todd stayed in the property. They signed a memorandum that Mr Todd would try to sell the house, and use the proceeds to buy somewhere smaller to live in. They each took £200 from the deposit paid by the buyer. No final agreement as to their finances was ever reached. Mr Todd died and Mrs Todd (now Mrs Nielsen-Jones) appointed Mr Fedden as a second trustee to enable the sale to be completed. Mrs Nielsen-Jones argued that she took the property by survivorship and was therefore entitled to the whole of the proceeds of the sale. Mr Fedden and the other defendants, who were the executors of Mr Todd's estate, wanted to know whether the sale proceeds could properly be paid to her in full or whether an appropriate proportion should be paid to Mr Todd's residuary beneficiaries. The judge held that there had been no severance of the joint tenancy. First, the memorandum did not amount to a 'notice in writing' as the intention manifested by the exact wording simply authorised Mr Todd to sell the property on behalf of both parties. Second, they had never reached a mutual agreement. Consideration was then given as to whether the inconclusive negotiations amounted to severance by a mutual course of conduct.

MR JUSTICE WALTON

There remains the third point: is it possible from the correspondence, more particularly from the determination therein manifested by both parties that their respective financial affairs were going to be kept separate, whether or not coupled with the fact that they were both negotiating as to what precise share of the proceeds of sale each should take, and whether or not coupled with the actual distributions out of the deposit paid by the purchaser of the Old Rectory, to say either (i) in accordance with the established authorities, that there was a sufficient course of conduct by Mr. and Mrs. Todd as to lead to the implication of an agreement to sever, and hence a severance? or (ii) to amount to a declaration by one or either of them of their intention to sever, which declaration, submits Mr. Essayan [acting for Mr Todd's estate], is also an established method of severance?

As to (i), I think I can take the matter very shortly. It appears to me that when parties are negotiating to reach an agreement, and never do reach any final agreement, it is quite impossible to say that they have reached any agreement at all. Certainly it is not possible to say that they have reached an agreement to sever merely because they have, in the course of those negotiations, reached an interim agreement for the distribution of comparatively small sums of money. It will be borne in mind that the total amount of the deposit was £1,000 - presumably paid to the vendor's agent, and not to a stakeholder. Had the whole of that £1,000 been distributed equally between Mr. and Mrs. Todd, this would at least have been consistent with an agreement that they should take the whole of the proceeds of sale in equal shares. But a distribution of part of that £1,000 only - I am not certain of the precise figure, but it was certainly neither the whole nor a sum calculated by any reference to the whole thereof that was distributed - appears to me to point away from any such agreement having been reached, rather than to the reaching of any such agreement. At the highest in Mr. Essayan's favour - and I think this distribution forms the high-water mark of his case on this aspect of his argument - it appears to me to be neutral in its implications.

 Link
See also Denning's comments in *Burgess v Rawnsley* [1975] Ch 429

As to (ii), I shall first of all assume in favour of Mr. Essayan that the correspondence does indeed disclose an unequivocal declaration by Mr. Todd to the effect that he wishes to sever the joint tenancy so as to make himself master of a one half share of the net proceeds of sale of the property. The question then is, can such a declaration - a unilateral declaration - ever be effective to sever a beneficial joint tenancy? It appears to me that in principle there is no conceivable ground for saying that it can. So far as I can see, such a mere unilateral declaration does not in any way shatter any one of the essential unities. Moreover, if it did, it would appear that a wholly unconscionable amount of time and trouble has been wasted by conveyancers of old in framing elaborate assignments for the purpose of effecting a severance, when all that was required was a simple declaration.

The judge said that re Draper's Conveyance was wrongly decided. The issue of the application for the property adjustment order was in his view insufficient to be a 'unilateral act' on her share; nor did it amount to 'notice in writing' under s 36(2).

Burgess v Rawnsley [1975] Ch 429

Panel: Lord Denning MR, Browne LJ and Sir John Pennycuick

Facts: Mr Honick and Mrs Rawnsley bought a house, comprising two separate flats, as beneficial joint tenants, each paying half of the purchase price. Mr Honick had thought they would marry but Mrs Rawnsley had no such intention. They never did marry, nor live together. In 1968 Mrs Rawnsley orally agreed to sell her share to Mr Honick for £750, but subsequently changed her mind and wanted £1000. Mr Honick died before anything was resolved. Mr Honick's daughter argued that the beneficial joint tenancy had been severed, and as he had died as a tenant in common, she took his share on his death.

LORD DENNING MR

First, Lord Denning MR said that there was a resulting trust in proportion to their respective contributions as, although was no *common* purpose which had failed, their *individual* purposes had nonetheless failed: his as a matrimonial home; hers to use the upstairs flat as a home for herself. He was not happy with basing his decision thus, so he looked at severance too. It is difficult, however, to see whether he based his decision on 'mutual agreement' or 'mutual conduct'.

The important finding is that there was an agreement that she would sell her share to him for £750. Almost immediately afterwards she went back upon it. Is that conduct sufficient to effect a severance?

Mr. Levy submitted that it was not. He relied on the recent decision of Walton J. in *Nielson-Jones v. Fedden* [1975] Ch. 222, given subsequently to the judgment of the judge here. Walton J. held that no conduct is sufficient to sever a joint tenancy unless it is irrevocable. Mr. Levy said that in the present case the agreement was not in writing. It could not be enforced by specific performance. It was revocable and was in fact revoked by Mrs. Rawnsley when she went back on it. So there was, he submitted, no severance.

Lord Denning MR explained why he thought that *Nielsen-Jones v Fedden* was wrongly decided:

The husband and wife entered upon a course of dealing sufficient to sever the joint tenancy. They entered into negotiations that the property should be sold. Each received £200 out of the deposit paid by the purchaser. That was sufficient. Furthermore there was disclosed in correspondence a declaration by the husband that he wished to sever the joint tenancy: and this was made clear by the wife. That too was sufficient. ...

It remains to apply these principles to the present case. I think there was evidence that Mr. Honick and Mrs. Rawnsley did come to an agreement that he would buy her share for £750. That agreement was not in writing and it was not specifically enforceable. Yet it was sufficient to effect a severance. Even if there was not any firm agreement but only a course of dealing, it clearly evinced an intention by both parties that the property should henceforth be held in common and not jointly.

SIR JOHN PENNYCUICK

It is not in dispute that an agreement for severance between joint tenants effects a severance. This is the rule 2 propounded by Sir William Page Wood V.-C. in *Williams v. Hensman*, 1 John. & Hem. 546, 557. The words he uses are contained in one sentence: "Secondly, a joint tenancy may be severed by mutual agreement."... The case falls squarely within rule 2 of Page Wood V.-C. It is not contended that it is material that the parties by mutual consent did not proceed to carry out the agreement. Rule 2 applies equally, I think, whether the agreement between the two joint tenants is expressly to sever or is to deal with the property in a manner which involves severance. Mr. Levy [acting for Mrs Rawnsley] contended that in order that rule 2 should apply, the agreement must be specifically enforceable. I do not see any sufficient reason for importing this qualification. The significance of an agreement is not that it binds the parties; but that it serves as an indication of a common intention to sever, something which it was indisputably within their power to do. It will be observed that Page Wood V.-C. in his rule 2 makes no mention of specific enforceability. Contrast this position where severance is claimed under his rule 1 by reason of alienation by one joint tenant in favour of a third party. We were referred to a sentence in *Megarry and Wade, the Law of Real Property*, 3rd ed., p. 418, where, under the heading of "Alienation in equity," it is said:

"In equity, ... a specifically enforceable contract to alienate creates an equitable interest in the property even though the legal act of alienation has not taken place."

That statement has, I think, no application to an agreement between the two joint tenants themselves. ...

Mr. Mummery advanced an alternative argument to the effect that even if there were no agreement by Mr. Honick to purchase Mrs. Rawnsley's share, nevertheless the mere proposal by Mr. Honick to purchase her share would operate as a severance under rule 3 in *Williams v. Hensman*, 1 John. & Hem. 546 , 557. That rule is stated by Page Wood V.-C. in the following terms:

 Alert

"And, in the third place, there may be a severance by any course of dealing sufficient to intimate that the interests of all were mutually treated as constituting a tenancy in common. ..."

I do not doubt myself that where one tenant negotiates with another for some rearrangement of interest, it may be possible to infer from the particular facts a common intention to sever even though the negotiations break down. Whether such an inference can be drawn must I think depend upon the particular facts. In the present case the negotiations between Mr. Honick and Mrs. Rawnsley, if they can be properly described as negotiations at all, fall, it seems to me, far short of warranting an inference. One could not ascribe to joint tenants an intention to sever merely because one offers to buy out the other for £X and the other makes a counter-offer of £Y.

 Alert

So the judge decided that severance took place by mutual agreement: there was an insufficient course of dealing to amount to severance by mutual conduct.

We were referred to a long series of authorities... culminating in the conflicting decisions of Plowman J. in *In Re Draper's Conveyance* [1969] 1 Ch. 486; and Walton J. in *Neilson-Jones v. Fedden* [1975] Ch. 222. Once it has been determined that an agreement was made, as in the present case, anything more one may say on this line of authorities must necessarily be obiter; but I think it may be helpful to state very shortly certain views which I have formed in the light of the authorities.

1. I do not think rule 3 in Page Wood V.-C.'s statement, 1 John. & Hem. 546, 557, is a mere sub-heading of rule 2. It covers only acts of the parties, including, it seems to me, negotiations which, although not otherwise resulting in any agreement, indicate a common intention that the joint tenancy should be regarded as severed.

    I do not overlook the words which I have read from Page Wood V.-C.'s statement, namely, that you must find a course of dealing by which the shares of all the parties to the contract have been affected. But I do not think those words are sufficient to import a binding agreement.

2. Section 36 (2) of the Law of Property Act 1925 has radically altered the law in respect of severance by introducing an entirely new method of severance as regards land, namely, notice in writing given by one joint tenant to the other.

3. Pre-1925 judicial statements, in particular that of Stirling J. in *In Re Wilks, Child v. Bulmer* [1891] 3 Ch. 59, must be read in the light of this alteration in the law; and, in particular, I do not see why the commencement of legal proceedings by writ or originating summons or the swearing of an affidavit in those proceedings, should not in appropriate circumstances constitute notice in writing within the meaning of section 36 (2). The fact that the plaintiff is not obliged to prosecute the proceedings is I think irrelevant in regard to notice.

4. Perhaps in parenthesis because the point does not arise, the language of section 36 (2) appears to contemplate that even under the existing law notice in writing would be effective to sever a joint tenancy in personalty: see the words "such other act or thing." The authorities to the contrary are rather meagre and I am

not sure how far this point was ever really considered in relation to personalty before 1925. If this anomaly does exist, and I am afraid I am not prepared to say positively that it does not exist, the anomaly is quite indefensible and should be put right as soon as possible.

6. An uncommunicated declaration by one party to the other or indeed a mere verbal notice by one party to another clearly cannot operate as a severance.

7. The policy of the law as it stands today, having regard particularly to section 36 (2), is to facilitate severance at the instance of either party, and I do not think the court should be over zealous in drawing a fine distinction from the pre-1925 authorities.

8. The foregoing statement of principles involves criticism of certain passages in the judgments of Plowman J. and Walton J. in the two cases cited. Those cases, like all other cases, depend on their own particular facts, and I do not myself wish to go on to apply these obiter statements of principle to the actual decisions in these cases.

Hunter v Babbage (1995) 69 P&CR 548

Panel: John McDonnell QC

Facts: Mr Babbage and Mrs Allen (formerly Mrs Babbage) owned their home as beneficial joint tenants. Mrs Allen left and in the course of the divorce proceedings, she applied for a property adjustment order. She suggested in her affidavit in support that the fairest way of dealing with the house would be for it to be sold and the proceeds split in such a way as to give her sufficient money to buy a small flat, with the rest going to Mr Babbage. After negotiations, an agreement was reached and the terms were incorporated in a draft consent order (often used in family law cases). The consent order had not been finalised when Mr Babbage died. The judge decided that there was no notice in writing, nor was there a mutual course of conduct evidencing an intention to sever. However, he held that reaching an agreement to deal with property in such a way which involves severance was sufficient to sever. The agreement itself, which was proposing a split other than in equal shares, was of no effect; but the making of the agreement was enough to sever into equal shares.

JOHN McDONNELL QC

In my judgment, the correct inference from the affidavit evidence, on the balance of probabilities, is that there was an agreement for severance in the present case just as there was in *Burgess v. Rawnsley*. The existence and terms of that agreement are shown by the letters from Mrs Allen's solicitor to the deceased's solicitors [on November 28] and to the court, dated December 13, 1989...

In *Burgess v. Rawnsley* Browne L.J. and Sir John Pennycuick both founded their conclusion that there had been a severance on the basis that there had been a finding by the judge at first instance that one joint tenant had agreed to sell her share to the other. They both held that that amounted to or implied a mutual agreement for severance within the second rule in *Williams v. Hensman* . As Sir John Pennycuick put it:

"rule 2 applies equally, I think, whether the agreement between the two joint tenants is expressly to sever, or is to deal with the property in a manner which involves severance."

It must follow a *fortiori* that the agreement between Mrs Allen and the deceased in the terms of the letter of November 28, 1989 had the same effect. That was an agreement for the sale of the property and payment out to Mrs Allen of a part of the proceeds, or alternatively for the purchase of her share, for the amount stipulated, as in *Burgess v. Rawnsley.*

Burgess v. Rawnsley shows that it matters not whether the agreement which includes or implies an agreement for severance is specifically enforceable. Miss Brownlow [acting for Mrs Allen] submits, however, that what makes all the difference in the present case is that the agreement was for terms to be embodied in an order by consent on the application for ancillary relief; and she rightly points out that that order would not be made unless the court was satisfied as to the matters required to be considered by section 25 of the Matrimonial Causes Act 1973, after investigation by the court in accordance with rules 77– 79 of the Matrimonial Causes Rules 1977, on the basis of the Statement of Information required by rule 76A.

I do not agree with this submission. The observation by Sir John Pennycuick in *Burgess v. Rawnsley* as to the submission that an agreement for severance must be specifically enforceable appears to me to be equally convincing as a reply to the submission by Miss Brownlow to which I have just referred. It will be recalled that Sir John Pennycuick said:

"The significance of an agreement is not that it binds the parties; but that it serves as an indication of a common intention to sever, something which it was indisputably within their power to do."

In order to appreciate the true import of that observation, it is necessary to recall the facts of *Burgess v. Rawnsley.* Not only was the agreement by Mrs Rawnsley for the sale of her share to Mr Honick for £750 not specifically enforceable, but no attempt was ever made to enforce or give effect to it. Mrs Rawnsley went back on it almost immediately after it had been made; and Mr Honick did nothing more about it. He simply remained in the house until he died three years later, when Mrs Rawnsley claimed it as her sole property by survivorship.

It was as at that point that it was held that the consequence of the agreement made three years previously was not that the parties had been holding the house since severance as tenants in common in shares corresponding to the ratio between the £750 and the balance of the value of the house, but that they had been holding the house in equal shares. In other words, the severance not only did not depend on the agreement being carried out, it actually operated independently to the extent of producing a result quite different from what the result would have been if the agreement had been carried out.

 Alert

To put it another way, if the agreement, the existence of which was the basis of the reasoning of the majority of the Court of Appeal in *Burgess v. Rawnsley*, had had any legal effect whatsoever as such, the tenancy in common which replaced the joint tenancy in equity should have been not in equal shares, as it was held to be, but in shares corresponding to the price which had been agreed for Mrs Rawnsley's share and the balance of the then value of the house.

...In the result I find that the joint tenancy was severed and that what severed it was the agreement made in December 1989. That agreement was never enforced as such; and the result is that the property was held by Mrs Allen for herself and the deceased's estate in equal shares and not on the terms which she had agreed, which appear on the figures to have been somewhat less favourable to her.

Gore and Snell v Carpenter **[1990] 60 P&CR 456**

Panel: Blackett-Ord J

Facts: Mr and Mrs Carpenter owned two properties as beneficial joint tenants, occupying one as their home. When the couple decided to divorce in 1985, Mrs Carpenter went to live in the other property. Between July 1986 and Mr Carpenter's death in early 1987 negotiations took place as to the division of the assets. Mrs Carpenter had agreed in principle to each of them taking one property absolutely, but a final agreement was not reached as there were other matters to be sorted out. Mr Carpenter did not serve a notice of severance of joint tenancy as he considered that this may have been construed as a hostile act. On his death, the question arose as to whether the joint tenancies had been severed, in which case Mrs Snell took his share of each property under his will. It was held that there hadn't been a severance.

MR JUSTICE BLACKETT-ORD

Going through those possible methods of severance and trying to apply the facts to the present case, first there is the method of a joint tenant dealing with his own share and I think it is right that that means dealing with his own share to a third party as against releasing it to the other tenant in common. There is no suggestion that Mr. Carpenter did deal with his share in that way. Any thoughts he may have had of doing it clearly came to nothing. Then there is mutual agreement between the parties. The correspondence does not, in my judgment, show any such mutual agreement. It is suggested that there was an agreement between Mr. and Mrs. Carpenter before he produced his draft separation agreement in 1985. But I have said that I believe Mrs. Carpenter's evidence as to the events leading up to the production of that agreement. There was not, in my judgment, any mutual agreement. Afterwards, when the discussion ranged more over the proposal that each party should take one house and that there should be a financial settlement, again there was no agreement reached. They were very near it— it was an agreement in principle— but I think each party reserved their rights and when the divorce proceedings had come on, if they had come on, it would have been open to them to have argued for some other provision.

Then, was there a course of dealing? There were negotiations, as I have said, but negotiations are not the same thing as a course of dealing. A course of dealing is where over the years the parties have dealt with their interests in the property on the footing that they are interests in common and are not joint. As, for instance, in the case of *Wilson v. Bell*, which was referred to by Vice Chancellor Page-Wood. But in the present case there were simply negotiations between the husband and the wife and again there was no finality and there was no mutuality. For severance to be effected by a course of dealing all the joint tenants must be concerned in such a course and in the present cast there is no evidence that Mrs. Carpenter was committing herself to accepting a tenancy in common... .

The judge referred to the remarks of Sir John Pennycuick in *Burgess v Rawnsley* to the effect that it is possible in certain circumstances to infer from negotiations a common intention to sever, even though those negotiations are ultimately inconclusive. He then continued:

It is, in my judgment, a question of intention and this applies also when it is a question of the fourth possible method of severance, namely the service of a notice under section 36(2) of the Law of Property Act. It is argued for the executors that the proposed separation agreement put forward by Mr. Carpenter amounted to such a notice. It will be recalled that the paragraph I read expressly refers to severance, but that was only part of the deed and the deed was never accepted. It was put forward by Mr. Carpenter, not in isolation but as part of the package of proposals, and was not intended in my judgment and therefore did not take effect as a notice under section 36(2). Later, as I have said, Mr. Gore was advising Mr. Carpenter to serve a notice or notices under the Act and Mr. Carpenter refused to do so. I think that there is nothing in the correspondence which can fairly be called a notice of severance. The result is, in my judgment, that the joint tenancies were not severed and the properties, No. 8 and No. 291, do not form part of the estate of Mr. Carpenter, but vest in Mrs. Carpenter by survivorship.

Davis and another v Smith [2011] EWCA Civ 1603

Panel: Lord Neuberger MR, Maurice Kay and Sullivan LJJ

Statute: Law of Property Act 1925

Facts: In 1989, Mr and Mrs Smith bought a house as beneficial joint tenants. In 2009, their relationship fell apart and in April, Mr Smith moved out of the house. Both parties appointed solicitors who advised their respective clients to serve a notice of severance on the other, although neither of them ever did this. A divorce petition was served in May, and correspondence between the solicitors followed regarding the parties' joint assets: the house, two bank accounts and an endowment policy. The solicitors agreed that the house should be sold and the endowment policy surrendered. In a meeting which took place in June, the solicitors agreed that more of the proceeds of the endowment policy should be paid to Mr Smith and that the 'lion's share' of the proceeds of the sale of the house would be paid to Mrs Smith. When the policy was surrendered, Mr Smith received £9,500 and Mrs Smith received £3,000. The house was also put on the market. There was no further substantial progress made before Mrs Smith died in October 2009.

The judge at first instance decided that the beneficial joint tenancy had been severed prior to Mrs Smith's death. Mr Smith appealed to the Court of Appeal.

LORD NEUBERGER MR

Lord Neuberger cited section 36(2) LPA 1925 and reviewed some of the relevant authorities on severance, including the obiter comments of Sir John Pennycuick in *Burgess v Rawnsley*.

14. Applying these principles to this case, it seems to me that there is obvious force in the point ... that neither the proposal nor the agreement to put the house on the market, nor even the acceptance of a subject to contract offer, could have severed the joint tenancy on their own. Even a sale could be said to have been entirely consistent, on the face of it at least, with the joint tenancy continuing and applying to the proceeds of sale. ...

15. This is not, however, a case where all that happened was that it was agreed that a jointly owned property would be placed on the market; nor is it even a case where the only relevant fact is that the house was put on the market and a subject to contract offer had been made and accepted. What passed between the parties went further than that.

16. First, there was what was stated in the correspondence and the 22 June meeting. More than once it had been indicated by Mr Smith's solicitor that the house should be sold and that the proceeds of sale would be divided. That had never been challenged by Mrs Smith's solicitors and it seems to me as a matter of inference, reading the correspondence as a whole, that both parties were proceeding on the basis of a common and expressed intention and expectation that the house would be sold and the proceeds of the sale would be divided equally between them, albeit that the division might include some balancing payment to reflect an unequal division in the proceeds of sale of the policy. The reference to "the lion's share" at the 22 June meeting would otherwise be difficult to explain.

17. Secondly, there is the background fact ... that each party was being advised, and each party knew that the other party was being advised, by solicitors, and they both would have known that, in this case of a long marriage and modest but significant jointly owned assets, a fifty-fifty split was inevitable. It seems to me that one should not put that fact out of one's mind when reading the correspondence.

18. Thirdly, there was not merely the attitude expressed in relation to the proceeds of the surrender of the policy, but the fact that the policy was actually surrendered and the proceeds distributed unequally between the parties on the clearly agreed basis that a balancing payment was then to be made to Mrs Smith to

reflect the fact that she had received less of the proceeds of the surrender of the policy. ...

19.   ...In other words, they had embarked on an exercise whereby they had not merely indicated to each other, but had actually acted on the basis that, the various properties that they owned, in particular the policy and the house, would be sold and the proceeds divided equally between them.

20.   In those circumstances the parties must have understood and assumed between themselves, irrespective of what they knew or did not know about the law, that they had negotiated and actually acted on the basis that their assets - and in particular the house, by far the biggest component of their assets - would be realised and the proceeds divided equally between them.

21.   In my view, therefore, applying the principles laid down in *Burgess*, the Judge reached the right conclusion. ...

22.   I should add one other point. There was other evidence to much of which I have not referred revealing what the parties wished to do, what they intended to do and what they were advised to do by their solicitors. ...Such evidence, in my view ... is simply irrelevant to the issue. As in most cases involving arrangements between parties, whether contractual or otherwise, the court should concentrate on what passed between the parties by way of words or actions, and what was known to both parties. It should not normally consider what was in the mind of one of the parties, or what was communicated between one of the parties and his or her solicitor or other adviser.

12.4 Disputes Relating to Co-owned Property

Before TLATA was enacted, anyone with an interest in a co-owned property could apply to the court for an order for sale under the LPA 1925 s 30. The courts generally upheld the principle of statutory trusts for sale by ordering a sale. The only basis on which courts would not order a sale was if the underlying or 'secondary' purpose for which the co-ownership had been created was still continuing. Although s 30 is now obsolete, the case law based on it is of assistance when dealing with applications for orders under the current law in TLATA s 14.

In re Buchanan-Wollaston's Conveyance [1939] Ch 738

Panel: Sir Wilfrid Greene MR, Clauson and Du Parcq LJJ

Facts: In 1928 four people bought a piece of land in Lowestoft between their houses and the sea in order to ensure that it was kept as an open space and thus preserved their sea view. The owners entered into covenants including one which said that they would not build anything on the land, or deal with it in any way unless there was unanimous agreement. One owner sold his house and wanted the land to be sold so that he could realise his share. The others did not agree to the sale so he applied for an order for sale under the LPA 1925 s 30, which was refused.

SIR WILFRID GREENE MR

… It seems to me that the court of equity, when asked to enforce the trust for sale, whether one created by a settlement or a will or one created by the statute, must look into all the circumstances of the case and consider whether or not, at the particular moment and in the particular circumstances when the application is made to it, it is right and proper that such an order shall be made. In considering a question of that kind, in circumstances such as these, the Court is bound to look at the contract into which the parties have entered and to ask itself the question whether or not the person applying for execution of the trust for sale is a person whose voice should be allowed to prevail. In the present case, Farwell J. approached the matter from that angle and gave a perfectly definite and unhesitating answer to it, with which I entirely agree. He said in effect "Here is a person who has contracted with others for a particular purpose, and the effect of the contract is to impose upon the power of the trustees to sell this land, certain restrictions." Without going into the question which I mentioned a moment ago as to overriding or not overriding those things, he said: "It is not right that the court of equity should in those circumstances, on the invitation of a person who has not acted in accordance with the contract, and is opposed by other persons interested, exercise the power of the Court and make an order for sale." That, of course, does not mean that in other circumstances, at some future time, the Court will not lend its aid. Circumstances may change. If all the parties died and all their houses were sold, I apprehend, for example, that the Court, if asked to enforce a statutory trust for sale, would not be disposed to listen to arguments against such a sale adduced by people who had no real interest in keeping this land unsold. Questions of that kind can be decided if and when they arise. In the present circumstances (and it is sufficient to confine my reasons to present circumstances) it seems to me that the appellant cannot ask the Court to help him in the way in which he desires.

 Alert

Jones v Challenger [1961] 1 QB 176

Panel: Ormerod and Devlin LJJ and Donovan J

Facts: Mrs Jones and Mr Challenger were formerly husband and wife. They owned their leasehold property as beneficial joint tenants. When his wife left him for another man, Mr Challenger continued to live in the property for three years. Mrs Jones applied for an order for sale under the LPA 1925 s 30. At first instance the judge refused to grant the order on the basis that it was unreasonable to turn Mr Challenger out of his home. On appeal, the order was granted.

LORD JUSTICE DEVLIN

After careful consideration of the authorities and some hesitation, I have come to the conclusion that the judge applied the wrong test, and that the question is not whether it is reasonable or unreasonable that the husband should be allowed to remain in the house.

At the front of his argument on behalf of the wife Mr. ap Robert put *In re Mayo*. In this case Simonds J. said: "The trust for sale will prevail, unless all three trustees agree in exercising the power to postpone." If that dictum governs this case, Mr. ap Robert must succeed. But he felt a difficulty in pushing his argument to this extent because of what was said by Lord Greene M.R. in *In re Buchanan-Wollaston's Conveyance*, where he laid down the principle more widely, and said that the court must ask itself "whether or not the person applying for execution of the trust for sale is a person whose voice should be allowed to prevail."

His lordship applied the wider test in *In re Buchanan-Wollaston's Conveyance*:

In the case we have to consider, the house was acquired as the matrimonial home. That was the purpose of the joint tenancy and, for so long as that purpose was still alive, I think that the right test to be applied would be that in *In re Buchanan-Wollaston's Conveyance*. But with the end of the marriage, that purpose was dissolved and the primacy of the duty to sell was restored. No doubt there is still a discretion. If the husband wanted time to obtain alternative accommodation, the sale could be postponed for that purpose, but he has not asked for that. If he was prepared to buy out the wife's interest, it might be proper to allow it, but he has not accepted a suggestion that terms of that sort should be made. In these circumstances, there is no way in which the discretion can properly be exercised except by an order to sell, because, since they cannot now both enjoy occupation of the property, that is the only way whereby the beneficiaries can derive equal benefit from their investment, which is the primary object of the trust. ...

I think that the result must be the same whether the test to be applied is derived from the language used in *In re Mayo* or from that used in *In re Buchanan-Wollaston's Conveyance*. Let it be granted that the court must look into all the circumstances; if when the examination is complete, it finds that there is no inequity in selling the property, then it must be sold. The test is not what is reasonable. It is reasonable for the husband to want to go on living in the house, and reasonable for the wife to want her share of the trust property in cash. The true question is whether it is inequitable for the wife, once the matrimonial home has gone, to want to realise her investment. Nothing said in the cases which I have cited can be used to suggest that it is, and, in my judgment, it clearly is not. The conversion of the property into a form in which both parties can enjoy their rights equally is the prime object of the trust; the preservation of the house as a home for one of them singly is not an object at all. If the true object of the trust is made paramount, as it should be, there is only one order that can be made.

In re Evers' Trust [1980] 1WLR 1327

Panel: Ormrod, Eveleigh and Templeman LJJ

Facts: A couple lived together and had a child. Her two children from her marriage came to live with them. They bought a cottage in joint names as beneficial joint tenants and they all lived there. Three years later the couple separated and the father applied for an order for sale of the property under the LPA 1925 s 30. The judge at first instance ordered a sale but postponed the sale until the couple's child reached sixteen. On appeal by the father, the Court of Appeal refused to order a sale.

LORD JUSTICE ORMROD

The section [s 30] gives the court a discretion to intervene to deal, inter alia, with the situation which arises when the trustees under a trust for sale are unable or unwilling to agree that the property should be sold. In such circumstances, the court can order a sale of the property, and, if appropriate, impose terms, or it can decline to make an order, leaving the property unsold, unless and until the trustees reach agreement, or the court makes an order at some future date.

The usual practice in these cases has been to order a sale and a division of the proceeds of sale, thus giving effect to the express purpose of the trust. But the trust for sale has become a very convenient and much used conveyancing technique. Combined with the statutory power in the trustees to postpone the sale, it can be used to meet a variety of situations, in some of which an actual sale is far from the intentions of the parties at the time when the trust for sale comes into existence. So, when asked to exercise its discretionary powers under section 30 to execute the trust, the court must have regard to its underlying purpose: see *In re Buchanan-Wollaston's Conveyance* [1939] Ch. 217 ...

 Alert

He then reviewed *In re Buchanan-Wollaston's Conveyance* and *Jones v Challenger*. He referred to *Burke v Burke* [1974] 1 WLR 1063 where once again the court looked beyond the statutory trust for sale, and considered the purpose for which the property had been bought. In that case, the judges gave no special importance to the children, because they said that the provision of a home for the children was not the underlying purpose of that trust. The general approach of all of the cases was to look at whether the underlying purpose was still capable of being carried out. On that basis, and following that approach, the court held that the primary purpose of this particular trust was in fact the provision of a family home.

This approach to the exercise of the discretion given by section 30 has considerable advantages in these "family" cases. It enables the court to deal with substance, that is reality, rather than form, that is, convenience of conveyancing; it brings the exercise of the discretion under this section, so far as possible, into line with exercise of the discretion given by section 24 of the Matrimonial Causes Act 1973; and it goes some way to eliminating differences between legitimate and illegitimate children in accordance with present legislative policy...

The irresistible inference from these facts is that, as the judge found, they purchased this property as a family home for themselves and the three children. It is difficult to imagine that the mother, then wholly responsible for two children, and partly for the third, would have invested nearly all her capital in the purchase of this property if it was not to be available to her as a home for the children for the indefinite future. It is inconceivable that the father, when he agreed to this joint adventure, could have thought otherwise, or contemplated the possibility of an early sale without the consent of the mother. The underlying purpose of the trust was, therefore, to provide a home for all five of them for the indefinite future. ...

> ... The judge was right not to order an immediate sale but the form of his actual order is not satisfactory.

The judge refused an order for sale but indicated that a further application could be made in future when the children were older or other circumstances had changed.

In re Citro (Domenico) (A Bankrupt); In re Citro (Carmine) (A Bankrupt) [1991] Ch 142

Panel: Nourse and Bingham LJJ and Sir George Waller

Facts: Two brothers, Domenico and Carmine Citro, were declared bankrupt. The only assets they had were their interests in their respective homes which, prior to the bankruptcies, they held as joint tenants with their wives. Domenico was separated from his wife, who lived in their home with their three children. The youngest child was 12. Carmine still lived with his wife and their three children, the youngest of whom was 10. The trustees in bankruptcy applied for orders for sale of the properties pursuant to the LPA 1925 s 30. At first instance, Hoffmann J declared that the beneficial interests of the trustees amounted to a half share in each property. He ordered the sale of both properties but due to the children's educational problems and fact that the wives would be unable to acquire other property in the area, the orders were postponed in each case until the youngest child reached the age of 16. On appeal the period of postponement was reduced to six months in each case.

> LORD JUSTICE NOURSE
>
> In the leading case of *Jones v. Challenger* [1961] 1 Q.B. 176 it was held by this court that on an application under section 30 of the Law of Property Act 1925 in relation to property acquired jointly as a matrimonial home neither spouse has a right to demand a sale while that purpose still exists. That is now a settled rule of law, applicable to property owned jointly by joint occupants, whether married or unmarried. But its application depends on the whole of the beneficial interest being vested in the occupants. If one of them has become bankrupt, so that part of the beneficial interest is vested in his or her trustee, there arises a conflict between the interests of the occupants and the statutory obligation of the trustee to realise the bankrupt's assets for the benefit of the creditors.
>
> In a series of bankruptcy decisions relating to matrimonial homes subsequent to *Jones v. Challenger* it has been held that the interests of the husband's creditors ought usually to prevail over the interests of the wife and any children and, with one exception, *In re Holliday (A Bankrupt), Ex parte Trustee of the Property of the Bankrupt v. Holliday* [1981]. Ch. 405, a sale within a short period has invariably been ordered.... .

In *In re Holliday* the unusual circumstances were that none of the creditors presented a bankruptcy petition: the bankrupt himself did. There was no doubt that the creditors would eventually be paid the money owed to them in full, with interest, so there was no real detriment to them in making them wait.

The judge surveyed the authorities in great detail in deciding whose voice should prevail.

The broad effect of these authorities can be summarised as follows. Where a spouse who has a beneficial interest in the matrimonial home has become bankrupt under debts which cannot be paid without the realisation of that interest, the voice of the creditors will usually prevail over the voice of the other spouse and a sale of the property ordered within a short period. The voice of the other spouse will only prevail in exceptional circumstances. No distinction is to be made between a case where the property is still being enjoyed as the matrimonial home and one where it is not.

 Alert

What then are exceptional circumstances? As the cases show, it is not uncommon for a wife with young children to be faced with eviction in circumstances where the realisation of her beneficial interest will not produce enough to buy a comparable home in the same neighbourhood, or indeed elsewhere. And, if she has to move elsewhere, there may be problems over schooling and so forth. Such circumstances, while engendering a natural sympathy in all who hear of them, cannot be described as exceptional. They are the melancholy consequences of debt and improvidence with which every civilised society has been familiar. It was only in *In re Holliday* [1981] Ch. 405 that they helped the wife's voice to prevail, and then only, as I believe, because of one special feature of that case.

With the enactment of TLATA, co-owned land is held on a trust of land with no duty to sell. Any person having an interest in the land may apply for an order under TLATA s 14. In reaching its decision as to whether to make the order the court must have regard to the factors listed in TLATA s 15, or the Insolvency Act 1986 ('IA') s 335A if the application is made by a trustee in bankruptcy. These factors extend beyond an analysis of whether the 'underlying purpose' still exists as was the focus of pre-TLATA case law. Therefore although decisions made on the basis of the LPA 1925 s 30 may be of assistance, they relate to a different statutory regime and should be treated with care.

The Mortgage Corporation v Shaire and Others [2001] Ch 743

Panel: Neuberger J

Statutes: Trusts of Land and Appointment of Trustees Act 1996 s 15

Facts: Mr Fox and Mrs Shaire lived together in a property formerly owned by Mr and Mrs Shaire as beneficial joint tenants, having purchased Mr Shaire's interest. After Mr Fox's death it transpired that he had forged Mrs Shaire's signature on a mortgage document in favour of The Mortgage Corporation ('TMC'). The loan, of which Mrs Shaire knew nothing, was in arrears. TMC applied for an order for sale pursuant to TLATA s 14. Mrs Shaire, who was still living in the house with her son, opposed the application on the basis that s 15 required the court to take into account wider considerations than simply the interests of the creditors. The judge concluded that Mrs Shaire held a 75 per cent interest as tenant in common. He said that pre-TLATA, save in exceptional circumstances, an order for sale would be made if an application was made by a lender or trustee in bankruptcy and that the interests of the family in occupation were unlikely to prevail. However, he said that s 15 had changed the basis on which decisions in such cases were made, and gave eight reasons.

MR JUSTICE NEUBERGER

To my mind, for a number of reasons, Mr Asif is correct in his submission on behalf of Mrs Shaire that section 15 has changed the law. First, there is the rather trite point that, if there was no intention to change the law, it is hard to see why Parliament has set out in section 15(2) and, indeed, on one view, section 15(3), the factors which have to be taken into account specifically, albeit not exclusively, when the court is asked to exercise its jurisdiction to order a sale.

Secondly, it is hard to reconcile the contention that Parliament intended to confirm the law as laid down in *Lloyds Bank plc v Byrne & Byrne* with the fact that, while the interest of a chargee is one of the four specified factors to be taken into account in section 15(1)(d) , there is no suggestion that it is to be given any more importance than the interests of the children residing in the house: see section 15(1)(c) . ....

Thirdly, the very name "trust for sale" and the law as it has been developed by the courts suggests that under the old law, in the absence of a strong reason to the contrary, the court should order sale. Nothing in the language of the new code as found in the 1996 Act supports that approach.

Fourthly, it is clear from the reasons in *Lloyds Bank plc v Byrne & Byrne*, and indeed the later two first instance cases to which I have referred, that the law, as developed under section 30 of the Law of Property Act 1925, was that the court should adopt precisely the same approach in a case where one of the co-owners was bankrupt (*In re Citro*) and a case where one of the co-owners had charged his interest (*Lloyds Bank plc v Byrne & Byrne*). It is quite clear that Parliament now considers that a different approach is appropriate in the two cases— compare section 15(2) and section 15(3) of the 1996 Act with section 15(4) and the new section 335A of the Insolvency Act 1986.

Fifthly, an indication from the Court of Appeal that the 1996 Act was intended to change the law is to be found in (an albeit plainly obiter) sentence in the judgment of Peter Gibson LJ in *Bankers Trust Co v Namdar* (unreported) 14 February 1997; Court of Appeal (Civil Division) Transcript No 349 of 1997. Having come to the conclusion that the wife's appeal against an order for sale had to be refused in light of the reasoning in *In re Citro* and *Lloyds Bank plc v Byrne & Byrne*, Peter Gibson LJ said: "It is unfortunate for Mrs Namdar that the very recent Trusts of Land and Appointment of Trustees Act 1996 was not in force at the relevant time"— ie at the time of the hearing at first instance. Of course it would be dangerous to build too much on that observation, but it is an indication from the Court of Appeal, and indeed from a former chairman of the Law Commission, as to the perceived effect of the 1996 Act.

Sixthly, the leading textbooks support the view that I have reached...

Seventhly, the Law Commission report which gave rise to the 1996 Act, Transfer of Land, Trusts of Land (1989) (Law Com No 181), tends to support this view as well. ...When commenting on the proposed equivalents of what are now section 15(2) and section 15(3) the Law Commission said, in footnote 143:

"Clearly, the terms of these guidelines may influence the exercise of the discretion in some way. For example, it may be that the courts' approach to creditors' interests will be altered by the framing of the guideline as to the welfare of children. If the welfare of children is seen as a factor to be considered independently of the beneficiaries' holdings, the courts may be less ready to order the sale of the home than they are at present." ...

Eighthly, to put it at its lowest, it does not seem to me unlikely that the legislature intended to relax the fetters on the way in which the court exercised its discretion in cases such as *In re Citro* [1991] Ch 142 and *Lloyds Bank plc v Byrne & Byrne* [1993] 1 FLR 369, and so as to tip the balance somewhat more in favour of families and against banks and other chargees. Although the law under section 30 was clear following *In re Citro* and *Lloyds Bank plc v Byrne & Byrne*, there were indications of judicial dissatisfaction with the state of the law at that time. ...

All these factors, to my mind, when taken together point very strongly to the conclusion that section 15 has changed the law. As a result of section 15, the court has greater flexibility than heretofore, as to how it exercises its jurisdiction on an application for an order for sale on facts such as those in *In re Citro*...

A difficult question, having arrived at this conclusion, is the extent to which the old authorities are of assistance, and it is no surprise to find differing views expressed in the two textbooks from which I have quoted. On the one hand, to throw over all the wealth of learning and thought given by so many eminent judges to the problem which is raised on an application for sale of a house where competing interests exist seems somewhat arrogant and possibly rash. On the other hand, where one has concluded that the law has changed in a significant respect so that the court's discretion is significantly less fettered than it was, there are obvious dangers in relying on authorities which proceeded on the basis that the court's discretion was more fettered than it now is. I think it would be wrong to throw over all the earlier cases without paying them any regard. However, they have to be treated with caution, in light of the change in the law, and in many cases they are unlikely to be of great, let alone decisive, assistance.

Link

to the Pascoe and Probert articles in the Further Reading section

The judge analysed the situation having regard to all the factors and made no final order, preferring instead to give the parties time to consider his suggestions.

12.4.1 'Exceptional circumstances' and human rights

The IA s 335A lists the factors which a court must take into account in determining whether to make an order under TLATA s 14 where the applicant is a trustee in bankruptcy. The IA s 335A(3) states that the interests of creditors should prevail if the application is made by the trustee more than one year after the bankruptcy, unless the circumstances are 'exceptional'. This follows the reasoning developed in cases such as *re Citro*.

Romano Barca v Malcolm John Mears Trustee of the estate of Romano Barca [2004] EWHC 2170 (Ch), [2005 2 FLR 1]

Panel: Nicholas Strauss QC (sitting as a deputy judge of the High Court)

Statutes: Insolvency Act 1986 s 335(A), Human Rights Act 1998 s 3(1)

Facts: Mr Barca lived in a property with his son Lorenzo, who had learning difficulties. Mr Barca's trustee in bankruptcy applied for and was granted an order for the sale of the property pursuant to TLATA s 14 and the IA 1986 s 335(A). The Deputy Registrar granted the order on the basis that the hardship caused to Lorenzo by a sale was not sufficiently 'exceptional' to refuse the sale in circumstances where the application was made more than one year from the date of the bankruptcy. On appeal, the judge agreed with the decision to grant the order. He then turned to Mr Barca's argument that ordering a sale breached his and his son's human rights:

NICHOLAS STRAUSS QC

He [Mr Barca] submits that the Deputy Registrar failed to take account of his or his son's right to family life, home and privacy, stating that in the 8 year period since he became bankrupt his son had grown to know him as his father and that his right to family life, home and privacy were important aspects of his development. He submits at paragraph 29.4 that "insolvency legislation in this area is particularly brutal and contrary to the average concept of fundamental freedoms and rights". ...Although it was not raised before the Deputy Registrar, it is a point which I am bound to consider on appeal since the court is itself a public authority which is bound to comply with the Convention: see HRA section 6.

The judge then quoted Article 8 of the Convention, Article 1 of the First Protocol and the Human Rights Act 1998 s 3(1) in full.

Mr. Gibbon submitted, in my view correctly, that where a court considers that a statutory provision, as interpreted before the Convention became part of English law, is incompatible with the Convention, it should seek to re-interpret the relevant provisions so as to achieve compatibility: only if this is not possible should a court consider granting a declaration of incompatibility... .

Mr. Gibbon made the following further submissions, which I also accept:—

(1) The right to "respect" for private and family life and the home is not absolute. The state must have regard "to the fair balance that has to be struck between the general interest of the community and the interests of the individual, the search for which balance is inherent in the whole Convention"...

Clearly, in many or perhaps most cases, the sale of a bankrupt's property in accordance with bankruptcy law will be justifiable on the basis that it is necessary to protect the rights of others, namely the creditors, and will not be a breach of the Convention. Nevertheless, it does seem to me to be questionable whether the narrow approach as to what may be "exceptional circumstances" adopted in re Citro, is consistent with the Convention. It requires the court to adopt an almost universal rule, which prefers the property rights of the bankrupt's creditors to the property and/or

 Alert

personal rights of third parties, members of his family, who owe the creditors nothing. I think that there is considerable force in what is said by Ms. Deborah Rook in Property Law and Human Rights at pp.203– 5 to which Mr. Gibbon very fairly referred me:

"It is arguable that, in some circumstances, [s.335A(3)] may result in an infringement of Article 8. The mortgagor's partner and children have the right to respect their home and family life under Article 8 even though they may have no proprietary interest in the house … therefore it is possible that the presumption of sale in s.335A and the way that the courts have interpreted it, so that in the majority of cases an innocent partner and the children are evicted from the home, violates Convention rights …

The eviction of the family from their home, an event that naturally ensues from the operation of the presumption of sale in s.335A, could be considered to be an infringement of the right to respect of the home and family life under Article 8 if the presumption is given absolute priority without sufficient consideration being given to the Convention rights of the affected family. Allen [Mr. T. Allen in The Human Rights Act (UK) and Property Law in "Property and the Constitution", Oxford, Hart Publishing, 1999 at p.163] observes that:

'As the law currently stands, the right to respect for family life and the home receives almost no consideration after the one year period. Whether such a strict limitation is compatible with the Convention is doubtful.' …

It may be that the courts, in applying s.335A … will need to adopt a more sympathetic approach to defining what constitutes 'exceptional circumstances'. If an immediate sale of the property would violate the family's rights under Article 8, the court may be required in compliance with its duty under s.3 of the HRA 1988 to adopt a broad interpretation of 'exceptional circumstances' … to ensure the compatibility of this legislation with Convention rights."

In particular, it may be incompatible with Convention rights to follow the approach taken by the majority in *re Citro*, in drawing a distinction between what is exceptional, in the sense of being unusual, and what Nourse L.J. refers to as the "usual melancholy consequences" of a bankruptcy. This approach leads to the conclusion that, however disastrous the consequences may be to family life, if they are of the usual *kind* then they cannot be relied on under section 335A; they will qualify as 'exceptional' only if they are of an unusual kind, for example where a terminal illness is involved.

It seems to me that a shift in emphasis in the interpretation of the statute may be necessary to achieve compatibility with the Convention. …

Nevertheless, even on the view of the law which is most favourable to Mr. Barca, and assuming in his favour that either 335A or section 337 applies, such an exercise would have to be undertaken, and on the facts of this case in my view the creditors' interests must prevail… .

The judge emphasised four factors in dismissing Mr Barca's appeal: there would be substantial surplus funds available to Mr Barca; postponing a sale to Lorenzo's educational needs would deny the creditors their money for at least three years; Lorenzo's special needs were not extreme, and Mr Barca's mother was able to assist him financially with alternative accommodation.

Link
See the Dixon article in the Further Reading section

Further Reading

Megarry and Wade, *The Law of Real Property*, (8th Edition), Sweet & Maxwell 2012, pp 495-526 and 529-541

Dixon, M, Trusts of Land, Bankruptcy and Human Rights, 2005 *Conv* 161

Pascoe, S, Section 15 of the Trusts of Land and Appointment of Trustees Act 1996 – A Change in the Law? 2000 *Conv* 315

Percival, M, Severance by Written Notice – A Matter of Delivery?, 1999 *Conv* 60

Probert, R, Creditors and Section 15 of the Trusts of Land and Appointment of Trustees Act 1996: First Among Equals?, 2002 *Conv* 61